Traynham

61-16621

2-6-62

Moscow Journal

MOSCOW

Harrison E. Salisbury

JOURNAL

THE END OF STALIN

 THE UNIVERSITY OF CHICAGO PRESS

Library of Congress Catalog Card Number: 61-16621

THE UNIVERSITY OF CHICAGO PRESS, CHICAGO 37
The University of Toronto Press, Toronto 5, Canada

© *1961 by Harrison E. Salisbury. Published 1961*
Composed and printed by THE UNIVERSITY OF CHICAGO PRESS
Chicago, Illinois, U.S.A.

For Janet

Contents

Introduction

The Moscow in which I arrived on March 8, 1949, was a Moscow deeply frozen in the cold war. More deeply frozen than I or any other foreigner could guess.

It was typical of those times that the first thing I did on Russian soil was to try to make a telephone call to a man whom I learned five or six years later had already been purged and, quite possibly, executed.

Those were days of suspicion and, often, of terror. The suspicion became habit, and the terror ebbed and flowed and, sometimes, seemed to vanish. But it always came back, and never more strongly than in the months just before Stalin's death. It was more usual than not that my picture of precisely what was happening—and why it was happening—was myopic. Yet, in retrospect, it seems to me that not the least remarkable aspect of Stalin's final years were the rich clues which they provided not only to what was going on—but to what has happened since.

Often enough in those times I could not decipher the full meaning of the evidence provided by my eyes and ears—as this journal of life in Moscow in the last Stalin years and the early days of the succession frequently reveals. I could not be certain, for example, exactly why the Ukrainian Party secretary named Khrushchev was brought to Moscow in late 1949. But I well knew that his transfer affected the power balance within the Politburo. When late in 1952 Lavrenti P. Beriya suddenly dropped several notches in the official iconostasis I recognized

1

this as political news of the first importance even if I could only guess at the reasons for his decline. Few people in Moscow could surmise the ramifications of political plots and counterplots which were afoot in Russia in 1948 and 1949. But no one who lived there could fail to sense that something sinister and complex was going on.

Yet, life in the Soviet Union even during the most grim of the cold war years was not just a journey through darkness. Day did not follow shrouded day. Unresolved mysteries abounded. Some still defy solution. But what surprises even one who lived through it all is the clear light which the record so often casts upon what was happening then. And, even more pertinent, the perspective which we may draw for analysis of the future. One of my most valuable discoveries in Russia was the insight into Stalin's rule which I could gain by studying that of Nicholas I. Often I was not able to travel as widely as I would have liked. Often my contacts with ordinary Russians were restricted or hampered. But if I delved into a diplomatic memoir of the 1880's, if I went to the Moscow Art Theater to see Tolstoi's *Fruits of Enlightenment,* or if I read a bit of Dostoevski's *Diaries,* I could find revelations of Russian character and psyche which explained what was happening in the Kremlin more perceptively, I am sure, than a member of the Politburo could have done.

I do not want to suggest that all of the pertinent facts about Soviet policy and practice are to be found in history and literature. But history is in a real sense the handmaiden of Russia's future, and I think that if this journal has virtue it lies in the pattern which is disclosed of the unity of Soviet practice and Russian habit; the persistence with which specific tendencies in policy emerge again and again with no more meaningful variation than those traced by the surf upon a sandy beach; the deep and tangled roots of never-ending conflict between those Russians who lean toward the West and those who act with hostility and a sense of Russian mission; the struggle of the conciliators and the intransigents who would carry their hostility to the brink of war or beyond.

What was the world like in February, 1949, when I set out to return to the Russia which I had first seen in wartime 1944? The picture had been sketched quite vividly in an open letter written on Christmas Eve, 1948, to Generalissimo Stalin by Edwin L. James, the late managing editor of the *New York Times*.

Contact between Russia and America, James noted, had almost ceased. Few Russians came to America. Almost no Americans were permitted in the Soviet Union. Diplomatic intercourse was at a standstill. East and West were locked in the grim combat of the Berlin blockade. The violent recriminations which followed the Kasenkina case (the Russian schoolteacher who jumped from the window of the Soviet consulate in New York City) had brought Soviet-American relations almost to the breaking point. The iron curtain had fallen on eastern Europe. Westerners had been expelled from Poland, Czechoslovakia, and Hungary. If there was a ray of hope anywhere in the world it was not visible to the ordinary observer.

In this forbidding situation James called for one small step toward a new effort at understanding. He suggested that Moscow permit the *Times* to send a correspondent back to Russia (where for a year and a half the newspaper had been without representation because of Soviet refusal to grant a visa). Within a fortnight word was received from the Soviet embassy that my pending visa application had been approved.

Thus, the portents were by no means optimistic when I set sail early in February for Moscow. Indeed, the picture was, if anything, even more forbidding than had been painted by Edwin James. The Soviet quarrel with Marshal Tito was smoldering dangerously. Actually, it was the only visible chink in the Soviet barricade, but suspicion was so deep in the West that many thought it was just a stage-managed row, a bit of Communist trickery. To the east, China's Communist armies methodically were taking over the land, step by step, ousting Chiang Kai-shek from one city after another. There was no longer much real doubt that Mao Tse-tung would triumph. Truman was President and Acheson was Secretary of State. The shadow of what was to become known as McCarthyism was beginning to rise. The North Atlantic Alliance was shaping up nicely, but Germany was still an occupied land. The United States was proud possessor of the atomic bomb, and warnings that the monopoly would not last much longer were scoffed at by those who firmly believed that Russia would require ten or twenty years to catch up.

This was the façade of the cold war world in the winter of

1949. As to what was going on behind that façade—this was what I was being sent to Moscow to try to find out. From a distance it was clear that Stalin ruled in dictatorial supremacy like some oriental potentate while life within the Kremlin was shrouded in impenetrable secrecy. I was to find almost as little knowledge of the inner workings of Stalin's cabinet within Russia as without. Even today we do not understand many obscure events of that period.

But we do know now, for example, that the reason I could not reach Mayor Popkov on the telephone in Leningrad was that he had already been dismissed and jailed. We know, too, that the reason why N. A. Voznesensky, chairman of the State Planning Commission, was dropped from the Politburo in March, 1949, was that he, too, was arrested. And we know that both Popkov and Voznesensky and many others as well were victims of the so-called Leningrad Affair, a political machination directed at supporters of the late Andrei A. Zhdanov, the powerful Politburo member from Leningrad who died, presumably of natural causes, August 1, 1948, about six months before I arrived in Moscow.

We know now that Stalin was on extremely bad terms with Mao in late 1948 and early 1949—that he was almost as suspicious of Mao as he was of Tito. In the light of this knowledge the meaning of the arrest (just before I arrived in Moscow) of the American journalist and Communist sympathizer, Anna Louise Strong, and of the old revolutionary, Mikhail Borodin, can be postulated. And the significance of a whole sequence of puzzling happenings in Soviet-Chinese relations becomes plain.

When I arrived in Moscow I found, stridently underway, a campaign against what was called "cosmopolitanism." It was obvious enough that this drive had anti-Semitic implications since most of the targets of attack were Jewish writers and intellectuals. But it was not until Stalin had been dead nearly three years that accurate details began to leak out which revealed the scope of the terrible anti-Jewish outrages which were carried out in 1948–50.

Much evidence of what was going on in Moscow inevitably found its way into the possession of foreigners who lived on the scene. The problem perpetually was to understand the nature of the pattern which underlay the frequently bizarre exterior.

Thus, in the final months of Stalin's life, we in Moscow could watch a complex and dangerous skein of events unwind. We could not guess that Stalin's own death would ring down the curtain on a kind of Communist Götterdämmerung. But the scent of impending catastrophe on a massive scale hung heavy in the air.

Yet, it is quite wrong to interpret the last Stalin years and the launching of the post-Stalin era as if it were all some kind of Grand Guignol played out on the world's stage. To be sure the terror, the mystery, the enigma, the drama was all there. But as one leafs through the years another picture emerges—that of a Russia which lives and works and laughs and cries and endures regardless of the high melodrama of the Kremlin. There is this stream of Russian life in the cities of Moscow and Leningrad, in the quiet villages of the pine forests, in the remote and picturesque lands of the Caucasus and of Central Asia which survives czar or commissar. This is the land of the Russian people who from one decade to another and quite without regard for world politics, cold war, the thaw, coexistence or the inevitability of conflict between capitalist imperialism and communism, yearn for a better life, for a world of peace, for freedom from the threat of war, for ease, for relaxation, for friendship with the Americans whom they persist in admiring and liking, regardless of what *Pravda* has said or Radio Moscow has broadcast during the past twenty years or more.

And there is another constant which emerges—the consistency of viewpoint and policy which characterizes Soviet attitudes, regardless of whether the man in the Kremlin is Stalin, a group of "collective leaders," Nikita Khrushchev, or his successor.

Thus, year after year, the figures disclose a steady and spectacular rise in steel production and heavy industry which makes Stalin's proudest boasts come true—ahead of time. There is the sharply defined emphasis upon science and technology, the patient and stubborn work of the laboratory men and the technicians which overcomes all of the handicaps—Russian backwardness, Soviet bureaucracy, material shortages, and even the octopus grasp of such political pseudoscientists as Lysenko. There is the endless controversy over agriculture—controversy which is fed by the harsh facts of Soviet farm production—production which, for one reason or another, never keeps pace either with the hopes of the Kremlin or the needs of a rapidly increasing urban population.

5

And, finally, there is the persistent ambivalence in viewpoint toward the outer world—the conflict of those who continue to fear the threat of attack by "capitalist encirclers" and those who feel that Communist strength is now so great that the danger of "imperialist war" has begun to recede. This dispute, so central to the evolving differences between Soviet Russia and Communist China, was precisely defined and vigorously debated within the U.S.S.R. long before Stalin's death and played its role in the maneuvering among his would-be successors. And so did most of the other arguments over Marxist principle which have harassed the Communist world in recent times.

Perhaps the most spectacular demonstration of underlying consistency in Soviet policy was provided in the first three or four weeks after Stalin's death in March, 1953. Almost all the main characteristics of the post-Stalin epoch made their appearance in that time: the de-Stalinization policy, the effort at a *détente* with the West, the reduction in power of the Soviet police, the relaxation in the field of the arts, the new emphasis on consumer goods and services, the first steps toward greater realism in discussion of domestic issues. From this period, too, dated the first steps of Khrushchev's rise to power, although it was to be several months before his rivalry with Malenkov was publicly defined.

The record suggests many hints for the future—the constant difficulty, for example, of translating a desire for less tension into reality. The U-2 incident of May, 1960, was not the only occasion when a plane flight or a calculated propaganda insult by one side or the other wiped out the hard-won results of months of patient investment in good will and negotiation. Indeed, there seems to be a fateful counterpoint which plagues the course of every effort to improve relations between Russia and the West and thus serves to emphasize the underlying dialectic in which both sides are so harshly imprisoned.

It is my hope that this journal demonstrates that the old-fashioned virtues of using one's eyes, ears, and, sometimes, one's nose to detect what is going on about him have not entirely lost their purpose; that it is possible under adverse, even painful, conditions to gain insight into the life and manners, the hopes and aspirations, of a great people and the difficult form of government under which they apparently prefer to live—a people with whom we share an ever smaller and more dangerous planet. This

6

Moscow journal is the record of one American's five difficult years in Russia. No one is more aware than its author of its many flaws. There were times when important events completely escaped my notice. There were other occasions when I was distracted by trivia or false scents. And there were times, especially in the months just before Stalin's death, when it did not seem wise to put down on paper in any form some of the things I knew or feared. But, with all this, the record does, I believe, convey accurately the flavor of five critical years, 1949–53, in Moscow—five years which did much to shape the future—and because of this may provide some hints which could make future relations of Americans and Russians a bit less difficult.

This journal is made up of extracts from a diary, memoranda, letters, notes, and dispatches to the *Times*. Many of the dispatches were killed by the Soviet censorship and never saw the light of day. Where such is the case I have noted this fact in the journal. Many times pertinent sentences or paragraphs of dispatches were cut by the censor. To give the reader some notion of the extent and variety of cuts made by the censor the excised passages are inclosed within brackets.

I

Back to Moscow

Stockholm, March 1, 1949

I have arrived safely in Stockholm. It was a fine trip over. The sea was calm, and there were no cases of seasickness that I heard about. The ship was not crowded, only about fifty first-class passengers, including a couple of kids, a girl and a boy, going to Moscow to be clerks in the embassy. The girl speaks a good bit of Russian.

I got into Stockholm yesterday after a pleasant trip up from Göteborg. Old medieval buildings, canals, narrow little streets. All very fresh and clean in the sharp winter air. I leave Thursday for Helsinki and am due in Moscow the eighth.

Moscow, March 12

I have been here nearly five days now and have not written before—not for lack of things to write or lack of desire but because I wanted to sort out some of my impressions before putting them on paper. There are many, many changes in Moscow since my days here in 1944.

Our little band left Helsinki Sunday night, the sixth. It was a long, slow journey down to Leningrad—didn't get in there until nearly 6:00 in the evening, principally because the train stops a long time at the frontier for customs examination, and it does not go very fast.

The Russian countryside reminded me of my last trip—the

familiar little peasant villages and the forests and the snow-covered land. I found Leningrad transformed since the war days. Crowds of people on the streets, traffic, electric signs, and many shops open—forerunners of what I was to find in Moscow.

I had wanted to stay over a night and a day in Leningrad but that proved impossible since Intourist already had my tickets on the Red Arrow, leaving that night. So after some argument I proceeded on my journey. The Red Arrow is a luxurious train, very comfortable. There were only three foreigners aboard—a man returning to the Italian embassy from Stockholm, a man coming to the Greek legation, and myself. We got into Moscow at 11:30 in the morning, and by noon I was back in the Metropole. My room, 393, is one which Alex Werth occupied during his long stay here—a pleasant large room.

A little bit about my troubles—and I have a lot. The biggest stem from my not knowing Russian, of course, which makes it hard for me to deal with people. I do not have a secretary yet—and won't until next week sometime.

The other problems are just the usual formalities—getting my press card, getting my telegraphic facilities, and so on.

The number of correspondents here is not large. That is, of American correspondents. It has diminished by two within the last year—not counting my arrival. The question is whether the group may not diminish more in the next year.

March 13

Russia is a preoccupied land today—preoccupied with concern lest a new war break out while the scars of the old are not yet healed.

Coming back to the Soviet Union for the first time since the victory days of 1944, my outstanding impression is of this concern. It seems to color almost every phase of Soviet life.

The reasons for this preoccupation are another story, but that the possibility of a new war appears real to the Russian people cannot be doubted. Almost the first words I heard spoken after crossing the Finnish frontier were those of a woman customs inspector, a Leningrad woman who had endured the horrible siege years of 1941 and 1942 and watched her eleven-year-old daughter's bright blonde hair turn gray under conditions of peril,

9

cold, hunger, and disease such as few other people have endured in our time.

This Leningrad woman said: "We people of Leningrad want peace. We have seen war. We do not want war with America."

It seems likely that this pleasant, efficient customs woman voiced the sentiments of all the Soviet's nearly 200,000,000 population in these brief words. The Russian people's desire for peace and the Soviet government's fear that a new war is in the making sharply color the whole Russian scene today.

Even the most casual observation reveals sound physical basis for Russian concern. Although vast strides have been taken toward reconstruction of the devastated cities and countryside, the country still faces gigantic tasks in erasing the marks of the most destructive war of modern times.

Moscow is not Russia—a fact which sometimes escapes foreign observers. It is Russia's capital, and it is natural that it should reflect more sharply postwar reconstruction than small villages and even other large cities. Furthermore, Moscow escaped the destruction which was visited upon Leningrad, for example, or Kiev and Kharkov, or any other city in European Russia. Soviet concern over a new war has a physical basis.

Dispatch to New York Times
March 14, 1949

The Presidium of the Supreme Soviet reveals that it has released from his important duties as chairman of the State Planning Commission and as vice-chairman of the Council of Ministers N. A. Voznesensky, one of the Soviet's outstanding economists.

[Only last spring Voznesensky was honored with the award of a Stalin prize of 100,000 rubles for his analysis of *The War Economy of the U.S.S.R. in the Second World War,* which was recently published in the United States. With the release of Voznesensky the Council of Ministers presents a substantially altered lineup.]

A week ago Molotov was released as foreign minister and Anastas Mikoyan as foreign trade minister. However, Molotov and Mikoyan continue in their positions as vice chairmen of the Council of Ministers. The Presidium's decree on Voznesensky also released him from his vice-chairmanship.

The Supreme Soviet approved other changes in government posts, including the release of Georgi Popkov from the Presidium of the Supreme Soviet on account of the fact that he "is no longer in Leningrad" where he had served as secretary of the Party. V. M. Andrianov was named Popkov's successor.

All the members of the Politburo with three exceptions have appeared at the Supreme Soviet sessions. The exceptions have been Nikita Khrushchev, who frequently does not attend because of his preoccupation with Ukrainian matters, A. A. Andreyev, who also is an infrequent attender because he is usually preoccupied with spring planting at this season, and Voznesensky. . . .

March 15

It is hard to convey the atmosphere of the foreign colony here. I should say, however, that it is the sort of thing that Oechsner and Beattie and Shirer were familiar with. Or Howard K. Smith, for example.* I would not say that the attitude of the foreigners is completely justified. In many respects I think it is not. But that is their attitude nonetheless, and it tends to color one's life quite rapidly.

Dispatch Killed by Censor
March 16

Speculation abroad about the probable early convocation of the first All-Union Congress of the Communist Party since 1939 has produced no reaction in the Soviet press.

In the past six months Communist parties have held congresses in virtually all the sixteen federated Union republics. In the past local congresses have always been followed by an All-Union meeting.

The last congress was held March, 1939, on the eve of World War II. Foreign diplomats have advised their governments that an All-Union Congress is likely some time this year but probably not before autumn.†

March 18

A letter from Mother and Janet (my sister) today—sent March 6. Not such bad time.

* Correspondents in Berlin on the eve of World War II.
† In fact, the Nineteenth Party Congress was not held until October, 1952.

There is just no comparison between the food situation now and when I was here before. The people look much better dressed. The city has perked up—lots of cars and traffic on the street. But my work is just as difficult as ever—if not more so. I can't help but see in it the reflection of the deterioration of relations between Russia and the United States. Not that I am surprised. I am still balked by inability to get a secretary.

Dispatch to New York Times
March 19, 1949

In a [penetrating] series of exposés carried out over the past six weeks the Soviet press has uncovered the existence [particularly within the intellectual circles of nests] of what are described here as "homeless cosmopolitans."

[The campaign has disclosed the fact that "cosmopolitans" have been harbored in a wide variety of intellectual circles, from poets to sports writers.] One of the most concise definitions of cosmopolitanism was offered by Konstantin Simonov, the Soviet author, who described it as a "desire to undermine national roots and national pride because people without roots are easier to to push over and sell into slavery to American imperialism."

The campaign had its inception within the Writers' Committee executive which last December considered [the theater's failure to carry out effectively the decree of the late Andrei Zhdanov for encouragement of] Soviet realism and problems of the day. The writers found the Moscow drama critics sabotaging such works, and their complaint was thunderously taken up by *Pravda* on January 28 with a four-column exposé of "anti-patriotic critics." *Pravda* dubbed them "parentless" cosmopolitans, but the phrase more generally used is "homeless" cosmopolitans.

[Punitive action has been taken against three leading] cosmopolitan critics, I. Altman, Fyodor Levin, and D. Danin—the first two of whom were expelled from the Communist Party. Danin was expelled as a candidate member. Levin was also expelled from the Gorki Literary Institute along with G. Brovman and P. Antokolsky.*

[The full list of cosmopolites is too long for reproduction, but

---

* Pavel Antokolsky, one of Russia's leading poets. He soon was restored to favor. Most of the critics did not reappear in print until after Stalin's death in 1953. Some never appeared again.

it includes, for example, seven Ukraine critics who were un-masked by *Pravda* of the Ukraine on February 19. The Ukraine *Pravda* listed them as J. Stebun (Katsnelson), L. Sanov (Smulson), A. Katsnelson, E. Adelheim, G. Helfandbein, Y. Burlachenko (Berdichevsky), and A. Gozenpud.

Similarly, in the field of sports writing the unmasked cosmo-politans include G. Yasny (Finkelstein), V. Viktorov (Zlochevsky), L. Schneider, and A. Svetov (Sheidlin).

Among the Moscow cosmopolites the one most frequently men-tioned is Ifrim Kholodov (Mayerovich).

In Leningrad cosmopolitanism has been uncovered within the Leningrad cinema production center.] L. Trauberg's cosmopol-itanism has caused him to fail in producing a movie "on the vivid and patriotic theme of the biography of the outstanding Russian scientist, Alexandr Popov." Popov, as is well known, is the Russian scientist who gave the world the invention of radio. Trauberg's close associate, M. Bleman, was disclosed to have described David Wark Griffith as "the father of world cinema," ignoring the well-known fact that Soviet scientists pioneered in cinematography.

One of the sharpest attacks was directed by *Komsomolskaya Pravda* against S. Altshuler. To quote this paper, ". . . everyone knows that the discovery of one of the most mighty instruments of contemporary science—penicillin—was the service of the re-markable Russian scientists, Polotobnov, Masassein, and Gukov-ski. But Altshuler affirms that 'the British scientist Fleming dis-covered penicillin.' "

The newspaper *Evening Moscow* unmasks another cosmopol-itan who apparently has been encouraged by the critic, Levin.

[This is Aleksandr Isbakh who writes under the pseudonym Isaak Bakhrakh and has published a novel entitled *The Years of Life*. In the words of the *Evening Moscow*: "What ideas does the author of this petty little book preach? In the first place exaltation of the Hebrew religion. The entire book from the first to the last page is permeated with the cult of religion. Isbakh slanders the Jewish people by asserting that for all Jews irrespec-tive of class origin and position in society all happiness lies in religion."

Isbakh's cosmopolitanism is even more clearly revealed by the

13

fact that he "openly propagandizes for Zionism and even reproduces the text of the Zionist anthem. . . ."]

Among the chief Western cosmopolitans are named André Gide, Bertrand Russell, T. S. Eliot, André Malraux, Arthur Koestler, Stephen Spender, Jean Paul Sartre, Simone de Beauvoir, Ezra Pound, and e. e. cummings. . . .

[Soviet criticisms uniformly point out the original names of those criticized in instances where Jews have adopted Russian pseudonyms.

A number of measures apparently have been found necessary to uproot cosmopolitanism among this racial group. The Jewish newspaper in Moscow has been suspended. The Jewish anti-Fascist committee has been dissolved. A number of changes have been made in the Jewish theater in Minsk.]

March 20, 1949

Outside the Metropole Hotel in Sverdlovsk Square workmen are busy all day long. They are putting up a great circular wooden fence which will enclose the central part of the square—an area as large as the infield of a small racecourse.

Once the fence is up other crews will tackle the job of breaking up and removing the pavement and creating a grassy park with flowers, trees, and benches where Muscovites can take the air on pleasant summer days and children can run and play hopscotch.

One of the first questions asked me by Russians is: "Do you notice any change in Moscow?"

The answer is, of course, there have been many, many changes, but most of them are summed up by the workingmen busy starting the park in Sverdlovsk Square.

I have wartime memories of Sverdlovsk Square . . . the singing of troops as they marched in companies and platoons in the evening snowfall . . . the chip, chip, chip of women's picks as they labored night and day to remove the snow and ice from the vast expanse of concrete . . . minutes of suspense as from the loud-speakers in the square came the chiming of the Moscow radio that always preceded the announcement of another *prykaz* —a victory communiqué.

There are other wartime impressions, too—the worn, tired faces of men and women on their way to the factories in the cold of early morning, the unheated flats with pipes burst from the grim winter of 1941–42, the long queues at the few shops, for many people the everlasting struggle to eke out more than a bare existence on the prevailing rations. . . .

It's against this picture that Moscow today presents such vivid contrasts. Now Moscow sparkles at night. Great red stars gleam in the evening twilight over the Kremlin walls.

One only has to look at the chubby-faced children and bosomy Moscow girls to see they're well fed. The gaunt, strained faces, so common during the war, have fleshed out.

Among the persons I knew in Moscow five years ago I have yet to meet one who has not put on weight.

Dispatch to New York Times
March 23

The Soviet humor magazine *Krokodil* today published a double-page spread of full-color cartoons under the title "Snob Cosmopolites."

This epitomizes the current ideological drive. One cartoon depicts a group of long red-nosed critics spattering ink on the famous sea gull curtain of the Moscow Art Theater. Another shows beak-nosed critics hurling saxophones and slinging ink at portraits of Tchaikovsky, Glinka, and Borodin. Another pictures Faginish critics holding D. W. Griffith's director's hat over the lens of a camera operated by a handsome Soviet cameraman. . . .

March 24

What do Moscow housewives talk about as they wait in line in the crowded stores to pay their checks? Like people anywhere they talk about the problems of the day.

What strikes home sharply to Muscovites is the question of the possibility of a new war.

They remember only too vividly the husbands, fathers, and sons struck down in the war against Germany. They remember the grim days when the Germans approached Moscow's outskirts and thousands of civilians—men, women, and children—thronged out through the suburbs to erect trenches and fortifications.

And the days when thousands marched from the factories to meet the initial impact of the German panzers. And they remember the thousands who did not return. . . .

March 28, 1949

This is a quiet Monday evening, and I have been sitting here listening to the radio—Voice of America and then some dullish BBC—and reading the *London Times*. It has been a sunshiny day today—second in succession. Almost springlike. They are selling mimosa in the markets, and you see people all over town walking along with bunches in their hands. Of course there will probably be several more blizzards before spring really comes, but it is nice to see the sun. There is so little light in winter that everyone blossoms when the sun comes out and starts to shine.

Now, the radio is tuned to Stockholm, and I am getting the Swedish version of the news in English. I just switched it from BBC where they were giving the news in Swedish!

How do I get the news when I still have no secretary? It isn't easy. I have to suck around the other correspondents, making myself a fine nuisance. Thank goodness, they are very decent about it. But I despise working this way. I hate not being on my own, and there is so much which I can't do.

The censorship is substantially worse than I have ever seen it. It is much worse than in 1944, and so far as I can judge from Middleton's and Atkinson's files* much worse than during their period. The other correspondents here agree.

I have sent Freedman† enough samples so that he can get a fairly good idea of the cutting which goes on.

Generally speaking, they cut almost anything which does not appear in the press. They also cut direct quotations from the press, often, in order to attempt to pervert our reports. An outstanding example is the consistent cuts of Semitic names from the reports on the cosmopolitan drive in order to conceal the strong anti-Semitic basis of this campaign.

Conclusions, analysis, speculation, etc., are automatically cut. Biographical material is almost always cut.

In referring to relations between the U.S.A. and the U.S.S.R. they pass sentences referring to "threats to the peace" but cut any reference to "possible war" or "war threats." They pass ref-

* Drew Middleton and Brooks Atkinson, previous correspondents of the *New York Times* in Moscow.

† Emanuel R. Freedman, foreign editor of the *New York Times*.

16

erences to damage during the war but no references indicating that damage has not yet been repaired.

As a result all dispatches from Moscow are automatically biased. They definitely misrepresent the news and distort it to fit the frequently incomprehensible Soviet propaganda line.

These dispatches are printed in the *Times* with no indication to the reader that they have been tampered with. Yet, the fact is they represent, first, my effort to anticipate the censor and phrase the dispatch in terms which he will pass; second, the censor's effort to slant the story into the Soviet line by judicious editing.

Therefore, I am recommending most strongly that all dispatches from Moscow carry a warning slug—"Passed by Soviet Censorship"—or words to that effect. I think that is the least the *Times* can do to protect its readers.

I feel very strongly on this.

One of the first things I did was to write a dispatch outlining the general conditions of work here. I wrote it on March 13. As might have been expected, it was killed by the censor.

Here is the story I wrote:

Moscow.—Few Americans are unaware of the dangerous deterioration of relations between Russia and the United States, but I doubt whether they realize fully the atmosphere this has created in Moscow.

Difficult and painful as the subject may be to discuss, it is important for our readers—now that the *New York Times* bureau has been re-established in Moscow—to understand the conditions under which it operates.

All foreigners in Moscow, and particularly Americans, are subject to restrictions. From the correspondent's viewpoint the chief of these is a rule whereby direct informational contacts with government officials are barred. All contacts must be arranged through the Foreign Office press department. . . .

This rule is bulwarked by regulations concerning state secrets which sharply restrict the type and kind of information which can be released by officials. Thus, correspondents to a considerable extent are cut off from normal news sources.

There are considerable restrictions on travel. Some highways leading from Moscow are banned to foreigners, and large areas of the Soviet Union are also banned. However, contrary to impressions in America, travel about the Soviet Union is by no means prohibited. Many regions, including Leningrad, Odessa, Kharkov, Pskov, Omsk, Tbilisi, and Stalingrad, have been visited by American embassy staff members or correspondents in recent months.*

There is an official censorship which has the twofold function of guarding against transmission of information regarded as restricted in the U.S.S.R. and preventing correspondents from presenting what are regarded as inaccurate or biased reports.

And there is what might be termed a psychological hazard arising from repeated suggestions by the Soviet press that the chief function of many foreign correspondents is spying and espionage.

In the case of Americans, this hazard has extended from the psychological to the physical by the expulsion of two correspondents—Anna Louise Strong and Robert Magidoff—within the past year. Both Miss Strong and Magidoff were charged with intelligence operations. These expulsions came before publication of Annabelle Bucar's book† contending that the American embassy, generally, was engaged in anti-Soviet activities.

March 31, 1949

There's not much evidence of active antagonism on the part of Muscovites toward individual Americans. True, there are occasional altercations, but the average Russian never sees an American because there are only a handful here.

April 1

I have been investigating the cost of living situation. Here is the way it adds up:

My costs for the hotel room and meals will run close to 5,000 rubles a month.‡ Meals run about 100 rubles a day in the hotel, cooking my own breakfast and some of my suppers. It is possible

* Much more extensive travel restrictions were imposed in January, 1952. In June, 1953, after Stalin's death, about two-thirds of the country was opened to travel. Additional areas including the Baltic states have been opened since then, but some regions opened in 1953 have been again restricted.

† Miss Bucar, a member of the U.S. embassy staff in Moscow, broke with the embassy in 1948. She married a Russian operetta tenor and in early 1949 published a book entitled *The Truth about American Diplomats.*

‡ The diplomatic exchange rate prevailing then was 8 rubles to the dollar.

to shave that slightly by importing food from the United States and Denmark and hiring a cook to prepare a midday dinner. My hotel room costs 1,860 rubles a month. That means food and lodging cost in dollars about $625 a month. For purposes of comparison, I paid $75 a month rent for a one-room apartment in New York, which was luxurious in comparison with the Metropole, and about $50–60 a week for food.

Needless to say all other costs are in proportion here—16 rubles ($2) to press a suit, for example.

I don't file a story about Moscow prices because the censorship uniformly kills all prices—and well they might!

II

First Impressions

April 2, 1949

Two letters today from Minneapolis, mailed March 14 and March 21. For some reason the mail seems to pile up and get here in gobs. I suppose it has to wait for a plane—or something.

Only this week managed to get a secretary. Now my work is going along better, and it should improve as time goes on.

April 4

Now, at last, a detailed report on some of the things which I find interesting . . . .

Changes in the government:

So far as anyone here has been able to discover, none of the changes are of real consequence with one exception—that of Voznesensky. Molotov, Mikoyan, and Bulganin are much in evidence, particularly Mikoyan. It seems pretty clear that Politburo members are generally being relieved of direct administrative jobs in order to concentrate on policy.

Kosygin remains at the head of light industry—to which he was named only last December. The other Politburo members are all out of specific cabinet posts. I thought before arriving in Moscow that the way was being cleared to let Uncle Joe retire and that Molotov would resume the premiership. I have changed my mind on that, however. I suspect that Stalin will continue in the premiership. Incidentally, Malenkov laid down the line for the relinquishment of cabinet responsibility by Politburo members pretty clearly in his speech at the Cominform meeting in Poland.*

Voznesensky:

He appears to be out not only of the government but of the Politburo. He has dropped completely from sight. No mention of him whatsoever in the press, and the censorship has killed all references to his membership in the Politburo while passing such references for Molotov, Mikoyan, and Bulganin.

There are two theories for Voznesensky's fall. One is that he sided against Varga and that Varga is coming out on top.† I am not sold on that one. Varga obviously is staging a comeback, but the evidence that Voznesensky opposed him is not precise. The other theory is that Voznesensky was a Zhdanov protégé and that Malenkov fixed him. There may be something in that. Voznesensky certainly was brought forward by Zhdanov, and there is

* Malenkov, speaking at the Conference of Communist Parties in Poland, September, 1947, said: "During the war party organs were frequently compelled to engage in operational work in directing the economy. This was correct under the circumstances. One can't help but see, however, that this engendered certain negative features in the work of party organizations, resulted in the weakening of intraparty work and at the same time in the replacement of state and economic organs. One of the fundamental tenets of Bolshevik leadership was violated." He also said the Party's central committee was working on a new basic program for the Bolshevik party. "The program of the Communist Party in effect now is long obsolete and must be replaced. Along with preparing a new program, work is under way for introduction of changes into the charter of the Party. The situation in the country and the Party has so changed during the past few years that a large number of paragraphs are obsolete." *Pravda* in March, 1949, said on the anniversary of the Ninth Bolshevik Party Congress that the central committee was preparing a new program designed to replace that of the Ninth Congress. In fact, the new Party program was never completed. When the Nineteenth Party Congress finally met in October, 1952, it named a committee to draft this program. Its work was not completed by the time of Stalin's death, March 5, 1953, and it then was quietly dissolved. Apparently, Malenkov's remarks about Party and state responsibilities and the new Party program were—like the seeming preparations for a Party congress in 1949—involved in some way in his bid for Party leadership. Malenkov's position with regard to Party and government functions was to have great significance after Stalin's death. Malenkov and his supporters in March and April, 1953, chose government rather than Party posts. But it was the Party, led by Khrushchev, which emerged supreme in the political control.

† Eugene Varga, Soviet economist, was the center of controversy in 1947 for his unorthodox view that the U.S. economy would not suffer an immediate postwar depression. By 1949 he had recanted and was again in favor.

plenty of evidence that Malenkov is now in the driver's seat and has gotten rid of a good many of the more ardent Zhdanovites.*

Incidentally, I think there will be several new candidate members of the Politburo soon. Suslov and Ponomarenko seem to be very good bets.

Cosmopolitanism:

There is a good story here which censorship is stopping and which, so far as I know, the foreign press has not picked up. That is the very strong anti-Semitic bias which the campaign has taken.

The original objective of the drive did not seem to be the Jews, but it has developed in that direction. The bitterest venom about persons "homeless and without kith or kin"—as the cliché has it—is preserved for victims with Jewish names.

In the cases of writers who employ noms de plume, the newspapers print the original Jewish name in brackets, thus drawing even more attention to their faith. Several Jewish writers have been singled out because of alleged pandering to Jewish religion and Zionism, and in these articles there have been many slams at the Jewish religion. The censorship has refused to pass these vile pieces.

At the same time there has been a big hubbub over the Jewish theater in Minsk and the Jewish critics there. As was reported abroad, I believe, the Minsk theater was closed for a time but has now reopened. Rumors circulated that the Jewish theater here would be closed but it has not done so. However, the Jewish paper here was closed and the Jewish Anti-Fascist Committee here was dissolved.†

Taking a cue from this official propaganda, a good many lesser government officials have conducted purges of their departments, removing all Jews, and additional official or unofficial barriers

* Voznesensky's fate did not become known until Khrushchev revealed in his secret speech to the Twentieth Party Congress, February, 1956, that he had been arrested, apparently in February or March, 1949. He was not executed until the following year.

† In fact, all Jewish cultural institutions, not only in Minsk and Moscow but also in the Jewish province of Birobidzhan, had by this time been closed. The members of the Jewish Anti-Fascist Committee had been arrested and in July, 1952, were tried and most of them executed. It was not until 1956 and 1957 that the principal details of Stalin's anti-Semitic campaign of 1948–49 began to fall into place. Much, however, is still unknown.

to the employment of Jews have appeared, particularly in the schools and universities.

It would be my guess that this activity on a lower level is unauthorized. But judging from the readiness with which ordinary Muscovites leap at any opportunity to gratify their latent anti-Semitic feelings, the government must have known very well what the results of this open propaganda against the Jews would be.

As to the motivation behind the campaign—I presume it is part of the all-out campaign to solidify the government's ideological and emotional bulwarks, and the Jews, in their eyes, represent one possible link with the outer world.

Foreign policy:

In spite of its rabid propaganda, there is no evidence that the government seriously is concerning itself with the possibility of an imminent outbreak of war.

The major domestic propaganda emphasis is on reconstruction and the improvement of general living conditions.

There is no way of telling, of course, what proportion of the Soviet budget is actually being devoted to military purposes. I can only judge by comparison with the war years, of course, and all the tangible evidence I can find indicates that there has been a really big shift over to peacetime economy. Our people here think that after an intensification of the war of nerves this spring the Russians will make some kind of an offer toward a settlement with the West.*

Anna Louise Strong:

What probably lay behind the expulsion of Anna Louise?† She had been talking pretty openly about what she was going to tell her friends in Communist China once she got out there— apparently advice à la Tito. She talked so freely that there is little doubt the Russians heard of it—in fact, she may very well have talked in the same fashion to such Russian contacts as she had.

* In May, 1949, the Malik-Jessup conversations in New York produced settlement of the Berlin blockade.

† An American woman who had been an early sympathizer with Soviet communism, and who had been in Communist China during the "long march" of Mao Tse-tung, was arrested in January, 1949. She was held in the Lubyanka prison for about a week and then deported with the announcement that she had been a long-time agent of U.S. Intelligence.

The theory is that she was smeared, not for domestic propaganda nor for any effect on the United States, but in order to destroy her possible influence with the Chinese Communists. I may be leaping at conclusions, but I can't help thinking the closing of the *Moscow News* and the disappearance of our old friend Borodin after all these years may in some obscure fashion be linked with the same situation.*

From all I can gather the Kremlin still is very unsure of the situation in China. It gets very scanty reference in the press, and even statements by the Chinese, laudatory of Russia and Soviet leadership, are handled most gingerly. My opinion is that the Kremlin has its fingers crossed about its Chinese friends and will keep them that way for some time.

Dispatch to New York Times
April 8, 1949

The *Evening Moscow* reveals that the world's first bicycle was built by a heretofore obscure Urals metalworker from Nizhni-Tagil named Artamonov. . . .

Dispatch to New York Times
April 9

Soviet physical and atomic science has again carried off top honors in the award of Stalin prizes. *Pravda* said "a great step forward" was taken in the past year toward the fulfilment of Stalin's statement of February 9, 1946, that "if we give proper help to our scientists they will be able not only to equal but to surpass in the nearest future science outside our country."†

April 11
Letter to Jacob Lomakin,‡ Foreign Office

Would it be possible for the Press Department to arrange for me to interview some of the Stalin prize winners? I should be deeply grateful for any interviews you might set up as I think there is

---

* Mikhail Borodin, old Bolshevik and principal Russian agent in the Canton Revolution of 1924, had been for some years editor of the *Moscow News*. The newspaper was suspended and (as it later transpired) Borodin and most of his staff arrested in January, 1949. Borodin was sent to a concentration camp where he died early in 1953. Borodin and Miss Strong were close friends and had been associated for many years on the *Moscow News* staff.

† September 23, 1949, President Truman announced that the Soviet Union had carried out its first atomic test.

‡ Acting chief of the press department.

great interest in America in all of the prize winners. . . . I realize that the list comprises the virtual elite of Soviet science and art and that some of the interviews may be difficult or impossible to arrange. . . .

April 12

I've just finished a current Russian novel called *Early Days,* by Konstantin Fedin, a story of life in Saratov, a Volga River town, back in 1910, and most charming. I have finished *The Idiot* and have started *Dead Souls.*

Went to the theater again. Saw *The Conspiracy of the Doomed.* It has a lot of ideological content, being about an American plot to stage a coup d'état in some country like Hungary or Rumania. Last night I saw *The Stone Flower,* a lovely color film about a bad fairy who lives in the heart of the Ural Mountains.

April 14 (Easter Sunday)

It has been a bright sunny day here. Of course, it's not Easter in Moscow until next Sunday, but there was a sort of holiday atmosphere in the air.

Ludmilla (my secretary) and I went to see *Uncle Tom's Cabin* at the Transport Workers' Theater—a show for kids. More fun than a picnic. The kids suffered agonies. I never heard so much bawling in my life as when poor Tom was auctioned off. Then, I came back to the office and wrote my story and walked over to the telegraph office with it and on the way back window-shopped in the bookstores. I practice my lousy Russian by spelling out titles of books.

April 16

Last night I saw *Swan Lake* for the first time since arriving here. First time I had been to the Bolshoi. Went with Dick Davis of the embassy. The Bolshoi as much a fairyland as ever.

April 17

Three jokes killed by the censor today—all from *Krokodil,* the humor magazine.

First joke:

"I can't understand—which tractor has been repaired and which one is to be repaired?"

"Run them."

"I tried that—neither of them run."

Second joke:

"Your report says that you made some profit. Where is it?"

"It was spent in drawing up and binding the report."

Third joke:

"I think the dress material is good, but I don't like the pattern."

"Don't worry, the pattern will disappear after the first washing."

April 20, 1949

What kind of stories do I have access to? The daily press, the weekly press, the monthly press, the quarterly press, the theaters, the movies, the books—and walking around Moscow and looking at the people and seeing what they do and how they eat and dress and what the stores are like.

April 21
Letter to Jacob Lomakin, Foreign Office

Mr. Simonov advises me that he has contacted the various Stalin prize winners with whom I requested interviews and finds that all of them are either too busy to see me or are not in Moscow at the moment. . . .

If your department believes that such interviews would be inadvisable in view of the state of Soviet-American relations, I should much prefer to have you tell me, since, to be frank, it is difficult to believe that every one of the Stalin prize winners— artists, writers, and poets as well as scientists and technicians— is so busy that he cannot spare an hour's time to discuss his work with a correspondent. . . .

April 25

Easter was quite pleasant. I went to services in the big cathedral. The first time I'd been to a Russian Easter service, barring the occasion in Odessa in 1944. Tremendous throngs in the streets outside. The car could hardly get through in spite of the best efforts of the scores of militia.

As midnight neared, the patriarch and his acolytes and attendants came out. The church was absolutely jammed. They were good-looking people, dressed well, many of them young, both men and women.

Just before midnight the patriarch offered a prayer for Russia and her people and for Stalin. Then at midnight they chanted that Christ had arisen and the congregation responded, Yes, He truly has arisen. Hundreds of people lighted candles just at midnight—I don't know the exact significance of that.

Dispatch to New York Times
April 27

The Communist successes in China are reported in brief dispatches without any special display. The China news is usually broken into two or three items of one hundred to two hundred words by Tass, crediting the Sinhua Agency.

[Due to lack of any editorial comment the events have not produced any major impact among Soviet readers. The China news is gratifying to readers, but their satisfaction is limited by the fact the dispatches do not proclaim final victory and thus far the extent of the Communist gains has not yet been analyzed.]

May 3

Frankly, as I have indicated previously to Edwin James (in New York), I do not think dispatches which are subject to a censorship as heavy as that which is being imposed here every day should be published without some warning to the reader.

Dispatch to New York Times
May 5

Special radio broadcasts brought news to the Russian people of the decision to lift the Berlin blockade and convene the Council of Ministers—news which was welcomed universally by Soviet citizens as tangible evidence that international tension has eased.

In the words of one Soviet citizen, the announcement was "the first good news we've had on the international front in so long I can't remember the last time."

May 6

There are two theories current as to what the Russians will propose at the Council of Foreign Ministers.

The first and more conservative theory is that they will bring no basically new plan to the conference, but will utilize the meeting as a forum to voice their well-known views on the unification of Germany.

The second theory is a radical one. It suggests that the Russians are making a basic change in tactics and are prepared to accept virtually all of the western position on Germany with these ideas in mind:

1. This would weaken seriously support of the Atlantic Pact, both in Europe and in the United States.

2. This would force early withdrawal of at least the bulk of American forces from Europe.

3. In exchange for what might be regarded as "paper" concessions in Germany the basic Soviet position might be vastly strengthened.

4. If a sweeping German settlement were achieved, the well-knit Communist Party in Germany would be in a strategic position to move forward toward the Soviet long-term goals.

5. American interest in both the Marshall Plan and the Atlantic Pact might well be materially decreased.

6. The easing of European tension would enable Russia to redirect her interest to the Far East where enormous stakes are in the balance of her touchy relations with the Chinese Communists.

Attractive as this second thesis is on the surface, I'm inclined to think it is too radical.

I am convinced that the top leadership actually believes there is more than half a chance that the United States might attack Russia. The reaction of the people to the lifting of the blockade was very significant. They were almost pathetic in their pleasure. . . .

Meanwhile, the censorship has slammed the lid on with a vengeance.

For the last week or so they have killed or radically cut all copy reporting anti-American propaganda. This includes a complete kill of the dirtiest anti-American piece which has appeared since I got here. This is a scene from a new play by Anatoly Surov, one of the top ideological dramatists who wrote the Stalin prize play, *Green Street*. His new opus is called *The Mad Haberdasher*. The play is set in a small Missouri town. The central character is an unsuccessful haberdasher who in appearance resembles Hitler. A gang of Missouri Democratic politicians, members of the Pendergast gang, decide to put the haberdasher in the White House.

One interesting thing. The great drive against "cosmopolitanism" has almost disappeared from the press. It seems to be over for the time being. The open attacks on Jews have disappeared. This followed a conference of the editors of the central papers, called by the central committee, at which, I understand, they were told to pipe down on the Jewish question.*

Nothing new has become known about Voznesensky. His picture was prominently missing on May Day. All other Politburo members were present, except for Khrushchev who was at Kiev and Andreyev who is supposed to be ill. Andreyev has appeared in public only once in the last year so far as I can learn. With the Politburo on Lenin's Tomb were Georgi Popov, Suslov, and Ponomarenko. It seems very likely that they are now candidate members.

The new film *Stalingrad Battle,* which is opening May 9 incidentally, makes much of Malenkov, who is pictured as being sent to Stalingrad in the direst days to take charge of the defense. His build up is going ahead steadily . . .

May 6, 1949

There is a lot of rough talk these days, particularly from some of the loudmouths in Washington and their counterparts over here. But the people are not interested in having a war.

This agreement on the Berlin blockade is very important. It is going to relieve the daily tension and, psychologically, it will mean a hell of a lot regardless of the foreign ministers' conference.

There will not be any war. These people do not want a war. They hate the idea and haven't the faintest intention of precipitating a conflict. Their feeling is that, generally speaking, history is on their side, running their way. They can afford to wait a while.

I was in the Red Square on May Day. The spectacle is terribly impressive. Run off with split-second timing. I think the masses

* Actually, by this time all Jewish cultural institutions in the Soviet Union had been closed down and scores of leading Jewish intellectuals were being held in prison for interrogation concerning a "nationalist-Zionist plot." Nothing of this was known in the diplomatic or newspaper colony in Moscow at that time.

of people moving through Red Square, plain people, are more impressive than the troops. The troops are smart, of course; the tanks are big and the airplanes fast—but any country could put that on. The people are another thing. About half of Moscow turns out and marches—all the kids, all the youngsters, and many middle-aged and older people. They carry thousands of red banners and flags of pastel colors—yellow, green, white, rose, pink. A moving mass of color. It goes on all day—from 10:00 in the morning until 4:00 in the afternoon.

Then, at night, the great squares are closed to traffic and there are bands and everyone wanders around and there is dancing and fireworks—just like the wartime victory salutes—and dozens of searchlights, like those in Hyde Park, shooting straight up into the air.

I wandered around among the people for a while. I was very lonely, walking by myself among half a million people.

On Monday I went out to the Novo Dyevichye Monastery and saw the grave of Stalin's wife.* It is lovely. The cemetery is reached through a huge gate in the thick convent walls—about twenty feet thick, I guess. The grave is off in one corner, surrounded by young evergreen trees. There is a simple shaft of marble with Alleluyeva's head carved at the top. There is just a plain inscription on it, giving her dates of birth and death and the fact she was a member of the Communist Party. Nearby is the grave of another member of her family—a brother or father.

Dispatch to New York Times
May 7, 1949

Pravda gave prominence today to a report from Peiping on the Chinese Communist government's declaration of prerequisites for establishing foreign diplomatic relations. . . .

[Of the two conditions—withdrawal of armed forces and severance of relations with Chiang Kai-shek's government—] the Soviet [already meets one requirement since it] has no military forces in China.

[However, the Soviet continues to maintain scrupulously correct relations with the Chinese Nationalist government and cur-

---

* Nadezhda Alleluyeva, Stalin's second wife, died suddenly November 6, 1932, under mysterious circumstances.

rently is engaged in diplomatic negotiations with the Nationalists concerning southwest China.

There has been no indication when the Soviet will withdraw recognition from the Nationalists and enter into relations with the new government. It is generally felt that such action would quickly follow occupation by the Chinese Communists of Shanghai.]*

Dispatch to New York Times
May 8

A new Soviet play, *The House on the Lane,* at the Lenin Komsomol Theater last night attracted a number of Moscow diplomats. It was based in part on the revelations of Annabelle Bucar's *The Truth about American Diplomats,* a current best-seller.

May 10

This has been one of those days when I haven't gotten many things done. A fellow came in who wants to work as a chauffeur. Maybe at long last I'll get my car operating. Two months since I came—and just getting to this point! Only yesterday was my outside telephone line installed.

Last night I saw the new film, *Stalingrad Battle.* It gives the best picture of Stalin's life and how he works inside the Kremlin and of the Politburo that has ever appeared.

There was a big moon over Moscow and lots of youngsters on the streets and in the parks with their accordions, singing and strolling. I walked part of the way home.

May 13

Today I went to the Fine Arts Museum. I thought they had some modern Russian paintings by young Russian artists. But it turned out they didn't. They have a pretty fair collection of eighteenth-century French—Fragonard, Boucher, or whatever his name is, and that ilk.

Event of events—I had my first Russian lesson yesterday. I don't think I'm going to be a very good scholar.

The trees are leafing out with amazing rapidity. The sidewalk café outside the Metropole is open, and there are others around the city.

* Actually, the Soviet recognized the Communist Chinese regime in October, 1949, after Chiang's withdrawal from the mainland.

May 20, 1949

Today is one of the rare occasions when my name appears in the Russian press. It appears in connection with the conference we had yesterday with Archibald Johnston.* One funny thing is that the censor cut out of my story my own question to Johnston. But here we find it bright and shining in the Tass account. . . .

May 23

This is the kind of spring morning you dream about—a fresh, cool breeze, smelling of flowers and blossoms, a blue, blue sky, and the sun not yet high enough to be hot; a day that makes you think of walking in the country along quiet lanes and under orchards bursting with blossoms; the kind of day you want to be lazy and lie back in the fresh green grass with a brook bubbling near by and the girl you love lying beside you, doing nothing but dreaming a bit and making love a bit and letting the rest of the world go about its dreary tasks.

Not a day for worrying about ideological studies, political problems, and international tensions. I will do a few chores and then what? Well, I don't know. I have spring fever. . . .

May 24

It has been suggested that censorship conditions have not changed materially here since Drew Middleton left. That is not my impression.

One of the most serious consequences of the censorship is that it has effectively concealed the real extent and bitterness of the anti-American campaign.

The campaign is having real effect. I saw an Indian film not long ago. It showed some officers dining in luxury while the Indians were starving. They were British officers. But the spectators sitting behind me promptly identified them as Americans and remarked about it. On May Day a car from the embassy which was flying an American flag drew boos, several times. . . .

The radio-jamming campaign is effective—at least in the Moscow region. . . .

And they are liquidating almost the only remaining direct contact of Russians with foreigners—the little Catholic church in

* Editor of the British government's Moscow paper, *Britansky Soyusnik.* Johnston resigned to devote himself to the cause of peace, as he put it.

32

Moscow. Father LaBerge's visa to return after he had gone to America was withdrawn. After many months there is still no action on a visa for his successor.

The church, meanwhile, has been conducted by Father Thomas, a French priest. Just over a week ago a deputation called on Father Thomas. They had an order from Mossoviet requiring Father Thomas to turn over the keys—which he did. The next move obviously is the appointment of a Polish priest.

Once this little matter is tidied up, no doubt it will be possible to grant a visa to an American priest, thus honoring the terms of the Litvinov agreement, but restricting his function to that of chaplain to the American community.*

Travel by diplomats to places on the non-restricted list continues amid a good many difficulties. The latest wrinkle is inability to get hotel facilities. With the exception of a trip which Eddy Gilmore made to Tiflis in March there have been no trips by correspondents.

The rub in the matter plainly is OVIR.† It is my impression that one result of the Strong case (and I expected as much from the slam that announcement made at the Foreign Office)‡ is that all visa matters now must have OVIR clearance, and the Foreign Office is virtually powerless in this matter.

It is now, incidentally, official policy not to grant re-entry visas to correspondents who leave the country. . . .

There are not many familiar faces from the wartime era still to be seen in Moscow. I have seen Ehrenburg at a couple of Foreign Office receptions and Simonov at one.§ They bow to their

* The Litvinov agreement of December, 1933, whereby the United States established diplomatic relations with the Soviet Union, provided that spiritual mentors for Americans in Moscow would be permitted to enter the U.S.S.R. Under this agreement Father Leopold Braun went to Moscow in 1934 and remained until 1947, conducting services at the Church of St. Louis. His successor was Father LaBerge. After the Church of St. Louis was placed in the hands of a priest from Riga in May, 1949, a visa was finally granted to the Reverend Louis Brassard (like his predecessors, a member of the Assumptionist order) from Worcester, Massachusetts. He arrived in Moscow in January, 1950, but was not permitted to serve at the Church of St. Louis.

† OVIR—the visa department of the Ministry of Internal Affairs.

‡ When the announcement of the expulsion of Miss Strong was made, it was said that she had been permitted to enter the U.S.S.R. through lack of vigilance on the part of the Foreign Office.

§ Ilya Ehrenburg and Konstantin Simonov, Soviet writers.

former friends in the press corps but do not converse with them. I've seen Palgunov once and talked with him. He seemed the same as ever, a little thinner and a little more pasty-faced. Lomakin I have not seen since May Day. All press department contacts are through Simonov.

The whole American press corps would disappear in a moment, if it could. Newman is waiting on a visa for his successor. Gilmore has an application in to transfer to Warsaw. Stevens would leave if he could sell his house—and probably will leave anyway in a few months. I don't know about Shapiro. Natalie Rene is in the hospital. She was hit by a truck in the Arbat about a month ago and suffered a serious spine injury. It is a great shame. It came just when Natalie was in very good form, too, still basking in the aura of her Kremlin letter. Parker seems in bad shape to me. I think he is tarred a bit with the same brush as Anna Louise. He has been selling off his library and getting his affairs in shape to leave the country. My guess is that he will be lucky to get out without serious trouble. I can't help but feel sorry for him. Another person who is having a rough time of it is Champanois. Margolis died some months ago. He had lost his job some time previously.*

Dispatch Killed by Censor
May 24, 1949

The rapidity with which the Chinese Communists are now moving raises pertinent questions in connection with the Japanese treaty. It appears likely that by the time the five-member Council of Ministers convenes on that question the Kuomintang no longer will be the recognized government of China and in its place will be the Communist regime. . . .

*Nikolai Palgunov, 1943–60, head of Tass News Agency. Jacob Lomakin, Soviet consul-general in New York, expelled at the time of the Kasenkina case in January, 1949; became acting head of press department of Foreign Office on his return to Moscow but soon transferred to Foreign Trade Ministry; died in 1958. Simonov, a subordinate official of the press department. Joseph Newman, *New York Herald-Tribune* correspondent; he left in June, 1949. Eddy Gilmore, Associated Press correspondent in Moscow; his wife and children were Soviet citizens, and Soviet authorities refused to permit them to leave the country. Edmund Stevens in 1949 was *Christian Science Monitor* correspondent in Moscow. Henry Shapiro was United Press correspondent. Natalie Rene, a Soviet citizen, was string correspondent for the International News Service; in January, 1949, she had gone to the Kremlin to receive a reply from Stalin to

May 28

For two weeks now we have had one fine hot clear day after another, and in the evening, frequently, thundershowers. Moscow is lush with green and filled with flowers. The nights are warm and made for lovers to walk in. I woke up at 3:30 this morning. It was quite light outside. It is close to the season of white nights that they have in Leningrad.

---

questions submitted by Kingsbury Smith of INS. Ralph Parker went to Moscow as *London Times* correspondent in 1942; in 1949 he was correspondent of the London *Daily Worker*. Jean Champanois was wartime correspondent of Havas and Agence France-Presse in Moscow; in 1949 he was correspondent for two left-wing Paris publications. Jack Margolis, a London cockney, was manager of the Hotel Metropole in the late thirties and until about 1948.

June 1, 1949

A hot sunny morning on the first of June. For some reason I woke up at 6:00 this morning. Maybe because it is a lovely day with a blue sky flecked with fleecy white clouds. We have had about three weeks of very warm weather; the trees are luxuriant; the parks are full of flowers; the people are all in summer clothes —the men, very often, in white linen and the women in gay prints of white cottons and linen with lots of embroidery.

I am still hoping to get a chance to tour the country a little. Everything is molasses slow. Meantime, the ministers debate in Paris without, as far as I can see, much chance of arriving at any sort of agreement.

Dispatch to New York Times
June 4

One of *Pravda*'s best-informed commentators on foreign affairs, M. Marinin, has made evident what was already apparent at Paris—that both East and West have presented mutually incompatible programs on the German question. . . .

[Implicit in his argument was the blunt fact that neither side was willing to give up the present status of Germany for any changed condition based on the ideas of the opposing powers.]

June 6

Yesterday afternoon I went out with Tom Whitney and his wife, a Russian girl, to a spot on the Moscow River just outside town and we sat in our bathing suits under the pine trees. I put my toes in the water, but it was cold and the river is not very clean.

Lots of Russians about—having a pleasant Sunday, sunning themselves, picnicking with their kids and tossing a ball around.

June 7

The Russians are trying to liquidate some of their political and economic commitments in Europe. They are trying it in their clumsy way at Paris on the German question and they would like to see something similar in Greece.*

Why do they want a settlement? Is the support of the rebels becoming too much of a burden on Albania? Is it connected with their plans for Macedonia? What bearing does the Yugoslav situation have on it?

I don't think that the end of the CFM (Council of Foreign Ministers) will end the Soviet "peace" offensive. . . . They are not likely to stir us up in the Far East by jumping on the bandwagon of the Chinese Communists—not by ostensible acts and moves that are likely to cause fireworks in the United States.

One thing I want to say about the Yugoslav situation. I think the Russians would like to drive Tito into the Western camp. The reason is simple. As long as Tito continues to follow Soviet foreign policy and Communist domestic policy he constitutes the biggest ideological threat to the Party theorists since Trotsky. If and when Tito abandons his tightrope act and moves toward the West, the ideological problem will be solved.

I take no credence whatever in any rumors that Tito and the Kremlin will make up. He cannot be taken back after the way he has been attacked. Nor do I think he is likely to be unseated easily or soon. . . .

Incidentally, they are beginning to show a little more confidence in the Chinese Communists. A few laudatory reviews are appearing, and they seem to have been working very hard with a group of intellectuals brought west for the Paris conference. Even so, they are still keeping their fingers crossed.

Baldwin† had a piece about ten days ago about "guerilla

* An active propaganda and diplomatic effort was then being made by the Soviet to liquidate the still continuing civil war in Greece. As matters developed it became apparent that these efforts were stimulated by the widening breach with Tito.

† Hanson Baldwin, military editor of the *Times*.

warfare" in the Caucasus and the Carpathian Ukraine. There probably are a few hideouts in both places but as a threat to the regime they are slightly less important than the Kentucky moonshiners are to the U.S.A. . . .

There is no doubt that a thorough weeding-out process is going on constantly in the Party. On the top level there is the Voznesensky-Popkov business with its possible relationship to Zhdanov and Malenkov and Kuznetzov. I don't believe that "purge" is the correct word to use so far as the upper levels are concerned.*

June 7, 1949
Letter to Edwin L. James,† New York Times

Gilmore of the AP told me today that he has received from his New York office an inquiry regarding the use of a slug on AP copy from Moscow to the effect that it has been passed by Soviet censorship.

I hope that this may mean that my suggestion for instituting such a rule on the *Times* is getting active consideration. . . .

My dispatches do not and cannot give an objective picture of conditions here nor of the propaganda which the Russians themselves issue. . . .

June 9

Is it hot! I'm here in the office with the late afternoon sun beating in on me, and it is like an oven.

These are very, very long days all right. I woke up about 3:00 this morning and it was almost full daylight.

Last night I went to the Robeson concert. It was thrilling. What a voice! The audience just about tore down Tchaikovsky Hall. They had the militia out to hold back the crowds. What do you suppose the audience shouted and shouted for him to sing? "St. Louis Blues"! They made the rafters ring. He didn't sing it; said his accompanist didn't have the music.

---

* Actually, Popkov, Kuznetzov, Rodionov, and others had been arrested early in 1949 in connection with the so-called Leningrad affair. This fact and confirmation of their execution were not forthcoming until Khrushchev's speech to the Twentieth Party Congress in February, 1956.

† Managing editor.

June 13

Within the Kremlin there's only one street—*Kommunistichi-skaya ulitza* or Communist Street.* It has no street numbers, but that is not necessary. If you drop a letter in the postbox outside Trotsky Gate it unfailingly will be delivered. The address: the Kremlin, Moscow, is quite sufficient.

June 14

Sunday afternoon I went swimming again. This time to a little lake about fifteen miles outside Moscow—Bear Lake, they call it. A pretty little lake, very shallow, lying in a meadow heavy with the rich smell of new hay. I swam for a while and then came out and lay on the soft green grass.

June 18

Here I am, second night in a row, confined to quarters, suffering from a foul and loathsome disease. My mouth is as sore as a raging boil, and I run a small fever.

Dispatch to New York Times
June 18

Moscow today is [the world's most beautiful city] the center of the world's most advanced industry, most advanced science, [most brilliant] art and [home of the world's happiest, most energetic, and courageous people].

So wrote Anatoly Surov, young Soviet playwright in the *Literary Gazette* today. "What can be more beautiful than the city in which lives, thinks, and creates the greatest genius of the earth, Josef Vissarionovich Stalin?" asks Surov. . . .

June 20

I am in a gloomy mood. I have been all but laid-up for several days with this virulent mouth infection. My mouth is a maze of fiery boils.

Dispatch to New York Times
June 21

The Soviet press today hailed the Paris conference as marking a sharp improvement in the international atmosphere and laying

---

* Actually, there are several streets within the Kremlin. None, according to current guidebooks, is called "Communist Street."

the groundwork for constructive creation of a peaceful postwar European solution. . . .

But Yuri Zhukov,* *Pravda*'s special correspondent in Paris [, warned that obstacles toward peaceful solution of the world's problems still exist. . . .

Zhukov's dispatch noted that the Soviet Union made a number of concessions on both Germany and Austria. Examination of the Austrian terms revealed that among the major concessions were abandonment of support of Yugoslavian territorial claims in Carinthia as well as Yugoslav reparations.]

June 21, 1949

This is a big anniversary here—the anniversary of the German attack on Russia. Eight years ago tonight I was sitting on the back porch in Mamaroneck in the hot darkness with the scent from the rose arbor very strong. Berney Geis and his wife were over—he was editor of *Coronet* in those days—and we were drinking. I had been telling them that I was sure the Germans were about to attack Russia. They didn't believe it. The conversation died away. Then the phone rang. It was the office. The radio had just reported the attack had been launched.

Well, it is a long way from there to here . . .

June 22

Midsummer night, the shortest of the year. It has been raining cats and dogs for hours. I just got back from a trip to Eddy Gilmore's *dacha*. It rained, rained, rained.

Dispatch to New York Times
June 26

Pravda expresses the opinion today that the Paris conference was "a bitter pill" for President Truman and characterized his statement on the agreement as "a mixture of immodest boasting and tendentious interpretation."

June 26

The new British ambassador got in this week. The new American ambassador comes in Tuesday. He is reputed to be flying in

* G. A. Zhukov, now head of the State Committee on Cultural Relations.

14,000 pounds of supplies and his wife and his son, who is nineteen and learned some Russian at Princeton last year and hopes to learn more this year in Moscow.*

June 28

The new American ambassador got in this afternoon. Saw him at the airport, just briefly. Must say I liked the initial impression. Seems bluff and hearty and has a sense of humor.

Last night I saw a hell of an interesting new ballet at the Bolshoi—*The Bronze Horseman*, by Pushkin. I wrote a story about it today but couldn't really say all I wanted to say because, in essence, the story is so expressive of the philosophy of this country—the sacrifice of individuals and the individual tragedies which go into the greater and broader purpose which is the building up of the nation.

June 29

A rainy, dreary afternoon, and now it is turning into a rainy, misty evening. Looking out of my window here on the square, I can see the rain-washed boards of the fence around the spot in the middle of the square where they are making a park. It is going to be a fine park with a fountain playing, nice concrete walks, trees, and benches for folks to sit on. But on this rainy evening the spot where the park is going to be is an angry-looking sore, a gash of raw earth and piled-up stone and tools. Maybe our lives are in that kind of state, a state of semi-construction, getting ready for better things to be. . . .

June 29
Letter to Edwin L. James, New York Times

A friend writes me that in the course of the *New Republic's* forum on the Soviet Union last month Y—— expressed the opinion that my dispatches from Moscow indicated either that I "was being taken in" by the Russians or was "trying to get in good with them."

Perhaps Y—— has been misquoted. Or possibly he is piqued. . . .

As I am certain you know, I am not currying any favor with

* Sir David Kelly and Admiral Alan G. Kirk arrived in Moscow in June, 1949, to serve, respectively, as British and American ambassadors.

these people; nor am I being taken in by them. If their g.d. censorship would permit me, that would be quite evident. No one is more aware than myself that my dispatches do not and cannot give a balanced picture of conditions here.

Dispatch to New York Times
July 4, 1949

An American pledge to work "unremittingly" for betterment of relations between the United States and the Soviet Union was made today at a Fourth of July ceremonial in the Kremlin at which the new United States ambassador Alan G. Kirk officially submitted his letters of credence.

July 6

Some rather interesting things seem to be developing here. Another big push toward prominence was given Malenkov over the weekend in connection with Dimitrov's death.* In all the radio accounts of the various ceremonies—the honor guard at the Dom Soyuzov, for example—his name was mentioned first after Stalin's. And Sunday morning it was Malenkov who led the six members of the Politburo who turned out to escort the body to the Byelorussian railroad station.

There seems hardly any doubt that Malenkov is firmly in the position of heir apparent. Molotov did not appear for the Dimitrov ceremonies. I believe there is a possibility that he is seriously ill. At the Supreme Soviet session in March I studied him closely through opera glasses and he looked unusually bad. His face always appears pale and waxy, but there seemed to me to be a radical change for the worse.

The other notable absentee was Andreyev. He is almost certainly seriously ill. He has not made a public appearance for a year and a half.

It is interesting to note that the announcement on Dimitrov bore seventeen names. There were the twelve members of the Politburo plus Ponomarenko, Georgi Popov, P. Pospelov, Suslov, and Shkiryatov. The names are listed alphabetically. I have suggested previously that it seemed likely that Ponomarenko and Suslov and possibly Shkiryatov and/or Popov might actually now

* Georgi Dimitrov, Bulgarian premier, died July 2, 1949, at the age of sixty-seven in a sanatorium outside Moscow.

be candidate members of the Politburo. The Dimitrov ceremonies gave one indication that they are not. When the Politburo turned out for the guard of honor at Dom Soyuzov it was in a body of old-line members: Stalin, Malenkov, Beriya, Voroshilov, Kaganovich, Mikoyan, Shvernik, and Bulganin—listed in that order. The other lads did their honor guard duty earlier in the evening and in a separate group. I think that is a pretty good indication that they have not yet been co-opted.

I thought Stalin looked extremely well in the photograph published of the Politburo standing by Dimitrov's bier. Beriya looked bad—tremendous paunch and very baggy and out of condition. I would bet money on Stalin surviving him. . . .*

When Kelly presented his credentials to Shvernik last week, Shvernik told him that Russia would not be unreceptive to proposals from Britain looking toward lifting of economic barriers and reviving trade. When Kirk presented his credentials, Shvernik told him virtually the same thing.

Just a word about the new ambassador. I should say he is a hell of a sound choice for the post. He has made a very, very good initial impression on people here and has come in with precisely the type of attitude which is necessary to meet the peculiarities of the Moscow situation.

July 7
Letter to Glavlit, the Soviet Censorship†

I have had no report from you on the disposition of my dispatch dealing with the Bolshoi Theater presentation of *The Bronze Horseman*.

I should appreciate some word from you as to whether the dispatch has been killed; passed; or is being held for future consideration.

I must say that the lengthy delay on a dispatch of this character seems unusual to me; but perhaps I do not appreciate all the factors and principles which underlie the censorship system.‡

---

* Stalin died March 5, 1953. The execution of Beriya was announced December 24, 1953.

† Glavlit, abbreviation for "Chief Literary Office."

‡ No answer was ever received to this communication. It was not the custom of Glavlit to reply to mail inquiries. The dispatch was, however, subsequently killed in its entirety.

Dispatch Killed by Censor
July 7, 1949

The magazine *Nature* reported today that research by the writer, Alexei Yugov, discloses that Achilles, hero of the Trojan War, was actually a Russian. . . .

July 7

The worst thing so far as daily existence is concerned is being confined to a grim and dreary room in the Metropole, moving aimlessly about the corridors, wondering whether somebody will say hello or go past without speaking. And the weary-faced little men leaning against pillars in the lobby and staring at you through slit-eyes and slinking out after you as you go through the revolving doors. . . .

July 9

At the moment two stories are being held in censorship without action. One is on a discovery that Achilles was a Russian. The other is on the arrival of a Latvian priest, Adamovitch, accredited by the Bishop of Riga, to take over the Church of St. Louis.

July 10

This morning I went up to the little Catholic church here, the Church of St. Louis. First time I had ever been there. A pretty down-at-the-heels kind of place, up back of the Lubyanka.

The congregation was diplomatic—about twenty of those—and the rest almost entirely old *babushkas* with white cloths on their heads and grimy, well-worn Bibles in their hands. The altar was banked with white flowers. Not cherry blossoms. Too late for them. Six candles were lighted on the altar and above it six electric tapers. The service was pathetic. So many old people. And all women. One very thin and spiritual little girl of about thirteen. She looked like those little French girls whom you see in French movies. Her face was somehow luminescent in the dim light. You could see that she had complete faith. Such a girl, I thought, might become a nun. Or have a great love for someone. Also a woman beyond middle age, very *ancien régime,* in black lace dress and holding a gold lorgnette.

44

Soviet astronomers have pledged themselves to fight relentlessly against cosmopolitanism, formalism, and particularly against the Western theory of "so-called relativist cosmology" and the "reactionary-idealistic" theory of a finite, widening universe. . . .

Soviet astronomers strongly attacked the theories of Jeans, Lemaître, and Eddington. . . .

July 17

I came in a little while ago from the airfield where I have been watching the big aviation show. I have a pinkish nose and a headache from staring into the sun trying to see the jets before they got into the next hemisphere.

An air show with jets is really very unsatisfactory from a spectator's viewpoint. Jets are too much like rabbits—almost before they have it they've had it.

July 19

Yesterday, I had a little bit of Russia—Russia that I love and enjoy. It was Tolstoi's Russia—Yasnaya Polyana. About 125 miles from Moscow to the south. I drove down and took the Whitneys with me. It was a bright morning, and we drove south over a straight highway through rich countryside. The wheat and the barley and the rye and the potatoes and the sunflowers have grown like rank weeds. Some small peasant villages look little different from the way they did in Tolstoi's day—wooden houses, often with thatched roofs. And a few sleepy provincial towns with swarms of goats tethered along the highway and masses of wildflowers everywhere.

We got to Yasnaya Polyana about midafternoon. It was Monday, which is the "free day"—the day the museum is closed. There is a gate house with a militiaman at the edge of the estate. We left the car there and walked up a long *allée* with tall pine trees on each side toward the house. Tolstoi describes it in *War and Peace*. The weather had changed, and we walked with the rain dripping steadily from the trees. It was easy to imagine that the clock had rolled back sixty years and that we were paying a pilgrimage to Tolstoi as thousands did in his lifetime.

The house is rather simple. There is a huge old-fashioned veranda where Tolstoi and his friends spent most of the summer. The impression was of peace and relaxation. A tall tree beside the veranda with a dinner bell—they used to ring it to bring Tolstoi back from a little *izba*, cottage, he had deep in the woods. And lovely flower beds, alive with dahlias and gladiolas and daisies.

There was no one else about. Sitting on the porch, with the rain dripping off the wet leaves of the trees, we found it easy to imagine we'd driven over from Tula in our carriage and found the Tolstois off on a visit to friends.

Finally a wonderful little man turned up. He was about thirty, I'd say. With a very intense air. He has dedicated his life to Tolstoi. Matter of fact, he is a Tolstoi—possibly a Tolstoi via one of the many peasant girls in the neighborhood. . . .

We talked with him down through the woods to the new-growth forest—"new" because the trees had been chopped down during the time of the Tartars so that their stumps would form an impenetrable barrier to the Tartar horsemen. . . . It's a long quiet path through birches and lindens and a few pines. Finally you come to a place where the path branches and goes down a gentle incline to a little grove within the forest, a half-circle of birches, very tall and very straight. And there a little green mound with rather sharp corners, but deep green turf growing on it. And on the top, as every day, a spray of fresh flowers. . . .

It was quiet and still. A few paces away there was a pretty, buxom militia girl standing guard, a good smiling peasant girl. The kind Tolstoi knew so well. It was very good. . . .

Making us promise not to tell anyone in Moscow about it, our young man opened up the Tolstoi house. It was just as it was when Tolstoi died in 1910. . . . A cluttered, lived-in look. Books and papers and the clutter of things that accumulate. Here a very old Remington typewriter—with the words in Russian on its case. Tucked away on top of a chest, what surely must be one of the very first Edison dictaphones—looking very new and shiny. I don't believe Tolstoi ever touched it.

Along one wall photos of famous people who made the pilgrimage to Yasnaya Polyana—and in the very center William Jennings Bryan. . . .

Dispatch Killed by Censor
July 21, 1949

If Poet Evgeni Dolmatovsky is to be taken literally, Russia possesses an explosive agent—"not *toluol* and not dynamite"—capable of disintegrating mountains in Siberia, and whose blast "rolls toward foreign coasts" as a "warning to enemies."

In the far-off Siberian *tiaga* there is a mountain of granite which has been prospected for twelve months by geologists.

"Then," says Dolmatovsky, "the plane brought professors. A detachment of sappers came. Their young officer, as duty required, placed a load of explosives. It wasn't tuluol and not dynamite. Now, in your country there is a substance stronger than that. I will not name it."

The explosion "turned the granite into smoke. And all around the tiaga was lighted by a golden light. . . .

"Let it sound like a warning to the enemies. Recently it was a fairy tale. Now it's reality. . . ."

July 21

On Ambassador Kelly's visit to the Kremlin censorship was almost completely relaxed. Obviously the copy had been referred to the Kremlin and apparently orders were sent down to censor lightly, presumably to encourage speculation which might be helpful to the Kremlin in testing the interest of the Western powers in further talks. . . .

I heard a good joke about the big row about genetics. It was explained like this: If a woman has a son and he resembles his father—that is proof of the theory of gene heredity. But if her boy resembles the next door neighbor—that shows that environment is the decisive influence.

July 24

Moscow does not give me a feeling of war tension or prewar tension. I noticed that as soon as I arrived, and the impression has steadily strengthened.

It is difficult and possibly dangerous to generalize, but the major emphasis clearly is on peacetime interests, peacetime pursuits, and a "return to normalcy."

Here, as well as in Europe, the fire has gone out in the cold war. Cautiously and slowly it is being discovered that we can speak a little back and forth without the heavens falling in.

Rather typical of this development, I think, is the fact that Stalin has received Sir David Kelly and, undoubtedly, is going to receive Kirk. I believe the diplomatic position of both the United States and Britain in Moscow has been materially improved by the new appointments. Sir David impresses me as a shrewd, intelligent, able diplomat. And, if I understand the situation correctly, his government is not adverse to dealing with the Soviets on such subjects as trade and others which, possibly euphemistically, they place in the category of "non-political" questions.

Sir David tells me he found Stalin able and as alert as ever—a man who is aging but who is well preserved and mentally most acute. Like most Stalin interviews the conversation followed a rather coolish pattern at first; then Stalin's interest seemed to rise; he contributed some points to the discussion, and the brief meeting wound up with some Stalin pleasantries. Stalin is still doodling. He doodled all through the discussion.

I will not attempt to compare Kirk to his predecessor except to say this: I regard him as a much more valuable man in this particular spot than Bedell. From the moment Smith was named I had the feeling that he was not a sound choice and that the predicate on which the choice was made was most unrealistic.*

But Kirk is a very, very able man. The State Department is really to be congratulated on its intelligence—from me, that is quite a compliment. . . .

The spy and security phobia here is abominable; that is, the latest outbreak of this endemic and chronic ailment from which Russia has suffered for so many hundreds of years. It is really something awful. To maintain it, of course, there must be a symbol—and we're it.

The manner in which they have ruthlessly rooted out and torn up every vestige of contact between scientists and intelligentsia with the West is something fearsome to behold; accompanied by such unutterably naïve propaganda works as Simonov's latest, called *An Alien Shadow,* in which the poor scientists are saved by

* General Walter Bedell Smith was named ambassador on the theory that the military would play a leading role in postwar Russia and that his wartime friendship and association with Marshal Georgi K. Zhukov would be invaluable.

smart Party people from turning over their great secrets to the Americans. . . .

Another aspect of the anti-American drive lies in the campaign to wipe out the generations-old Russian inferiority complex. This is widely advertised by the hilarious game of "priorities" in which everything from the toothpick to the wheel is claimed as the product of Russian ingenuity. . . .

It is my opinion that this attitudinal drive will not really replace the inferiority complex. The complex will still be there, but masked by a sort of adolescent superiority attitude.

Ed Stevens is winding up his affairs. Like everything he does, his departure is clouded with a good deal of vagueness. But the fact is he really doesn't expect to be back here for a long time. Maybe never. That will leave me the only non-agency correspondent here. . . .

Voznesensky is out as RSFSR education minister as of last week. I believe he is a brother—but can't swear to it.*

July 25, 1949

Today is the start of another week—fair, blue, cool, a little brisk. Yesterday was so different. Rain, rain, rain. It started early in the morning and stayed that way. You could hardly see across the square. In no time water was awash the sidewalk outside the Metropole, and the trolley buses set up great waves that lapped up toward the entrance.

I finished my work early, caught up on some of my correspondence, and went back to my room, No. 393, and read and read. I finished *The Train*. Lydia, my faithful childlike courier, came in. Said my psychology story has not come out of the censorship yet. How much of my work ends up in nothingness. Well, *ça va*. . . .

July 26

The last three mornings I've had no bath. For reasons unknown to me there is no hot water in the hotel.

---

* A. A. Voznesensky, released as RSFSR education minister, July 15, 1949, was the brother of N. A. Voznesensky, the purged State Planning Chief.

IV

The Yugoslav Crisis

July 27, 1949

What a puritanical life I lead these days. It astonishes me a bit —no wine, no women, and only an occasional song. I must say, though, that Russia without vodka is to be preferred to Russia with vodka.

July 29

I am fed up with this squirrel cage. Round and round and round—and never coming out anywhere. The office all day. The papers which never say anything new. The same Metropole meals. The cocktail parties. Same people. Same talk. Little piddling rides into the country. Same bumps on the same cobblestones. Arguments with customs. Eternal letters to the press department. Same old gossip. Same old talk. . . .

Dispatch to New York Times
July 31

[The Soviet Union's first formal diplomatic negotiation and agreement with any portion of newly liberated China was revealed today with] the announcement of a trade pact between representatives of "The Manchurian People's Democratic authorities" and the Soviet Union.

The announcement did not state what officials represented the Soviet Union in negotiations with a Manchurian mission headed by Mr. Gao Gan.* It was noted by Moscow diplomats that the agreement was with "The Manchurian People's Democratic authorities" rather than with the Chinese Communist government.

The Soviet Union maintains correct diplomatic relations with the Chinese Nationalist government and has given no indication that any change in diplomatic status is under consideration.

One question which caused observers some speculation was the relationship of "The Manchurian People's Democratic authorities" to the Central Chinese Communist government.

[So far as is known here Manchuria constitutes merely an administrative division of the Chinese Communist government. The "People's Democratic authorities" of Manchuria, therefore, would be subordinate to the Chinese Communist regime.

China's most important industrial facilities are located in Manchuria, and rapid expansion and rehabilitation of the Manchurian industrial plant is vital to the general revival of the Chinese economy.

However,] the extent of Soviet assistance was not indicated in the brief announcement. The agreement was on a one-year basis [, indicating that it will be subject to re-examination and renegotiation on the basis of Chinese developments.

Some quarters speculated that the time is drawing closer when the Soviet Union will undertake a general review of the China situation in light of the fact that the Chinese Communist government now controls all of the country with the exception of the southern and southwestern regions.]

July 31

This is incredible. Today, once again, we have had an amazingly hard rain. Still the country looks not bad. Potatoes look good, and the cabbages are big and green. Grain is another thing. How can it ripen and be harvested?

Last night I took some friends to the Arogvy. The headwaiter there is like something out of a Grimm fairy tale. He wears a pince-nez, a page-boy bob, tail coat, and white waistcoat—like

* Kao Kang, leader of the Manchurian Autonomous Area, committed suicide under mysterious circumstances in 1955. The official announcement of his death intimated that he plotted to detach Manchuria from Communist China. Some persons have speculated that the "plot" was engineered by Stalin and directed against Mao Tse-tung.

someone out of Dickens. The band plays Georgian songs. They have very good *shashlik* and a curious hors d'oeuvre made from turkey with a sauce of ground nuts and horse-radish.

August 1, 1949

Rain again today. It rained all yesterday. It rained almost all night. Depressing.

Dispatch to New York Times
August 2

Entrance examinations were in progress today throughout the Soviet Union for hundreds of thousands of young men and women seeking places among the 190,000 who will be admitted to entering classes of Soviet universities and higher educational institutions this fall.

There are 2,000 openings in twelve Moscow University faculties. . . .

August 2

I'm mean and restless and cantankerous . . . like I wanted to chew somebody's ear off. What I need is to go out into rough country and hike from morning till dark.

August 4

I have had more difficulty with the censorship than usual. They have killed five dispatches in the last ten days and mutilated several others.

One was a résumé of a Komsomolskaya *Pravda* article on how to handle religious beliefs in children. The point was that religion is being inculcated in many youngsters by their grandparents.

Another dispatch reported a discussion of Soviet divorce laws. A third dealt with the poem in *Novy Mir* hinting that Russia already had atomic explosives.

The trade deal with Manchuria got the works from the censors, as I expected. Lord knows I know little enough of what the real implications of the deal are; but the possibilities are considerable, as I tried to point out. . . .

As of this date Kirk still hasn't had an invitation to see Uncle Joe. I don't know what the implication may be.

August 10

It is just after midnight, and I've come back from a long, lazy stroll around the Kremlin on this warm August night. I had a late supper and then went over to Red Square. I sat there on the concrete platform between Lenin's Tomb and the Spassky Gate for a long time. A great orange-red moon came up across the Moskva River and threw St. Basil's into silhouette . . . the big red star gleaming against the sky high over Spassky Gate . . . the red flag flying over the Supreme Soviet building . . . the lights in the big row of offices across the square . . . and the people, thousands of them, walking in the quiet dusk . . . girls by twos and threes and fours . . . boys in little clusters . . . girls who wanted to be picked up . . . girls who don't want to be . . . youngsters hand in hand. . . .

Three sunburned guards came marching out of the Spassky Gate just as the clock struck the hour. Their boots went slap, slap, slap on the pavement, and their long rifles gleamed. . . .

Not much like the guards changing at Buckingham Palace. I listened to the murmur of Russian voices and wondered why the girls all seemed so healthy and robust with their sturdy hips and big breasts and why the boys all looked puny and runty. . . . Russia is a great matriarchy . . . a country of mothers. . . . The men are like the male bees, just a biological adjunct. . . .

I strolled down to the river. A steamboat passed with its lights glittering like a Christmas tree. There were dozens of couples leaning on the balustrade in the quiet warm night. . . . Finally I came back to the hotel. . . .

Dispatch to New York Times
August 11

Pravda, in the first Soviet comment on the American White Paper on China, today characterized the State Department recital as "one failure after another! One foolishness after another!"

It predicted further American policy failures in the future. . . .

Noting the State Department's characterization of the Kuomintang as "corrupt and rotten," *Pravda* said this discovery was made by the Chinese people long before the American diplomats. . . .

August 11, 1949

Yesterday I went swimming at Bear Lake. It had been two months since I was there. There were few folks around—mostly kids from the kolkhoz nearby. And the kolkhoz folks were busy threshing their barley. Peaceful and rural. It seemed a long, long way from Moscow.

Dispatch Killed by Censor
August 12

Diplomatic relations between the Soviet Union and Yugoslavia today moved a step closer toward formal severance with an official Soviet declaration that the Yugoslav government is now regarded "not as a friend and ally but as an enemy and adversary of the Soviet Union."

The new note gave formal notice that Russia considers the Yugoslav-Soviet alliance nullified by the antagonistic acts of the Tito regime. It was the frankest in an increasingly frank exchange between the two countries.

Diplomatic observers believed the next step would be the formal withdrawal of ambassadors.

August 14

Here it is Sunday morning again, and again I am sitting in my office with the sunshine bathing the square outside and in my ears the ring of hammers chipping away at stone paving blocks. There is a lilt and ring to those hammers as the steel chips against the stone; like a gentle anvil chorus. It soothes like the beat of surf on the seashore.

Dispatch to New York Times
August 15

Pravda devoted five of its seven foreign-news columns to reaction to the latest Soviet denunciation of Tito and new reports of Belgrade's gravitation into the Western camp. . . .

Dispatch to New York Times
August 15

The American ambassador, Alan G. Kirk, held a forty-minute Kremlin conversation with Generalissimo Stalin tonight—the first

54

personal discussion between the Soviet leader and an American diplomat in almost exactly a year. . . .

Dispatch to New York Times
August 16

Diplomatic opinion in Moscow characterizes the Kremlin meeting of Stalin and Ambassador Kirk as an important step toward what some describe as "normalization" of relations between the United States and the Soviet.

The substance of the conversation was a closely guarded secret. . . .

Dispatch to New York Times
August 20

The Soviet Union tonight placed Yugoslavia under *solemn* warning that it will be compelled to "resort to other more effective measures" in order to protect its citizens in Yugoslavia unless the Tito regime promptly corrects its present "inhuman practices."

[It made evident that the Soviet has virtually reached the end of its patience so far as exchange of notes is concerned and is now looking toward application of more practical methods. . . .

While the Soviet and Yugoslavia still maintain formal diplomatic relations the Soviet ambassador to Belgrade, Lavrentiev, this week was named vice-minister of foreign affairs, leaving the Belgrade post vacant. It seemed apparent that the Soviet Union did not have diplomacy in mind in referring to "more effective measures."]

August 22

It's a beautiful September morning here. I know it's only August. But it is a crisp day after yesterday's rain, with a hint of chill. The flowers in the big square outside my window look especially fresh and sparkling. All summer they have worked on that square, and now that fall is almost here the square is almost finished. . . .

For the last week the Yugoslav crisis has been gathering momentum rapidly. The most important conclusion to be drawn from the fourth and fifth Soviet notes to Belgrade, those of

August 12 and August 20, is that the Soviet has decided most firmly that Tito must go.

All that remains to be elucidated is the method of his going. Obviously, the most convenient thing would be a coup d'état. It would be even more convenient if Tito were not shot but captured and placed on trial.

I realize that nothing from Belgrade indicates that a coup impends; nor that the Soviet has the kind of organization there which could carry one out in the face of Tito's vigilance.

Nevertheless, the latest note with its curt statement that the Soviet will be forced to employ "other more effective means" leaves no doubt that a definite plan of action has been prepared.

What means does the Soviet have at its command?

First, and most obvious, would be reprisals against Yugoslavs here. Diplomatic relations could be broken. A Free Yugoslav government, here or in Bucharest, could be recognized.

A complete embargo by Russia and the satellites might be proclaimed. I believe that that is not at all unlikely.

Mass arrest of Yugoslav diplomats in the Soviet Union might be carried out, simultaneous with discovery of a "plot" against the Soviet.

Finally, there is the possibility of direct military action. I think it must not be ruled out. . . .

One Russian said to me: "Tito is finished, and he knows it. There isn't room for a little lump of clay between the two cliffs of America and Russia. Only a great power can permit itself the luxury of behaving as he does, and there are only two great powers—Russia and America."

The only thing that would deter them from military intervention would be fear of war with the United States. I cannot see us going to war if they blitzed Tito in a week.

One interesting sidelight on the fifth note is that it bears considerable internal evidence, so I am told, of having been written by Stalin himself.

There continues to be security jitters in this country. In mid-June several thousand persons of foreign origin were moved out of Baku and the surrounding area, presumably to Central Asia and Siberia.

Apparently this sort of transfer is still in progress. There is a report that Jews with relatives in the United States and Britain have been removed from Odessa; that persons of Greek origin have been removed from Georgia. How many persons are involved in these transfers is not known.

Curiously enough, there has been no confirmation of reports originating apparently in Jewish circles in America about a month ago of large-scale Jewish transfers from White Russia. It would be my guess that this report has been garbled or exaggerated. Information regarding Jews seems to travel very fast (through the Jewish colonies, I suppose), and it seems invariably to reach foreign sources quite rapidly. Since no information has reached the best-informed foreign quarters in Moscow, I am inclined to doubt it.

I think there was also published abroad information about large-scale transfers from the Baltic states. So far as I can judge there is no movement involving the Baltic now. There was, of course, a couple of years ago.

On the literary-critical front the pendulum is swinging back. The most violent purgers are now getting it in the neck. The *Literary Gazette* has been apologizing and admitting its sins. K. Simonov as editor of *Novy Mir* has been criticized for publishing a play called *Bekitov's Career,* which is ideologically dandy but constructed like a piece of hack work.

More than usual attention has been paid to British personnel by the appropriate Soviet agents since the Johnston affair. There have been at least three overt approaches. Occasional nibbles are made at American embassy people.

The press corps continues to dwindle. Ed Stevens leaves Wednesday. Now Shapiro is talking about leaving and turning the UP file over to Ludmilla.

One bit of encouraging news. Four and a half months after I first applied to the press department I have just received permission to make a trip to Stalingrad.

Dispatch to New York Times
August 23, 1949

The Soviet press made plain today that Tito is regarded not only as an enemy and an antagonist of the Soviet Union but of the peoples' democracies as well. Foreign dispatches cited in particular a growing threat by Belgrade against Albania. . . .

Dispatch to New York Times
August 29, 1949

Pravda today revealed that the Council of Economic Mutual Aid, comprising the Soviet Union and six eastern European states, has just concluded a meeting in Sofia. . . .

[In light of the general deterioration of relations between council members and Yugoslavia it was thought likely that the Sofia conference discussed the question of whether further trade relations with that country should be maintained. . . .]

August 29

Perhaps it is this lovely, early autumn day with its high white clouds against a pale blue sky, the hot sun and the lazy drone of bottle flies against the window, the pink and white flowers blooming in the park outside. . . . Perhaps it is a lazy weekend with mushrooming in a white birch forest and peasants busy with their haying and spreading golden grain to dry along the hot tarmac of the highway . . . whatever it is, for today, at least, I do not feel gloomy.

Dispatch to New York Times
August 31

The Tito clique has been placed on notice that Soviet public opinion now regards Belgrade not only as an "enemy and adversary" in a "state of war" against Communist parties throughout the world but as "a deserter of the very worst type."

[It hardly needs to be noted that there is a vast difference between methods of dealing with "a deserter" and with an ordinary enemy. The penalties for desertion are simple, well-known, and do not differ the world over. Desertion automatically brings imposition of the severest penalty and obviously robs the deserter of any possible defense. . . .]

September 2

The censorship pattern on Yugoslavia has been quite interesting. It has been rigorous throughout. I believe I have had more material cut from my dispatches on Yugoslavia than on any other issue since I arrived.

Generally, the cuts seem designed to allow the dispatches to carry a threat to Yugoslavia—but without allowing the threat to be stated in specific terms.

September 3
Letter to Emanuel Freedman, New York Times

The failure of censorship to clear my dispatch on the latest note to Tito uncovered a rather extraordinary situation which the Russians have now corrected.

My Tito dispatch was turned in at the telegraph office at 2:00 A.M. It did not clear until around 1:30 P.M. the next afternoon. It seemed obvious to me that the censor on duty had knocked off work at 3:00 A.M.

I sent a blistering letter to Glavlit, which runs the censorship. It struck me that somebody probably would get in dutch since the censorship failure held up a story on which the Russians are itching to get the widest publicity.

Sure enough. Yesterday Glavlit telephoned to say that "my request" that the censors stay on duty after 3:00 A.M. had been "granted."

Dispatch Killed by Censor
September 13

The case of a girl who deliberately married a schoolboy sweetheart whom she didn't love in order to escape the boredom of life in a remote city and get back to Moscow was presented today by the newspaper *Moscow Komsomolets.*

Ludmilla wrote to her former schoolmate, Boris:

"Hello, Borya. After I graduated from the Technicum I was sent to Margelan. A distance of 3,500 kilometers separates us, but I know you love me. I am willing to marry you and come back to Moscow. Awaiting your answer impatiently."

Guileless Boris went to Margelan and married Ludmilla. She was released from the factory, and the couple returned to Moscow. Two weeks later Boris came home to find a letter from his wife, saying:

"Farewell, Boris. I am tired of this comedy. I'm leaving you forever. Frankly I never loved you, but how else could I get out of Margelan."

59

September 13, 1949

We have just finished liquidating Joe Newman's effects. A depressing chore. I don't like to see such a tiny press corps here. There are five Americans left now, all agency men except me, and all with a personal reason for staying here except me.

September 16

I don't believe I ever got around to writing about the peace congress toward the end of August. It was held in the Dom Soyuzov, which is kitty-cornered across the square from the Metropole. I can see it from my office window.

There's an interesting story in that. It relates to Dimitrov's death in early July. It was a hot, dull Saturday afternoon when I looked out the window and noticed that a cordon of militia had been thrown across the street by the Dom Soyuzov, cutting off traffic coming from the direction of the hotel and the Bolshoi. A few minutes later I left the hotel to drive over to the embassy. By this time the militia were in great force, and in the big square there were scores of trucks drawn up. My chauffeur found out that it was Dimitrov who had died. He had been ill for some time at a sanatorium about twenty miles outside Moscow.

Not one of the correspondents had heard the news although it had been broadcast more than an hour earlier. That gives some idea under what conditions news is gathered here.

To return to the peace conference. It was held in the large hall —the one which is truly called the Hall of Columns.

The most impressive figures were the famous Red Dean of Canterbury and the Metropolitan Nikolai—and, of the two, Nikolai was the more impressive. He is a handsome bearded man in his late fifties, a fine speaker—the only man at the conference who spoke without text or notes. His speech was filled with the rich imagery and symbols of the church. . . .

Perhaps, to me, the most interesting figure was Mikhail Sholokov who wrote *The Virgin Soil Upturned* and *And Quiet Flows the Don*. Far and away my favorite Soviet author. The first day of the conference the chairman called Sholokov's name. Nothing happened. A dead silence. No Sholokov. Another speaker was called. The next day the chairman again called for Sholokov. There was a titter. But this time he appeared. He is youngish looking. Very handsome, with a Budenny mustache. Wore the old Party uniform, simple khaki tunic, cavalry breeches, and boots. He spoke briefly, apologizing that he was a writer and not a speaker. Made a poetic kind of speech, referring to Stalin as a gray eagle. Seemed diffident and almost shy. . . .

Vanda Vasilevskaya* spoke. She is a fiery orator, of course, in full vigor. She impressed me with her apparent ruddy health. Looked quite handsome. When I was here before she was practically dead of t.b. Her husband, Alexander Korneichuk, the Ukrainian poet and playwright, also spoke.

Dispatch to New York Times
September 17

Under headlines "Rajk and his accomplices—agents of American intelligence—ties of Tito, Rankovich, and others with the intelligence organs of the United States," the Soviet central newspapers published a full-page report of the Budapest trial of former Hungarian Minister of the Interior Laszlo Rajk today. . . .

The Soviet press made plain that the real defendants in the proceedings were the men who stood behind Rajk—in other words the Tito clique of Belgrade and American intelligence agents. . . .

Dispatch Killed by Censor
September 18

Konstantin Simonov, secretary-general of the Writers' Union and leading Soviet poet, playwright, and novelist, was criticized sharply by the *Literary Gazette* for "restoring the worst traditions of decadence" in a newly published poem entitled "A Few Days."

Simonov's poem deals with a man and his "tortured love" for a woman. The poem describes their meeting on New Year's Eve in Moscow's Koktail Hall on Gorki Street. Later they spend the night together.

"One can understand from significant dots which separate the description of night from the description of morning that he quickly and energetically realizes his 'masculine claims,'" the criticism said. "Is this Soviet youth, its characteristic manifestation of love?"

---

* Well-known Soviet writer, author of "Rainbow" and a founder of the Union of Polish Patriots.

V

Return to Stalingrad

September 19, 1949

I have had rather more copy than usual killed and held in censorship the last ten days. For instance, my cable rounding up more instances of "feudal attitudes toward women" out in Central Asia. The censorship has been holding since September 7 a rather long dispatch which I filed on the opening of the famous play *The Mad Haberdasher.*

September 21

Saturday I'm going down to Stalingrad for a brief visit with Ambassador Kirk. I finally got permission to make the trip. He was planning a trip there too, so we are joining forces.

Dispatch Killed by Censor
September 22

The Soviet press today publishes a comprehensive report from Peiping on the convocation of a Peoples' Political Consultative Conference as a preliminary to creation of a Central Peoples' government for China.

The assembly raises the immediate question of action by the great powers including the Soviet Union on the recognition of the new government.

Thus far no government has been more careful of the requirements of diplomatic protocol than the Soviet with regard to relations with the Nationalist government. . . .

At present the Soviet ambassador is absent from his post with the Nationalist Chinese government, and the Chinese ambassador has not returned to Moscow after going home to consult his government. The representative of the official Chinese news agency, Central China News, left Moscow a couple of weeks ago.

September 22
Letter to Edwin L. James, New York Times

I think you might be interested in a report on *Pravda's* attack on the United Press last week which may indicate that the diminishing band of American correspondents here is going to have some more difficulties.

You will recall that *Pravda* jumped on an item published by *Il Tempo* of Milan and attributed to the UP giving some purported quotes from a *Pravda* editorial. The quotes, *Pravda* charged, were fabricated.

It seems apparent that this gratuitous reference had some specific purpose in mind:

1. Further general intimidation of correspondents.

2. A veiled warning that a "censorship of responsibility" may be imposed. . . .

3. Intensification of public resentment and suspicion of foreign correspondents.

Serving as an American correspondent in Moscow in these times is very much like living under siege behind the enemy lines. The idea is hammered into the mind of the public that we are spies.

In my judgment it is only a matter of time before another "spy" case is tagged on the American press corps here.

September 22

I've done a story about the puppet theater's production, *To the Rustle of Her Eyelashes,* ribbing Hollywood, but it was pretty sharply cut by the *Times.*

I saw another of their shows, called *Ordinary Concert,* the other night. Obratsov is the founder and guiding genius of the theater.

The night I saw him it was cold and the performance was in a summer theater in a park. I nearly froze. One of Obratsov's cleverest acts doesn't involve puppets at all. It is an argument between his left hand and his right hand, with just the hands appearing over the rim of the booth.

Dispatch to New York Times
Stalingrad, September 28, 1949

Ambassador Kirk today concluded a three-day visit to the hero city of Stalingrad. . . .

He arrived Monday morning after a thirty-six-hour train trip from Moscow. He was housed in a new and comfortable suite in an Intourist hotel just across the street from the basement headquarters where Von Paulus finally surrendered on January 31, 1943. Its yellow brick walls are still pockmarked with shellfire and bullet holes.

On the spot where Von Paulus surrendered now rises a busy six-story central department store which opened its doors only ten days ago. . . .

Traces of defense lines are fast being obliterated, and scattered along the river bank are new whitewashed cottages in which women peacefully go about their chores [washing laundry in back yards fenced with bits of iron and metal drawn from war's scrap heap, chopping wood for fires, and minding swarms of young children who play busily oblivious of the fact that the ground they scurry over is historic soil].

September 28

I had hoped to send Mother a postcard from Stalingrad for her birthday. But there wasn't a card in town.

Stalingrad, September 29

It was pleasant sitting in the park with the warm September sun flooding the broad walks and the bright banks of orange and yellow marigolds. The sky was deep aquamarine and flecked with high white clouds.

Watching the children tussling in the sandpile beside the silent fountain it was hard to imagine that on another September day seven years ago the Nazi blitzkrieg reached a zenith beside the placid Volga.

The first time I saw Stalingrad, nearly a year after the siege was lifted, it was covered with ice and snow. The first impression was that not a structure in the city had escaped damage—and the first impression was correct.

Stalingrad lay then as if dead. . . .

Today a dark-haired schoolgirl sauntered through the park with schoolbooks under her arm. A war veteran strode down the path with two companions, gesturing excitedly. "It was right here!" he said.

Where the beds of nicotiana, petunias, and snapdragons blossomed had been a network of German trenches.

Dispatch to New York Times
September 29

The Soviet announced tonight that it has formally denounced its treaty of friendship, mutual assistance, and postwar co-operation with Yugoslavia. . . . Only *pro forma* diplomatic relations remain between the Soviet and Yugoslavia. . . .

Dispatch Killed by Censor
September 30

Soviet authorities imposed an unannounced incoming censorship last weekend on President Truman's announcement of a Soviet atomic explosion.

This was the first time such a censorship had definitely been revealed. . . . All outgoing dispatches and service messages of correspondents for the past two years have been censored by Glavlit, which customarily has censored out all references either to censorship or to its own existence. . . .

September 30
Letter to Mr. Yeregin, Central Telegraph Office

I wish to make a formal protest against the imposition of an incoming cable censorship in connection with inquiries directed to me by my New York office concerning President Truman's announcement of September 23 concerning an atomic explosion in the Soviet Union.

Two cables were directed to me from New York, one filed at 11:57 A.M., New York time, and the other at 4:01 P.M., both on September 23. On both of them the "receipt" time has been carefully inserted with a typewriter, differing from that used in

65

copying the message. This time is given as "0540" on the twenty-fifth, which I understand is the time of the Tass communiqué on the Truman statement. In one of the messages the erasure of the original, actual time of receipt is plain. . . .

I do not question the right of the Soviet government to impose an incoming censorship if it so desires. I do protest its imposition without notice. . . .

Dispatch to New York Times
October 3, 1949

The Soviet press today greeted the formation of the new central Chinese government and published a declaration by Mao Tse-tung proposing general establishment of diplomatic relations. . . .

[The vast revolutionary implications of the establishment of the People's Republic in China were widely analyzed by the press, which pointed out the implications of this new victory for communism upon the struggle of the peoples of Indonesia, Vietnam, Malaya, Burma, and other regions of Asia. . . .

The Soviet has maintained diplomatic relations with the Nationalist Chinese government. Establishment of the new central regime raised the question as to continuance of these relations. . . .

October 3

I put most of Stalingrad into my stories and what is left over I will do for the magazine. I hope they may use this piece. I have done half a dozen for Markel since I've been here. He has used none of them.

It was a real blessing to get away from Moscow even if for only four days.

We had a pleasant ride to Stalingrad by train. We took our own food as there is no diner on the train. Scads of people selling food at stations all along the way—cooked chickens for 10 rubles, turkeys for 30, tomatoes, melons, smetana, cheese, milk, apples, *pirogi* (pastry shells with meat inside), etc.

We had a compartment in the one "soft" car—a clean car and a pleasant if slow journey across the autumn countryside—the crops mostly in, the fields plowed for fall planting, and winter wheat green in many fields. We passed through lots of sugar beet country and carload after carload of beets piled up for the mills. It is not interesting country—rather like the Dakotas or Kansas, flat or gently rolling. You can see for miles.

In Stalingrad I was impressed by the tremendous devastation and the tremendous rebuilding which has already been done. Ruins and barren fields are everywhere, but one gets the impression of a busy, hard-working, normal city rather than a wounded war convalescent. Housing is a terrific problem, and many people still live in the cellars of destroyed buildings. They have electricity and stoves and seem to manage surprisingly well.

One thing you know well after talking to a few Stalingraders. They know war and want no more of it. We had a young woman as our guide who was a native Leningrader who lived and worked in Stalingrad before the war. She was there with her husband and three-year-old boy when the Germans attacked. She told us the German planes came over on August 23, 1942, and in hardly any time the whole center of the city was in ruins. Water and light were knocked out. They lived in the cellar and drank water from the boiler. When that was gone, they carried water from the Volga. Luckily much food was stored in cellars so that did not run out. The civilians began to leave the city, crossing the Volga. Many, many were killed by German dive bombers.

This girl finally left Stalingrad the first week in September with her youngster. Her husband stayed and was killed. When the war was over she returned to her old job in Stalingrad. As she said, no one who saw the suffering would ever want to see it inflicted on another people again.

Just before we left for Stalingrad, Truman made his announcement about the atomic explosion. It is my conviction that this should be a considerable help toward getting somewhere with a realistic solution of our postwar problems.

Dispatch Killed by Censor
October 7

The Central Committee of the Uzbek Communist Party has ordered a special concentration of forces to liquidate a serious lag in harvesting cotton. . . .

Dispatch Killed by Censor
October 8, 1949

A shocking breakdown in Communist Party leadership in Uzbekistan is revealed by the Tashkent *Pravda* of the East. Fulfilment of the republic's enormous cotton production pledge is jeopardized. . . .

October 9

I've been here long enough now so that I feel as though I had some idea of the public pulse. I should say that folks here are feeling better this fall. The international scene looks somewhat improved, and domestic conditions steadily improve. Nothing changes rapidly here, and Ivan Grozny would recognize a good many things in Moscow. But there is much he would not recognize. The capital is getting attention from the builders and beautifiers.

October 10
Letter to Edwin L. James, New York Times

My feeling that the Russians would be imposing some new restrictions on the press has been speedily confirmed. We are now being subjected to a blind, incoming censorship. . . .

My guess is that we must expect in the future that most messages from New York will continue to be delivered with considerable delay. I also expect that messages dealing with what Russians might consider sensitive topics will merely "disappear."*

You can make one interesting deduction from the Russian action. Truman's announcement obviously caught them very far off base.

October 10

Ambassador Kirk plans to make other trips around the country and plans to include a correspondent in his party when he goes. It remains to be seen whether the Foreign Office and militia will approve such correspondents' travel.

I had requested permission to go to Stalingrad last spring. After four and a half months' delay I was still waiting when

---

* These fears never bore fruit.

Kirk decided on his trip. The militia had still not cleared my departure, but they finally did after being called by the Foreign Office.

We were given every courtesy at Stalingrad. They were unable to fulfil two requests which the ambassador made—one was to purchase some fresh caviar; it was the wrong time of the year; the other was to see a model of the plans for reconstruction of the city; apparently they couldn't get hold of the proper people.

We did not see the famous tractor plant, except from the train. It was obviously working hard. The railroad yards were full of flatcars loaded with new gray tractors. Also some carloads of light antiaircraft guns. . . .

There are still large numbers of Stalingraders living in rubble-topped cellars with smokestacks poked through the rubble fields. . . .

The goods in the newly opened department store are very, very shoddy. Only four styles of men's hats; eight styles of women's hats; three types of men's shoes; four varieties of radios.

One morning we saw a riot outside the store. Several hundred women fighting to get in, and a dozen militia pitching them off the steps. It was a sale of carpet material. (Recently there was a queue at the Mostorg that reached from the fourth floor down to the first and out onto the street. They had oilcloth on sale.)

It would be my guess that Truman's announcement caught Moscow by surprise. However, here is an interesting fact. About three weeks before the announcement one of the lecturers at Moscow University told his students there would be such an announcement soon. I do not know whether this gentleman merely happened to make a lucky hit or whether word had been passed around in Party circles.

The lecturer's analysis of the significance of this news, together with the establishment of the new government in China, is also interesting. He told his students that relations between the Soviet Union and the United States would now begin to improve.

Again, that may be wishful thinking. Probably the intellectuals continue to wish and hope for improvement of relations with the United States. I strongly suspect the government would be pleased with some improvement. But what *quid pro quo* they may be prepared to offer—if any—I do not know.

It would be my guess that the Russians would now be prepared to explore in private conversations the possibilities of some form of atomic controls.

I think it should be understood that they are not going to agree to any system which would restrict the employment of atomic energy for industrial or non-military purposes. I think this pretty well eliminates international atomic authority under the UN. The most they could be expected to agree to would be some international plant inspection. But it should not be overlooked that they continue to talk about "control."

After months and months of soft-pedaling the Chinese Communists, the papers finally gave them a sunburst with the creation of the new government. I think this means a modus vivendi has been worked out.

I believe this has taken a good bit of negotiation both here and in Peking. There has been a succession of Chinese delegations here.

I have heard that there will be a state visit of Mao Tse-tung and possibly Chou En-lai or maybe just Chou very shortly. Presumably it would be for the purpose of signing a treaty of alliance and friendship. And I expect an economic delegation will come along too.*

Dispatch to New York Times
October 10, 1949

Two Soviet newspapers today published reviews of a book by the British newspaper correspondent Ralph Parker. He charged the British and American embassies in Moscow with active preparation of a new war against the Soviet. . . .

Parker's book sells for seven rubles. It was issued in an edition of 50,000 copies, and bookstores reported stocks exhausted forty-eight hours after publication.

October 11

For more than a month now censorship has been holding my dispatch on the première of the play *The Mad Haberdasher*.

My effort to predict the recognition of the new Chinese Communist government met another dead kill. I thought the cut in a

* Mao Tse-tung did, in fact, arrive in Moscow in December, 1949. The agreements were signed February 14, 1950.

later dispatch concerning the revolutionary implications of the Communist victory and its importance in other Asiatic countries was interesting. . . .

October 12
Letter to Edwin L. James, New York Times

My formal protest to the Foreign Office concerning the incoming censorship on message dealing with Truman's atomic announcement has, surprisingly, stirred up the Foreign Office.

I was called yesterday to a conference with Frantzev,* chief of the press department—the first time I had had the privilege of meeting him since he succeeded Lomakin last May.

Frantzev told me that "there is no incoming censorship." The holdup on Truman's announcement he described as "unauthorized action" on the part of some telegraph office employee, identity as yet "unknown." They are making a full investigation, and the guilty party will be "reprimanded and fined."

He expressed some indignation that I should "generalize" an individual instance of delayed delivery of cables into an "incoming censorship." He said he felt it rather rude of me. I told him I was sorry but that I found the action of the telegraph office "very rude."

October 12
Letter to Glavlit, Censor

I should appreciate it if some action could be taken on my September cables dealing with the play *The Mad Haberdasher.* If these cables are not to be passed, I should appreciate it if you would kill them and advise me of the fact.

Dispatch Killed by Censor
October 14

About the time of the first World War Russia's leading writer of children's verse, Korei Chukovsky, published a children's poem about a revolt by the animals of the St. Petersburg zoo.

The revolt was led by the crocodile and his two sons, and it remained unquelled until a little boy, Vanya, armed with a

---

* U. P. Frantzev, head of the press department of the Foreign Office, 1949–53. Now a leading member of the Marx-Lenin-Engels Institute.

wooden sword, conquered the crocodile and compelled him to submit.

In return for sparing his life the crocodile promised Vanya to devote himself to good deeds and to righting wrongs.

Under these circumstances it was natural that when a new Soviet satirical journal was launched in August, 1922, it was given the name *Krokodil.*

In a land as big as the Soviet Union *Krokodil* is bound to find an almost inexhaustible supply of material.

Here is a *Krokodil* joke which caught on very quickly. It was published under a drawing of a milkmaid:

"Why do you add water to the milk?"

"Because I want everybody to have some."

Another sample of *Krokodil* wit:

A man is talking to a secretary:

"This is the third day I've been waiting to see the director."

"Well, this is the fourth day he's been waiting to see the big boss."

Dispatch to New York *Times*
October 17, 1949

Lillian Hellman's play *Another Part of the Forest* was given a distinguished première at the Moscow Drama Theater this week and was enthusiastically received by a sold-out house. . . .

Dispatch Killed by Censor
October 22

Soviet girls must be distinguished for their "inner beauty" and not the polish on their nails.

That's what the newspaper *Moscow Komsomolets* replied to Olga Kochik who asked whether Communist Youth members should manicure their nails.

"You are asking whether pupils of the tenth grade, Komsomols and particularly Pioneer Guides, should manicure their nails? There can be only one answer to this: No."

October 24
Letter to Edwin L. James, New York Times

You will be interested to learn that the Moscow press corps will be further reduced in about six weeks. Reuters is closing its bureau and withdrawing its correspondent and will henceforth rely on string coverage.

The move stems directly from devaluation (of the pound)—plus the fact that Reuters has been increasingly relying upon the Soviet monitor* in London for its spot coverage. *Exchange Telegraph,* which has been receiving a small Moscow file, is terminating its string arrangement. The Reuters bureau will probably be closed December 1.

The Western press corps has practically been halved in the time I have been here.

In withdrawing its correspondent from Moscow and relying on the Soviet monitor in London, Reuters has placed itself completely in the hands of a branch of the Soviet propaganda machine. . . .

I should not be surprised if the American agencies were tempted to follow Reuters' example.

October 24

I have written James about Reuters. I am very sorry to see this happen. The Western press corps has literally fallen apart in the nine months I have been here.

The loss of each correspondent diminishes the effectiveness of those who remain. There is little information that any one of us can gather. But by pooling we had a fairly respectable body of knowledge. With only four left the total amount of news will be sharply reduced.

A most serious loss is the virtual destruction of the secretarial corps. With all the faults which this largely female group possessed, it constituted a hell of an asset so far as looking beyond the iron curtain was concerned. They had their prejudices, but by and large they were an alert, interested group of Russians.

As of today they have practically vanished. There are only three secretaries still working. With Dallas' departure the number will drop to two—possibly to one.

It certainly must make the Russians laugh at our talk about their propaganda, freedom of the press, access to news, etc., and then to watch the agencies feed right out of their hands by relying on the Soviet monitor in London for the sound capitalistic reason that the Russians provide the service more cheaply.

* A monitoring service provided by the Soviet embassy in London.

That reminds me of Parker. Last spring he told me he was pulling up stakes, probably for good. He sold off most of his library, tried to get me to hire Valentina, and was in a dither to be off. But he had trouble getting an exit visa. He was very nervous and upset. Obviously afraid he couldn't get out. I think he had plenty of reason for nervousness because he had been close to Anna Louise Strong. Then, all of a sudden he calmed down. His nervousness vanished. I marveled greatly.

Well, I think the answer was provided ten days ago by his book. It bears the writing date of March–June. . . .

The book solves his financial problems, which have been acute. It had an initial edition of 50,000 copies and will doubtless go through two or three editions. . . . The book is devoid of any startling revelations. It rakes up a good many gossipy charges, mostly dating back to the Clark Kerr era. He also has some nasty pages on Pop Hill.*

At the Tolbukhin funeral Molotov looked much better than last spring and seems to have put on some weight. I guess my theory about his being ill doesn't look so good.

---

* Lord Inverchapel, then Sir Archibald Clark Kerr, was wartime British ambassador to Moscow. Captain George (Pop) Hill, British intelligence agent in the Soviet Union in early Bolshevist days, returned as military attaché of the wartime British embassy in Moscow.

Return to Leningrad

Dispatch Killed by Censor
October 25, 1949

Outside Pavlodar the newspaper Kazakstan *Pravda* has discovered a small settlement where the voice of Soviet Russia hardly penetrates.

The settlement houses some 5,000 workers. It has no school. It has no drugstore, no movie, not a single book or newspaper stand, and doctors seldom penetrate its isolation.

"Underground witch doctors and other obscurantists and charlatans have not failed to take advantage of this forgetfulness," the paper observed. . . .

October 30

Tomorrow I'm off for Leningrad. It will be good to get away. I've been beating my brains out for news the last couple of weeks.

October 31

The Mad Haberdasher story sets a record. Filed September 7, it was killed October 15.

November 5

For the last few hours I have been writing stories about Leningrad. Now while it is fresh in my mind I want to set down some things about my trip and the feeling which I have for Leningrad.

The imperial grandeur of the city . . . the majesty of the buildings . . . the dark tragedy and fantastic glitter of its past . . . the drama of the Revolution . . . the horror of the winter of 1941–42 when people starved and froze and died in the city—not by thousands but by hundreds of thousands.

There is no city in the world which has seen more life, more death, than Leningrad. During the war what impressed me was the pride and heroism of the Leningraders. How straight they walked, how firmly they shook your hand, how directly they looked you in the eyes. Here were people who had survived. Each was a hero. To be alive did not mean individual heroism. You could not live or die in the city without being a hero every day. To live was merely a chance, an accident.

These people then were the survivors . . . alert, conscious of their strength, not boasting. Quietly resourceful. They knew that nothing which they would encounter in life would be more of an ordeal than what they had passed through.

They were proud. They have always been proud. That goes back to Peter. Always it has been the most advanced, the most resolute, the most progressive city in Russia. A gathering place of bold spirits, men and women of genius, artists, writers, thinkers, freebooters, revolutionaries.

No other city has such a heritage. Only the Paris of Louis XIV, of Napoleon and the Encyclopedists, bears much relation to Peter's city. But the parallel peters out by mid-nineteenth century.

Petersburg was a city ruled by tyrants, and the spirit of revolt which it fostered was almost a function of that tyranny—had not the tyrants been so ruthless there could hardly have come into being fighters, revolutionists, protestants so single-minded and so resolute.

I have steeped myself in a good bit of Russian history. Enough to get the flavor of the city—the imperial strain, the freebooting mercantile traders, such as the Stroganovs. The incredibly wealthy landowners. The brilliant intelligentsia, feverish in their pursuit of ideas, their preoccupation with moral and philosophical questions.

All this . . . painted in colors that bewilder the imagination. Everything was too intense in Petersburg. The buildings were enormous. Their cost staggers the imagination. There were no small tragedies there. No small comedies. No little defeats. No modest victories.

I suppose you capture here the essence of Russia and all its qualities—the terrible magnification that occurs because of the sheer size and weight and wealth of the country—the narrow, narrow pinnacle of power—as vast as the distance from Warsaw to Vladivostok at the base and as narrow as a single man's breeches at the top.

I returned to Leningrad this week with this kind of mixed emotion. I had had a glimpse of the city as I came into Moscow. But just a glimpse. Now I returned with a good deal of excitement.

My impressions of Leningrad are mixed. For one thing, they have done a good job of reconstruction. I stressed that in my dispatches, and rightly so. Particularly in going out to the Kirov works I was satisfied that they have done that job magnificently. It was important for me to see that because, judging by a thousand externals, I would have formed a different conclusion.

These externals are what strike you first—the general over-all shabbiness and dowdiness, the paint peeling off, the stucco cracking, the grim and desolate interiors. You see the famous Winter Palace. I don't know what those words mean to others. To me they mean thousands of starving, freezing people straggling across a vast open square on an icy Sunday in the winter of 1905 with a shaggy priest (a police spy) at their head . . . a row of troops in flashing uniforms drawn up before the grim palace . . . a quietly voiced order . . . a flash of gunfire . . . the crowd rushing back in panic, leaving its dead bleeding on the pavement behind. . . . To me the Winter Palace means the Czaritza and those fantastically foolish fatal letters to Dear Nicky, and Rasputin slinking in and out of the corridors. . . . It means scenes from the operas . . . ballrooms glittering with silks and velvets and brocades and acres of diamonds and pearls and emeralds . . . Catherine and her lovers . . . the mad Paul . . . a procession of characters such as imagination could not conceive.

So I saw the Winter Palace this week, painted green and white and the paint peeling off. It didn't look imperial. It didn't look like a palace. It looked like an astonishingly baroque pavilion erected for the world's fair. . . . And then the Hermitage collections, so colossal they fill page after page in the 1914 Baedeker that is my bible. And outside the main entrance, closed, dirty, and dusty, a wooden platform erected for some forgotten repairs. Shabby. And the buildings of the Nevsky Prospekt . . . shabby . . . like an impoverished gentlewoman who no longer has the energy to brush off the dinner stains from her gown.

Inside, the Hermitage is lovely and fine—except for the lighting, which was so gloomy that we had to leave at 4:00 in the gathering dusk. But there was another thing about it, too. This is an impression almost too tenuous to put into words. I couldn't help feeling that the city has stopped growing, gone static or stale, or maybe just tired. Maybe it is because Moscow is the capital and exercises such a terrific pull on Leningrad, pulling away its best artists, best minds, best talents. True, the Mariinsky still prides itself on being superior to the Bolshoi. But I'm not so sure that is true. The première ballerinas are at the Bolshoi. Trained at the Mariinsky—but they perform at the Bolshoi.

This is somehow typical of Leningrad. It is slowly but surely losing ground.

It is still brisker, brighter, gayer, somehow more adult, more "cultured," as the Russians like to say, than Moscow. But it seems to be living on the glories of the past.

Industrially, I doubt if that is true. I think it is still pre-eminent in industrial technique, the traditions which make "Made in Leningrad" a recommendation anywhere in the Soviet Union.

I wanted to visit some of the historic spots of the Revolution. I wanted to see Smolny Institute where Lenin lived and worked in 1917. Lenin's office can be seen—but it was being repaired and wasn't open. But the rest of the building is closed to visitors. And the Tauride Palace where the Duma met, where Lenin said on the night of the Revolution, "We will now proceed to construct the socialist order," isn't open at all.

Another thing, quite symbolic: The Soviet regime has made little external change in the center of the city. The big grocery store—fancy groceries—was the same before the Revolution. The big department store was the big department store in 1917. The big bank building now houses a Soviet bank. And so on.

The big changes are outside the city in the suburbs and workers' quarters. . . .

It wasn't a good time to visit the city. The place is lovely in late spring or summer, and sometime I hope I can have the pleasure of seeing it that way. Maybe tomorrow I'll write a few more lines. Now it's late, and I'm tired.

Dispatch to New York Times
Leningrad, November 5, 1949

To one who saw Leningrad five years ago when the great Russian offensive was just driving Germans from the environs of the city the contrast between then and now is astonishing.

Five years ago the journey by roundabout rail route required almost forty-eight hours over rough tracks and wooden bridges. Today's Red Arrow makes the run in twelve hours. . . .

[Soon the city is to have a subway system, and the Leningrad papers every day or so report progress in construction—no small task in view of the swampy terrain which Peter the Great picked for his "window on Europe."]

When the great maroon and gold curtain of the Mariinsky Theater rises on the new Soviet ballet, *The Bronze Horseman,* you know that the spirit of Peter the Great still burns in the heart of Leningrad.

[The ballet eulogizes Peter the Great and his driving force which created not only Leningrad but the modern Russian state.

Leningrad is proud of Peter and proud of the glories of its days as Russia's capital. . . .]

Dispatch to New York Times
November 6

Georgi Malenkov, speaking at the October Revolution ceremony at the Bolshoi Theater, tonight said that American warmongers want to turn the world into an American colony. A third world war, he said, would "dig the grave" of the world capitalist system.

[It was the first time the anniversary speech had been presented by Malenkov.

Malenkov warned that a new war would not be confined to Europe and that the American continent would not go unscathed if conflict again broke out. . . .]

Victory of communism in China, he said, has opened a new era not only for China but for all colonial peoples in Asia.

A few more notes about Leningrad. . . .

One day we took a little suburban train out to Tsarskoye Selo to see Catherine's great palace, which I had seen in 1944 and which was burned by the Germans. The line from Petersburg is the first railroad line built in Russia. I couldn't help wondering if the old wooden train with wooden seats and luggage racks made the first run.

The train was filled with peasants going back to the country, clumping in their great warm *valinki,* carrying great sacks and string bags of bread and provisions and empty milk cans. A good cross-section of country people, chubby red-cheeked girls, laughing and singing . . . a long mournful ballad about a boy whose mother died and whose father hadn't looked after him and how he fell into crime and was brought up for trial before his own father who sentenced him to hang—an old ballad which their grandmothers probably sang. A blind beggar making his way through the car, collecting great handfuls of kopecks. Two more blind beggars who sang another loud and mournful song. A rather supercilious army officer, neatly dressed and carrying a brief case. A tired official with mournful eyes and a battered brief case. A peasant worker with his pockets stuffed with bread, tearing off pieces and stuffing them into his mouth.

Tsarskoye Selo surprised me. When I'd seen it, it was a ruin. Now there is a brand new railroad station. The lovely park around Catherine's palace is neatly tended and almost as good as new. The palace, of course, remains to be repaired.

We made a thorough tour of the shops because Ludmilla wanted to buy some things. They have good porcelain. We visited the bookstores. Leningrad is famous for them. There is supposed to be more selection than Moscow. But we didn't find it so. I picked up one thing—a supplement to the Bolshoi encyclopedia, which is valuable.

One thing irritated me—not being able to get decent postcards and photos.

The crowds in the stores are less rude and shoving than in Moscow. Part of the business of the city being more "cultured."

Tonight I've been to the Bolshoi for the Revolution anniversary meeting. Gay and glittering. All the big shots there. Women in evening dress, wearing fine necklaces and jeweled earrings. The stage decorated with red banners and a huge bank of chrysanthemums. Malenkov made the speech. A political event. The first time he has made it. His star has risen fast in the last year. He is a good speaker. Trained his shots on the United States.

A three-day holiday today, tomorrow, and Tuesday. Tonight the town is decorated. Rows of electric lights on big buildings. Loud-speakers blaring music in the streets. Big portraits of Stalin, Lenin, and the Politburo. Thousands of people strolling. In the square outside the hotel the big park whose construction I've watched for months opened today. The telegraph office a blaze of blue and red lights. Looks like a Christmas tree.

I must stop now. It's late, and I must be up early for the big show in Red Square tomorrow.

November 7

Tonight there is a reception at Spiridonovka House. Very shortly I must begin dressing for it. I am going to wear my tails. I bought a set in New York, but it has seemed too silly to wear them up to now. Tonight I'm going to take the plunge. . . .

November 8

There is no getting around it. There is a thrill in being in Red Square and watching the troops march by and the tanks clanging through. The square vibrates with their passage, and the vibration from the roaring motors rumbles in your lungs.

I think I like best the crack cavalry units. They have wonderful horses. With the bright sabers gleaming in the sunlight it is a spectacle to make a small boy's heart dance with joy. Mine is enough of a small boy's to give a leap or two.

There is the excitement of anticipation. Who will be on the Tomb? Will Stalin be there? You crane your neck to see which members of the Politburo are mounting the steps. And there are the planes sweeping overhead—will there be anything new? Yesterday there wasn't.

After the military comes the civilian demonstration. What they call the "spontaneous demonstration." About a million people massed with banners. Yellows, blues, white, greens, purples, orange. . . .

After a couple of hours in Red Square I made my way through

81

the militia lines over to the embassy on Mokhovaya. They have open house there. From the windows of the embassy you get a wonderful view of the parade.

Yesterday was a football day. Cloudless blue sky, sparkling crisp air. But your feet got cold on the cold concrete. At the embassy I was treated to a wonderful lunch of *pelmeny,* meatballs wrapped in dough and cooked very quickly in boiling water and served with some of the juice and lots of pepper, sour cream, and vinegar.

Last night was the big reception at Spiridonovka. Gromyko was the host. The party was dominated by the Soviet marshals. They are the biggest, bulkiest bunch I've ever seen anywhere outside of Minnesota football. Enormous in their huge gold epaulets, gold collars, sea-green coats, and fancy blue-and-red-striped trousers. Each chest weighted with medals.

The new Chinese were there. Much the center of attention.

What struck me were the Soviet ladies. There were many ladies, and they *were* ladies, elegantly gowned, elegantly jeweled, good hair-dos, good figures, and good manners. I think it's a trend. You should have seen the ballroom and the orchestra and the fancily dressed officers and their ladies dancing on the polished floor.

Dispatch to New York Times
November 11, 1949

The All-Union Art Exhibit of 1949 opened this week at the famous Tretyakov galleries with six hundred works by Soviet artists. [Nearly seventy of] the works entered in the exhibition depict some phase of Stalin's life. . . .

Dispatch to New York Times
November 12

Soviet Art today criticized Lillian Hellman's *Another Part of the Forest,* which is being presented by the Moscow Drama Theater, for failing to present "a merciless and scornful exposé of the awful capitalist reality."

November 12

Well, it's 10:00 of a Saturday evening and snowing. Out in the square it is all white, and the wind is blowing and swirling up little snow clouds. Maybe Moscow will look like winter in the morning. It's about time. I remember when I was a kid I always used to think it was bad if there wasn't snow on the ground by my birthday.

November 14

My birthday today. Outside it is drizzling. The sky is gray, and the clouds hang low over the city. The snow we had the night before last has vanished in dirty slush. It is dull and dreary and gray.

Tonight I will have a little celebration. I will go with a couple of friends to the new Kiev restaurant which opened over the holidays.

November 16

It has been foggy here since Sunday. No air mail has come through.

November 16

Here are some of the advertisements I saw on a bulletin board just off Sverdlovsk Square.

For Sale: Opel car in good condition.

For Sale: Technical automobile library, 1,500 books and magazines.

Construction office wants messenger.

Perfumery project: Wants three stokers.

Exchange: Rooms in Erevan for Moscow.

Experienced maid wants position in small family, no children.

Moscow auto factory wants: locksmith 700–1,500 rubles; repairman 600–1,500 rubles; assembly workers, 800–1,700; turners, 600–1,200; polishers, 600–1,200; body finishers, 650–1,500.

For sale: Dental chair.

English lessons.

November 17

Moscow has been practically fog-bound since Sunday. Not quite as thick as a London pea-souper but thick enough so that some evenings you couldn't see the red stars glowing atop the Kremlin towers. I've had no mail all week—except steamer mail.

I took the Whitneys to the new Kiev restaurant in Mayakovsky

Square for my birthday. The restaurant is run by the Ukraine Ministry of Trade, one of a series to be opened in Moscow. There are now three—the Arogvy, which is Georgian, the Riga for Latvia, and now the Kiev.

We had pork with a cold, rather spicy sauce for hors d'oeuvres. For the main course pork smothered in blankets of grated cabbage and onions and carrots. We had some Ukraine vodka of which I drank a thimbleful.

After the dinner we drove around town—a long, slow drive. It was a foggy night, the kind of night when you can make up dreams about Moscow and it looks as though they might come true. We talked a long time about love and life and fate and other good Russian subjects.

November 17, 1949
Letter to Edwin L. James, New York Times

It occurred to me this week that it would be interesting to discover whether the decision of Reuters to close their bureau and the departure of Newman and Stevens had any impact on the Russians. So I persuaded Gilmore of AP to join me in a letter to Gromyko.

Yesterday we received a hurried call to a conference with Frantzev, head of the press department. He said Gromyko had asked him to receive our proposals.

We made these specific suggestions:

1. That the Foreign Office resume calling in correspondents and issuing announcements to them instead of putting them out on Moscow radio for distribution via the Soviet monitor in London.

2. That arrangements be made with Glavlit for speedy clearance of copy based on these announcements.

3. That facilities be granted for interviews with foreign delegations and visitors; that facilities be provided for coverage of meetings, convocations, conventions, congresses, etc.

4. That measures be taken to facilitate trips to Soviet institutions. I have put in fifty to sixty such requests. So far one has been arranged.

5. That the Foreign Office reconsider its decision not to grant correspondents re-entry visas.

Frantzev took careful notes. He assured us with rather sheepish eagerness that "I will give Mr. Gromyko a full report on this later this afternoon."

November 19
Letter to Lester Markel,* New York Times

I want to apologize for two things: the wooden style and glaring omissions in the magazine material which I have sent you and the great delays.

The style is dictated entirely by the idiosyncracies of the censorship. Particularly do they beware of bright and casual leads. Please try to remember that *no comparisons* are passed. *Never.*

Generally speaking, the material I must omit is the most interesting part of the story.

The delays are inevitable. Ordinary facts may take a week of digging—or longer. It is unusual for the censors to pass magazine material in less than a week. . . .

November 19

There has been no air mail for eight days. Bad weather has grounded planes. It is the kind of delay one must anticipate during the winter. People coming in from Prague have had to shift to trains. Yesterday, a plane got to Lvov, I heard. But no regular service yet.

I have finally, only tonight, sent off a couple of Christmas parcels. They will be very late arriving.

This week we have been able to cover the International Women's Democratic Federation. Not much of a story. The best was La Passionara's† outburst at reports she had been arrested in Prague. She is a dramatic figure—a middle-aged, gray-haired woman, but still full of fire. Very black eyes. The Prague story was an INS report that she had been arrested for Titoism. The very same day she spoke here, blasting hell out of Tito. But she had been in Prague, for some heart treatments. . . .

November 19
Letter to Edwin L. James, New York‡Times

Cy has reported to me that you feel very strongly that I should not go out of the Soviet Union on leave because of the very real danger that the Russians would not allow me to return.

* Sunday editor of the *New York Times.*
† Dolores Ibarruri, a Spanish Communist and long a resident of Moscow.
‡ C. L. Sulzberger of the *New York Times.*

85

I want you to know that I respect your decision and will, of course, abide by it despite my very strong feeling that a "breather" is close to a vital necessity to any correspondent who has worked many months in the poisonous atmosphere which prevails in this country. . . .

November 20, 1949
Letter to Mr. Omelchenko, Chief, Glavlit

I want to call your attention to an example of what I regard as unsatisfactory action by the censorship.

This concerns a dispatch about the All-Union Art Exhibit. I included the sentence: "Nearly seventy of the works entered in the exhibition depict some phase of Stalin's life."

The censor deleted the first part of this sentence, making it appear the exhibition was entirely devoted to works concerning Generalissimo Stalin.

Dispatch to New York Times
November 22

Pravda today sharply criticizes the Soviet Institute of Paleontology for "indifference to the principle of Party spirit in science and failure to struggle actively against reactionary, obscurantist foreign paleontology. . . ."

Dispatch to New York Times
November 23

The *Literary Gazette* said today that the All-Union Geographical Society's publication should devote more attention to the "drastic differences between Soviet and bourgeois geographical science. . . ."

Dispatch to New York Times
November 25

The newspaper *Soviet Moldavia* reports that modern historical science has proved "beyond dispute" that Jesus Christ never existed. . . .

November 26

Winter seems to be setting in. This morning it is blustery and wintry. The square is white, and snow is silting down in small particles. It looks like the Moscow I remember best from the old days.

The people look like black ants as they cross the white square. It was snowing when I came home last night from the Bolshoi. I went to see that wonderful ballet, *The Fountain of Bakchisari*. The mad, wild orgy of the Tartars. Thrilling, swirling masses of colors and bodies.

Sunday I'm going to Zagorsk again. I went there a couple of months ago to see the fabulous old monastery, the one with walls twenty feet thick. It used to withstand sieges of the Poles and the Swedes back in the fifteenth and sixteenth centuries.

November 30
Letter to Will Lissner, New York Times

I think it might be useful if I outlined briefly the types of controls under which correspondents work in Moscow.

1. All foreign correspondents are accredited to the press department of the Foreign Office. All our official business is handled through this agency.

2. Except for fire, police, and hospital cases, purchases of consumer goods, and entertainment tickets, all contacts with government officials must be through the press department.

3. Soviet officials are forbidden by law to deal with foreigners, including correspondents.

4. General surveillance. This is carried out by the MVD or Ministry of Internal Security. The MVD provides the plain-clothes men assigned to each ambassador and the details on duty at every important public function. The MVD also provides the plain-clothes men who intermittently shadow correspondents and diplomats. The shadowing should not be conceived of as continuous. It is irregular. However, the fact that at any time it may be applied causes one to assume that at all times he is being shadowed and govern his movements accordingly.

5. Specific surveillance. This is carried out by all Russians with whom the foreigner has regular contact—hotel staff, secretaries, chauffeurs, maids, etc. These people are not required to report every little item about a foreigner but merely those which strike them as suspicious. They must be ready to provide minute-by-minute information should the MVD desire it.

6. Communications. All communications at all times are sub-

ject to scrutiny and surveillance. There is a continuous tap on all hotel and embassy telephones. All incoming and outgoing mail is opened, scrutinized, and, presumably, photostated. There is some evidence that they employ only spot checking. Some mail arrives without the telltale heavy gum which they use to reseal envelopes.

7. Telegraphic communications. All outgoing news and service messages are subject to censorship by Glavlit. The same is true of telephonic communications. Personal cables and telephone calls are not subject to censorship but are subject to scrutiny. Incoming service messages are subject to scrutiny.

8. Travel. There is no published law, statute, or regulation governing travel by correspondents. The statute limiting movement specifically applies only to diplomats. In practice, however, correspondents are subject to severe restriction. They cannot purchase a railroad ticket without presenting their Soviet residence passport. No ticket will be sold unless it bears the travel permit of the MVD. The MVD in turn will not grant a travel permit without a request by the Foreign Office press department. There is no published statute, either, forbidding correspondents to motor around Moscow and its environs. But in practice correspondents, like diplomats, are halted by the MVD militia at control points on all highways leading out of the city. The greatest distance which may be traveled on any of these is fifty kilometers. Most of them have been cut down to ten or fifteen kilometers.

You will notice that all of the more important controls are in the hands of the MVD, which has gradually taken over from the Foreign Office. This tendency has been marked during the continuing spy hysteria here, particularly since the public criticism of the Foreign Office which was contained in the announcement of the Strong case. . . .

VII

Stalin's Birthday

Dispatch to New York Times
December 2, 1949

The teachers of the Moscow Boys School No. 315 have set themselves a special task—to see that every boy has a good mark both in study [and in conduct] by Stalin's seventieth birthday, December 21.

As an example of the maturity of the children's patriotism, Director Pavlenko declares that "when the question of cosmopolitanism arose even the smallest children were tremendously indignant. . . ."

December 3

I wrote a Christmas letter to the folks in Minneapolis today. I hope it gets there by the twenty-fifth.

Dispatch to New York Times
December 4

Spurred by the approach of Generalissimo Stalin's seventieth birthday, all branches of Soviet economy are setting special production tasks to be fulfilled by December 21. . . .

[From Warsaw came the report of the planting of fifty fruit trees in honor of Stalin's birthday. . . .]

Soviet Art said that "an inexhaustible source for the creative inspiration of the masters of art is the life and activity of the Great Leader. . . ."

December 9, 1949

This is a gray, foggy morning with hardly any light in the sky. We will be working under electricity all day. Now that we approach the shortest days of the year there is a perpetual half-gloom about Moscow.

December 11

Another gray Sunday. Yesterday there was sun for the first time in a couple of weeks. I hope the break in the clouds will bring in a batch of air mail in a few days. Ship mail has been getting here ahead of air mail.

Dispatch to New York Times
December 11

The circulation of Stalin's writings in the Soviet Union has now reached 539,000,000 copies in 101 languages. . . .

Dispatch to New York Times
December 15

Trofim Lysenko, writing about Stalin's contribution to agrobiology, said in *Izvestia* today that Soviet agrobiologists in 1949 transmuted wheat into rye. . . .

Dispatch to New York Times
December 16

Mao Tse-tung arrived in Moscow today. . . . [His initial visit to Moscow since establishment of the new Chinese Republic was for the purpose of attending Stalin's seventieth birthday, December 21. He was the first of the distinguished visitors expected for the unprecedented ceremonies.]

Mao expressed appreciation for the aid and assistance rendered in the past thirty-three years by the Soviet to China. . . .

Mao's visit has two purposes. The first is Stalin's birthday. The second is to lay the formal diplomatic framework of relations between China and Russia. High on the list of subjects for discussion are treaties of friendship, alliance, trade, and mutual defense.

[The Bolshoi Theater has announced a special production for Stalin's birthday, a revival of the ballet *The Red Poppy*. The score has been brought up to date with events in China and will be given its première December 21. . . .]

Dispatch Killed by Censor
December 18

Negotiation of a Russo-Chinese treaty of friendship, alliance, and mutual defense is one of the prime objectives of the visit of Mao Tse-tung.

A community of interest will be worked out in conferences by Mao and Soviet leaders headed by Stalin and including Molotov, Malenkov, and Bulganin. The Soviet press emphasizes the fact that China takes the Soviet Union as its model. . . .

The Japanese question is one of the most complex which must be discussed by Mao and the Soviet leaders. China is insistent that it be granted a full voice in the Japanese treaty. . . .

Dispatch Killed by Censor
December 18

A vision of the future when the world calendar will begin on the date of Stalin's birthday and will be celebrated as a Day of Thanksgiving was presented in *Pravda* today by the writer Leonid Leonov. . . .

Dispatch to New York Times
December 18

Announcement was made today of the transfer of Nikita Khrushchev, veteran Politburo member [and one of the Soviet Union's ablest administrators,] from his duties as Communist Party secretary in the Ukraine to a similar post for Moscow. He was also elected as a secretary of the central committee. . . .

Khrushchev succeeds Georgi M. Popov, also one of the secretaries of the central committee. Other secretaries include Stalin, Malenkov, A. A. Kuznetsov, Suslov, Ponomarenko, and Shkiryatov. . . .*

Born in a coal-mining village in the Donbas in 1894, Khrushchev has been a Party member since the Civil War. [In assuming the post of Moscow regional secretary he is returning to a job he held in the days when he was first rising to great Party prominence. His first important post was that of secretary of the Moscow Party committee in 1931.] From 1935 to 1938 he was secretary of the Moscow regional committee. He played a leading role in

---

* Actually Kuznetsov had been arrested nearly a year before.

the conduct of the war on the Ukrainian front and was particularly active in the organization of Partisan warfare behind the German lines. . . .

December 20, 1949

It looks like a snowy Moscow for Stalin's birthday. Yesterday it started, and today it is still swirling across the square. The rooftops are white, and the snow machines are busy in the streets.

I hope we will have a Moscow Christmas card scene for the holidays. This Stalin celebration makes it more of a holiday. All the buildings are decorated with red, and there are pictures of Uncle Joe on the walls. They've put platforms in the squares—for dancing and music. How they will manage in the snow I can't imagine.

Christmas trimmings are under way, too. They have some Christmas trees up, and there are decorations in some shops. There will be more a bit later because the holiday here is New Year's rather than Christmas.

Dispatch to New York Times
December 21

In a special article written for Stalin's seventieth birthday Georgi Malenkov today recalled Stalin's repeated declaration that capitalism and socialism can live peaceably together for a lengthy time.

Malenkov's article was published in a special twelve-page edition of *Pravda* which contained articles on Stalin by each member of the Politburo as well as Shkiryatov and the Chief of Stalin's secretariat, Lieutenant-General A. Poskrebyshev. . . .

Malenkov declared that the Soviet considers "the road of peaceful competition with capitalism as quite acceptable." Stalin has declared repeatedly that the Soviet proceeds from the fact of the unavoidable coexistence for a lengthy period of the two systems—socialism and capitalism. . . .

Mikoyan's article paid special tribute to Stalin in connection with China and Germany. He declared that Stalin long ago developed in detail the tactics and strategy of the Chinese Revolution. "That is why the Chinese Communist Party recognizes Comrade Stalin as its great leader," he said. . . .

Poskrebyshev revealed that Stalin was a scientific innovator who played a leading role in developing frost-resisting citrus for the Black Sea coast and encouraged the planting of eucalyptus trees. . . .

At the Bolshoi Theater tonight Mao Tse-tung greeted Stalin as "the teacher and friend of the Chinese people. . . ."

[Stalin did not speak. His only words were to interrupt the Polish representative Yozyaik to say: "Why don't you speak in Polish?"]

Dispatch to New York Times
December 22

Stalin believes the capitalist system is destined to exist for some years to come and that the world is large enough for both Communist and capitalist states to live and work in.

This was the conclusion drawn from the analysis of Stalin's views presented in *Pravda* yesterday by Georgi M. Malenkov. The fact that of all possible subjects Malenkov chose to present Stalin's conviction that the world must expect communism and capitalism to endure side by side for a considerable time added to the interest. . . .

December 25

Ramon, a little Argentine boy who lives in the hotel, popped in while I was starting to decorate my tree. He went for the ornaments like a duck to water. . . . I talked to my sons tonight. Mike asked who was calling. I told him—me. He said, Well! Gosh! He got all his things including his box. Stephen said Merry Christmas in rather unintelligible fashion. . . .

December 28

A little bit about my Christmas. Last week a continuous round of cocktail parties at the embassy. I have a tree in my room. On Christmas Eve there was a big buffet with carols at Spaso for the American colony. Lots of people went to the little Catholic church for midnight mass. Christmas morning I went to Spaso for services conducted by an English minister who came down from Helsinki. Then, dinner at Eddy Gilmore's. The weather continues warm with only light snow on the ground. Russian Christmas doesn't come until January 6. Their big holiday is New Year's Eve. . . .

Decembr 29, 1949

This morning, if Ramon will spare me too many interruptions, I'll write a bit more of Christmas in Moscow. He has been turning the third floor of the Metropole into a chamber of horrors, prancing around, blowing a bazoo which I gave him. He is equipped with a bicycle and roller skates. Six years old and a Wonderful Menace.

Christmas was complicated by the fact that the Dallases, my good friends, left in the middle of it. Just before they were to leave Frankie came down with an infection. She had a temp of 104. They finally took off last Friday night with the prospect of Christmas on the train from Leningrad to Helsinki.

There were some angles about their departure which were sort of upsetting—things which I will not tell now. I guess all is well. I surely hope so. But there was a point where Dallas and I were not so sure. . . .

I have a cook now and three of us eat in my room. Our Nina makes a difference. She is a lovely youngster and constantly thinking up good things to cook. She does the laundry, too, and keeps my room neat as a pin and shines my shoes. We gave her a sweater for Christmas and a box of soap and some lipstick and rouge. She is one of the good things about Moscow.

Christmas Eve we sang carols at the embassy. There was a great log fire crackling in the fireplace and a huge Christmas tree. The post office Christmas afternoon was crowded with all kinds of folks calling home—Hungarians, Poles, Czechs, Rumanians, and a contingent of Mongolians.

Dispatch to New York Times
December 31

The victory of Chinese communism was honored last night on the stage of the Bolshoi with a new presentation of *The Red Poppy*, which had not been seen for fifteen years. Moscow's première ballerina, Galina Ulanova, danced the star role of Tao Hwa. . . .

Tonight all over Russia, from Kamchatka to the Kola Peninsula, Ded Moroz, Grandfather Frost, was busy on his rounds of bringing presents to good Soviet children. . . .

At the big celebration at the Hall of Columns Ded Moroz told the children: "With the name of Comrade Stalin on our lips we lived through last year with glory. . . ."

December 31

Ludmilla neglected to get her New Year's tree until yesterday, and they were all sold out. So I undecorated my tree and lent it to her for Aresha. I took the tinsel ornaments and the beautiful bird and gave them to my courier for a tree for a little girl in her flat. I don't quite know if that was a gift or a loan.

January 4, 1950

It was a kick to talk to Mother and Janet on New Year's Day. Their voices sounded exactly as though I were calling from downtown Minneapolis. . . .

I sent E. a cute old man from Zagorsk—a wooden man whose head comes off. There is a great artists' center there, center of the Russian toy-carving industry. They teach craftsmen to make the traditional toys and dolls native to different regions of Russia.

Our cook is a honey. She is about nineteen, and this is the first time she has been a cook. Nearly every day she turns up some surprise. She makes pie on our little *pletkas,* electric plates. She gets good meat at the market. Fresh vegetables—carrots, cabbage, potatoes. Uses lots of sour cream. Makes us blini. Wants to darn our socks. God knows what she doesn't do. Always chipper and pleasant.

The censors were unusually touchy on Stalin's birthday. A few of the most horrible examples of fulsome praise were cut. The most severe carnage occurred in human-interest material. Much copy was subject to great delay. It was my impression every line was submitted to the Kremlin Secretariat.

It is significant, I think, that my analysis of Stalin's views on coexistence was passed without a deletion—after a delay of thirty-six hours. It was allowed to pass because it expounded exactly the point they wanted to put across. . . .

Dispatch to New York Times
January 4

The Soviet press made plain that the new Chinese government of Mao Tse-tung can be certain of the full support of the Soviet in its efforts to establish sovereignty over Formosa. . . .

January 5, 1950

I got a card from Mike. He said: "I'm sorry we didn't get your present off before but I have been very bissy. I know how to drive the tractor and I have shot a rabbit, a squirrel, and a possom."

Weather much milder for a change. Today is warm and almost melting.

January 6

The Kirks have been in Leningrad. The ambassador particularly wanted to see Leningrad in the winter because he had always thought of it as a winter city. When I think of Leningrad I think of the snow and the cold and dim street lamps glowing down narrow streets and granite buildings and troikas and beautiful young women in furs and fighting at the barricades in snow. . . . I wish they still had troikas here. Maybe they do in the country.

January 8

My courier brought me a special piece of Christmas cake this morning. The cathedral on Christmas Eve—night before last—was jammed. Christmas Eve begins with the first star in the sky at twilight. Services go on all night.

Looking out my window this frosty Sunday morning I can imagine troikas swirling around the square and noble ladies swathed in ermine. It is about 30° below centigrade—about 22° below Fahrenheit. Crisp cold. The sky is almost clear. The sun in shining on a glittering bank of snow. A cloud of white steam billows out of the ventilating shaft for the subway. People all bundled up are hurrying down toward the Lenin Museum. It is a cold Russian scene.

I love to walk the streets at night now with the frost so strong and the snow crunching and the full moon with a great halo around it and the buildings looking very Russian and mysterious.

I see the militiamen bundled up with fur caps and collars turned high, standing on the corners and swinging their arms, talking together. People hurrying back home and to work at all hours of the night. And long, black Zis limousines slinking around the streets at forty miles an hour. . . .

Here are some Russian jokes which are popular. There are two kinds. One variety is the Georgian toast. The other is the Armenian story.

The Georgian toasts are long and spun out. Here is an example:

A handsome young man was walking by the river when a frog spoke to him.

"Please, young man," said the frog. "Pick me up."

"Why should I pick you up?" said the young man.

"Please do, young man," said the frog. "You won't be sorry."

So he picked the frog up.

"Please, young man, wrap me in a nice clean handkerchief and put me in your pocket and take me home," said the frog.

"Why should I do that?" asked the young man. "Why should I wrap up a frog in a clean handkerchief and take him home?"

"Please do, young man. I promise you won't be sorry," said the frog.

So he wrapped up the frog and took it home. When he got there the frog said, "Please put me in your bed."

"Why should I put a frog in my bed?"

"I promise you won't be sorry."

So he put the frog in bed.

Then the frog said: "Please undress and get into bed with me."

"Why should I do that?" the young man asked. "Why should I get in bed with a frog?"

"Please do," the frog said. "You won't be sorry."

So he did and the frog said: "Please kiss me."

And he did and the frog turned into a beautiful young woman.

Just then the young man's wife walked in and found him in bed with the young woman.

So . . . let's all drink a toast to those good wives who believe the stories their husbands tell them!

Then, the Armenian joke in the form of a riddle:

"What is it that is long and green and is hanging in my living room—and squeaks?

"You can't answer it?

"The answer: a herring!

"Why? But, of course. It is hanging in my living room because I hung it there. It is long because it is a herring. It is green be-

97

cause I painted it green. And it squeaks—well it squeaks just to make it difficult for you to guess what it is!"

And then the Armenian joke to tell after telling half a dozen of them:
"Why are Armenian jokes so silly?
"Of course. Because the Russians make them up!"

January 9, 1950

We are in a quiet period so far as news is concerned. The only thing on the horizon is Mao Tse-tung and his conferences with Stalin and Molotov. I expect very soon there will be an official announcement so that speculation is rather pointless.*

It has been indicated in Mao's statement to Tass that the treaty basis of relations between Russia and China will be founded on the 1945 treaty. I should imagine it might be slightly revised—possibly on its military clauses, which are now limited to Japan. The two countries will probably pledge to come to each other's defense against aggression from any source.

There will undoubtedly be an economic agreement of considerable scope; probably an outright loan by the U.S.S.R. to China for reconstruction and rehabilitation and for the provision of Russian technical aid and assistance. I do not think all the clauses will necessarily be made public. . . .

So far Mao's visit has been cloaked in privacy. He was given a big welcome, but his known semi-public appearances have been limited to the Stalin birthday meeting at the Bolshoi—at which he drew applause second only to that for Stalin—and to the Stalin birthday reception at the Kremlin. I expect his tours to Russian cities will take on the nature of a semi-triumphal progress.

The fact is that we do not even know for certain where Mao is staying. He is not at the embassy. I threw the embassy into a dither by going out to try to find out some details about Mao. . . .

In all the Chinese and Russian statements about Formosa they mention Tibet in the same terms. I think you can write it down

* Actually it was five more weeks before the agreements were completed.

as absolutely certain that they will occupy Tibet at the earliest possible moment. . . .

It is hard to tell at this distance Washington's intentions regarding Formosa. But I gather from Truman's statement that opinion is inclining toward abandonment of the island. . . . I should think it probably would suit the Chinese and the Russians very well for us to become preoccupied with the Formosan question since it diverts us from the real crisis which is, of course, Southeast Asia. . . .

Actually Southeast Asia is so rickety that when it starts to crumble it will be damn difficult to halt it short of India and the Philippines. That is why we should be devoting more attention to that area than to the Formosa red herring. . . .

There is a decided difference in propaganda about China and the satellites. China is presented on the level of "an equal partner." The identity of China and Russia in foreign policy is always emphasized.

Whether the Russians will be able to restrain their overweening tendency to Russianize or attempt to Russianize China is an open question. . . .

What interests the average Muscovite a good deal more is the question of price reductions. For more than a month Moscow has been buzzing with rumors of an impending price cut. . . . There are three prices which are too high and which affect ordinary Russians. These are the prices of bread, butter, and meat.

With the plentiful harvests of this year and last there is no reason why bread should not be brought down to the prewar price. I think the price of butter could be cut by one-third.

I expect there will be reductions probably some time this month in bread, butter, and meat. There may be other cuts too. . . .

As regards U.S.–U.S.S.R. relations, we seem to be in another of the more and more frequent "waiting" periods. Malenkov in his Stalin birthday article told us, in effect, that Russia is ready to talk business with us on a long-term basis. Now they are waiting to see if we are interested.

I have no idea how Malenkov's remarks were taken in the State

Department. But I am convinced this is the point they wished to get across.

Dispatch Killed by Censor
January 13, 1950

Anyone equipped with a pencil, paper, and rudimentary arithmetic today could prepare a rough estimate of today's Soviet population.

The last Soviet census in 1939 showed a total of 170,000,000. Estimates abroad of present population generally range in the neighborhood of 200,000,000.

Now it is announced that the Soviet this year will have 671 election districts. Each district represents 300,000 citizens. By simple multiplication a rough total of 200,300,000 citizens can be obtained. . . .

Dispatch Killed by Censor
January 13

The death penalty was reintroduced in the Soviet today, just two and a half years since its abolition. The new decree limited its application to "traitors" to the motherland, spies, and "subversive diversionists."

January 14

The stores here really had a lot of stuff for the New Year's holiday, and I think everyone settled back and enjoyed himself without too much worry about the international situation. After all, why should they? With China percolating nicely, the atoms brewing away, and things not too bad in the satellite countries. . . .

Dispatch to New York Times
January 14

Uzbekistan's cotton growers have pledged themselves to deliver to the state several hundred thousand tons more cotton than in 1949. But the announcement made no mention of their pledge to Stalin to deliver 500,000 tons above plan in 1949. However, it is no secret that cotton deliveries did not fulfil expectations. . . .

Dispatch to New York Times
January 15

A friendly discussion was conducted last night at the Kremlin by Stalin and India's ambassador, Sir Sarvepalli Radhakrishnan. . . .

The generalissimo was described as appearing in excellent health. The discussion was marked by a "very pleasant atmosphere." The fact that the meeting occurred while Mao Tse-tung is in Moscow attracted interest. . . .

[Mao's departure from Moscow will be marked by a very strong Sino-Russian declaration concerning the political and territorial integrity of China. It will also carry a challenge against what are alleged to be Anglo-American imperialist efforts to maintain the status quo in Southeast Asia. . . .]

VIII

The Chinese Treaty

January 15, 1950

This is a snowy, snowy Sunday morning. The big cold wave has ended, and the snow has sifted down, turning Moscow into a picture-postcard land.

I get so immersed in political thought that it is refreshing to take a little glimpse at the kind of Russia which lies behind the *Pravda* façade.

For instance . . .

At New Year's time a Muscovite went to the German cemetery to look at his family's grave. He comes from a one-time upper-class family. Nearby is the burial place of a prominent pre-revolutionary merchant. A small black figure of the Virgin has long stood in a niche in the wall beside the grave.

There was a queue of about thirty people in front of the statue, each with a small cup. From the Virgin's head trickled a small stream of water. An elderly cemetery attendant said the water was miraculous and had worked many wonders and, believing the statue was on the man's family plot, suggested that they go into partnership, put up an iron fence around the statue, and charge each believer ten or twenty rubles for a few drops of water. He said every day people put money on the grave. Some days there were thirty or forty rubles there. The man declined the proposition.

The next Sunday he returned to the cemetery. The Virgin was

gone, but there were notes scribbled on the grave: "Thank you for returning my husband"; "Thank you for giving back my health"; "Thank you for making Ivan love me."

The attendant said a priest had come from the Patriarchy. There had been a quarrel over the statue and finally it was ordered taken to Zagorsk. . . .

Here is something which happened in an isolated village within fifty kilometers of Moscow last summer. Crime is practically unknown. People don't lock their doors. Then there was a sudden outbreak of theft—clothing taken from one house, food from another. The villagers traced the crimes—or thought they did—to three teen-agers from Moscow who were vacationing there. They seized the youngsters and methodically beat them to death. This form of village justice is—or is thought by Muscovites to be—fairly common. Moscow people are a little queasy about traveling deep into the remote countryside, particularly the back Volga areas. They fear getting too far into the land of the "dark people."

Here is another of the typical Stalin yarns which has made the rounds. An old character around town has as a hobby the study of Kutuzov. He finally crowned his obsession with success. He published a brief, popular pamphlet about Kutuzov. One day when he came back from lunch, his secretary told him the Kremlin had called, but the old man wasn't going to be taken in by this practical joke. The next day his secretary told him the Kremlin had phoned again and asked him to call a certain number.

He was still skeptical but on the way home that night thought, well, he would just see. He went to a public phone booth and made his call. Stalin's secretariat answered, yes, they had been trying to reach him. Please wait a minute. He waited. He waited some more. Outside the line of people grew longer and more indignant. Finally a voice came on the line. Stalin, of course. He congratulated him on the pamphlet. By this time folks were opening the door of the booth and shouting at him. Stalin could hear the rumble and asked what the trouble was. The old man told him. Stalin laughed and invited him to his office the next day for a chat.

It is interesting that I have not heard a single anti-Stalin joke from a Russian and few remarks tinged with anti feeling. . . .

There are three types of jokes in general circulation. Each has a racial basis, and each displays a measure of Great Russian chauvinism. These are the Georgian toast, the Armenian joke, and the simple anti-Semitic story.

A typical Jewish joke: A Jewish boy falls through the ice. A Russian jumps in to save him. He dives three times and brings up the boy. The boy's father appears on the scene. He says: "You rescued my boy? You dove in three times to bring him up? Then why didn't you bring up his cap, too?"

A dreary anti-Semitic joke. Which reminds me of Newman's stuff on anti-Semitism. The specific things he mentioned all happened. There was a spate of anti-Semitism; they did use the cosmopolitanism campaign to put a crimp into most of the surviving Jewish organizations and to knock off a certain number of Jewish critics and intelligentsia. But the roots of that drive were wider and deeper than merely the Jews. . . .

Dispatch Killed by Censor
January 20, 1950

The lengthy negotiations of Mao Tse-tung with Stalin, Molotov, and Malenkov drew toward a conclusion today. In the broad discussions it was believed they talked of the role which atomic energy will play in the development of Soviet and Chinese industrial potentialities. . . .

There has been no official report of the scope and progress of the discussions. . . .

It is in connection with the long-range problem of solving China's economic tasks that the question of atomic energy has arisen.

Dispatch to New York Times
January 21

Foreign Minister Vishinsky today denied that the Soviet has infringed on the territorial integrity or independence of China and denounced Secretary of State Acheson for a false and "crudely slanderous" attack. This was a reply to Acheson's declaration before the National Press Club in Washington, January 12.*

Vishinsky denied that Outer Mongolia had been incorpo-

---

* Acheson had charged that four areas of China—Outer Mongolia, Manchuria, Inner Mongolia, and Sinkiang—had fallen under Soviet control.

rated in the Soviet Union and said ". . . normal people cannot doubt the fact that Manchuria, Inner Mongolia, and Sinkiang continue to be part of China territory."

Dispatch to New York Times
January 21

Capitalism and imperialism are no longer capable of halting the revolutionary movement of millions of Asiatic peoples inspired by the successes of communism in China and the Soviet Union.

This analysis was made tonight at the Lenin anniversary meeting by Pyotr Pospelov [, one of the Party's leading theoreticians].

China's Mao Tse-tung has been in Moscow for nearly five weeks. Last night he was joined by Chou En-lai, accompanied by a distinguished delegation including the top figures in the new Northeast China government, established in Manchuria. . . .*

[It was understood that the general basis for the broadest Sino-Russian understanding has been laid in extensive conferences between Mao, Stalin, Molotov, Malenkov, Mikoyan, and others. The task of Chou and his mission will be to reduce these understandings to specific agreements and treaties. . . .]

January 22

This is one of those bright, sunshiny Sunday afternoons in Moscow. The kind when you dress your kids in their white furs and take them for a sleigh ride in the parks; and then take pictures of them, all bundled like little round fur balls. They *do* so dress their children here. And babies are swathed. . . .

January 27

Last night at the big Indian reception I talked with Pavlov, the little man who translates for all the big conferences—Tehran, Yalta, etc. He said he was entirely self-taught. Learned German first, then English and French. He thought Pushkin's stories were one of the best things for a foreigner learning Russian. He's just finished reading Stettinius' book. He didn't agree with S., of course, but said his report of Yalta was extremely accurate. "I ought to know," he added, "because I was there. . . ."

I've begun to hear a little gossip about the ouster of Georgi

* The leader of this Manchurian government was Kao Kang.

Popov as Moscow Party secretary. Khrushchev was brought in to fill his regional post. M. A. Yasnov was brought down from Leningrad to fill the city secretaryship.

The word I get is that Popov was fired because of nepotism and "careerism." His demotion is independent of the shifts connected with Zhdanov's death and the rise of Malenkov.

Moscow was said to be full of "Popov pets." What brought the situation to a head I do not know. Since November 7, however, when Malenkov devoted a good deal of attention to "criticism and self-criticism," there has been a campaign aimed at mismanagement and bureaucracy. One suggestion was that there was a connection between Popov's ouster and the poor showing made in opening up the new subway line. I am inclined to doubt this. The opening was announced for September 25. It finally did open January 1, 1950.

The effects of Popov's ouster are beginning to be felt. One of the first victims is the playwright Anatoly Sofronov, one of Popov's pets and, according to rumor, his cousin. He was particularly strong in his anti-Semitism. Always presented, inversely, in the form of "We Russians can handle this question."

Sofronov's play *Bekitov's Career* was greedily published and highly praised by the sycophants. Then No. 1 play critic, Mr. Stalin, read it and said it stank. So it was torn to ribbons. . . .

The situation is the talk of the Moscow intelligentsia. . . .

I don't know any inside information on the visit of Mao and Chou. No one here knows a damn thing about what is going on. We can guess, and my guess is that the Chinese are good bargainers. But I think any suggestion of real trouble between Mao and Stalin is just wishful thinking. They have too many interests in common at the moment to clash on basic principles. . . .

Meanwhile, the Soviet flirtation with India goes warmly ahead. Not content with Stalin's reception of the Indian ambassador (an event which I am sure made Madame Pandit gnash her teeth— she wasn't received and dearly wanted to be), the Russians went out of their way to honor India at the independence day reception yesterday. . . .

January 29, 1950

If there is a pleasanter way of spending a dullish Sunday morning in Moscow than watching the Moscow Drama Theater put on

Mark Twain's *The Prince and the Pauper* for young Moscow children and their parents, I have yet to find it. . . .

Dispatch to New York Times
January 31

The portrait of an American political boss, Thomas Brown of Kansas City, who rules by bribery, lynching, and corruption, has been added to the gallery of American scenes now being presented on the Moscow stage. The story is told in the play *Missouri Waltz*, by Nikolai Pogodin. . . .

Dispatch to New York Times
February 1

A series of denials was issued by Chinese sources of American reports concerning negotiations in Moscow between Mao Tsetung and Soviet leaders.

Background material issued by the State Department was termed "fiction" in a report by the Chinese Sinhua Agency. So-called Harbin and Moscow agreements allegedly entered into by the Russians and Chinese were called "an invention by the insane."

Among the reports specifically denied by the Chinese were the following:

That the Chinese Communists would be permitted to retreat to Soviet territory across northern Korea.

That the Soviet would allow the Chinese Communists to establish air bases in Siberia and northern Korea.

That the regions of Liaotung and Antung would be detached from Manchuria and garrisoned with Korean troops and later transferred to Korea.

That the Soviet will be permitted to station troops in Manchuria and Sinkiang.

That the Soviet will be permitted to name the commander-in-chief of the Chinese Communist army. . . .

February 3

Today is the day after ground-hog day. Yesterday was dull and grayish. Not a shadow for the G.H. And today is sunshiny and almost springlike. The idea of winter's end is exciting. I've had enough at this point.

I'm a little weary after surveying the wreckage of my January file at the hands of the censorship. Here is a list of dispatches killed outright:

January 3. *Izvestia's* demand for action by Gorki prosecutor in false-arrest case.

January 4. *Izvestia's* attack on legislators in the Grodno region.

January 5. Exposé of graft and corruption in the Moscow taxi service.

January 5. Exposé of corruption and red tape in the Moscow drugstore system.

January 7. Exposé of corruption and red tape in the Moscow housing exchange bureau.

January 8. General story on press campaign against graft, inefficiency, and red tape.

January 12. Story on the Dnprpetrovsk labor scandal.

January 13. Analysis of Soviet population on basis of electoral districts.

January 13. Dispatch on reinstitution of death penalty.

January 20. Speculative story on Sino-Russian negotiations.

January 22. Soviet restrictions on Father Brassard.

January 29. Another exposure of corruption in Moscow housing exchange bureau.

I omitted from my list another roundup on the Uzbek cotton situation. I have lost count how many stories I've done on cotton —all going into the censor's wastebasket.

I have sent the *Times* some corrections of identification in a photo they ran January 24. Pospelov is a former editor of *Pravda* and is now director of the Marx-Engels-Lenin Institute. Suslov is a secretary of the central committee. The correct name is N. S. Khrushchev. He is Party secretary for the Moscow region and not "mayor of Moscow" as the *Times* had him. The mayor of Moscow, newly appointed, is M. A. Yasnov.

Dispatch to New York Times
February 3, 1950

The Soviet government, in the opinion of some Moscow diplomats, is prepared today and, in fact, has been prepared for the last year to meet with the United States in a two-power effort to solve major problems. . . .

The Soviet Union strongly favors international control of

atomic weapons production and, in fact, abolition and prohibition of all atomic arms. It also favors an international inspection system and utilization of United Nations machinery for control.

The strongest Soviet objection against the American atomic plan has long been against those features which Moscow regarded as involving intervention by capitalist powers in the basic socialist economy. . . .

Against this background it can be seen that if the United States expects the Soviet to give serious consideration to American atomic proposals it must be prepared to give equally serious consideration to Soviet views on the subject. . . .

February 4

Naturally we are all interested in the China thing. But we don't know anything. Everybody in Paris, Washington, and Hong Kong seems to think he knows what they are talking about. But to be honest there isn't anyone here who has the faintest whisper of an idea.

February 5

I am relieved that Mike is again with his grandmother and aunt. I hope he has his skates. Minneapolis is a swell place for skating. Of course, so is this. They flood the parks, just as they do in Minnesota, and the kids are out every afternoon and evening. They have loud-speakers wired for music, and they skate to music and play hockey. You can walk along almost any back street of Moscow in the evening twilight and find the kids playing hockey. Jan writes that the temperature in Minneapolis has been 15° below. We had minus 37° just after New Year's. . . .

Dispatch to New York Times
February 7

Never in recent history has the head of a major foreign state paid a visit so prolonged as that of Mao Tse-tung to the Soviet Union.

Equally it may well be that never in recent history have two major states undertaken so searching an examination of the whole range of political, social, and economic problems which they share.

There has been intensive speculation in the world press. [This speculation has intensified as Mao's stay in Moscow, where he arrived December 16, has been prolonged. There has been a paucity of official information on the progress of discussions. . . .

While no date has been indicated for Mao's return to China there is general belief that his nearly two months' stay has given ample time to lay the groundwork for future relations. . . .

It seems reasonable to presume that Chou En-lai may remain to complete negotiation of specific agreements after Mao's departure. . . .]

Dispatch Killed by Censor
February 8, 1950

Mao Tse-tung's extended visit to Moscow has provided an opportunity for searching examination of the question of revision of the existing Sino-Russian treaty of friendship and alliance. . . .

In Mao's statement to the Tass News Agency he gave first priority to the question of the Sino-Russian treaty. In its present form it provides for an alliance against Japan, and the article is to remain in effect until the United Nations assumes responsibility for "prevention of further aggression on the part of Japan."

The 1945 treaty envisaged the alliance as basically temporary and directed primarily toward prosecution of the war which was then in progress.

It seems apparent that both the Chinese and Russian interests require revision of this clause to cover threats of aggression not only from Japan but from other sources. . . .

The revision probably will take the form of a generalized alliance, with mutual pledges against threats of aggression from any quarter. . . .

Examination of the collateral agreements signed by the Soviet and China in 1945 covering the status of the Changchun Railroad, Port Arthur, and Dairen, the territorial integrity of China's three northern provinces and Sinkiang, and the recognition of the independence of Outer Mongolia does not indicate necessity for current revision.

The terms of agreement on the railroad, Port Arthur, and Dairen are for thirty years. . . .

There is no doubt that the economic discussions concern the establishment of credits of billions of rubles to be expanded over a long-term period. . . .

February 9

Next week I think I will go down to Odessa for a few days. Permission for this trip which I requested at the end of summer has finally come through.

February 10

I've been dousing myself in Russian theater this week. Last night I saw *Boris Godunov* at the Bolshoi. A blaze of color and Old Russian tradition. Night before I saw *Ivan Grozny* at the Maly. Tonight I'm going to see Gogol's *Inspector-General*.

Dispatch Killed by Censor
February 12

A new picture of Generalissimo Stalin in which he is shown happily cultivating fruit trees in the peaceful country just before the outbreak of war in June, 1941, is presented in the film, *The Fall of Berlin*.

The sound-track carries a gay song of skylarks. The camera swings down to focus on Stalin. Wearing a white summer tunic, he is busy with a hoe, cultivating twenty young fruit trees, just set out.

The scene is Stalin's country dacha. He has invited an outstanding young steel worker, Alexei Ivanov, to lunch.

Ivanov, bashful, says: "How do you do, Comrade Josef Ivanovich." Stalin, eyes twinkling, gravely corrects Ivanov. "My name is Josef Vissarionovich," he said. "That was my father's name."

Dispatch to New York Times
February 15

Signature of a thirty-year Russo-Chinese alliance of friendship and mutual assistance, provision of a $300,000,000 credit, and agreement for return of the Changchun Railroad to China was announced early today.

The new alliance replaced that of 1945 and includes broader security provisions. Under the new agreement both parties pledge mutual aid in event of aggression not only by Japan but also in event of aggression by "any other state, directly or indirectly associated" with Japan. . . .

Russo-Chinese consultation is provided in all cases of important international questions affecting their interest. . . .

Dispatch to New York Times
February 15, 1950

A strong new effort by the Soviet Union and China for early conclusion of the Japanese peace treaty was indicated today. . . .

The Soviet is presently declining to participate in the work of the United Nations and its affiliates and in the work of the Far Eastern Commission because of the refusal of these groups to unseat the Kuomintang representatives. . . .

February 17

I hope that I'll be back in New York City by April 1. James has been very nice. He has written me, withdrawing his previous objections and telling me, in effect, to submit a new schedule for coming back. This is the anniversary of my last evening in New York. It all seems a little blurred.

IX

A "Peace" Balloon

*Excerpts from Dispatches to New York Times**

The important scholarly journal *Soviet State and Law* has called attention to the "exceptional interest" which attaches to Stalin's statement that "peaceful settlement of disagreements between the U.S.S.R. and the U.S.A. not only is possible but is also absolutely essential in the interest of general peace."

Particular interest was directed to this expression because of a series of suggestions from the United States that the time is approaching for another effort to seek resolution of international conflicts. . . .

It is not to be deduced from the silence of the Soviet press that the government is not actively studying both the atomic question and the issue of new diplomatic discussions with the United States. . . .

With, as *Pravda* said, international relations entering a new stage as a result of the Sino-Russian alliance, the press has displayed an interest in the rapidly evolving "American question."

There seemed grounds for belief that the Soviet would welcome a new effort at resolving Soviet-American differences. But whether this would be evidenced in concrete manner was another matter. . . .

*Filed February 13, 14, 16, 17, cleared by the censor just before midnight, February 17, 1950.

Dispatch to New York Times
February 18, 1950

In the rapidly widening discussion of atomic controls and Soviet-American problems a careful examination of the background against which Moscow assesses these developments may be useful.

Five factors seem important:

First, the Soviet continues to adhere strongly to its conviction that American foreign and military policy is aggressively directed against her and, if followed to a logical conclusion, will lead to war.

Second, the Soviet has given no indication that its position on atomic controls and disarmament has changed.

Third, there have been no private exchanges recently between American and Soviet diplomats. Nor has there been any informal "feeler."

Fourth, the Soviet regards its strategic and diplomatic position as stronger than at any time since the Bolshevik Revolution and feels this strength is on the threshold of further epochal development.

Fifth, the Soviet would welcome an opportunity for a careful and serious examination of Soviet-American problems. . . .

[Despite all the talk by American statesmen and the press about relations with the Soviet nothing tangible has occurred. For that matter not a word of the whole discussion has yet been printed by the Soviet press. . . .]

February 20

Suddenly, they are allowing me almost complete freedom to write and speculate on the subject of the atom bomb and Soviet-American relations. This development stems from my dispatch of February 3, stating that the Soviet is prepared to meet in a two-power effort to resolve atomic and other differences. That dispatch was held for about thirty hours and then passed without the deletion of a single word.

It is obvious that the dispatch had been referred to the Kremlin. It became, in essence, a trial balloon by the Russians. And so was interpreted by various *Times* writers and the State Department.

A whole series of dispatches written since February 3 has been passed by the censorship with only minuscule cuts. In each instance the dispatch has been held for a minimum of twenty-four hours and a maximum of seventy-two hours—showing that it has been referred to very high authority.

Most surprising to me has been the passing of accurate statements about the failure of the Soviet press to publish a single line of current developments on this situation; speculation as to the cause of non-publication; speculation as to the attitude of the Kremlin.

In truth, none of this is sensational material. But such material has never in recent times passed the censors. More interesting is the fact that there has been no particular relaxation of censorship for other correspondents. A number of speculative dispatches written by AP, for instance, have been killed. . . .

One possibility is that the Russians may not have made up their minds what line to follow. In any event the situation is worth watching closely. . . .

February 20
Letter to Edwin L. James, New York Times

Thank you very much for the understanding and consideration expressed in your letter of February 6. I want you to know that I shall welcome the opportunity of serving in this post for another year or even two, provided only that it proves possible to get out occasionally for much needed fresh air.

February 21

We had a big snowstorm over the weekend. The biggest of the winter. The town is covered with a new blanket of snow. Last night I went out for a long, long walk. It was cold—cold wind and the temperature about 10° or 15° above. I enjoy winter. But by this time the prospect of another six or even eight weeks before a break in the season seems grim. You can't really figure spring hitting Moscow before mid-April. . . .

There is much speculation here, as I gather there is in the States, as to whether the time may be at hand when the U.S.A. and the Soviet will make another periodic effort to come to an agreement about something.

One of the most interesting things I've done lately is to read Wallace's *Russia*.* It is fascinating to see how many tendencies which are in the forefront of Russian philosophy and politics today had their precise counterpart in the mid-nineteenth century. I only wish I had Wallace's opportunity of traveling about the country. I have to get my Russia secondhand. And, surprisingly, it is from such things as Wallace's book that real light is let in on some current subjects, such as the drive against cosmopolitanism last year. . . .

I propose to write during the next few days several dispatches dealing with atomic control, security, the general climate of suspicion in this country, etc. Each dispatch will deal with some subject on which the Russians are touchy. It will be most revealing to see how they handle such copy. My own suspicion is that the controls will be clamped on, but quick.

I noted with interest *Pravda*'s criticism of Andreyev.† I don't know any gossip on that. But as I envisage the Politburo situation there are certain natural internal stresses resulting from the rise of Malenkov and the liquidation of Zhdanov's influence.

I would presume that before Zhdanov's death his influence was second to Stalin's and that the majority of the members supported him because he was Stalin's fair-haired boy. With Zhdanov's death and (we presume) Stalin's selection of Malenkov, some Politburo members probably had difficulty in making the transition.

It is fair to assume, I think, that they had committed themselves against Malenkov.

I should suppose that now two processes are going on. First, Malenkov is seeking to consolidate his strength. Second, there is probably a quiet effort by some Politburo members to create a counterbalance to Malenkov.

I think it is within some such framework that we should assess the transfer of Khrushchev from the Ukraine to the seat of power

* D. Mackenzie Wallace was correspondent of the *London Times* in Moscow from March, 1870, to December, 1875.

† On February 19, 1950, Andreyev was criticized for use of the team rather than the brigade system in collective farms. Subsequently he was released as chairman of the government council on collective farms and dropped into the background.

in Moscow (and the ouster of Popov and breakup of his personal machine) and, now, the quiet, restrained but deadly criticism of Andreyev.

Anyone's guess is good as to how the two moves fit in. But I think it not impossible that Khrushchev's move into Moscow was designed to strengthen the anti-Malenkov forces who probably represent an "old guard" faction.

In this hypothesis, the criticism of Andreyev could be viewed as a sharp left jab by the Malenkov faction. It seems apparent that Andreyev is not going to be completely disgraced. But I shouldn't be surprised to see him lifted out of his job as chairman of collectives.

We may know more about that shortly. I think it is incumbent upon him to make public acknowledgment of *Pravda*'s criticism and to confess his sins. If that doesn't follow quickly I look for further developments and, possibly, his being dropped from the Politburo.

One thing has been proved by the current election campaign. Molotov is definitely No. 2. Every single election nomination lists Molotov first after Stalin. Then, Malenkov. The rest of the listing is Beriya, Voroshilov, Kaganovich, Mikoyan, Andreyev, Khrushchev, Bulganin, Kosygin, and Shvernik.

That supports the theory that if Stalin dies Molotov will become premier and front man, with Georgi holding the reins and the gray figure of Beriya looming strongly in the background.*

It is interesting that in the *Stalingrad Battle* movie released last spring Malenkov gets very special attention while Molotov is a background figure. In the new movie *The Fall of Berlin* it is Molotov who is at the leader's side and Malenkov has a secondary role.

Could it be that we have the emergence of two Politburo groupings, one centering around Molotov, the other around Malenkov? Or are they just the Gold Dust Twins of the Stalin epoch?

I can add nothing very thrilling to what has been published about the Russo-Chinese negotiations. The outstanding aspects

---

* On Stalin's death Malenkov became premier, Molotov foreign minister, and Beriya minister of the interior. These three were the main figures at Stalin's funeral.

to me were the extreme chinchiness of the financial assistance (so typical of the Russians); the multiple possibilities for difficulty and deadlock in the very vague provisions for the restoration of the stuff the Russians grabbed in Manchuria; the obvious inability of both sides to agree at this time on what to do about Dairen; and the general one-sidedness of the agreement, loaded with concessions to the Chinese but not revealing the *quid pro quo.*

I have no way of knowing whether there are secret protocols putting Russians in charge of the Chinese army or turning over Manchurian ports and things like that. I would certainly be extremely doubtful of anyone who claimed he had found out provisions like that in Moscow.

Security on the negotiations was as airtight as could be imagined. The satellite economic groups are still here. The Chinese left negotiators behind, presumably to clean up talks with the satellites. Among those left behind was the Sinkiang representative as well as members of the Northeast China administration.

There are conflicting theories about Mao. My own impression is that agreeable and eager as he may be to see eye to eye with Moscow so far as foreign affairs are concerned and, probably, so far as revolutionary prospects in Asia go, he is not to be considered as a puppet or mere Russian agent.

I don't think any potentate could have had more plush treatment than Mao was offered in the two months he spent here. I am sure that Mao is extremely friendly with Moscow. But I also think he conducts himself as the head of a state, albeit a Communist one.

Rumors continue of impending price reductions. Last week for several days the main stores were empty because housewives were sure that "in a few days" there would be price reductions. Now they talk about the first week in March. . . .

The food distribution system, incidentally, continues as archaic as ever. This week no eggs are to be had in Moscow. The reason is that last week was *maselnitza,* the pre-Lent blini feast. All the eggs in town were bought up for blini. Collective farmers have been celebrating the holiday too and have fewer eggs to bring to market.

118

Nothing new about Yugoslavia. I think the Russians are bound to pick at it, the way a kid does with a festering sore.

Dispatch to New York Times. Filed February 20, Cleared by Censor February 22, 1950

Interest turned today to the practical question of whether either the American or Soviet atomic proposals contain the essence of a compromise which might be acceptable. . . .

[Despite the definiteness with which both sides have stated their positions, it is equally plain that any real effort at control would require concessions from both parties. . . .]

The principle deadlock exists over the question of international ownership of atomic facilities. The United States insists on this point. The Soviet rejects it on grounds it would give capitalists a voice in Soviet economy. [The fact that it would give Communists a voice in American capitalist economy has not attracted much attention. . . .]

Dispatch to New York Times February 24

Many Soviet newspapers today published reports of what they described as a growing movement for revision of American foreign policy.

[This is the first time news has been brought to Soviet readers on a topic of greatest interest to all of them—the question of whether a possibility exists for effecting an improvement in world chances for peace and of removing some of the conflicts in Soviet-American relations. . . .]

February 24

A year ago I was six days at sea. All around was gray water and gray clouds. Ahead of me lay a great unknown—new tasks, new problems, new life. I felt rather lost. I could not look forward and see things with any clarity. And looking back brought only an ache in my heart.

Now, the year is almost over. I have been sitting and thinking here in my smoke-filled office. It is 11:00 at night, and I've decided I'm very tired of Moscow. . . .

Dispatch to New York Times
February 25, 1950

The Soviet press drew attention today to the fact that a movement is under way in the United States toward a new approach to the question of a Soviet-American agreement. . . .

[One veteran Moscow diplomat summed up the present situation regarding U.S.-U.S.S.R. relations with the following anecdote:

"The United States and Russia are like two small boys standing on the bank of a stream on the first warm sunny day of spring. They both want to get into the water and both know that it's still really too cold to swim. It is just a question of time before one jumps in and the other follows immediately.

"Both of them know that. But for the moment they are still standing on the banks of the stream—hoping the other will plunge in first."]

Dispatch Killed by Censor
February 25

A glimpse of the future in which Soviet atomic-powered interplanetary space ships will penetrate into the unknown corners of the universe was provided by a Soviet popular science writer in the magazine *Pioneer* today. The article said there were still many problems which must be solved before atomic energy can be harnessed for such peacetime uses. . . .

February 25

At a conference with Simonov of the Foreign Office press department yesterday I made a formal request for a re-entry visa. Simonov explained the rule is not a Foreign Office rule but a regulation of OVIR, the visa-issuing department of the MVD. He volunteered the information that he felt there would be no question of any difficulty in my case.

February 27

I am taking off this afternoon for Odessa. I don't look forward to this jaunt at all. All that is good about it is that it will take up a week of time. . . .

March 8

I can't say that my trip to Odessa was particularly fun. It takes two days to get there on the train. Trains run slow here. Hardly ever more than twenty-five to thirty miles an hour. This train had no dining car—in fact most don't. They don't have observation or club cars either. And no strato-domes like those on the train from Chicago to Minneapolis. They have three kinds of cars—hard cars, soft cars, and international cars. The hard cars have shelves on which the passengers sleep. They bring their own bedding. The soft cars have berths. The international cars are the best—very much like our fine compartment cars.

The nicest thing about Russian trains is that they have a samovar going most of the time, day or night. You can have a glass of hot tea whenever you want. I take along a supply of Nescafé and get hot water from the *provodnik* (porter) and brew myself coffee.

Odessa, on the Black Sea, is much warmer than Moscow. It is just on the verge of spring down there. The snow is gone and winter wheat is green, but it will be another two or three weeks before it is really warm. The wind off the Black Sea was rather raw and damp, and the sun didn't shine much.

It was about the first of April when I was last in Odessa. Just after the Germans were chased out. The weather was balmy and warm.

Probably the most interesting thing about Odessa are the catacombs. The city is built on limestone, and these caves were started by quarrying stone for the buildings. In the old days they were used by smugglers and gangsters and hoodlums. During the war they were used by Russian partisans. They had printing presses and schools and hospitals and little factories where they made bullets and bombs—and even a drill ground in a big cave. Now, of course, they are all shut up. . . .

Dispatch to New York Times
Odessa, March 9

Standing on the Potemkin staircase overlooking Odessa's busy harbor, it is hard to realize that just six years ago this port was a smoking, twisted jungle of broken steel.

I saw Odessa in April, 1944, a scant seventy-two hours after the Soviet army re-entered the city. Revisiting the port provides new evidence of the extent to which the Soviet has made good the vast war damage. . . .

Here and there in the city's center bombed-out buildings still stand, and there are occasional rubbleyards. . . .

Dispatch to New York Times
Kiev, March 9, 1950

From the Black Sea northward through the rich *chernozem* the Ukraine fields are green today with sprouting winter wheat.

Spring has come early to the fertile Ukraine breadbasket. Snow has vanished, and there are great vistas of rich black soil, fresh turned by tractor-drawn gangplows. . . .

The last time I saw the Ukraine was in 1944. [Then hand plows were being dragged through the fields by women and children because the cattle had been killed by the Germans and tractors were not to be had. . . .]

March 12

Under the new ruble rates our telegraphic deposits are being credited as of March 1 at the rate of 4 to the dollar, instead of 5.3 as previously. The press rate is 30 kopecks a word, which now works out at 7.5 cents per word, instead of 5.66—an increase of about 33 per cent. My general expenses are now being financed at the new 6 to the dollar diplomatic rate. The offset in reduced local prices is negligible since there has been no cut in costs of office rent, telephone, books, newspapers, magazines, gasoline, paper, postage, and supplies.

As of July 1, when the diplomatic rate is eliminated and all rubles must be provided at the 4 to the dollar rate, our general expenses will rise precisely 100 per cent over their cost at the 8 to the dollar rate. . . .

Dispatch to New York Times
March 15

How do the leaders of the Soviet estimate the present world situation?

A detailed answer to this question is provided by the election addresses delivered by eleven members of the Politburo. The most detailed review was presented by Molotov.

Each Politburo member stated in the strongest terms the Soviet's' dedication to the cause of peace and each asserted that, should war come, its result, as Beriya phrased it, would be that "its inspirers and organizers will perish in it."

Molotov warned that "so long as imperialism exists there exists also the danger of fresh aggression. Given the existence of imperialism, wars are inevitable."*

But other Politburo members expressed confidence that the forces of peace would prove powerful enough to prevent war. . . .

March 20

There has been little change in the general situation in the last week or two. I would say things are still dominated by the question of whether any move is to be made to explore the possibility of some improvement in the situation between the U.S. and Russia. The Russians have made plain that they would welcome the move.

They have again demonstrated their political ineptitude with regard to the United States. For instance, the young firebrand, Surov, author of the masterwork *The Mad Haberdasher,* was allowed to spew gutter language all over Acheson's Berkeley speech† before anyone else had a chance to comment on it. An asinine performance.

I think the Russians would like a Japanese peace treaty for obvious reasons. Japan represents one of the "situations of strength" of which Acheson speaks. For the same reason I think they would be quite satisfied not to negotiate about Germany. They do not think our position there is so strong.

So far as the atomic problem is concerned I think they would like an agreement a good deal more than they have indicated. . . . I think the cost of an atomic arms race is a considerable factor in Russian desire for a control plan.

However you add up Russia's objectives, it is apparent to a

* The Molotov thesis was being strongly echoed by the Chinese Communists in 1959 and 1960.

† Speaking at Berkeley, California, March 17, 1950, Acheson proposed a seven-point program for coexistence of East and West.

child of six that she could obtain them much more easily if "normal, peacetime" conditions rather than cold war prevailed.

I have not been able to uncover any signs that the hydrogen bomb talk has affected Russian public opinion. This is probably due, in part, to the effective blacking out of the Voice of America and the BBC.

It was a surprise and a disappointment to the general public that Stalin did not speak on the night before election. Why he did not talk is a mystery. In the week leading up to that Saturday night the censorship had passed stories saying flatly that he would talk Saturday night. The speeches of the other Politburo members were arranged in build-up fashion—Voroshilov, Malenkov, and Molotov on Wednesday, Thursday, and Friday. Then came the blank Saturday night, although the radio schedule contained a place where the speech was expected to fit in.

Monday's papers all carried huge page-one pictures of Stalin voting, obviously to scotch rumors he was ill. I wrote a story saying he didn't appear to be ill and suggesting that he hadn't spoken because of the delicate state of relations between the U.S.A. and U.S.S.R. I tried to get over the idea he didn't want to lay down any gospel until he was more certain he knew which way the cat would jump. The yarn was passed without deletions.

One of the interesting things about the election speeches was that it was again Malenkov who threw out the peace feeler while Molotov took the harder line. And Malenkov again emphasized the criticism and self-criticism line which fits so well with his cleansing of the Party organization.

To return to the question of why Stalin did not speak. This is his second recent break with tradition so far as public utterances go. He did not reply on his birthday to the greetings of the nation as he did on his sixtieth and fiftieth birthdays. And now he has not spoken in the election as he did in '46 and '37.

One suggestion has been made that he has now been elevated to such a cloudlike position that only his disciples will carry forth The Word. I doubt that myself. He may have had the grippe, although he looked spry enough in the pictures—if they were taken on election day. His general health seems good enough. He has made three appearances this winter and was described each time as looking very well.

Here is an interesting item about the election: The returns revealed the existence of seven special military voting districts, compared with twenty-six in the 1946 elections. These are created for military forces serving outside the Soviet. In the 1946 election it was possible to establish that about 2,800,000 votes were cast in the special military districts. If the districts are of comparable size, then the present Soviet occupation forces would be between 700,000 and 800,000.

Neither Litvinov nor Maisky was a candidate for the Supreme Soviet. I thought Vasily Stalin might show up as a candidate. But he didn't. I have heard reports that there has been a shake-up in the Soviet air force. I would not expect it to affect Vasily—but it may have.

An interesting agricultural development, and one which the censorship has been very touchy on, is a drive announced by Khrushchev in his Moscow election speech, for the enlargement and consolidation of kolkhozes in the Moscow area. This drive is now under way. It ties in directly with the campaign in favor of the brigade rather than the team, a campaign which was kicked off through the criticism of Andreyev.

Both of these have a common purpose: to make agriculture more nearly a large-scale enterprise, to put it on a mass-machine basis.

These are, I venture to say, the opening moves in what will probably be a long and gradual drive over a period of years to move away from the basic kolkhoz system and on to an industrial system of agriculture.

I think they will go easy on this. After all there is a hell of a lot of private initiative and enterprise built into the kolkhoz system. So far the censorship has killed any stories trying to point up the long-term trends involved in agriculture. . . .

Another program with which they are going to move forward is housing. I judge this because Khrushchev devoted a good deal of attention to it in his speech, as did Molotov. God knows they need it.

I hear that in Soviet playwriting circles there is talk that the anti-American espionage and skulduggery theme has been run into the ground. I hope that may be true.

The new ruble exchange rate proves quite a blow to the Moscow diplomatic colony. There is talk about cutting staffs, and some of the smaller countries will fold up operations after July. The blow hits satellite countries just like the others.

The satellite diplomats are harder to see and talk to than the Russians themselves. They are scared to talk to Western newspapermen. In many ways they are even more deeply distrusted than our people.

An example: A few weeks ago a satellite delegation came to Moscow. Before the group visited a Soviet plant the Russian workers were called in by their chief. He told them to wear their best clothes. The girls were to have their hair done and use good make-up. New curtains were put up in the workshops and potted plants were brought in. The best-looking workers were put into one room as a special show unit. The workers were warned not to get into private conversation with the satellite people; on no account to give any technical information; and to do all talking through the interpreters. One girl forgot her instructions and got into a conversation in French with visitors. There was hell to pay over this, and she drew a severe reprimand.

The old Potemkin technique undiluted. . . .

X

Spring and a Breather

March 24, 1950

I have delayed my departure for a month or two. I expect to be back in the United States in late May.

Spring is coming on fast. It is warm, and most of the snow in the city has gone. Out in the country the fields are still covered.

March 27

I guess they have had their first pussy willows and cowslips and crocuses and maybe even violets in Minnesota. I was driving outside Moscow a couple of days ago. The trees are beginning to look green in the distance, and soon the snowdrops will show up in the woods. One of the things I love about Moscow is that the woods are at the doorstep. As soon as you get out of the city limits they begin. Not like New York.

Last night I went to the Moscow circus. It is a permanent thing, shows twice a day, four times a day on Sundays and holidays. The best act was the last. A woman lion-tamer—a handsome woman with coal-black hair and a costume of black gloves, black boots, black shirt, black riding breeches. She worked with four lions in a cage. They let her put her head in their mouths, and she pulled one around by his tail. She made them all lie together and threw herself full length on them and lounged there.

Two firemen with high pressure fire hoses stood ready to turn the nozzle if the lions acted up.

Dispatch to New York Times
March 30, 1950

The journal *New Times* today characterized Mao Tse-tung's victory in China as "essentially an agrarian revolution."

It has the basis and the contents of a bourgeois democratic revolution, the journal said. It based itself on Stalin's theories of the Chinese situation evolved in 1926 and 1927.

The journal [sharply] differentiated between the present revolution in China and the Soviet Revolution of 1917. It suggested that the present Chinese revolution more properly was to be compared with that [which the Russian revolutionaries unsuccessfully attempted to bring about] in 1905. . . .

Dispatch to New York Times
April 2

The magazine *Ogonek* has published five poems by Anna Akhmatova, the veteran Soviet poetess. The poems are from a cycle which Akhmatova calls "Glory to Peace." One is dedicated to Stalin's birthday.

[The verses are the first Akhmatova has had published in the Soviet since] 1946 when her work, together with that of some other Leningrad writers, was severely criticized by the Communist Party central committee and by the late Andrei Zhdanov at a writers' meeting in Leningrad.

Her poem on Stalin declares, "Where is Stalin there is freedom, peace, and greatness of the earth. . . ."

[In the *Ogonek* poems her verse is not "empty and apolitical." Nor is it "art for art's sake." It does not reflect "gloomy tones of hopelessness." Nor is it marked by "mystical emotion mixed half and half with eroticism." These were the criticisms directed at her by Zhdanov and the central committee.]*

April 3

The tag end of a dull, quiet April Monday. I have been doing literally nothing. I have had a long talk with two of my colleagues, and I have looked out my window at the spring sun-

---

* These are excerpts from Zhdanov's address to the Union of Soviet Writers, August 21, 1946.

128

shine and the park beginning to turn green. Natalie Rene just dropped in. We had a gossip about Moscow literary life. Somewhat remote from the vital issues of the day.

April 5

How can I put a dream down on paper?

I can't, that's plain.

The only thing to do is to come to Moscow, come to the Bolshoi and see Ulanova in *Giselle*.

It is incredible, fantastic, perfection perfected, the most delicate dream come true, a butterfly brushing your eyelashes, a dress of sheerest cobweb and diamonds, a poem so beautiful it makes your heart ache, a song murmured in your ears.

It is the most thrilling and beautiful thing I have ever seen.

Don't expect this to make sense. I'm still at the Bolshoi watching toes twinkling like stars and bodies fluttering like hummingbird's wings.

But it is silly to try to write about it.

Foolish people talk about the seven wonders of the world. This *is* the wonder of the world. . . .

April 6

There's a thin Aprilish sun oozing through the clouds today. They are gray purplish clouds, full of April showers. What a shower we had yesterday! I was driving in the country. It came down so hard you could hardly see the highway. Only a few patches of snow left in odd corners and along the snow fences. The country is a sea of mud. The woods where we picked mushrooms last summer and fall are soggy as a sponge. But the birches look greenish, and there are bushes turning red, and soon there will be a few leaves here and there. I am sure there are snowdrops blossoming back in the woods, but it is too soggy to hunt for them.

I have effected some radical economies in an effort to balance the increased costs of the new ruble rate. I have held down filing secondary copy, and I have reduced salaries, discharging my second secretary and courier and cutting the pay of my secretary and chauffeur.

April 6, 1950
Letter to Maxim Litvinov, Ministry of Foreign Affairs

As you are aware, April 12 will be the fifth anniversary of the tragic death of President Roosevelt.

I wonder whether you would care to prepare a brief memoir of Mr. Roosevelt for publication in the *New York Times* on the anniversary, based, perhaps, upon your knowledge of Mr. Roosevelt and acquaintance formed during the important Soviet-American negotiations which you conducted with him.

April 10

Easter is a great thing here. It has never meant much to me. I suppose I am rooted too strongly in heterodox Protestantism. But here, of course, it is the church festival of the year. It may be hard for some to feel that there can be a deep and almost universal holiday of the faith and the spirit and the creed in a country which we are so used to reading about as godless Russia.

And, I suppose, many think of the church here in terms of people stealthily creeping to small hidden doorways, furtively ducking into tiny, almost deserted chapels. Or of police agents remorselessly tracking down the believers.

What a difference between the legend and the reality!

Last year I didn't get much of the Easter feeling. This year was different. Our Nina baked us a *kulich* and made a *paskha*. So we had them in 393, decorated with pink paper flowers and sprays of evergreen and asparagus grass. And she made us colored eggs—the brown kind that you make using onion skin for dye, with the K.V. marked on them for *Kristos Voskres.*

I went to the commission shops and found some old Russian Easter eggs, the kind that everyone used to make presents of at Easter time. They are bright and colorful—porcelain ones from the imperial porcelain works at Peterhof.

The weather was and still is gorgeous. Saturday evening a bunch of us drove to Zagorsk—riding along in the early twilight with the sky sparkling like a diamond mine. Along the road, throngs and throngs and throngs of people, thousands of them, taking to the churches their *kulichi* and *paskhi* in white cloth bags—taking them for the priests to bless. And in every little village the knot of people and the queue at the church waiting for the blessing. The miles people walked! We would see a little church, its yard filled with people, and then drive for fifteen or twenty minutes and even that far away people would be walking to the church with their cakes.

Godless Russia!

At Zagorsk . . . everybody in town was at the monastery, and there were thousands from the countryside. I haven't seen such crowds since I used to go to the Minnesota State Fair on Labor Day. And some of the same spirit.

Riding back from Zagorsk through the quiet night with the stars brighter than I can ever remember them, even brighter than the desert, I felt close to the Russian countryside. All the way there were the villages with the churches and the crowds, still worshiping and, perhaps, just standing in the courtyards. And in the little houses on the highway the lights burning although it was close to three in the morning—the people home from church breaking their fast with the traditional feast.

April 11

I think that the place to keep an eye on these days is Washington rather than Moscow. I say that because I am a little skeptical that the belated steps being taken to restore the shaken political basis of our foreign policy will succeed in giving us real freedom to handle the problems we have.

It seems to me that the position has been so weakened that any decision is wide open to political attack on personal grounds. I think this is extraordinarily unfair and unfortunate, but as Stalin once said, facts are stubborn things.

I realize very well that McCarthy has been spouting a lot of nonsense. But he would not have gotten so far and done so much damage if a great deal of damage had not already been done.

This would not be so serious if the situation did not require that we take certain steps.

What I am thinking about is this: Acheson will be meeting in May with the foreign ministers. They are going to have to decide some things, chiefly Germany. They probably will decide on another meeting of the CFM. And they should decide something about the Far East.

But, unless I miss my guess, every decision is going to be smeared politically in Washington despite Dulles, Cooper, et al.

That means, in effect, that at this critical stage of affairs our policy is close to one of paralysis.

The German situation and the arms situation are the only specific troublemakers which I see on the horizon. Of course the Kremlin may get active again against Yugoslavia.

To turn to the Far East. The more I look at the China situation, the more certain I am that we are our own worst friends.

I think that we could provide more genuine concern and embarrassment for the Kremlin by recognizing Mao and treating him in friendly fashion than by any other single act.

Tito's history seems to me to demonstrate that all we have to do to send the Kremlin into a tailspin is to treat Mao in friendly fashion and, if possible, prevail upon him to accept some gifts from us. It doesn't make any difference what. It doesn't make any difference how. Just give him something. As much as he can be persuaded to take. With no strings.

Once he has taken something from us, no amount of argument would ever convince the Kremlin that it was a freewill gift. The little worm of suspicion would be planted. Once that worm starts working in the Kremlin it never stops.

I might add that the same game can and should be worked in all of the satellite countries. To put it crudely: Kill them with kindness. The Kremlin can't stand for its friends to be on speaking terms with anyone else.

Give me a free hand, and I could cause more midnight oil to burn in the Kremlin in one day than they employ in a month now. All it would take would be some sweet words and a little ingenuity. . . .

Well, I'm not Acheson, thank goodness. I realize that the last thing in the world he is capable of doing in his present state of weakness is to recognize China—much as he would doubtless like to.

One more thing about Acheson. I think it was evident from the frantic reaction in the local press that they realize that if the Asiatic policy which he laid down in California is implemented it would constitute a far more effective barrier to the spread of communism than anything yet.

They know that as long as our Asiatic policy consists in sending gunboats to Saigon and letting Chiang use our bombers we are making more friends and allies for them every day than they could possibly make with a million agitators.

But they know that if we follow Acheson, recognize the national aspirations of the Asiatic peoples, throw our weight against colonialism, and support moderate governments like Nehru's and Indonesia's they will be stopped in their tracks.

They understand this because it fits their Marxian concept of the nature of the struggle of the colonial peoples. This was strikingly illuminated in the *New Times* the other day when they proclaimed the Mao revolution "national bourgeois." They have gone back to Marxist as opposed to the Leninist theory of the development of revolutions in Asia.

They do not think—and it was supported in a similar study a few days later in *Questions of Economy*—that Asia can leap in one jump from colonialism to socialism.

This means the revolutions which they hope to see in Indochina, Malaya, Burma, will be bourgeois revolutions. They hope, as in China, to give these bourgeois revolutions Communist leadership.*

I heard a lovely story the other day. The wife of a general was complaining about her sixteen-year-old daughter. Said she didn't know what she was going to do with the girl. The youngster gets fine marks in school—all fives. So do her friends. They come home from school together, finish their studies in an hour, and disappear. They have half a dozen American records, and they spend every evening doing the boogiewoogie and other American dances. The girl says: "Why, mother, you know all the smart youngsters in Moscow are doing this."

Apparently the jitterbug craze got its impetus from Red Army kids coming back from Germany.

There is plenty of crime in Moscow—and plenty of interest in it—regardless of the little you see in the papers.

A youngster of seventeen and some friends were celebrating a holiday—last November 7, I think. They had a lot of vodka to drink. They got tight and went to visit a friend. On their way upstairs a man came out in the hall and told them to be quiet

---

* This same line on Asia and colonial revolutions was being iterated by Moscow in 1960.

The seventeen-year-old whipped out a Finnish knife and stabbed the man to death.

He was held for trial and the lawyer made a point of the fact that he had never had a drink before, was a good boy, good student, etc. He pleaded for a two- or three-year sentence. But the boy got eight years in camp.

The police have a drive on against rowdyism or hooliganism. However, you can hardly walk any distance in central Moscow after 11:00 at night without encountering a drunk or two.

Dispatch Killed by Censor
April 12, 1950

Because of the strain and tension already existing between the United States and the Soviet Union the disappearance of an American plane off the Baltic coast is viewed in a most serious light.

The plane vanished after an exchange of gunfire with Soviet fighters. . . .

April 12

Rumors we have in Moscow by the bushel. But hard news is hard to come by.

At this point an inside story on the missing B-24 would be good. Naturally, I have a theory of what happened. It would be my bet that the plane was shot down by the local lads, although it might just have been so badly disabled it fell into the drink. What it was doing flying around the Latvian coast is another question.

I got a letter from Maxim Litvinov today. I sent him a note April 6 suggesting he might like to write us a little memoir on President Roosevelt. Under date of April 19 he replied: "My dear Mr. Salisbury—I have received your letter of April 6, transmitted to me by the Ministry of Foreign Affairs, in which you suggest that I write a memoir of the late President Roosevelt. I regret being prevented by indisposition from complying with this request which otherwise I should be glad to do."

It is signed with his usual bold signature. The letter is typewritten neatly in English on a sheet of paper torn from a perforated pad. Could be that Ivy* typed it for him.

* Ivy Low, Litvinov's English-born wife.

It is the first written reply I've had from a Russian to any letter I've written since coming to Moscow. It is good to know that Maxim is still around. Maisky is still working in the Foreign Office. He is editing a diplomatic dictionary. . . .

I have never gotten around to putting down some of my impressions of Odessa. For one thing they do not jibe well with those of some visitors last summer. They reported the Jews in Odessa were terrified of speaking with foreigners; that many were being removed; etc.

Nowhere since I have been in the Soviet Union have I encountered so many people, eager and willing—almost embarrassingly so—to enter into conversations. I heard more English in Odessa than in all the time I've been in Russia. All voluntary and spontaneous. Every day someone came up and started a conversation. A number of these were Jews.

I must say Odessa impressed me as it did in 1944 as a friendly, rather Westernized place with a minimum of emphasis on ideology and a maximum on living a warmer and more comfortable life.

Here is the sort of thing I ran into: I found it almost impossible to get a copy of the newspaper there—either the Odessa papers or the Moscow papers. They were not to be had. Nor did I see people reading them. Finally I located a handful of papers in the Central Post Office—*Pravda, Red Fleet, Merchant Fleet,* and the local Odessa job. The Odessa paper has a tirage of only 23,000! In a city of about 700,000.

One thing shocked me—the poor quality and quantity of consumer goods. The stores are small and inadequate for so large a town. I noticed in a local paper that they had only 79 per cent the number of stores they had before the war.

Food was plentiful and good. Except they had queues every day for white bread. Plenty of dark bread. But folks said white bread was always on short supply. The Odessa market was fabulous. All kinds of food. Oranges at ten rubles each, flown in from Sochi and sold by speculators. Other food prices about 60 per cent of the Moscow price.

Restaurants were lousy. Though there were stacks of fresh fish in from the Black Sea in the market—not a fish to be had in the restaurants.

Easter was impressive. It is astonishing what a comeback the Orthodox Church has made. My impression is confirmed by a report I picked up on a talk given the week before Easter by a member of the Society for the Propagation of Scientific and Political Knowledge. This man was telling of the need for more work to spread scientific ideas. He told of a sermon preached by a priest just before the election in which the priest said that never before had the church been so pure and so godly; that now it was not in politics at all; it tended only to God's business; that this was thanks to the wise Stalinist government; and that it was the duty of all believers to go out and vote 100 per cent for the wise government!

The speaker said not a week went by but that Comrade Stalin received letters from villages asking permission to reopen the old church or to build a new one. And, of course, he said Comrade Stalin always grants these requests. These letters were accompanied by statements that the peasants would pay the expenses of refurbishing the churches. The church is collecting remarkable sums of money. You should have seen the stacks of rubles raked in at Easter time.

The speaker said the time had passed when they could employ the old-fashioned anti-religious propaganda of the Godless League days. But they must work harder to spread the scientific viewpoint, especially among the young.

Dispatch to New York Times
April 13, 1950

The extreme seriousness with which the Soviet regards the Libau plane incident was emphasized by *Pravda*'s publication of a special two-column article on page one saying the "insolent" Americans received a proper lesson. . . .

Pravda said the plane's action was reminiscent of the Hitlerites.

Dispatch Killed by Censor
April 14

Moscow's skies were gloomy, gray, and forbidding today. There was a chill in the air which seemed to imply winter's return after the balmy Easter weekend.

Perhaps it was the leaden skies and raw April weather. Perhaps

136

it was the weather's warning that the long Russian winter has not yet loosed its icy grip, that spring's eager promise may still be delayed. But whatever the reason Moscow today appeared to be gray—gray in color and gray in spirit.

But if Moscow's weather was gray and gloomy the same could not be said for the language of fire and flame which illuminated the Soviet press.

Moscow editorialists heaped words of scorn, anger, and contempt on the United States. . . .

All Moscow newspapers printed an item announcing awarding the Order of the Red Banner to officers of the military air force of the Soviet Army for "fulfilment of their service duty." There was no description of the manner in which the duty was fulfilled. . . .

There was nothing new in the newspapers on the fate of the American aircraft or the ten missing American airmen. As *Pravda* summed it up yesterday, "the impudent fellows received a proper lesson."

April 21

It can be taken as axiomatic that no Russian citizen wants war or can contemplate the prospect of war with any emotion other than the deepest foreboding. In that connection I have heard of no instances of anger or resentment being displayed toward individual Americans as a result of the plane incident.

April 24

We have been having a wonderful spring, really extraordinary. Especially the last few days. Temperatures around 70° and sunshine. The whole land is glowing as the spring buds come out.

The balmy air and sunny skies have brought people out of their winter cocoons of heavy overcoats, fur caps, and *valenki* or felt boots.

In the parks people sit contentedly against a background of sprouting greenery. In the lengthening twilight young couples stroll slowly, bemused by the distant strain of balaliakas and the more lively chords of the *bayan*. Moscow's atmosphere this spring is one of peace and quiet.

There can be no doubt of what the word "war" conveys to the Russian people. War to the Russians means the thatched roof of his kolkhoz cottage going up in thick brown smoke while the cattle wail and the children thinly scream as the bayonet does its bloody work. It means cold. It means hunger. It means hardship. It means sorrow of oceanic proportions. It means the death of husband, wife, and brother, death of sons and daughters.

Dispatch to New York Times
May 1, 1950

The greatest demonstration of Soviet air strength ever placed on view over Red Square today marked the annual May Day celebration. . . .

The celebration was notable for a new type of twin-jet aircraft of fighter-bomber type never before shown. The flight was commanded by Lieutenant General Vasily Stalin, son of the Generalissimo and commander of the military air force of the Moscow military district. . . .

Dispatch Killed by Censor
May 4

The question of the restoration of co-education in Soviet elementary and secondary schools has been raised in vigorous fashion in a discussion sponsored by the *Literary Gazette*. . . .

Separate schools for boys and girls were established in 1944.

Dispatch to New York Times
May 11

Trygvie Lie, United Nations secretary-general, has arrived for conferences with [Generalissimo Stalin and other] Soviet officials designed to break the log-jam between the East and West. . . .

Dispatch to New York Times
May 13

Trygvie Lie's visit to Moscow provides an excellent opportunity to determine whether practical diplomatic means can be devised to translate Soviet declarations in support of world peace into concrete action.

Lie tonight held his second conference with Foreign Minister Vishinsky. He was accompanied by his assistant, Konstantin Zinchenko. . . .*

* Zinchenko, Soviet assistant to Lie, vanished soon after Lie's visit. He did not emerge until 1955, having been sent to the Siberian concentration camps for reasons never made clear.

Dispatch to New York Times
May 15

Trygvie Lie carried his proposals for easing cold war tensions to Generalissimo Stalin tonight. He conferred with Stalin for more than an hour and a half. . . .

[Lie outlined his plan for China representation which would end the five-month stalemate over this issue in the U.N. He made a plea for a plenary meeting of the UN Security Council which would be attended by heads of state, including Stalin if possible.

It was believed Stalin indicated that there was no insuperable barrier to his attendance at such a meeting. . . .]

Dispatch to New York Times
May 16

Trygvie Lie's mission to Moscow has achieved a real measure of success despite his own statement that it is causing more headlines than it deserves. . . .

Among the achievements are a new and important demonstration of Soviet support of UN principles, fresh affirmation of Stalin's belief in the prospect of long co-existence of the two systems—capitalist and Communist—[and tangible progress toward the solution of the question of Chinese representation in the United Nations. . . .

There was reason to believe Lie had grounds for optimism that the China problem is nearing solution. . . .]

Dispatch to New York Times
May 17

Trygvie Lie describes Stalin as "just as healthy and lively as he was in 1946." He called rumors about Stalin's health "lies and maybe wishful thinking."

Dispatch to New York Times
May 18

It appeared today that the most important consequence of Trygvie Lie's visit to Moscow was establishment of the fact that the Soviet leaders are willing to negotiate problems which divide the East and West. . . .

He did not expect spectacular results. The greatest barrier

which he encountered [is that of fear and suspicion—fears and suspicions so deep-rooted that they tend to color the reactions of statesmen even to the most objective proposals and non-controversial facts.

He found that neither East nor West has a monopoly on suspicion. . . .]

His discussions convinced him that while this is not 1945, nor yet 1947, equally, it is not 1939 nor, for that matter, 1937.

May 19, 1950

Today I leave Moscow. Tomorrow I will be in New York.

XI

A New Look at Russia

During my four months' absence from Moscow much happened.
On June 25 North Korean troops attacked South Korea, and the
United States—with United Nations backing—promptly intervened. For the next year or more the ebb and flow of the Korean
conflict was to dominate Soviet-American relations, bringing frequent crises and intensification of the cold war.

Within a month of the start of the war, in July, 1950, American
forces were almost driven out of Korea, but after the Inchon
landings in mid-September U.S. troops rapidly recovered and
drove north. Ignoring repeated warnings by the Communist Chinese, MacArthur crossed the 38th parallel in late September and
a month later reached the vicinity of the Yalu River boundary.
Chinese "volunteers" then intervened and throughout November and December, 1950, drove south, once again almost pushing
the Americans into the sea. This precipitated a grave crisis, but
by mid-January, 1951, MacArthur had estabilized his lines and
in March had gotten back to the 38th parallel. In May—after
President Truman had dismissed MacArthur—Moscow proposed
a cease-fire. After considerable acrimonious negotiation, a truce
was finally negotiated, and talks opened July 10, 1951.

As I left New York in late summer, 1950, the question in everyone's mind was: Will Korea prove to be a prelude to a general
East-West conflict? What are the chances of an extension of hostilities to Europe? Is Moscow planning any new move?

It was to this problem that I applied myself as I returned from America to resume my post as Moscow correspondent of the *New York Times*.

August 21, 1950
Aboard Liner "Queen Mary"

I've had a wonderful crossing. We've just left Cherbourg and will dock at Southampton late today. Up to London to the Savoy tonight and over to Paris toward the end of the week.

September 9
Aboard Orient Express, in Poland

We are rolling across the flat Polish plain at a great clip, and this afternoon I'll be in Warsaw. My hopes for the kind of excitement for which E. Phillips Oppenheim made this train famous have been disappointed.

As it has turned out I got a first-class compartment—and no wonder. I am the only Paris-Warsaw first-class passenger. There were a few who dropped off at Bavarian points and a woman and her six weeks' old baby who got off at Prague.

Germany looks like a rich, fat land. Few signs of war in Bavaria. It made me angry, rolling across that country and watching the industrious Germans repairing their railroads and putting up factories as though nothing had ever happened.

I didn't see much of Czechoslovakia. We crossed the frontier about 6:00 and into Prague around 11:00 P.M. Today we roll across Poland. It is very like Russia. Flat plains and pine forests and open fields. The country looks prosperous and the chimneys in the factory towns are belching smoke. The people on the train are nice, as Poles always are. I get the same kind of nostalgic feeling from the Polish countryside as from the Russian. It reminds me of Minnesota—northern Minnesota—although Poland is more populated.

Now that I'm on the move my depression has lifted.

September 12
Aboard Kuriersky Express, en route to Moscow

It is fun to write and while away the long hours going across this flat, uninteresting countryside. I am sitting in a little compartment, writing, while the long, slow miles of Russian country-side go by. We are getting near Vyazma, which is where one of the very big battles was fought in the German drive on Moscow. A while back we stopped at Smolensk. That was where we went in '44 for the Katyn forest inquiry. A famous expedition. A fancy train. Kathy Harriman and all. Well, the town has changed a lot. Then, there was only one building which hadn't been wrecked by the Germans when they got out. The one they used as their headquarters. Now it is a bustling place with lots of new build-ings, a big railroad yard, factories, and so forth. It is a good example of the rebuilding of devasted areas.

Just now the *provodnik* has come and stopped outside my door. He is fascinated to see me working my *mashinka,* as they call typewriters. Probably never saw one on this train before. The little customs lad yesterday at Brest was much interested, too. He particularly wanted to see how it worked, and I think he wondered about the ribbon whether it had writing on it or some secret message.

I spent yesterday in Brest. My train from Warsaw got in in the morning and the express didn't pull out until 6:30 so I had the whole day. Spent the morning looking at the town and the after-noon snoozing. I will be writing all this up for the *Times.* Brest is a pleasant provincial Russian town, quiet and restful, with a good many parks and pleasant boulevards. I sat for a long time in the park and smoked cigarettes in the sunshine and watched the kids play. . . .

The little customs lad at Brest couldn't pass my books because he didn't know English, so they had to go on to Moscow for the customs people there. All I have had to read is *La Vie de Bohème.* This is a pleasant trip. There's a diner which was gay last night with jolly toasting and even some songs. A youngster in the air force shared my table, and we made out a little conversation in my punk Russian. His only other language was German. All in all, a jolly Russian train.

I haven't many rubles so today I am on a peculiar diet—bread and apples, *pâté de fois gras,* and Nescafé. I should have realized in Warsaw that I would have a money problem and bought food for the trip. But I didn't. Luckily, I had a can of *pâté* which I picked up in Paris—a present from Cy. I had the coffee and

143

bought a bag of apples in Warsaw. So I bought some bread and
have been living on this lush, if peculiar, diet.

Dispatch to New York Times
Brest, September 13, 1950

These are my impressions, returning after a summer's leave in
the United States.

The date line of this dispatch will awaken uneasy memories in
minds which remember the first World War and the start of the
second. This provincial town on Russia's western border has figured only twice in world headlines—[both times unhappily].

Returning to the Soviet after several months' leave, my first
impression of this border city is one of hustle and bustle. The
freight yards are filled with long trains. . . .

The absence of any scars of war is not the only notable fact
about Brest. Equally notable is the absence of any indications
that the citizens of Brest are fearful that war again looms on the
close horizon.

[There are no war headlines on the billboards, nor did I hear
any conversations about war.

Naturally, there are many men in uniform in Brest; as a junc-
tion point for troops passing to or from the Soviet zone of Germany this is natural. Casual impressions are not always trust-
worthy. But some contrasts are striking enough. Unlike Warsaw
or even Paris, the walls of Brest are not plastered with angry
appeals and protests concerning Korea. . . .]

Travelers in the Brest station were breakfasting on borsch,
shashlik, and Wiener schnitzel, accompanied by vodka, beer, or
even champagne. Blonde waitresses in short black silk skirts and
billowy silk blouses waited on the diners, many of them military
men returning from Germany or going west to join the Soviet
occupation forces. . . .

Brest's finest street is Lenin Boulevard. Here are located the
Brest regional Communist Party committee, the state bank [and
the offices of the MVD and MGB].* On this street, too, is located
an imposing Roman Catholic church [somewhat dilapidated and
down at the heels from disuse].

* The MVD was the Ministry of the Interior and the MGB was the Ministry
of State Security.

It is precisely 1,104 kilometers from Brest to Moscow, and my outstanding impression of that distance is one of building, building, building.

Seldom is one out of hearing of hammers, the slap of trowels on mortar, and the burr of saws cutting through fresh pine lumber.

The route of the Kuriersky Express is the German's main invasion route of nine years ago. To call the roll of the cities—Brest, Baronovichi, Minsk, Orsha, Smolensk, Vyazma, Mozhaisk—is to call the roll of the major battles of the summer and autumn of 1941.

Today a new battle is being fought—the battle of construction . . .

Too much weight should not be given to impressions even though they may be the impressions of an experienced and reasonably quick-eyed observer who has traveled tens of thousands of miles across the Soviet Union.

But alongside the specific evidence of the huge postwar reconstruction effort now under way in Byelorussia and western Russia should be placed another bit of testimony. Along the entire 1,104 kilometers of route from Brest to Moscow I did not see a single troop train. I did not see a single tank, tank destroyer, or artillery piece loaded on a flatcar or awaiting shipment along the right of way.

The plain fact is I did not see a single piece of military apparatus of any kind outside of an occasional bayoneted rifle or tommy gun.

Naturally, one correspondent's railroad car window view is not conclusive. But it is recorded for whatever value it may have and in a reasoned effort to present a strictly objective account.

In view of the present state of the world's nerves it seems that this is a fact worth recording and possibly even underlining. . . .

I got into Moscow night before last. So, here I am for another tour of duty. We will see how it goes. . . .

Dispatch to New York Times
September 16, 1950

This has probably been the greatest clean-up, paint-up, and construction summer in the eight hundred years since the ancient boyars first founded Moscow.

At least that is the way it seems to me, returning to Moscow after a summer's absence. . . .

Taken in its proper context this is important news—news which should be carefully digested and studied against the background of world events. The economy of the Soviet is carefully planned and directed. During this summer hundreds of millions of rubles, tens of thousands of man-hours, and vast quantities of industrial output have been poured into a program for the beautification of Moscow.

It is hard to believe that the Kremlin would continue a program on this vast scale if it seriously believed that atom bombs might be falling in the near future on Soviet territory. . . .

Dispatch to New York Times
September 16

What have the people of Moscow been talking about in this critical summer of 1950?

Well, naturally, there has been the Korean war and the state of relations between the United States and Russia.

Another topic of conversation is the government's vast new hydroelectric program. To the ordinary Muscovite, here is concrete, specific evidence on a mammoth scale of the government's confidence in its ability to maintain world peace.

[The Moscow man in the street may be wrong. The Soviet government may be wrong.] But the Moscow man in the street regards his conclusion as reasonable. . . .

Some 30,000 to 50,000 people last weekend attended the greatest dog show ever held in Moscow. [Possibly, the most interest was drawn by three new crossbreeds, displayed for the first time. They were the Moscow great Dane, the Moscow watchdog, and the Moscow retriever. . . .]

[All Moscow is humming and singing a new song, called] "On the Wide Volga." [It has been popularly christened the Sormova song. It is about a boy and a girl in love in Sormova, a suburb

146

of Gorki. "There are many books but none to tell you how much I love you," the girl says.

Men and women have been able to buy summer shoes and sandals without encountering seasonal supply difficulties. . . .] The prices of Soviet automobiles have been somewhat reduced. The standard Pobeda—in the Chevrolet class—[has been reduced to 16,000 rubles from 17,500 rubles]. Penicillin can now be obtained in drugstores at 3 rubles, 30 kopecks for 200,000 units. . . .

Dispatch to New York Times
September 17

Here are some conclusions drawn from Soviet life which are particularly interesting in view of the tension between the United States and the Soviet Union.

There are no queues in front of foodstores in Moscow. The price of butter has not risen. There is no hoarding of sugar. There are more shoes for sale than last spring. Prices are lower and quality has improved somewhat.

These statements are not Soviet propaganda. They are plain, everyday truths vouched for by this correspondent.

Their importance is this: whatever may be the cause and whatever may be the underlying factors, there is not today in Moscow anything which an honest observer could possibly describe as a war scare or war hysteria.

So far as I can determine there is no feeling among the Moscow populace that war with the United States is imminent.

There are no recruiting posters, nor have there been any calls for recruits. No additional Soviet classes have been called to the colors. No reservists have been summoned to duty.

[To this let me add one qualification: if any such action has been taken it is not a matter of public knowledge among Soviet citizens nor of private knowledge within the diplomatic corps.]

Evidence exists on every side that the Soviet government has not made any radical alteration in its economic program as a result of the summer's events and growing Soviet-American tension. Food supplies are as ample as last spring and quantity and quality have improved. This is true of meat and vegetable oils— two categories which are extremely sensitive in any shift from peacetime to wartime economy. There has been an increase in quantity and quality of household goods, particularly such items as aluminum pots and pans, copper and brass samovars. These items are excellent barometers. . . .

[This is not to suggest the Soviet is neglecting its military defense.] The government is spending substantial funds on the armed forces and military establishment. The Soviet army is large.

Not that people are ignorant of rising tensions. [They worry about the outcome. When the Korean war started there was natural concern lest the conflict spread and result in general hostilities. The fact that Korea has remained local has given the public increased confidence that general was is not an immediate possibility.

Nevertheless, the Korean outbreak has served to emphasize to all Russians that the possibility of war is genuine.

Possibly the two events which drove this threat home most sharply were the Korean war and the Baltic plane incident. The plane incident was genuinely shocking to Muscovites who recalled only too vividly the plane incidents which preceded Hitler's attack on Russia in 1941.]

Dispatch to New York Times
September 19, 1950

What is the United States doing in Korea? That question is the most frequent one which Americans in the Soviet Union encounter in their contacts with Soviet citizens. . . .

Soviet citizens uniformly blame the United States for the Korean conflict. . . .

[There should be no particular surprise in the United States at this situation. Soviet citizens obtain their information on the world situation from the Soviet press and radio. . . . From what they hear or read there is nothing to justify the actions of the United States. . . .

The circulation of American press and magazines in Russia is no larger than that of the equivalent Soviet organs in the United States. No American would seriously suggest that *Pravda* has

148

sufficient subscribers in New York to affect the American viewpoint on such matters as Korea. . . .

Paradoxical as it may sound in New York or Washington,] the Russian reaction to the Voice of America frequently is that it is "just American propaganda."

Dispatch Killed by Censor
September 23

Here are some Soviet prices and wages. Butter prices in state stores range from 34 to 42 rubles a kilo. In the peasant markets butter is several rubles cheaper. Sugar sells in state stores at 12 rubles a kilo for granulated sugar and 13.80 for lump sugar.

The price of men's shoes ranges from 60 rubles to 260 for the highest quality.

Most Soviet wages are based on production quotas per worker. The more productive workers are able to earn considerably more than the less efficient.

Here are examples of wages per month: unskilled worker, 300 to 600 rubles; ordinary office clerk, 500 to 700; carpenter, 600 to 800; locomotive engineer, 1,000 to 2,500; subway engineer, 2,000 to 3,000.

September 24

There have been no changes since I was last here in opportunities for mutual discussions by Russians and Americans. The situation is neither better nor worse than it was last spring.

American correspondents are not very popular with the Soviet public. In many plays and movies they have been pictured as busying themselves with espionage, sabotage, and plotting. Naturally no good Soviet citizen is interested in associating with foreigners who he thinks have his worst interests at heart.

September 27

I have been out to our dacha a few times since coming back. The weather was bad all summer so Tom and Julie didn't get as much fun out of the place as they should have. But the first week I was back it was Indian summer, and we went out two or three times. I have been out once since.

September 28, 1950
Letter to U. P. Frantzev, Press Department

In line with our conversation of yesterday I am submitting to you a list of proposals which I should like to carry out.

The list is rather lengthy, and I do not suppose all of these things can be done at once. Some may prove impossible.

I would like to propose the following interviews:

1. With the minister of education with particular reference to longer terms of compulsory education and co-education.

2. With the Stalin Prize winner Olga Lepeshinskaya with regard to her cellular discoveries.

3. With any of the leading architects with reference to the movement for simplicity of design as exemplified in the tall new Moscow buildings.

4. With the Moscow city housing authorities. . . .

5. With Mikhail Sholokhov with reference to the new novel on which he has been working so long.*

6. With directors and engineers who will be building the great Kuibyshev, Stalingrad, Turkmenian, and Ukraine-Crimea projects.

7. With Dmitri Shostakovich.†

8. With Professor A. G. Ivanov-Smolensky on the Pavlovian theory. . . .

9. With a leading Soviet penologist or criminologist on the role of corrective labor.

10. With S. I. Vavilov, chairman of the Society for Political and Scientific Knowledge, on the question of religious beliefs.

I would like to propose the following trips:

1. A two- or three-day trip to a collective farm.

2. A bus trip on the Moscow-Kharkov-Simferopol route.

3. A visit to the Stalin auto plant.†

4. A visit to the Moscow television studios.

5. A visit to a corrective labor camp, etc. . . .

When I was in the Soviet Union in 1944, I had the pleasure and good fortune to accompany Eric Johnston on his trip to the Urals, Siberia, and Central Asia. If it could be possible to visit

* The sequel to *The Virgin Soil Upturned,* completed and published in 1960.
† Obtained in 1954.

the cities then visited—Magnitogorsk, Sverlovsk, Omsk, Novosibersk, Alma Ata, Tashkent, Samarkand*—I have no doubt the articles I would write would provide a major contribution to Soviet-American understanding. . . .

October 2

I wrote a hell of an important series on my return here which the paper hasn't printed yet. I am pretty upset about it. For many good reasons. I haven't final word on what they are going to do.

Dispatch to New York Times
October 3

The *Literary Gazette* today published a list of "enemies of mankind." It listed the "names of all those monsters and cannibals who openly preach the destruction of millions of human lives."

The names included "the political businessman, Henry Wallace. . . ."

Dispatch to New York Times
October 4

Within a month the Council of Ministers has announced plans for four of the largest and most ambitious public works ever projected in this or any other country.

The plans call for construction at Kuibyshev and Stalingrad on the Volga of two hydroelectric stations which are larger than any others in the world, one of the world's greatest canals—a 1,100-kilometer channel linking the Amu Darya or Oxus River with the Caspian Sea—and an elaborate system of canals, power, and irrigation works in the south Ukraine. . . .

The Kuibyshev dam will have a capacity of 2,000,000 kilowatts; Stalingrad will have 1,700,000.

[Moscow's available power supply will be doubled.]

Special labor forces are being assembled for the new projects—the design and planning of which has been placed in charge of Sergei Y. Zhuk. . . .†

* I visited Alma Ata, Tashkent, and Samarkand in 1953, Sverdlovsk and Novosibersk in 1959.

† Whom I revealed in 1952 was a high official of the MVD, which was in charge of constructing these projects.

A message from Turner yesterday. I am afraid it indicates they are not going to run the series. I feel very strongly that the dispatches are worthy of publication.

The main point is that there was no evidence of a step-up in Soviet military preparations in the past four months and a general lack of war psychosis here.

I think those points are very important. And I think I must have made it clear that these points were not straw-hat conclusions but based on careful sifting of all available evidence. I might add that these conclusions are shared by every responsible diplomat I know in Moscow, including those of our own and the British embassies.

I went to considerable difficulty to maneuver my entry into the Soviet via Brest so that I could cover the rail route in through Byelorussia and western Russia. My trip across the country was the first made by a correspondent in four years.

I did that because any military build-up in Poland or Germany must be fed by this route; also, this was one of the most devastated war areas, one which I saw when I was here in 1944, and I wanted to see what they had done with the country.

Well, the trip answered both those questions. I could detect no sign of military build-up. I don't care how good the Russians are at concealment (and, frankly, they are not very good at it), the railroad couldn't have been as clean of military stuff if anything important was going on.

Equally striking, although I couldn't mention this in the series, was the experience of the ambassador and his party on their trip out to Irkutsk and Lake Baikal last June, which bracketed the time of the start of the Korean war. They got no evidence of any major troop or military movements along the Trans-Siberian.

Of course, there were aspects of the situation which I could not deal with through the censorship. One point is that the standing military establishment is very large—but large as it is, certainly, if the Kremlin thought war was about to break out they would be busy enlarging it.

Nor could I go into detail about the ignorance of the Soviet public as to the American viewpoint. I thought that by my emphasis and re-emphasis on their dependence upon the Soviet press and radio for information that I put the point over obliquely. And I tried to suggest that the Voice of America doesn't reach them. It can't in Moscow because of the blanket jamming, and the number of listeners outside Moscow can't be more than a handful.

Prices and wages were cut out of the stories by the censorship. They always are. I noticed they let the penicillin price through, apparently because it actually is fairly cheap.

Censorship also cut out a rather delicate attempt I made to get across the point that people in Moscow really worry when there is a crisis in relations with the U.S.A.—such as the Baltic plane incident and the outbreak of the Korean war. People here are frightened when they think of war with the U.S.A., and the present absence of war hysteria is plainly due to the very successful effort the government has made to convince them that bad as things seem there won't be war.

Dispatch to New York Times*
October 7

The Soviet, in the opinion of some, would welcome an opportunity for a frank discussion of Soviet-American problems with a representative group of American citizens. . . .

The willingness of the Soviet to enter such talks should not necessarily be interpreted as indicating that the proposal of Harold Stassen for conversations between himself and Stalin is likely to evoke any warm response on the part of the Kremlin. . . .

Just a month ago the *Literary Gazette* placed Stassen on the list of those who would be tried ultimately as international war criminals. . . .

Dispatch to New York Times
October 11

There is a growing disposition in Moscow to believe that [no early end of the Korean war may be expected and that] the North Koreans are adopting the "tactics of prolonged war" mentioned October 1 by Chou En-lai. . . .

* Killed by me after being held two days without action by the censor.

October *12, 1950*

Another big worry resolved. This week at long last the *Times* is running the series which I wrote in the first ten days I got here. I can't say how glad I am, for three reasons—because the pieces are so important, because of my relations with the *Times,* and because of the situation here.

XII

A Korean Crisis

October 16, 1950

Today there is an autumn sun. It is burning through an early frosty haze. I can look across the square and see a patch of green and flowers and people in the street.

Dispatch to New York Times
October 20

The Soviet press directed a slashing attack upon Harold Stassen today, with *Pravda* calling him a political speculator. . . . The attack occupied three columns. . . .

October 24

That series about Moscow for the *Times* gives my impressions on getting back here as well as I can put them down. There is not a great deal to add. The material welfare of the people has gone up rather sharply this year, and so far there is every sign that it will continue in the same direction.

Europe, generally, is much more calm and peaceful than the U.S.A. This applies not only to the U.S.S.R. but also to western Europe where there is very little of that "on the verge" feeling which was so current in America when I left and, indeed, in London and Paris I found not a little resentment at the general air of excitement in New York and Washington.

October 24, 1950
Letter to Edwin L. James, New York Times

I want to give you a rather detailed picture of the expense situation here since the revaluation of the ruble.

I estimated last April that after making all possible economies bureau expenses would run in the neighborhood of 7,000 rubles monthly. That is borne out by current expenditures. . . . In spite of this, actual dollar costs are up nearly 50 per cent. . . .

If you translate what I have to pay for goods and services into dollar terms, you obtain some completely fantastic results.

To take a few random items for September: $125 for three not very good luncheons; $10 for a hotel porter for carting luggage from the lobby to the third floor; $4 for a cheap scrapbook which would cost not more than 20 cents in Woolworth's.

Some of my own costs: My hotel room costs me 60 rubles a day or 1,600 rubles a month. I pay my cook 700 rubles a month, and local provisions average 400 rubles a month. I pay 200 rubles a month for electricity for a refrigerator and two electric hot plates —$50. The cost of having a suit cleaned is 36 rubles—$9. One of the cheapest items here is a haircut. Only 7 rubles—$1.75. . . .

Dispatch to New York Times
October 28

Two [very important] changes in the Council of Ministers have been announced.

The new minister of state control is V. N. Merekulov, minister of state security until October, 1946, when his deputy V. S. Abakumov, former NKVD chief in the Rostov district succeeded him.

Merekulov succeeds Lev Z. Mikhlis, who was relieved of his post because of illness.

The other change was of equal importance. This placed [one of the Communist Party's most brilliant young figures,] Panteleimon K. Ponamarenko in charge of procurement of agricultural supplies. . . .

Dispatch to New York Times
November 2

The press made plain today that the Chinese People's Republic has full Soviet support in its Tibetan operation, which was described as a legitimate measure to complete unification of the country. . . .

November 3
Letter to J. V. Stalin, President, Council of Ministers

I wonder whether you would care to suggest what action might best be taken at this time to end the grave threat to world peace which exists in the Far East?

Is the Soviet Union prepared to mediate between the United States and powers associated with it in the United Nations, on the one hand, and China and North Korea, on the other hand? . . .

Dispatch to New York Times
November 6

Marshal Bulganin tonight said that the United States and England show that they do not seek the path of international co-operation and intend to unleash a new war. . .

He spoke at the Bolshoi Theater. Among those present were Molotov, Mikoyan, Kaganovich, Shvernik, Andreyev, Khrushchev, Voroshilov, and Kosygin. Others present included Suslov, Ponamarenko, and Marshal Budenny. [Generalissimo Stalin was not present. Nor were Malenkov and Beriya in attendance. . . .]

Dispatch Killed by Censor
November 7

Under weeping leaden November skies a parade of Soviet armed might and the shortest civilian demonstration in recent years marked Moscow's celebration of the 33rd anniversary of the Bolshevik Revolution.

An icy autumn drizzle soaked the paraders and high Soviet officials who witnessed the procession from Lenin's Tomb. A foggy ceiling which obscured the bulbous spires of St. Basil's and the slim elegance of Spassky Tower forced cancellation of the customary air demonstration led by Lieutenant General Vasily Stalin.

So cold and wet was the weather that the massive civilian demonstration was drastically curtailed. . . .

Dispatch to New York Times
November 11

The press publishes the first reports describing the participation of Chinese volunteer units in Korea. It cited Chinese declarations that aid will continue to Korea until "the American aggressive troops are fully destroyed, Korea and Taiwan fully liberated, and the threat to national defense fully removed. . . ."

It appeared the Chinese will give full support to the volunteers until the Americans are driven from Korea. . . .

November 12, 1950

It's a cold, wet, wintry day. The sidewalks are wet, there's a little dirty snow in the park, and the sky is gray. I have a cold, and I'm blue.

Dispatch to New York Times
November 13

Dispatches from China make clear beyond any reasonable doubt that the Chinese volunteers now entering Korea have as their purpose the complete liquidation of the threat to China's security which Peking says arises from American operations in Korea.

It is clear that events in the Far East have reached an important turning point. . . . Certain conclusions are apparent. First, Peking has concluded that the American actions in Taiwan and Korea and the bombings in Manchuria constitute "a direct threat to Chinese security." Second, the participation of the Chinese volunteer force is a serious and considered action designed to liquidate that threat. [Third, prospects for settlement of the Korean conflict by diplomatic means are sharply reduced because of the diametrically opposed views of China and the United States. . . .]

The purpose of the Chinese volunteers, clearly, is to drive the "American interventionists into the sea."

Dispatch to New York Times
November 16

The increasing gravity of the Far Eastern situation was emphasized by dispatches which included charges of extensive Japanese participation in the Korean war.

The dispatches charged that a secret military agreement was being negotiated between General MacArthur and the Japanese government. The Chinese asserted the United States was seeking to carry the war to China proper.

[In this connection it is worthwhile to recall the provisions of the Treaty of Friendship, Alliance, and Mutual Assistance between China and the U.S.S.R., signed in Moscow last February 14.

The military provisions of this pact become operative in event of attack by Japan or states allied with her. . . .]

November 16

I have had a bittersweet birthday. All day the 14th I was blue. But I knew it was kind of phony. Tom and Julie had arranged a birthday party for me. So, being bitter, I could throw myself into it and forget my troubles. That made it twice as good. Just a little bunch of us. Charley, Tom and Julie, and a couple of girls from the embassy. We went to the Arogvy for a wonderful Georgian dinner—caviar, *sotszivi, shashlik pakarski,* and vodka. We danced, and the Georgian music played, and it was fun. And better for me because I had my fine, burning secret bitterness at it all.

It is still warm. Especially the last couple of days. No real winter yet.

November 18

What is life like in Moscow? It's lots of things. It is my aluminum coffeepot and three cups of coffee to wake up with in the morning. It is the BBC news at 9:00 A.M. and "Program Parade," the latest hits. Then a bath while my bacon and eggs are cooking.

After breakfast—to the office and mulling over the papers. Gossip with my colleagues. The embassy. Gossip there. Work in the afternoon.

Or maybe just go out for a ride in the country. The fields all November brown and barren and the trees naked and the peasants' little huts gray and dull against the landscape. Not a spot of color. A kind of inverse beauty about it. Like the slagheaps of Pittsburgh, perhaps. . . .

Winter is almost here. Vasily, the chauffeur and weather prognosticator, says winter will begin on St. Michael's Day. That is Sunday, tomorrow. We will see.

November 22, 1950

The general attitude toward the press is a little better than it has been. The press department has bestirred itself to organize some piffling trips—a bakery, the Lenin library, a regional hospital. Hardly worth writing about.

When I came back, I had a long, bare-knuckles talk with the press department people. I told them they had debased the Moscow date line. That it wasn't worth a continental. That as soon as people saw it they said "more Moscow propaganda."

I told them public opinion was about as antagonistic toward Russia as it could be short of war. I said, that being the case, they might as well realize that even if they had a good, honest story to tell they had made it virtually impossible to get it across.

I blamed the censorship for a great deal of this. I challenged the whole basis of the censorship (the idea that it was supposed to stop anti-Soviet propaganda and misleading stories about the Soviet Union). I told them I thought it served exactly the opposite purpose.

Frantzev, chief of the press department, said he thought I would find some improvement in censorship and fewer difficulties "from now on." That was demonstrated to some extent in their treatment of the series and, particularly, in my replies to Catledge's inquiries.

We have an addition to the local press corps—Joe Clark of the New York *Daily Worker*. He came in about six weeks ago with his wife and two youngsters under three. He is a quiet, studious type who tells me he has been a member of the Party for twenty years. They are living in the Metropole and are learning quite a few things about life in the Communist state which never were printed in the *Short History*.

Eddy Gilmore went back to the States on leave. I have my fingers crossed. He left on the basis of one brief phone talk with Simonov of the press department. He has now been in the States about five weeks, and his visa to return has not come through.

An interesting thing happened with Parker. He didn't show up on November 7, either in Red Square or at Gromyko's party, which led me to suspect something was going on. A couple of nights later I went to a small dinner at which Parker and Valentina were guests. Ralph was very glad to see me but seemed a bit upset. Finally he burst out and said he was going to issue "a joint statement to the *New York Times* and *Pravda*." He said he was the "Howard Fast of Moscow." The Russians had refused to give him an exit visa to go to the Sheffield Peace Conference!

For three weeks he had been trying to get a visa. He wanted to see his mother in England, and he had been invited to address the peace conference. All day November 7—and quite a few other days—he had been sitting in the OVIR office, waiting to see the militia. The press department had promised that the visa would be forthcoming. He had his ticket to leave. But no visa. . . .

I tried to reassure him, but he would have none of it. The fact is, I thought they would give him a visa, and it turned out I was right. About thirty-six hours later he got his visa and took off for England. . . .

A visitor in October was Iris Morley, Alaric Jacob's wife, who was here when I was here during the war. Iris was with a peace delegation. I believe she is now a member of the Party. But she doesn't mind taking some cracks in private. I saw her several times, and she said her hosts, the Anti-Fascist Women's Committee, were going bugs—because she was seeing me.

What really got her down happened at a big reception in the Metropole dining room. They had all the usual intellectuals out in force. But whenever one of them approached the British delegates, the big-bosom babes of the Anti-Fascist Committee swung into action and protected their charges from indelicate contacts.

Iris is a blonde who regards herself as pretty attractive. She never got to dance with a single man all evening. Every time one of the intellectuals looked like asking her, one of the bosomy madames cut in first.

November 22
Letter to Emanuel Freedman, New York Times

I enclose a copy of the story you ordered on the increase in living costs for foreigners under the new dispensation here.

I am afraid it is the only copy of it that you will get a chance to see since there isn't a chance in Hades that the censors will let it through. . . .

Dispatch Killed by Censor
November 22, 1950

One of the most curious anomalies of present life in Moscow is the fact that living costs for foreigners are almost twice as high as a year ago while the cost of living for Soviet citizens has been sharply reduced.

The anomaly arises out of the financial measures which were announced last March by the Soviet government. At that time sharp reductions were made in retail prices, averaging about 26 per cent. At the same time the ruble exchange rate was greatly increased. Prior to March 1, American dollars could be exchanged for rubles at a diplomatic rate of eight to one. As of March 1, a temporary rate of six to one was established, and a four to one rate has been in effect since July 1.

The ruble change had a radical effect on the five hundred foreigners who comprise Moscow's diplomatic colony. The reduction in Moscow retail prices had comparatively little effect on the diplomats, including Americans, since their purchases of consumers goods in Moscow are small.

A year ago a cook or a maid could be hired for 600 to 800 rubles monthly—$75 to $100. Today the wage is the same in rubles but in dollars it is $150 to $200.

Virtually no foreigners have Moscow driver's licenses and therefore must have a chauffeur for their cars. Last year a chauffeur's wage was about 2,000 rubles or $250. Now it is $500.

Another ruble expenditure is theater, opera, and ballet tickets. A pair of tickets to the Bolshoi costs 52 to 60 rubles—$4.50 to $7.50 last year. It is double this year.

Costs in Moscow are now so high that two countries, New Zealand and Iceland, decided to eliminate their representation.

Dispatch to New York Times
November 22

[The re-examination of basic Soviet sciences with a view to eliminating Western bourgeois ideology has extended to] the field of organic chemistry where a sharp attack is directed by *Problems of Philosophy* against Soviet supporters of the theory of resonance advanced by the American scientists Pauling and Wheland. . . .

Winter hasn't really set in. We had a couple of crisp days over Thanksgiving with some snow and cold. But it is warm again. Most un-Russian weather.

November 26
Letter to Arthur Hays Sulzberger, New York Times

I ran across a bit of information the other day which I thought was interesting.

A Norwegian woman journalist was taken to visit the new journalism courses at Moscow University. She tells me that one of their basic routines is a comparative study of the *New York Times* and *Pravda*. The students read both papers carefully, paying particular attention to items which appear in the *Times* and not in *Pravda* and vice versa. Where *Pravda* and the *Times* carry stories on the same event the stories are carefully analyzed for differences in treatment and content.

It was the visitor's impression that both the professors and students hold the *Times* in the highest regard and regard it as a model of what a newspaper should be like.

Dispatch to New York Times
December 2

The press reports that the American public is puzzled, confused, perplexed, despondent, and nervous over Korea.

This atmosphere, it is said, has spread to the Pentagon, the State Department, Congress, Lake Success, and Wall Street. The papers publish a two-column summary by Tass regarding the American attitude toward the Korean events. . . .

The American high command in Washington was said to have recommended to Truman that he employ diplomatic means to remedy the deteriorating military situation. However, the Pentagon was said to feel that diplomacy cannot be expected to operate rapidly enough to assist the retreating American forces. . . .

Dispatch to New York Times
December 3

Pravda asked today "who but the insane" could now believe in the peaceful intentions of President Truman.

It said that "Truman needs war and not peace." These were the conclusions of a three-hundred-word statement published in the upper right-hand corner of *Pravda's* front page under the headline: "On Truman's Statement at His Press Conference— New War Hysteria."

Pravda's declaration was unsigned [but it required no signature. No one could read the statement without instantly recognizing the unmistakable Stalin logic and unmistakable Stalin style. Nor was there any mistaking the importance of the comment].

The statement said:

"Why did Truman reject the peaceful proposals of the Koreans and the Chinese if he actually strives for peace?

"Truman accuses the Koreans and Chinese of 'aggression.' This can only cause a smile. Did the Koreans or the Chinese attack the United States? Is it not United States troops that are in Korea and on Taiwan? Who is the aggressor if not Truman and his friends, MacArthur, Harriman, and the others?

"Why should China which borders on Korea have no right to defend its frontiers, and the United States, which is 5,000 miles from Korea, have the right to 'defend its security' at a distance of 5,000 miles from its border?

"Where is logic? Where is justice? Who but the insane can after this believe in the peaceful intentions of Truman and his friends? Truman needs war and not peace. This is why he starts a new war hysteria."

December 3, 1950
Letter to Generalissimo Stalin, President,
Council of Ministers:

In this morning's *Pravda* there appears a statement regarding Mr. Truman which, if I do not mistake the style of language and ideas, comes from your pen.

I wonder whether I might have your permission to attribute this statement to you, personally, in writing a dispatch for my newspaper.*

Dispatch Killed by Censor
December 6

Little comfort though there may be in the fact, nonetheless it should be interesting to the American public that the present

* No reply was ever received.

serious crisis in Korea comes as no surprise to anyone who has been reading the Moscow newspapers since November 1.

The fact is that events in the Far East have taken the precise course which the press suggested they would.

The accuracy of the Soviet press in indicating the trend of Far Eastern developments can be established by rereading two dispatches filed by myself in mid-November. One was sent November 11 and a more comprehensive analysis was transmitted November 13.

The dispatch of November 13 said that the Far Eastern situation had reached "an important turning point," that there was no reason to suppose the Chinese had entered Korea with only a limited objective, and that their apparent intention was to drive the Americans into the sea.

Nothing which has been published by the press since that time has given the slightest reason for revising that conclusion. . . .

Probably the most important military conclusion which can be drawn from this is that the Chinese intervention in Korea is designed to be decisive—on a scale of strength sufficient to liquidate the American military position in Korea. . . .

Dispatch to New York Times
December 7

[No support is given by the press to suggestions that China's interest is confined to protection of the Yalu River power installations.]

To the contrary—the emphasis throughout is on the threat to China's integrity and security which arises from American military operations in Korea. . . .

Dispatch to New York Times
December 10

Against the historic background of the Russian Revolution it can be seen that the leaders of Communist China naturally anticipated a military effort by capitalist powers similar to that directed against the Bolsheviks during the Interventionist period.

The Chinese Communist leaders regard the possibility of armed intervention by the United States and other capitalist powers as a great potential threat.

It can be said firmly that they view all military and diplomatic moves in the Pacific region, especially those close to their border, with the possibility of armed intervention foremost in mind.

One has only to quote the essential passage from the notorious Tanaka memorial as the *New Times* did yesterday to see very clearly what memories and chords are stirred in Chinese minds by the present developments.

Tanaka wrote: To conquer the world one must first conquer China. To conquer China one must first conquer Manchuria and Mongolia. To conquer Manchuria and Mongolia one must first conquer Korea and Taiwan.

The pattern of events in the Far East seems to Peking to fit the Tanaka memorial like a glove on the hand. . . .

December 13, 1950

Generally speaking, censorship has been of medium severity since my return in September. The most interesting cuts in my series were the deletions of practically all price or wage figures. There were inconsequential cuts in details of military traffic to and from Germany and, somewhat more important, the wrecking of my attempt to give some idea of the state of mind of Muscovites in view of the war threat.

December 18

There are two important features of the current Soviet line. The first is the shattering blow which, in their view, has been dealt to our basic "strong" policy. The second is the thesis that Truman is trying to meet this by increasing "war hysteria."

The war hysteria theme is extremely important. It was laid down in *Pravda*'s brief and striking first page editorial of December 3, which almost certainly was written by Stalin himself. There are unmistakable evidences of his literary style. It does not use the ordinary *Pravda* editorial writer's jargon. It is brief, pithy, pointed.

I said in my dispatch of December 3 that it had been written by Stalin and repeated this on the 4th and subsequent days. Of course, the censors deleted this information. I went so far as to write Stalin asking if I could publicly attribute the article to him. But, again, no response.

166

Dispatch to New York Times
December 22

An authoritative Soviet publication describes the theoretic possibilities of obtaining atomic energy from hydrogen as of "tremendous importance."

It says that once the dangers of war have disappeared nuclear fuel will solve "fantastic scientific problems." This is the view presented by an article in the *Bolshoi Soviet Encyclopedia.* . . .

December 23

Last night I had a Christmas party. Wonderful! Vasily got me a fine tree which almost reaches the fifteen-foot ceiling. The night before Tom and Julie and I decorated it. All the lovely things from America and Charley Russell's strings of lights. How pretty it looks with great dabs of cotton snow!

Just had the room lighted by the tree and eight candles—a real Christmas room, heavy with the smell of the fir and the soft light of candles.

I moved my central table out and found that Mr. Charleton's heavy mahogany table comes apart. It made two lovely half-moon tables for serving drinks.

There were sixty people at the party. What excitement! For two days my cook has been making hors d'œuvres—hot *pirozhki,* those little hot meat-filled rolls, caviar, red and black, cheese and onion and egg canapes—God knows what.

Things are quiet here. Unearthly quiet, I might say, by contrast with the U.S.A. Which doesn't mean much but is at least pleasant.

Dispatch Killed by Censor
December 24

DEAR MIKE:

I guess you'll think this is a kind of funny way for me to say Merry Christmas, but it's a long way from Moscow, U.S.S.R., to Galatia, Illinois, and I hope the editors of the *New York Times* and the gentlemen over on Gorki Street don't mind my using their facilities for this cable.

You know I've been sitting here in the Hotel Metropole listening to "Silent Night" over the radio from the Voice of America. It's Christmas Eve in Moscow just as it is out there on the farm in Illinois. And I'll tell you a secret, son—the kind of a secret they don't often print in newspapers—there's not much difference where you are, whether it's New York or Moscow, you'll still find the spirit of Christmas.

Out there beyond my window in Sverdlovsk Square the snow is swirling down and the whole world looks white and Christmasy. And if you could talk Russian and could walk up to the first person you saw and ask him whether he believed in peace on earth, good will to men—guess what? He would say "Da," which is the Russian way of saying yes.

You know, Mike, that our government and the Russian government don't get along very well. They have lots of things they disagree about, but it would be pretty hard to find anyone here who didn't think that the policy laid down in Bethlehem nearly two thousand years ago was the best one for the world.

Mike, I'm talking pretty frankly to you in this cable, but these are things which I think a little boy out on an Illinois farm ought to know about.

That's a pretty important state—Illinois. It wasn't far from where you live that Lincoln used to practice law. They know about Lincoln over here, Mike, and they think that in our country we have forgotten him. You know better than I do that we haven't forgotten him, but it just goes to show how mixed up grown-up people can get sometimes.

This afternoon, Mike, I drove out in the country to a place called Leninsky Gorok. That's a country house where Lenin used to live and where he died. The folks over here think the same thing about Lenin that we think about Lincoln.

All the way out in the country I saw kids your age with their sleds. They were sliding on the fresh snow, and in the villages they had little skating rinks and were cutting figure eights just as fancy as you please.

Somehow, Mike, I have an idea that those kids and their parents would a lot rather concentrate on snow and sleds and skating and Christmas than some of the things we hear so much about these days—for instance, atom bombs and the third World War.

Of course, Mike, I could be wrong, but maybe it wouldn't be such a bad idea if the men that live in the White House and the

168

Kremlin took Christmas afternoon off and went out to the country and listened to what the folks sliding down the hills and skating on the ice had to say.

I think they'd find that in Russia just as in the United States on Christmas Day it would be pretty hard to discover anybody who wanted to start a third World War.

Merry, Merry Christmas to you, Mike, and to Steffie, too.

Dad

P.S. I hope you got the fifty bucks. What kind of a horse did you buy?

Dispatch to New York Times
December 31, 1950

On New Year's Eve the press triumphantly proclaims that in the second half of the twentieth century "all roads lead to communism."

XIII

Again, Leningrad

January 4, 1951
Letter to Major George Fielding Eliot

I have just seen your letter of December 18 regarding the Tanaka memorial. I must congratulate you on uncovering a clever Russo-Chinese propaganda twist.

The possibility of a distortion did not occur to me. . . .

Interesting as the distortion is, I should not let that divert your attention from the much more important fact which is that Japan did, actually, launch its effort against China first by acquiring Formosa, then Korea, then Manchuria, etc. This provides a parallel for use by the Communists in convincing their people that we are following the same road. . . .

January 7

Merry Christmas! This is Christmas. By the Orthodox calendar. I'm celebrating by taking down my Christmas tree—a poor moth-eaten thing it is by now.

Come look out my window. Fine white snow is silting down, and the square looks lovely in its white dress. It has snowed every day for a week or more. Looks wonderfully wintry and still not cold.

January 11

Today has been the loveliest of winter's days—a steel-blue sky, golden-bright sunshine, and dazzling white new snow from last night's blizzard.

The sun has just set and from my window the sky is azure and clear and the first yellow lights in the gathering gloom look like twinkling jewels. It is good to be alive on a day like this.

Dispatch to New York Times
January 11

President Truman's state of the nation message attracted considerably less attention than Senator Taft's criticism of American foreign policy.*

The *Literary Gazette* called Truman's message "hypocritical, pharisaical, and swindling. . . ."

January 12

It is ten minutes of three in the morning. A lovely hour. This has been one of many lovely nights I have had in Moscow. Just now I am alone in my room and the Rachmaninoff concerto is playing. To me there is nothing in the world like it. I can sit here —as so often I do—and it carries me off to the clouds, never alone. . . .

The first step in love is listening to the concerto. . . .

Dispatch to New York Times
January 12

In the next ten years the Soviet Union can be expected to double its steel production, which is now running at a rate of close to 30,000,000 tons annually.

Stalin said just after the war that Soviet steel production would be brought up to 60,000,000 tons by 1960. [This would be only one-third short of America's record steel production.]

January 17
Letter to Emanuel R. Freedman, New York Times

. . . On the matter of qualifications. Sometimes they are removed by the censors. Perhaps more often what you refer to is my use of a typical Russian phrase to describe a situation such as "intervention in Korea." If I preface that with "alleged" the whole

---

* On January 8, 1951, Senator Taft proposed that the United States withdraw from Korea and establish a defense perimeter based on Formosa and Japan.

phrase goes out—clip. I try to use "what the Soviet press describes as" or "as it is called here." But I hate to burden the cables with such awkward phrases.

Please have no hesitancy to insert qualifications where needed. Working through the tightest censorship my copy frequently *needs* editing. . . .

I have read the Harsch article* with closest interest.

I agree with the main thesis, i.e., that the Russians do not want general war (at this time) and that they feel peace works more to their advantage. As he notes, their doctrine contends that capitalism will inevitably fall of its own contradictions. They also believe in giving it a shove, from time to time. . . .

About Korea I think Harsh is partly right and partly wrong. I think he is right in believing the Russians have improvised policy there, just as they generally improvise a lot more than our deep thinkers seem to believe. I think Korea was originally conceived as a hit-and-run operation that would not produce American military counteraction. When we did react, a new improvisation took place—sort of a stringing along to see what might develop.

At that point they went to work on their propaganda in Asia, hitting the line that white Americans were bombing Asiatics. They began working on the Chinese, emphasizing the danger of intervention along the lines of what occurred in Russia in 1918–20.

I think Harsch is right again in saying that when we crossed the 38th parallel we handed the initiative back to them.

This I know for a fact. The Soviet propaganda by no means convinced Russians that the U.S.A. or South Korea started the war. When the attack came, Russians were shocked and scared stiff that it would mean an attack on Russia by the U.S.A. They knew damn well who started it. When no attack came, the Russians quieted down.

When I got back here in early September, I was told by Russians that apparently their government had judged the situation correctly because we were being driven out of Korea (as we were at that time).

The Inchon landing and sweep north by MacArthur came as a

* An analysis of Soviet policy by Joseph Harsch, the correspondent of the *Christian Science Monitor.*

shock to the Russians. As we moved north, I was asked by many Russians if we would stop at the 38th parallel. I naturally said I didn't know. They made no secret of their belief that if we did stop at the 38th parallel it would "mean that you were right and that we started it."

It is hard in New York to realize what a blow that would have been at the naïve faith which these people have in their government. It would have been a major moral defeat. And moral defeats—as they always have historically—mean a lot in Russia.

However, we missed that bet. Now the question of who started what and who is to blame is buried too deep ever to have much significance to the ordinary Russian.

Another point on which I agree in part with Harsch is his statement of the Soviet desire and need for peace. I am certain they need peace politically and economically. It is constantly overlooked in the U.S.A. that the place where the peace campaign and peace propaganda are strongest is right here in this country.

That does not mean that the Red Army will not march in Europe. But it does mean that it cannot march until the people here are convinced that the atom bomb is going to be dropped tomorrow morning.

I do not share Harsch's opinion that the regime fears the people or a popular uprising. It is true that the regime has a phobia about security. But, if it has such a fear of its people today, I can only say I think it very mistaken.

Regardless of what happened in the Ukraine during World War II (and I would not like to see us exaggerate that in expectation that it might repeat itself) or in the Crimea or among the small northern Caucasian tribes, the outstanding fact about the last war was the patriotic unity of the people. Victory in the war strengthened the regime, and the postwar era has strengthened its popular support.

You might suppose that Muscovites these days sit around and talk about nothing but fear and the threat of war. The fact is, the favorite topic of conversation is the possibility—they think of it as a certainty—of another big cut in consumers goods prices March 1. . . .

I accept Harsch's final conclusions with the deletion of one sentence which says: "The regime is hated at home." It is hated, of course, by some people. But not by many. Granted Russia is a prison—the prisoners have lived in it so long they no longer notice the bars, and they do notice the new linoleum on the floor and the better slumgullion. . . .

Dispatch to New York Times
January 17, 1951

The most important news published today—and for a considerable period of time—was the announcement that Generalissimo Stalin has agreed to stand as a candidate for the RSFSR Supreme Soviet from the Kirov election district of Leningrad.

Perhaps the importance of the announcement may not be immediately apparent. . . .*

Leningraders have great pride in their city as the cradle of the Bolshevik Revolution.

[Their civic pride probably has no equal in the Soviet Union. Moscow, of course, is the capital and in recent years has tended more and more to overshadow Leningrad. . . .

It is a truism to say that such a decision by Stalin is not made without the most serious thought and study. This means the decision evolves from a close examination of the whole political, social, and economic situation. There will be some who in their search for understanding of the decision will turn to the political side of the question, to questions of party organization. . . .]

January 17

I hope this year may bring peace on earth and good will to men. I have a feeling it may prove better in that respect than it might appear on the surface. But don't ask me to explain that logically. It is just a feeling.

Dispatch to New York Times
January 21

Generalissimo Stalin and other leaders of the Soviet Union tonight listened to the bitterest attack upon American imperialism which has been made from a Communist Party forum within recollection.

---

* It was not apparent then nor is it now fully apparent. Most probably it bore some relationship to the aftermath of the purge of the Leningrad Party of 1949–50.

Speaking on the Lenin anniversary at the Bolshoi Theater, Pyotr Pospelov declared that the Russian people will never forget that their blood is on American hands. He said that any new third world war was doomed to the same fate as befell Hitler's attack on Russia.

Pospelov had one theme—America and what he called its unswerving, imperialist, adventurist interventionist role in Russia. He traced this back to the days of the February Revolution in 1917 before the Bolsheviks came to power. . . .

January 23

I think one thing should be kept in mind. Not yet has the government here introduced a propaganda line which indicates that war is immediate or inevitable. The line still is that "Peace will conquer war."

The "vigilance" note was introduced immediately after the early December events (the Korean crisis). It represented a definite step toward increasing war preparedness. But the specific "vigilance" line has not been carried on. It was emphasized a few days and then dropped. My impression is that there were jitters in the Kremlin in early December, but they have now calmed down. . . .

I would judge that the short-term analysis of the Kremlin now is that war is a danger in 1951 but not a probability. . . .

Of course, the Pospelov speech the night before last marks a new advance in anti-American propaganda, and a very disturbing one. He has laid the basis for a "hate" campaign, broader and deeper than anything previously attempted.

His thesis, simply put, is that the Americans have always been No. 1 sons of bitches. They led the intervention, they built up Hitler and Germany. Now they are leading the pack against Russia themselves.

My impression is that this—like most of the hate propaganda (atrocity stories from Korea, the succession of ugly items about American conduct at home and around the world)—does not take well. The Soviet propagandists are up against reversing a long, deep, and historic feeling of good will and admiration toward America. . . . It resembles the difficulty the Russians had after the Nazi-Soviet pact in trying to sell the public on Hitler. . . .

It is pathetic, sometimes, when a Russian asks you why the

175

Americans did this or that, almost pleading that you tell him it isn't true. (Sometimes, unfortunately, the item is true.)

The Russians generally feel, why should the Americans dislike us? Why aren't the Americans friendly? They can't understand that their government's policies have created fear and hatred in the U.S.A.

I think the Party in advancing the intransigent Pospelov line has bit off somewhat more than it can digest—at least for quite a while. . . .

If I am correct, it means the government still has a long—a very long—way to go before it will be able to mobilize public support for offensive action against the U.S.A.

January 24, 1951

At long last a Christmas package from Minneapolis. Everything came through in fine shape. Over here we have had a mild winter. Only a couple of days down to zero. But since Christmas there has been lots and lots of snow—which I like although the girls who have to shovel it off the Moscow streets probably don't think it is such a blessing. But the city looks wonderful under a deep snow. I've been out in the country a couple of times, and I think it is at its best with the snow on the ground and little one-horse peasant sleighs jingling along the road and everywhere kids sliding on their sleds or skating on the village ponds. Real old-fashioned country scenes. Something like New England a century ago—except of course the *izbas* hardly look like trim New England houses.

February 1

If you were to ask a person in Moscow what new opera he has heard lately, the answer is likely to be *From the Depths of the Heart,* which had its première recently at the Bolshoi.

If you ask him what new play he has seen, he is just as likely to say *From the Depths of the Heart*—now being put on at two Moscow theaters. And, if you ask him what novel he has lately read, the answer might also be *From the Depths of the Heart.*

All kinds of performances are popular in Moscow this winter of 1951, but *From the Depths of the Heart* is the most popular. It isn't hard to see why. Maltzev is discussing just those problems of social adjustment to postwar life which millions of Russians have had to face—problems of personal daily life and basic morality and the meaning of human existence. . . .

February 7

I think it would be perfectly practical for Janet to come over next year. She has had a lot of negative advice on the subject. But there will be no war—that is what is all important.

February 8

Seldom has a more loathsome and revolting photo display been published than that in the *Literary Gazette* under the caption "American murderers in Korea and at home." It resembles Nazi wartime bestiality and is designed to evoke hatred of America. . . .

February 14

I am in Leningrad on a sentimental mission. I am seeing many things, but what I really came for was to follow the trail of Zhelyabov and the young people who assassinated Alexander II. I found the place, No. 14 Malaya Sadovaya, where they set up the cheese shop and put the mine under the emperor's route. It is a bakery now. Next door on one side is a militia station and on the other a photo shop. There is no sign or placard to indicate what happened here—just half a block from the busy Nevsky. . . .*

Dispatch to New York Times
February 16

Generalissimo Stalin tonight said that war is not inevitable, "at least for the present." But he said the United Nations is becoming a weapon of aggressive war. It was his first statement on the international situation in twenty-five months. It was made in reply to questions by *Pravda*. . . .

He left no doubt that the world situation has undergone substantial deterioration and that the threat of war has grown more dangerous since his last statement in January, 1949. . . .

February 17

We must face a new contingency—the possibility that a further reduction of the dollar-ruble rate will be made shortly. I sincere-

---

* On March 1, 1881, Alexander II was assassinated in St. Petersburg by members of the Narodnaya Volya, headed by Andrei Zhelyabov.

177

ly trust that the Russians will not again tamper with it, but the town is full of rumors that a new adjustment, probably to something like the old czarist rate of 51 cents to the dollar, is contemplated.

Dispatch to New York Times
February 17, 1951

Generalissimo Stalin's statement has opened an intensive campaign by the Soviet calling on the peoples of Western countries over the heads of their governments for a change in basic foreign policy. . . .

His statement does not concern itself with such matters as direct conversations, for instance, with President Truman. In effect Stalin writes off the United Nations as an instrument of American policy. . . .

It is noted that he has not excluded the possibility of peaceful settlement of Korea. . . .

Another event which was foreshadowed plainly by Stalin was continued reduction of retail prices.

Dispatch to New York Times
Leningrad, February 18

This week on the hoardings of Leningrad has appeared a new poster entitled "We" and "They."

The poster "We" pictures Soviet engineers with blueprints of new power projects and bears the legend: "We—are turning deserts into flowering country."

The poster "They" shows war and bombs ravaging the countryside and says: "They—are turning towns and villages into deserts."

It is a dramatic illustration of the dichotomy which in the Soviet view exists between East and West.

I saw Leningrad first seven years ago this month. The iron siege ring had just been broken.* The city's architects and builders displayed their plans for conquering the devastation left by the Germans.

* Leningrad was under seige for 872 days. The siege was formally lifted on January 27, 1944, after an eight-day offensive.

178

Today Leningrad presents a lively and majestic appearance. Streets are thronged with traffic. Stores are thronged with shoppers. The famous Nevsky Prospekt looks brighter and fresher. Every building on the street has been repainted. The Mariinsky theater sparkles with fresh gilt and robin's egg blue. . . .

The biggest construction project under way is the Leningrad subway system. No date for completion has been announced. . . .

Watching hundreds of youngsters with their skates and skis sliding across the River Neva a stone's throw from the Winter Palace, mingling with the thousands jamming the galleries of the Hermitage on a sunny winter's afternoon, listening to the thunderous applause of the young balletomanes in the upper galleries of the Mariinsky, or sitting amid the dancing and drinking in one of the Leningrad cafés, the grim war days seem like a nightmare of another world. . . .

Dispatch to New York Times
Peterhof, February 18

It is seven years almost to the day since I last tapped out the date line "Peterhof." That was in February, 1944. The Nazi siege of Leningrad had just been broken, and the Red Army had just recaptured the famous palaces of Peter the Great in this Baltic seashore town, twenty-five miles east of Leningrad.

It was bitter cold that February day. Bodies of fallen Germans lay frozen and dusted with snow in the fields. Youngsters with dog teams probed the highway shoulders for mines and occasionally touched one off with a roar and pillar of black smoke.

That day Peterhof lay gaunt and shattered—possibly the greatest single monument to Nazi vandalism on Russian soil.

On that day the great palace—more than three-hundred yards long—was a gaunt shell with only the walls and chimneys remaining. Dugouts and gun emplacements spattered the snow-swept lawns. The Cascade was a frozen Niagara from burst and broken pipes.

Today under the February snow Peterhof presents a striking contrast. The palace remains a gaunt façade surrounded by wooden paling. But all forty or fifty statues, including the Samson, are back in place, sparkling nakedly in their bright gilt against white snowdrifts. . . .

179

February 19, 1951

There have been a few changes in the press corps lately, but the total is about the same. Cyril Ray, of the *Sunday Times* of London, came in on a trade for a Russian correspondent's visa to London. Natalie Rene has gone out of business. She never has gotten over that very bad accident in which she was knocked down by a truck in the Arbat a year and a half ago. She quit work on January 1 and has been in bed ever since. Probably she will have to spend at least a year in a sanatorium. I miss her. She knew everything about the Bolshoi because of her speciality in ballet. A curious woman and an interesting one.

A couple of items of ballet gossip. Ulanova fell during a ballet in January or late December and injured herself badly. One report is that she broke her leg. She hasn't danced since and isn't expected back this season.

Another item. About Lepeshinskaya. They were making a special documentary of the Bolshoi for use in connection with the 175th anniversary next month. Lepy discovered they had about two hundred feet of Semyonova and only one hundred feet of her. She protested that this wasn't fair. The movie people said nothing could be done about it. Finally they came back and took some more footage—enough to even things up—and Lepy footed the bill of upward of 20,000 rubles. Ballerinas don't differ much, wherever they are and even if they are leading Party members.

In Leningrad I talked to about twenty Russians—conversations ranging from a few minutes up to all evening long in two instances. In no case—except at the Hotel Astoria—was I taken for an American. I was recognized as a foreigner, to be sure. But Russians don't expect to meet Americans. I was taken for a Balt, a Pole, a German—most frequently for a Balt. In no case when the Russians discovered that I was an American did it evoke any antagonism, resentment, or rudeness. On the contrary, the usual reaction was one of amazement, surprise, and pleasure.

In not one of these conversations was I asked a single question about foreign policy, American policy, prospects of war, or anything bearing on the international situation.

I spent one evening talking to a girl on the Red Arrow. She didn't even inquire about my nationality, and when I mentioned that I was an American after about an hour and a half of small talk, mostly about her work and about Leningrad (she was a Leningrader), she merely said, "That's interesting," but offered no further comment. I don't believe these people steered away from the question of war out of a feeling of tact. My impression was that the idea of war is not very likely in their minds—certainly not so much as questions of better living, more consumers goods, possibility of a price cut March 1 (they all talked about that!), sports, theater, etc.

The questions I got about the U.S.A. were about the movies (No. 1 topic by far—they wanted to know what has happened to Deanna Durbin, Bing Crosby, Shirley Temple, and Charlie Chaplin), about American skyscrapers, American literature—what were our new novels, new plays.

Why wasn't the war question uppermost? I think the No. 1 reason is Soviet domestic propaganda. It shifted into new ground with the Pospelov address in January, of all-out vilification of America going way back to the days of the Indians. But the new line hasn't had time to have much effect, and I doubt if it will—except possibly among school children and the komsomols, etc.

There are two reasons for this. First, the inhibiting effect of thirty years of propaganda. It is like the radio commercials. After a time you don't hear them any more. The second reason is they have to start from scratch on the anti-American line. The U.S.A. has never done anything to the Russians. The Russians know this. Their reaction is not one of hatred—it is one of questioning —can this really be true, how could we really do this, etc. People just don't believe it.

The third reason is that in their thirty-three years of Revolution the people have known only two easy times. The first was in the late thirties. The second is now. It is silly for us to blind ourselves to the fact that bad as is the standard of Russian living by our standards—they have never had it so good here. In over-all terms. True, in '39 prices were lower. But wages today are considerably higher even if the worker has to work harder. (God knows he does not work hard by our standards. . . .)

The Russian is enjoying this. Why shouldn't he? He sees every sign that there is more of this pie to come. Note Stalin's insistence on the policy of lowering prices being continued. Everyone takes that to mean a new cut March 1. Uncle Joe has played hell with retail trade for the next ten days. No one will buy anything till March 1 has come.

I actually feel some embarrassment in reporting the state of Russian public opinion because people in America seem to resent the fact that Moscow isn't all stirred up.

One story comes to mind. The Hotel Astoria restaurant has a damn good jazz band. The best I've heard in Russia. At least 80 per cent of its music is American jazz, some of it fairly recent. The place is crowded with youngsters—where they get the money I don't know. It isn't cheap. The kids favor long, shaggy haircuts, zoot-suit jackets reaching almost to the knee, and pleated pockets. They don't have dog chains dangling from their pockets, but they dance in the best humped-over style of St. Germain des Près or the jive spots of New York. Poor Zhdanov. He must be turning over in his Kremlin urn at the decadent bourgeois goings-on in his old bailiwick.

Dispatch to New York Times
February 21, 1951

A careful study of Generalissimo Stalin's remarks on the military situation in Korea last week has led some diplomats to advance some interesting suggestions. . . .

They take Stalin's words to indicate that in his opinion the door has by no means been finally shut on the possibility of peaceful settlement of the Korean conflict. . . .

[Noting Stalin's words about Anglo-American generalship in Korea, it appeared to some that Stalin had said in effect that there could be no real question of considering a defeat in Korea as a stain upon the military record of even the most brilliant officer since the controlling factors were political and psychological rather than military.

Thus it could be argued that regardless of the ebb and flow of battle results MacArthur's military reputation, for example, should not be regarded as tarnished if diplomats step in and work out a solution of the conflict. . . .]

February 22

Some more about Stalin's answers to *Pravda*. An important bit of background is the toast which Molotov offered at the Chinese embassy reception, here at the Metropole, on the anniversary of the Soviet-Chinese treaty. His toast was: "To the Chinese and Soviet Armies—to Mao Tse-tung and Chu Teh!"

This came after the Chinese ambassador had made a conventional, rather flowery speech about Sino-Russian leaders with no mention of Korea. The blunt and enigmatic remarks of Molotov have stirred lots of speculation. The Chinese invited to the reception all countries with which they have complete diplomatic relations—but not the British, for example, or Pakistan. The Israelis, Swedes, Finns, etc., were there.

I don't offer any interpretation of Molotov. Maybe his purpose was to make people wonder; maybe, in an oblique way, to call attention to the military force behind the alliance.

But Molotov provided the psychological atmosphere into which Stalin introduced his letter. . . .

The prevailing interpretation has been to fit the letter into a theory that the Russians are concerned about Western defense plans and, thus, more amenable to reason. I do not get this feeling. My dominant feeling is that the letter is designed to provide a propaganda framework for the failure of negotiations.

I don't find any great significance in the passage on the UN. I don't think the Soviet Union will give up its UN membership. . . .

Most interesting were his remarks about the American generals. They seems to be directed at MacArthur. He is saying that MacArthur's military honor is not at stake in achieving a victory on the field of arms in Korea. It is somewhat parallel to Eisenhower's assurance to the Germans that their military honor was not compromised in the war—that they were good soldiers (some of them) and that it was the Nazis who were bad. . . .

For the last two weeks my file hardly shows a censor's pencil. I even managed to slip through the fact that they aren't showing their Picassos any more, although they killed my message that the Museum of Western Art has been closed since the start of the war. I understand the collection of Western art is now in the Tretyakov in several special galleries which are occasionally shown to distinguished visitors on special request.

No one here shares the concern which seems to be rising in the West about a possible attack on Yugoslavia this spring. . . .

Around Moscow the most impressive thing is the activity of Khrushchev. I don't believe the Party has ever had so active a local leader. Hardly a week goes by without his addressing some local group. It is one pep talk after another. Only a few of these talks get reported in the papers. And those which are reported are not especially interesting. He is spending much time with the kolkhozes. They are trying to make the consolidations in the Moscow *raion* a model for the country. It is a good place for such activity as the average Co-op in the Moscow *raion* was decidedly small. But it is easy to imagine the bugs in such a program. He spends a lot of time with the Moscow builders. The building program is so large and unwieldy and in the hands of so many competing organizations that all kinds of troubles develop from outright graft to lush cost-plus construction setups.

Probably the most interesting Party development was Stalin's decision to run in the Kirov district of Leningrad. One motive I had in going to Leningrad last week was to see if I could figure out why he did that.

There are two possible interpretations. The first, and the one I favor, is that it is a move designed to tie Leningrad closer to Moscow and the central Party apparatus. Or, to put it a bit differently, to give Leningrad more of a sense of participation in the national picture.

Leningrad has been neglected in the postwar situation. They continue to grab off one academy or institution after another and transfer them to Moscow. They lit into Leningrad's intellectuals (Zhdanov). They are keeping its population down. The program for beautification of Leningrad is peanuts.

In other words, Leningrad is treated by the Center with a good deal of prejudice. On the other hand, Leningrad is damned important. It is the home of the country's best machine plants. Its best electrical works—in fact practically all high-quality precision manufacture—is in Leningrad. It continues to be the home of the most brilliant intellectuals—those who are not siphoned off to Moscow.

There is a good deal of evidence—little things, some of them intangibles, others negative items—to suggest that Leningrad has been in something like a sulking mood. Certainly Leningrad is well aware of what has been going on.

So, I should not be surprised if Joe were saying to Leningrad in effect—Look, maybe the bureaucrats have forgotten you, but your Old Uncle Joe remembers. I, personally, will represent you.

So, perhaps, the move was designed to pep up Leningrad and

to try to patch up what I really think is a pretty serious underlying antipathy between Leningrad and the Center.

If that is its purpose, I doubt it has succeeded. I talked to a
good many Leningraders and mentioned the election and Stalin's
candidacy. None of them seemed much interested. Their faces
didn't light up the way Muscovite faces light up (they really do)
when they talk about the Great White Father. The Leningraders
with their greater sophistication didn't indicate any emotion one
way or another.

I noticed that Leningrad was not plastered with Stalin pictures the way Moscow is at all times.

There were plenty of pictures of Kirov and of Zhdanov—more
than of anyone else. And it is interesting that they are both dead.

The other theory about Stalin's running in Leningrad is that
it is a rebuke to the local Moscow Party organization and, perhaps, to the Stalin district group for falling down on production
quotas or something of the kind.

I don't believe that is so.

It may be that the move has some connection with the delicate
balancing act going on inside the Politburo these days.

I would not pretend to suggest what the connection might be.
But if the theory I advanced last year has any validity—that
Khrushchev came into Moscow rather to represent the Molotov-
Voroshilov group as opposed to the Malenkov group—the transfer of Stalin's candidacy out of Khrushchev's area into a city
which probably fell into Malenkov's pocket when Zhdanov died
may have some bearing on these maneuvers.*

February 26, 1951

We have had a mild and decent winter with only occasional
days under zero. The worst has been a little more than 20° below.
That was when I was in Leningrad. I was out walking one day
and couldn't figure out why my face got so cold. Nearly froze.
Finally had to hop a bus and go back to the hotel. It wasn't until
the next day that I found out how cold it was.

* At the time this was written, I had no idea of the "Leningrad affair" or
more than the most cloudy impression that there had been a bloody purge
of the Leningrad Party apparatus in 1949–50.

XIV

Another Spring

Dispatch to New York Times
March 7, 1951

The 1951 state budget was presented in the Supreme Soviet tonight in the presence of Stalin and the Politburo, including Molotov, Malenkov, Beriya, Voroshilov, Mikoyan, Bulganin, Khrushchev, Andreyev, Kosygin, Shvernik, and Kaganovich. . . .

Stalin was among the last to enter. He appeared very fit and very trim. He wore a smartly tailored tunic of deep maroon or russet shade which was new to foreign eyes. His color was good and his steel gray hair added to his brisk appearance. . . .

Dispatch Killed by Censor
March 11

The Supreme Soviet today approved Russia's 1951 budget including an estimate of 96 billion rubles for the armed forces. . . . The budget provides a 51.3 per cent increase for the Soviet navy and a 15.6 increase for the army and air force. . . . No details of the large Soviet naval building program were provided. . . .

Dispatch Killed by Censor
March 12

At the bottom of the column on the back page of *Pravda* today appeared a brief, black-bordered notice announcing the death yesterday of Olga Evgeyevna Alliluyeva.

Madame Alliluyeva was the widow of the distinguished early Bolshevik revolutionary, Sergei Ya. Alliluyev, who was associated with Stalin in the days of Caucasian revolutionary activity. It was in Alliluyev's house in Petrograd that Lenin first took shelter in the stormy days of July, 1917. Stalin lived in the same house.

Madame Alliluyeva was the mother of Nadezhda Alliluyeva who in 1919 was married to Stalin, dying suddenly in 1932. . . .

March 16

My fears about a change in the ruble-dollar rate were not confirmed March 1, and we probably are safe on that score for another year. But it is a virtual certainty that there will eventually be further revaluation of the ruble, presumably restoring the old czarist two-to-the-dollar rate.

Dispatch to New York Times
March 20

The foundations for a new structural organization of Soviet agriculture based on large farming units, centering around "agrogorods," have been substantially laid in the past year.

In 1951 it should provide substantial gains in crop and livestock yields. . . .

Figures thus far published indicate there has been a reduction of nearly one-fifth in the approximately 254,000 collective farms which existed at the beginning of 1950. . . .

This year great steps are planned toward physical consolidation of smaller peasant villages into new large units which are already being called agrogorods or agrocities, although the name "Kolkhozny Poselok" or "collective farm settlement" has been suggested as a more appropriate designation by Politburo member Nikita Khrushchev, who personally has been directing the amalgamation.

In the Moscow oblast 6,029 collective farms existed at the beginning of 1950. The total now is 1,541. . . .

March 25

We finally carried a story on the project for the integration of the collective farms. There were a couple of points out of focus. There hasn't been any censorship on that story, but there would be if I went into the whole thing.

I don't think the plan will reduce farm production this year—
it probably didn't last year, although some crops were below
plan. But it will slow down expansion of production for a couple
of years.

They are working very carefully and cautiously, avoiding the
harsh methods and bad reactions of the collectivization days. But
local frictions are inevitable. They are trying to attach weak
farms where possible to big strong ones. This increases the earnings of farmers from the weak farms—winning their support. But
it dilutes the earnings of the workers on the big successful farm.

So far as peasant land plots are concerned, they are not eliminating them. I am sure they want to eliminate them and eventually will. But that is a long way in the future.

As the peasants are moved into new agrogorods the idea is to
give them new plots—a small plot surrounding the new cottage
and the remainder in a field set aside for all the peasants. This
will enable them to use mechanical cultivation on the bulk of the
peasant acreage.

Obviously, the next step will be to incorporate the big peasant
acreage into the collective, leaving him just a small garden at
his cottage.

All of this will take considerable time. Except for a few
Ukraine regions, they have hardly gotten started on building
new towns, and the job is envisaged as requiring a minimum of
five years, and ten is a more likely figure. One other area where a
good deal of consolidation of villages has taken place is the
Baltic, where they have been moving farmers from individual
houses and creating villages in the Russian style.

Integration of the collectives is important and a big step toward wiping out the class difference between the peasant and the
proletariat and toward "industrializing" agriculture.

They are also working hard at the livestock position. This is
the weakest spot.

I have been pressing the press department for a trip to Siberia.
I want to go all the way to Baikal. That would provide some
good copy and revive my flagging spirits. I'd like to get in a good
bit of travel this year—Georgia, the Volga to Astrakhan, some
Ukraine points, and possibly a couple of Ural towns that are
open. . . .

I saw Stalin twice at the Supreme Soviet sessions. Of course, we sit so far back that we don't get the best possible look, but my impression was that he had aged somewhat since a year ago. He dawdled about sitting down in the fussy way of an old man. At the first session he seemed fidgety—crossed and recrossed his arms and drummed his fingers. Beriya, as usual, spent his time gabbing and apparently storytelling. Every time I've seen him he gives the appearance of being the life of the Party.

Spring is coming here—we have had three heavy, wet snowfalls in the last week and today a miserable all-day drizzle. . . . I had a "near miss" on the death of Mme Alliluyeva. When I saw the tiny death notice in *Pravda*, I deduced that she would be buried out at Novo Devechye in the family plot with her husband and Nadezhda. So Tom Whitney and I hotfooted out and found they had posted a notice that the cemetery was closed for the day. So we went outside and followed the wall around. Presently, we ran into a gate which, by chance, was open. We popped in and found ourselves right at the plot where a bunch of husky gravediggers were at work. We stood watching the scene, and an old militiaman came up. He inspected us carefully, uncertain whether to question us or not. I could see the indecision in his eyes. Finally, he decided that it was the better part of prudence to say nothing since obviously only someone important would come to the graveside.

This was about noon. I went back a little before 3:00, hoping to catch a glimpse of the cortege. However, all was quiet. I decided the funeral would not be until tomorrow. That was a fatal mistake. The next day I found Madame's grave heaped high with flowers.

This initiative went for nothing. My story was killed *in toto* by the censor.

March 29, 1951

Russia certainly has nothing on Minnesota when it comes to snow and cold. A few days ago I saw in the *Times* a picture of the latest Minnesota blizzard—tunnels with twelve-foot drifts in the main streets. There has been nothing like that here. We have had a fine snowy winter with no blizzards and no real cold. One time it went down to about twenty below. Now it looks like spring.

I drove out into the country the day before yesterday. The ditches beside the road were full to brimming with run-off water.

On lines in front of every cottage were all the winter clothes, getting their first spring airing. The birches were beginning to green, and in the open patches of field you could see the green clover.

My Siberian trip is still in the works but probably won't come through for a while. Meantime, I hope to go down to Georgia.

I haven't changed my views about the immediate prospects on the international scene. It seems that we will get through another year without much change. But the long-term factors don't look good.

Dispatch to New York Times
March 30, 1951

Russia may achieve an oil production of 60,000,000 tons a year, substantially ahead of the target year of 1960 fixed by Generalissimo Stalin.

[Last year about one-quarter of Soviet oil production came from the Bashkir fields—about 9,000,000 tons. . . .]

Dispatch to New York Times
Klin, April 3

In a driveway outside a big maroon house on the outskirts of Klin two chubby youngsters were playing. In the past few days of the quick Russian spring the snow has almost disappeared, and the children walked gingerly to keep the mud off their shoes.

"Whose house is that?" a stranger asked them.

"That's grandpa's house," the older lad replied.

Actually, the sign on the gate reads simply: P. I. Tchaikovsky—reception on Mondays and Thursdays from 3:00 to 5:00. Nobody home. Please Don't Ring.

To be accurate it is not really "grandpa's house." Tchaikovsky died a bachelor, and three-year-old Lev and five-year-old Georgi Davydov are the great-great-nephews of the composer. But, while Tchaikovsky's home is now a museum, it is still grandpa's house to the small boys who live on the grounds with their mother who is a member of the museum staff. . . .

April 5

The press did not publish Speaker Rayburn's assertion that non-Chinese troops are massing in Manchuria and that there is "gravest danger of a new war."

My check did not show any diplomat who felt a new military crisis was arising in the Far East. There does not appear to be any diplomatic information to bear out Rayburn's statement. . . .

Moscow has seldom presented a more quiet and peaceful aspect. Winter came to a sudden end just a week ago, and the city has been basking in bright sunshine and temperatures in the sixties and even seventies in sunny corners.

For the next few weeks peasants all over Russia will be busy with the spring planting. The maximum of Russian man- and woman-power is needed. It's not exactly a convenient season so far as this country is concerned for any project that would divert manpower away from this essential task. . . .

Dispatch to New York Times
April 7

An official Tass-agency statement declares there are no Soviet troops in Manchuria. This raises a question as to whether Soviet troops have been withdrawn from Port Arthur ahead of time. . . . It was possible the statement referred only to such "concentrations" as had been mentioned by Rayburn. . . .

Dispatch to New York Times
April 11

Western diplomats said today that General MacArthur's dismissal may create "the political and psychological preconditions" for settlement of the Korean hostilities. . . . If, as some Moscow observers have contended for some time, the Chinese would be receptive to a well-conceived plan for ending the Korean war, it seems that the time has come for testing out these possibilities. . . .

Dispatch to New York Times
April 13

Generalissimo Stalin tonight attended the opening of the Supreme Soviet of the Russian Republic—his fourth public appearance within a month. . . .

He looked well and vigorous. He stayed in his aisle seat for exactly an hour and a half. During much of the session he read papers and documents, making rapid notations as he worked. . . . He exchanged batches of documents with Malenkov and conversed with him several times. . . . At other times Beriya and Malenkov engaged in vigorous discussion. . . .

191

April 15, 1951

We have had such wonderful spring weather that I have been playing hookey and going for long walks in the country or have been sitting in the parks in the afternoon, soaking up the sunshine. God, how good it is to get the sun back again! I am going to Georgia at the end of this week. Still haven't gotten out to Siberia. Probably that will be next month.

Dispatch to New York Times
April 16

Sergei Prokofiev, one of the great geniuses of Russia, celebrates on April 23 his sixtieth birthday and forty-odd years of creative work.

The event which the musical world is now awaiting with impatience is Prokofiev's new ballet, *The Stone Flower*. It was first mentioned for possible production in the 1950 season. . . .*

Dispatch to New York Times
April 17

Soviet industry has laid a broad foundation for the greatest industrial expansion in Russian history during the new five-year plan. The plan will be presented to the Supreme Soviet, probably in June.

[The new plan will take Russia at least two-thirds of the way toward fulfilment of Stalin's objectives of 60,000,000 tons of steel, 500,000,000 tons of coal, 500,000,000 tons of pig iron, and 60,000,000 tons of oil annually by 1960. . . .]

Dispatch to New York Times
April 19

The Soviet opera of collective farm life, *From the Depths of the Heart,* was condemned today by *Pravda* as a "serious failure."

The composer, Herman Zhukovsky, the librettists, A. Bamet and A. Kovalenkov, the Bolshoi Theater direction, the Union of Soviet Composers, and the Committee on Art were sharply criticized.

Pravda's critique was contained in a half-page unsigned article published just a fortnight after the production had been wit-

* It did not have its première until 1954.

nessed by Generalissimo Stalin and other members of the Polit-buro.

Stalin attended the performance April 5. This is the second Soviet opera in recent years to attract sharp official criticism. The other production was Vano Muradeli's *Great Friendship*, presented in autumn, 1947. After Stalin viewed it, *Great Friendship* was condemned as a tasteless example of formalism and Western bourgeois concepts. This was followed by a critical re-examination of the work of such figures as Shostakovich, Prokofiev, and Khatchaturyan. . . .

April 20

The ancient Hebrew festival of Passover was celebrated to-night in Moscow's crowded central synagogue. At sundown the voice of the famous Cantor Barkan sounded sonorously in the solemn chants commemorating the exodus of Jews from Egypt. . . .

The synagogue was filled. Later in the evening, in thousands of Moscow orthodox Jewish homes, the feast of unleavened bread was eaten.

Dispatch to New York Times
April 25

Two important figures in the world of music and art were dis-missed today as a consequence of the roles they played in the pro-duction of the opera *From the Depths of the Heart*.

The men were P. I. Lebedev, chairman of the All-Union Com-mittee on Arts, and Alexandr V. Solodovnikov, director of the Bolshoi Theater. Lebedev was replaced by N. N. Bespavlov, Solo-dovnikov by A. I. Anisimov.

[The dismissals removed from leading roles in Soviet artistic life two men who came to the fore three years ago at the time of the Communist Party's criticism of the Bolshoi Theater for the production of the opera *Great Friendship*, by Vano Muradeli.

At that time Solodovnikov replaced Leontiev as director of the Bolshoi when Leontiev suffered a heart attack and died, shortly after Stalin and members of the government witnessed his production of *Great Friendship*.

It is expected that the Union of Composers will conduct an ex-tensive discussion of *Pravda*'s condemnation of *From the Depths of the Heart*. It seemed likely that there would be other changes in the world of music and art.]

Dispatch to New York Times
April 28, 1951

Moscow tonight starts one of the biggest and most pleasant holidays of recent years due to the fortuitous conjugation of the Orthodox Easter celebration with the Soviet May Day holiday.

Crowds thronged the shops and promenaded in hot April sunshine. The temperature was in the seventies. The whole city was alive with red bunting and portraits of Lenin, Stalin, and members of the Politburo.

The Orthodox Easter ceremony reaches a climax at midnight tonight. . . .

Dispatch to New York Times
Zagorsk, April 29

The iron bells of Troitski monastery today pealed out the eternal tidings of Christ's resurrection to thousands of believers.

The ceremonial was little changed from that observed in what was then a remote and desolate Russian forest by the founder of Troitski, Saint Sergius Radonezhsky in 1350. . . .

The most ancient cathedral, Troitski Sobor, was built seventy years before Columbus discovered America, and here in a magnificent silver catafalque rest the bones of Sergius himself. . . .

In the lavishly decorated Trapezhaya chapel hundreds of believers formed double lines waiting for priests to bless their Easter cakes—kulich and paskha—and their brightly colored Easter eggs.

Presently a dark-bearded young priest carrying a golden cross and holy water passed down the line, blessing the cakes, while an acolyte with a great wicker basket accompanied him to receive the offerings of the believers. . . .

As the midnight hour approached, the great doors of Uspensky cathedral swung open, and a procession of priests carrying glittering icons, sacred church banners, flambeaus, and swinging censers made its way through the ranks of the believers whose candles glistened like fireflies. . . .

May 8
Letter to U. P. Frantzev, Press Department

I am distressed and bewildered to learn that Mr. Simonov has departed for Tbilisi without word to me that plans for our trip had been changed. . . .

On May 3 I spoke with Mr. Simonov by telephone to confirm the train accommodations, and we agreed that we would leave May 10 by soft car on the 3:55 P.M. train for Tbilisi.

Now, with no word, notice, or suggestion to me, it would appear that these detailed arrangements have simply been abandoned, and Mr. Simonov has gone south and left me to go ahead by myself. . . .

In discussion with Mr. Simonov of the places we would visit, he mentioned the following: Tbilisi, Gori, Mtskhet, and Tsinindali. Today I received my Soviet passport and found that Tsinindali had been omitted.

I asked Mr. Khlopikov about this and he said OVIR would be able to advise me why Tsinindali had not been included. I telephoned OVIR and was told: "We will not validate the document for Tsinindali." They referred me back to your department for an explanation.

In all frankness, I regard this action by OVIR as rude and discourteous in the extreme.

May 10

I am scurrying around to get away for Tbilisi this afternoon. But I want to make a few brief notations. . . .

With regard to the Andreyev rumors—I think there is nothing to them. He appeared with the Politburo both at the Supreme Soviet meeting in March and at the RSFSR meeting in April. He was not on the reviewing stand on May 1, being the only Politburo member absent. But I do not regard that as significant. He often is absent, presumably due to poor health. It may be true, however, that he is somewhat in the doghouse since his line on agriculture was rejected and Khrushchev took over most of his agricultural functions.

It is my impression that some of Schwartz's pieces on the farm program have given the indication of more urgency and controversy than actually is occurring. It seems to me they are handling this program with kid gloves, moving slowly and cautiously and taking precautions not to stir up the sort of hornet's nest they had on collectivization.

Except for the Ukraine the "consolidations" are almost entirely paper. I draw this impression in part from the Moscow *raion*. This *raion* under Khrushchev is supposed to be a model for the whole country. Yet, I have driven out on each of the seven highways we are allowed to go on, and I have also driven to Klin and Zagorsk in the last month or so. In none of the villages is there the slightest evidence of any physical consolidation.

Another point: while the general line for consolidation is hard and fast, the methods of achieving it are being kept deliberately flexible. I think this is the way to interpret *Pravda*'s action in labeling Khrushchev's article "for discussion" and the action of the Georgia CP.*

* Actually, it soon became apparent that there was a sharp dispute within the Politburo on agricultural policy. Andreyev was displaced by Khrushchev as chief farm adviser. Then, the Khrushchev proposals were disavowed by *Pravda* and attacked by the Georgian and Azerbaijan Communist secretaries, probably at the instigation of Beriya and, perhaps, Malenkov. For months thereafter no Khrushchev speeches were published.

XV

Stalin's Georgia

Dispatch to New York Times
Rostov-on-Don, May 12, 1951

A 1,400-kilometer journey across Russia's breadbasket reveals that the Soviet is due to harvest a bumper crop if spring's indications are fulfilled.

Never have the rich, black Ukrainian fields looked more fertile with lush fields of winter wheat, gleaming green across the undulating steppes. . . .

To a native Midwesterner the trip is reminiscent of one across Indiana, Illinois, and Iowa. . . .

May 17

Here at Mtskhet, one of the most ancient towns in Georgia, there's a yellow statue of Lenin and Stalin, seated side by side, which stands on the banks of the Kura River. The streets are cobblestoned and the houses, brick and plaster. Some have red tile roofs. The mountains form a backdrop. Around the ancient cathedral, swallows soar toward the blue sky.

Some kind of yellow flowers, fragrant white flowering tobacco, and red poppies grow beside the eleventh-century bell tower. There is a little Christlike figure of a child in a niche in the wall. The scent of mimosa is heavy in the air. An old attendant comes out in black shawl and scarf. And then a funeral cortege . . . the women in black, weeping. Against another wall there is a picture of Stalin and the slogan—Forward to the Victory of Communism.

May 18, 1951

At Gori I saw Stalin's report card for the school year 1894–95. He got all fives—the highest grade—in writing, Russian, history, math, and Georgian language. He didn't take Latin. A photograph of him taken in 1892 shows him a spirited, alert youngster, considerably younger and smaller than his classmates. . . .

Stalin was born and lived in a one-room house, partly of wood and partly of plaster. It has been surrounded by an ornate roof. But the room is still sparsely furnished. I wrote down the inventory: a wooden three-quarter-length bed with three bolsters, an oriental rug, a wooden stool, a small chest covered with a *montarki,* or Georgian scarf, three wooden stools, a wooden table with a linen cloth, two cupboards, a brass samovar, a small mirror, a kerosene lamp, a glass, an earthen pitcher called a *toki* and a colored towel. . . . Next door to the Stalin museum there is a house exactly like that in which Stalin lived. There people are still living in the same poverty. . . .

May 20

I called on the eighty-five-year-old patriarch, Kalistrat Tsinsadtze, of the Georgian Orthodox church, in his second-story apartment on the grounds of the Zion cathedral in Tbilisi which since the seventh century has been the principal Georgian church. . . .

He poured out glasses of Georgian brandy and set out a feast for me—heaping mounds of spring strawberries, as big as plums, dishes of candies, plums, preserved grapes, pickled melon rind, all kinds of candies and cakes. . . .

I asked him whether he had ever met Stalin. He chuckled and said: "Yes, indeed. I met Comrade Stalin on two occasions, but it was many years ago. It was when he was a student in the seminary here in Tbilisi. At that time I was a school examiner and it was my duty to examine the students on their progress. On two occasions Stalin appeared before me—once for an examination in the Russian language and once in Russian history."

The patriarch said Stalin was a very bright student. "I must admit," he said with a twinkle in his eye, "that in those times I never could have guessed what the future would bring."

The patriarch was very proud of his new ZIM car. It is the first one in Tbilisi.

Dispatch to New York Times
Tbilisi, May 23

Georgi Natizov, a carpenter, rested his gnarled hands on the green baize of the director's table in the Tbilisi silk factory and said: "Do I remember Stalin? Of course I do."

"I remember him very well," Natizov said. "I was just a young worker in those days. I got forty kopecks for a twelve-hour day. Stalin used to come out here—to this very building. He would talk to us. ['Why do you work twelve hours? Eight hours is long enough. Forty kopecks a day isn't a living wage. You must receive more.' He'd talk to us like that."]

Dispatch to New York Times
Ateni, May 24

In the cool and sand-floored Ateni wine vault, the director of the winery raised a glass of pale yellow wine to his lips and sipped reverently.

"It's mother's milk," he said. Ateni is a light, dry table wine resembling Graves. It is the most famous wine of the region around Stalin's birthplace [and each year the directors of the winery send a gift to Stalin at the Kremlin of the year's best wines].

May 25

In the yellowing files of the Georgian State Library at Tbilisi I found six documents of greatest interest—the earliest published writings of a sixteen-year-old seminary student whom the world knows today as Stalin. . . .

To me the most interesting of Stalin's poems was that published by the magazine *Kvali* in 1896 called "Old Man Ninika."

The verses tell of old Ninika who has labored all his life. Now he is old and sick. He had been strong in his time, but his strength has been exhausted in ill-paid labor. "Now, old man Ninika has nothing. He is lying ready to die and no one helps him. At first he is envious, seeing young men full of strength, going about their labors." But then, Stalin writes, his heart grows happy. He feels the young men will get the happiness in life which was denied him.

The poem was signed "Sozeli." This was a typographical error for "Soselo"—Stalin's nom de plume, a diminutive in Georgian of his name, Josef.

Stalin's first published work was a short verse published in *Iberiya*, January 14, 1895. It carries no title and was signed I. G. Dash Shishvili. Here is the verse:

> The rosebud is opening
> And all around are bluebells.
> The iris, too, has awakened
> And all nod in the breeze.

> The lark flies high in the sky
> Chirping and singing.
> The nightingale with great feeling
> And quiet voice sings:

> Flourish, my dear country—
> Wed and be happy, my land of Iberiya—
> Motherland of Iberiya.
> And, you men of Georgia,
> May your studies wed
> You to your homeland.

Iberiya is the ancient name of Georgia.

Two of Stalin's poems convey somewhat the same thought. Both employ the moon as the central symbol, conveying light to a world in darkness.

"To the Moon," published on October 11, 1895, opens with these lines:

> Now it is always night
> Let the moon serve to awaken all people
> Poor people live under the moon in cold and ice.

Dispatch Killed by Censor
Tbilisi, May 26, 1951

In a narrow side street of one of the most ancient quarters of the city stands a former synagogue which now houses a Jewish ethnological museum. It contains undoubtedly the finest exhibition of Jewish tradition and culture in the Soviet Union.

The museum was established in 1933 at the initiative of Lavrenti P. Beriya as part of a program for raising the cultural and economic conditions of Georgian Jews.

The plight of the Jews was so serious that Beriya directed the organization of a special Jewish committee for the poor, attached to the Georgian government.

Jews came to Georgia as early as the fifth century before Christ under the protection of the Georgian kings. But, in centuries of war with the Turks, Persians, and Mongols, they fell to a position worse than that of livestock. Paintings in the museum show beautiful young Jewish women being sold as slaves to Turkish harems in the seventeenth and eighteenth centuries and being traded for fine Caucasian sheep dogs in the early nineteenth century at a rate of three women for one dog.

Under czarism Jews were permitted only a few trades. They were banned from education, and the only way a Jewish girl could come to the city was to get a yellow ticket—a prostitute's certificate. At the time of the Revolution only 4 per cent of Georgian Jews were literate. One of Beriya's first acts was to establish a special school in Tbilisi for illiterate depressed Jews.

The Jewish museum has preserved a record of how the Jews once lived in Georgia. There are representations of Jewish feasts, synagogues, and celebrations. . . .

There are circumcision scenes and those depicting the traditional widow's right of *xalitza*. . . . One of the most interesting paintings shows Stalin conferring with the Jewish leader, Reginashvili, who served under Stalin until he was killed by the czarist police in 1906. . . .

The museum has a special exhibit of famous Jewish generals and World War II heroes. There is a section on Nazi persecution of the Jews and a photograph of Albert Einstein.

There are two synagogues in Tbilisi—one for Georgian Jews and another for Russian Jews. There are about 50,000 Jews in Georgia today. . . .

Dispatch to New York Times
Tbilisi, May 26

It is thirteen years since Beriya left Georgia, but monuments to his work in Georgia are to be seen at every hand.

Most of the modern features of Tbilisi are associated in one way or another with Beriya. The modern university quarter of the city was started under Beriya. Along the muddy Kura River there is a fine esplanade named for Stalin. It was built under Beriya. On

Rustaveli Street there is a handsome marble and granite Marx-Lenin-Engels Institute. It was planned by Beriya. . . .

Under Beriya's direction the huge old bazaars were torn down. "Beriya was a very practical man. He was a great builder. He put Georgia on its feet," Georgians will tell you.

May 28, 1951

I have been thinking about the experience I had the other night when I saw *Othello* with Georgia's leading actor, Akady Horava, at the Rustaveli Theater. A group of visiting Finnish actors said it was the most powerful characterization they had ever seen, and I am inclined to agree. . . .

I am convinced that in this very performance of *Othello* can be found certain keys to Georgian character which, when applied to the most famous of all Georgians, unlocks many curious and important secrets.

I won't labor the point because it is obvious enough. And simple enough. It consists in the fact that suspicion, jealousy, plots, and intrigues are deep in the blood of the Georgian people. . . .

I suppose I have seldom been so moved in the theater as I was that night. I could not understand a single word of Georgian. But that wasn't necessary. I could feel the suspicion grow when Iago started in on Othello. Not just on the stage. In the audience, too. It was almost a physical thing. . . . I looked at the audience. I was sitting up in the gallery in an eight-ruble seat. Their eyes were glazed. They were breathing rapidly with flushed faces. . . .

Dispatch to New York Times
Tbilisi, May 28

On the eve of World War I, Baedecker said the most interesting sight in Tbilisi was its vivid street scenes—colorful bazaars, Caucasian mountain costumes, and oriental atmosphere.

The bazaars are long since gone and replaced by blocks of modern stores and offices. Occasionally, you see mountain women in bright red, yellow, and black blouses, kerchiefs, and skirts.

There are still medieval buildings and courtyards, overhanging balconies, ancient walls, and outdoor cooking stoves. But the new Tbilisi of modern streets and boulevards is much bigger. . . .

How do the Georgian people live? Pleasantly, it seemed to me.

They are hospitable almost to the point of embarrassment, courteous, and fond of conversation....

May 29

I have just come to Mineralnye Vody by train from Dzaudzhikau and by bus over the famous Georgian military highway from Tbilisi....

We had a big genial bus driver—an open bus—a jolly crowd. There was a very pretty girl with nut-brown cheeks, ruby lips, a beautiful smile, new red nails and lipstick, a new diamond and a new garnet ring. She was with a dark, runty husband who wore a new suit and overcoat. One of the old women complained about the girl's lipstick....

We stopped at least twenty times to let past herds of sheep—karakul, merino, black, brown, white, and shaggy. There were ferocious white Caucasian sheep dogs, drovers with enormous sheepskin coats and wheeled carts, many burros and mules. The bus stopped a couple of times to let the passengers bargain for sheep. A youngster offered 100 rubles. The old drover wanted 250. No deal. We stopped at a hot spring, and everyone filled their bottles with *narzan*. It had a strong taste of iron. Mount Kazbek was hidden in the clouds. In a few minutes we passed through rain, snow, sleet, and out into sunshine again.

The highway is a good hard-surfaced road with stone retaining walls, but it is hard to keep it open in the face of constant rock slides. Particularly in the spring, huge avalanches roar down.

Dispatch to New York Times
June 6

Two Soviet authors were taken sharply to task today for spreading "pseudoscientific theories" that the famous Tungus meteorite which fell in Siberia in 1908 actually was an atomic space ship....

June 9
Letter to Mr. Simonov, Press Department

In line with my conversation of the day before yesterday I want to make a trip to Siberia, leaving about June 20. I would like to visit the following points: Sverdlovsk, Omsk, Novosibersk, Tomsk, Irkutsk, and Sludyanka. . . .*

June 15, 1951

The Georgian trip was grand. Best I have had in this country. I was gone nearly three weeks and had a great time scouring around Georgia, which is no more like Russia than Mexico is like the U.S.A. Mountains and swift streams and lush valleys. Mostly sheep in the part I was in, but they have horses and cattle as well. Tbilisi is a Mediterranean city. A place to sit in garden cafés and drink wine and listen to music and watch the play of the sunshine through the leaves of the trees. Flowers everywhere. The mountainsides, just carpets of them.

Fresh strawberries, all the green stuff you can imagine. A wonderful ride down on the train. I shared my compartment with three Red Army officers. We messed and drank together. Hopping off the train at little stops to buy mounds of fresh onions and radishes, pickles, cucumbers, strawberries, cherries, whole roasted chickens, fish near the Black Sea. It was fun, and three days of solid Russian conversation—none knew English—unlimbered my Russian.

Tom and I have put in a big vegetable garden at the dacha. Almost everything is up, and we have our fingers crossed. Weather has been fine, warm, sunshiny with just enough showers. If it keeps up, we will have a swell crop. We have bought tomato plants and flower sets in the local market at Saltikovka.

It is wonderful to wake up at 5:00 in the morning with birds singing all around, roosters crowing, and the sun streaming in my balcony window.

Dispatch to New York Times
June 22

Suspension of the Paris Big Four talks has launched relations between East and West into a new epoch of doubt and uncertainty [which in Moscow was marked by a slashing press campaign].

The press offensive was unprecedented in its sharpness [and in the sweeping nature of the allegations which were presented].

* Permission for this trip never came.

Dispatch to New York Times
June 23

Under a headline "Savages in Yasnaya Polyana," the *Literary Gazette* charges that ten American embassy staff members have desecrated the grave of Lev Tolstoi by boisterous, drunken behavior. . . .

Dispatch to New York Times
June 24

Western diplomats express hope that the way toward ending the Korean war may have been opened by Malik's cease-fire proposals. . . .

[What interested observers especially was that in outline Malik's statement comes very close to paralleling the terms for ending the war which Acheson and Marshall advanced in the congressional hearings on MacArthur's removal. . . . They regarded Malik's statement as possibly the most important break since the start of the Korean war.]

June 27
Letter to Edwin L. James, New York Times

I would like a little guidance on making further trips around Russia.

I notice that my articles on Georgia drew a very sharp letter from Mr. Bagration, head of the Georgian-American League. And I recall the fuss over the articles I wrote last fall on returning here, and it is my impression that the articles I wrote on Leningrad last winter attracted some hostile comment.

There are two questions to be considered. The first is that under the censorship practically nothing but the favorable side is allowed to go through. The second factor is that conditions in places which I have visited are not as black as seems to be generally supposed by the public.

I certainly don't want to place the *Times* in the position of being accused of pro-Soviet propaganda, and I do not want to make myself the object of such criticism.

The fact is that these trips are difficult to arrange and hard to carry out. The negotiations for the trip to Georgia went on over three months.

Dispatch to New York Times
June 27, 1951

U.S. Ambassador Kirk conferred today with Gromyko, seeking clarification of the Soviet cease-fire proposals for Korea. . . . It was assumed he wished to ascertain whether the Soviet was prepared to support a cease-fire on the basis of withdrawal of troops from both sides of the 30th parallel. . . . After many past disappointments, diplomats kept their fingers crossed. . . .

Dispatch to New York Times
June 29

In *Pravda* today Lieutenant General of Aviation Vasily Stalin, son of the generalissimo, said that the Soviet people call their fliers "Stalin's falcons."

July 1

Since coming back from Georgia in late May, I have been spending most of my time out at the dacha with Tom and Julie Whitney. It is the same one we had last year, about twenty miles outside town in a little village called Saltikovka. There are no other foreigners in the village, so we get the Russian atmosphere practically unadulterated.

It is a simple summer cottage, and we have only the minimum of furniture. Our garden is about fifty by one hundred and fifty feet. Ate our first radishes two days ago. We have lettuce and carrots and cabbage and corn and peas and beans and cucumbers and squash. There has been a spell of unusually fine weather—only one rain since we went out about a month ago, so things are getting dry, and every night we haul about twenty buckets of water from the well down the lane. They don't have individual wells. There is a communal well for every group of a dozen or twenty cottages.

We have lots of flowers, mostly plants which we buy in the little village market. Market day is Sunday. We have a small pig to fatten for fall slaughtering. And we may buy a goat. Everyone has a goat. We get country eggs and milk and vegetables in the market— all fresh and right out of the earth.

There is a little lake about fifteen minutes walk from the cottage where we go swimming. It is a wonderful contrast from Moscow.

Dispatch to New York Times
July 1

Chu Teh, the commander of Chinese military forces, has given an unequivocal pledge that the island of Formosa "will be liberated from American imperialism. . . . The statement attracted considerable interest because [of the cease-fire proposals that are under way].

Dispatch to New York Times
July 7

Ambassador Kirk transmitted to the Soviet government today a personal message from President Truman, expressing friendship and the good will of Americans for all peoples, including those of the Soviet Union. . . .

July 13

Things are quiet at the moment. I expect there will be a loud yammer from the Russians over the draft of the Japanese peace treaty. I would not be surprised to see them go to our peace conference, under strong protests, make a presentation of their case, call for admission of the Chinese and then, having made a big propaganda show, walk out dramatically à la Molotov at the time of the Marshall Conference in Paris.

So far as one can judge, they seem to be sincere in wanting to wash-up Korea. They are playing all developments pretty straight, although trying to make out that we were forced to accept the idea of an armistice.

I believe the principal factors in their desire for an armistice are the impending Japanese treaty and the revelations of the MacArthur hearings, which laid clear so plainly the fundamentals of our policy in the Far East vis-à-vis Russia. The most impressive facts in the hearings were the plain evidence that we didn't want to fight Russia and China in the Far East and that we are prepared to fight Russia if they open up a new threat of the Korea type in Europe or possibly the Middle East.

The Communist Party has launched [a sharp and sweeping campaign] to eliminate "serious ideological faults and mistakes" in the Ukraine. . . .

The central committee of the Ukraine Party acknowledges its responsibility for the errors and pledges itself to eliminate them. [The campaign in the Ukraine recalls in its intensity and sweeping nature the general campaign against cosmopolitanism and bourgeois ideology which was carried on throughout the Soviet two years ago.]

Among the prominent writers who have been criticized are Vanda Vassilevsky, Alexander Korneichuk, and the well-known poet V. Sosyuri, whose verses "Love the Ukraine" are attacked as nationalistic in character. Another writer singled out for special criticism is M. Rylsky. The work of the Kiev opera theater was said to be of such a character that "any enemy of the Ukraine people from the nationalist camp, let us say, of Petlura or Bandura" could subscribe to it. The opera *Bogdan Khmelnitsky,* by Vassilevsky and Korneichuk, was sharply criticized. . . .

July 14

Here are some lines from Sosyuri's poem, "Love the Ukraine":

> Love the Ukraine,
> Like the sun, like the light,
> Like the wind, like the grass and water;
> Love the eternal expanse of the Ukraine,
> Be proud of your Ukraine—its new and eternal beauty,
> And its nightingale tongue. . . .

Dispatch to New York Times
July 15

There was a sharpening conviction tonight among diplomats that the Korean truce initiative may be only the first of a number of moves by the Soviet with the general purpose of reducing international tensions. . . . The most intriguing development was the appearance in Moscow of a new publication called *News,* published in English and having as its stated purpose "closer understanding with the Anglo-Saxon world. . . ."

Dispatch to New York Times
July 18

The imprimatur of the government's own newspaper, *Izvestia,* has been placed on the policy of friendship between the Soviet and the Anglo-Saxon nations advanced in the new magazine *News.*

Izvestia today republished the leading article from the magazine, presenting the thesis that there is no basis in history or present-day economic and political conditions for strained relations between Russia and Britain and America. . . .

July 20
Letter to Generalissimo Stalin

If I am not mistaken there exists in the world today a feeling that the time may be ripe for the Soviet and the United States to try once again to settle some of their conflicts.

Would you care to make some comment at this time upon the basic reasons why the Soviet Union and the United States should, in their own selfish interests, co-operate for peace? . . .

May I once again suggest a personal interview? . . .

Dispatch Killed by Censor
July 20

Moscow diplomats are beginning to wonder whether the Soviet at some early date may make a new and important move in support of the current campaign for friendship between Russia and the Anglo-Saxon nations. . . .

One lesson which has been well learned by Moscow displomats is that few reputations are ever won by forecasting the actions of the Soviet government. . . .

If there is a desire on the part of the government to emphasize a new policy, there exists a rather convenient method. For the past week there has been in Moscow a delegation of members of the Quaker faith from England. They would like a frank and open conversation with the Generalissimo. . . .

Dispatch to New York Times
July 24

The uncompromising nature of Molotov's Warsaw speech today tends to counterbalance the favorable impressions derived from the new emphasis which had been put on friendship with the Anglo-Saxon nations. . . .

[Contrasting Molotov and the magazine *News*, Moscow observers inevitably recalled the famous policy of the carrot and the stick, but in this case the stick seemed to be considerably more evident than the carrot.]

Dispatch to New York Times
July 27, 1951

The Soviet made a new and important statement of basic foreign policy in a declaration to a visiting delegation of British Quakers by Jacob Malik.

Malik's statement included a reassertion of Stalin's famous 1936 declaration that "export of revolution is nonsense."

This was in reply to a point raised by the Quakers as to whether the Soviet was willing to give pledges of non-intervention in action or in spirit and directly or indirectly in the internal affairs of non-Communist governments. . . .

[Stalin's declaration made to publisher Roy Howard in March, 1936, is not one which has been frequently cited in the Soviet press. The question which this raised in diplomatic minds was whether this was designed as a disavowal of participation in or responsibility for revolutionary struggles by national Communist parties in bourgeois countries.]

July 29
Letter to Emanuel R. Freedman, New York Times

You will recall that I messaged you a number of times regarding transmission and censorship of the Georgian dispatches, noting the slowness. I also advised you I had written twelve dispatches and after you had received nine told you you would get no more.

My purpose was to advise you as closely as possible what the censorship was doing to the pieces. And I thought I had made it clear that three stories—the ones I described as "the best"—were killed by the censorship.

Now, it seems to me that it would have been much better to have prefixed to the Georgian dispatches an editorial note, pointing out that one-fourth of my copy had been killed and that there was internal evidence of other censorship mutilations. . . .

July 29

I am now in the curious position of having directly contradictory guidance on the question of further trips in the Soviet Union. I have a letter from Cy suggesting that I go ahead so far as possible with plans for trips to Lake Baikal, down the Volga and the Ukraine. And I have a letter from Manny recommending that I forego further trips in view of the censorship situation.

I am holding further plans in abeyance until the matter is cleared up.

July 31

The most interesting current development is the great freedom with which speculation and discussion is being permitted on the question of a change in Soviet foreign policy in the direction of an effort at better relations with the West.

I thought Harry Schwartz's discussion of this change in last Sunday's *Times* was excellent and touched on most of the main points. What is most interesting to me is that we are being permitted to make comparisons with past attitudes and with contradictory material which is appearing in the press.

XVI

Inconclusive Diplomacy

August 1, 1951
Letter to Mr. Simonov, Press Department

For some time Mr. Whitney and myself have been endeavoring to get a telephone installed at the dacha which we share at Saltikovka. This is a vital necessity if our work as correspondents is to be carried on satisfactorily.

I wonder whether the press department might exercise its influence toward expediting this matter. . . .*

Dispatch to New York Times
August 1

[For the first time in many years—possibly for the first time since the Bolshevik Revolution—] an opportunity seemed to be presenting itself for [a comparatively] open debate before the bar of Russian public opinion on basic questions at issue between the Soviet and the West. . . .

There were two important developments—first, the publication by *Pravda* of Foreign Secretary Morrison's excellently conceived message to the Soviet people and the tacit invitation by the English-language journal *News* to the *New York Times* that its columns stand open to any contribution which the *Times* deems likely to promote friendly relations between the two countries. . . .

---

* The telephone was installed after about six months of negotiation.

Dispatch to New York Times
August 7

Millions of Soviet citizens tonight heard over the Soviet radio system President Truman's friendly greetings to the Soviet people. . . . It was the first time since the end of World War II that the Soviet radio had brought to the people a message of good will and friendship from the President of the United States. . . .

August 11

Moscow diplomats are wondering whether it would be desirable from several points of view to put to a practical test recent Soviet pronouncements of a desire for more friendly relations with the West. . . .

Dispatch Killed by Censor
August 14

Some Moscow diplomats felt that Gromyko's forthcoming trip to the United States might provide an insight into the Soviet's new policy of attempting to better relations with the West. . . .*

Dispatch to New York Times
August 15

The English-language magazine *News* takes issue with observers who see in its publication any change, turn, or evolution of Soviet foreign policy which, it said, "needs no changing." . . .

Dispatch to New York Times
August 23

In his speech at Bucharest yesterday, Marshal Voroshilov for the second time in a month put the Politburo on record with an unequivocal denunciation of American policy. He used terms even stronger than those of Molotov at Warsaw. . . .

September 7
Cable to Arthur Hays Sulzberger and Edwin L. James,
New York Times

Seriously concerned by reports of proposed legislation directed at Tass correspondents. Proposal obviously well-intentioned but

* Gromyko went to the United States for the concluding talks on the Japanese peace treaty. He made no significant peace overtures.

fear likely create new worse incidents here. . . . Action against Tass invites Soviet retaliation against five American correspondents here who unlike Tass have no diplomatic immunity and literally no protection against Soviet reprisals. Also unlikely reprisals here be limited to expulsion or further working restrictions. . . .

Dispatch Killed by Censor
September 14, 1951

There was a growing conviction in Moscow tonight that neither the Chinese nor the Soviet governments any longer entertains any substantial belief that the Kaesong negotiations will lead to the end of the Korean war. . . .

Dispatch to New York Times
September 18

The Soviet stands today approximately at the halfway mark toward creation of the industrial and agricultural basis on which it is hoped to replace the present Socialist economic system with the planned goal of a Communist society. . . .

[According to most reliable estimates Soviet production is approximately halfway toward meeting the marks of 50,000,000 tons of pig iron, 60,000,000 tons of steel, 500,000,000 tons of coal, and 60,000,000 tons of oil set by Stalin for 1960. Steel this year is expected to top 30,000,000. Pig iron is expected to be a little short of half Stalin's goal. Coal is pushing toward 60 per cent, and the same is true of oil. . . .]

Dispatch to New York Times
September 22

In one of the most sharply worded articles since the outbreak of the Korean war, the *Literary Gazette* attacks General Ridgway as a "bloody executioner," "an American Rommel," and a "repulsive mountebank."

[You will look in vain in the current issues of the central Soviet press for any echo today of the appeal launched with so much fanfare only a few weeks ago by the magazine *News* for effort at closer understanding with the Anglo-Saxon peoples.]

September 22

It is very difficult for me to analyze the Korean truce situation from here. What has been published has been consistently along the line that the North Koreans and Chinese want the talks while the United States is trying to delay, block, and disrupt them.

My personal guess is that two factors are involved—jockeying for propaganda positions and questions of face. The interlude in the talks has been occupied by the Chinese-Korean side almost entirely in denouncing the United States. It is quite possible this reflects genuine fears. But any suggestion from me is hardly more than a guess and not a very well-informed one.

Dispatch to New York Times
September 23

The leading Soviet philosophical journal proclaims that one of the best known Marxist theses—the inevitability of war in the epoch of imperialism—no longer holds true in the present historical period.

This doctrinal assertion is made in the journal *Questions of Philosophy* in a discussion of whether a new world war can be prevented. The article concludes that, in fact, war is not inevitable and sharply rebukes those who regard Marxism as a collection of dogma whose "conclusions and formulae are suitable for all epochs and periods."

"If one does not take into consideration changes in the conditions of development of society," said the journal, "then one can by blindly grabbing hold of one or another thesis of Marx relating to a definite historic epoch make a very crude mistake. . . ."*

September 30

It has been a pleasant summer for me—lots of time in the country, healthy and relaxing. So relaxing that I practically gave up writing except for my dispatches. Now that fall is here and I am getting back to the city, I must resume my old habits.

What a difference it makes to live in a pleasant little village where the air is fresh and the countryside is made up of pine trees

---

* This, in almost the same words, is the precise argument directed against Peking by Soviet ideologues in 1960.

and birches and cows and cottages and flowers and potato gardens.

I have become a real gardener. This year we raised some fine tomatoes, excellent peas, more beans than we knew what to do with, loads of lettuce, carrots, beets, turnips, Swiss chard, cucumbers, broccoli, etc. Even some pretty good cabbage. The only things which didn't quite make it—because of the short growing season—were sweet corn and Brussels sprouts.

For the last week we have been having light frosts in the country so the days are numbered. Maybe we will have another week. Maybe not.

Life in Moscow continues quiet and peaceful. Food and other living conditions improve. It seems curious in view of the unsettled state of the world, yet it is true. We hear echoes of the din and thunder only rather dimly here. It is something which newcomers to Moscow constantly remark on.

Dispatch to New York Times
October 2, 1951

The press asserts that President Truman's affirmation of his Library of Congress declaration that agreements with Russia are not worth the paper on which they are written makes plain that the United States has embarked on a policy of "dictation, violence and aggression." . . .

[The commentator's language made the rash of newspaper speculation appearing in western Europe on the possibility of some new Soviet high-level move to end the cold war look like wishful and rather misguided thinking.]

Dispatch to New York Times
October 3

Soviet experts on jet and rocket propulsion have reached the conclusion that space ships for travel to the moon and nearby planets as well as the creation of artificial earth satellites are scientifically possible.

This conclusion was presented by one of the Soviet's leading experts, M. K. Tikhonravov, a corresponding member of the Academy of Artillery Science. . . .

He left no doubt that Soviet scientific development in the field of jet and rocket propulsion is advancing rapidly, and suggested that this science in the Soviet Union has reached a level at least equal if not exceeding that in Western countries. . . .

He suggested the first step might be establishment of an artificial earth satellite. . . .

Dispatch Killed by Censor
October 4

There was no immediate Soviet comment on President Truman's announcement of a new nuclear explosion in the Soviet Union. No comment was expected for at least another twenty-four hours and possibly longer. . . . While there has been nothing in the press to suggest that Russia has developed a hydrogen bomb, Soviet scientists are fully aware of the theoretical capabilities of such a weapon. . . .

Dispatch to New York Times
October 4

On the eve of his departure from Moscow, Ambassador Kirk said that the period of his service in Moscow has been marked by a progressive deterioration of relations rather than the improvement he hoped to achieve on his arrival here twenty-seven months ago. . . .

With the blunt honesty of a veteran naval commander, Kirk recalled that when he arrived he said he would work unremittingly to better relations. . . .

"Well," he said, "it hasn't worked out quite that way. Relations are worse than when I came—not better."

He noted, however, that the ability of an American ambassador to influence the course of relations should not be exaggerated. He has traveled about 16,000 kilometers in Russia. His most extensive trip was in June a year ago when he visited Lake Baikal. . . .

He feels that one of the basic factors in the relationship between the two countries is the vast difference in historic, cultural, and social heritages. He is convinced this factor is not widely understood in the United States. The same might equally well be said on the Russian side. . . .

Dispatch to New York Times
October 6, 1951

Generalissimo Stalin confirmed today that the Soviet recently tested one of its types of nuclear bombs. Diplomats felt his statement that bombs of different calibers would be tested in the future indicates the Soviet is moving stride-by-stride in atomic development along the same path followed by the United States. . . .

Dispatch Killed by Censor
October 7

Stalin's reference to testing bombs of various calibers leads some military observers to conclude that Russia can be expected to place major emphasis upon tactical rather than strategic atomic weapons. This would be in line with basic Soviet military doctrine. . . .

Dispatch Killed by Censor
October 9

Diplomats suggested that analysis of Stalin's atom statement should be made on the basis of his fundamental assessment of the military value of atomic weapons which he made five years ago.

Speaking in 1946, he expressed the view that atom bombs were not such all-powerful weapons as they were regarded in the West, that they would not prove decisive in warfare, and that their chief effect was to intimidate. There was nothing in Stalin's statement of last Saturday to indicate any alteration in his views. . . .

October 14

Censorship of my copy in the last few days has been unusually severe, and it has eliminated a very important point which I have tried to make regarding Soviet atomic development.

It has been a long time since my copy has been so chewed up. The point I have been trying to make is that on the basis of what we know about Soviet military doctrine, particularly air doctrine, it is reasonable to suppose they have concentrated on tactical

218

atomic weapons and will continue to do so. Nothing but a bare hint of this has gone through the censorship.

The second point which I tried to make was that there is little or no serious talk here about negotiating on atomic control or any other international issue. Stalin in his last two *Pravda* statements has made not a hint of such an approach.

Dispatch Killed by Censor
October 18

The British embassy announced that it has protested to the Foreign Office the disappearance of one of its women employees after attending a performance at the Bolshoi Theater twenty-four hours ago.

Deputy Foreign Minister Feodor Gusev promised Chargé d'Affaires Paul Grey he would investigate.

Mrs. Ira Ricketts, a Soviet woman who during wartime years married a British sergeant on duty in Moscow, had been employed for several years by the British embassy.

On the evening of October 16, accompanied by a member of the Australian embassy, she visited the Bolshoi Theater. At the end of the performance, just as she stepped into a taxi and her escort was about to follow, two or three men boarded the taxi and drove off, followed by two tan-colored Pobedas.

A nearby militiaman refused to intervene. The scene of the incident is one of the most important public squares in Moscow— the steps of the great Bolshoi Theater.

Nearly a dozen men were involved in the matter. Mrs. Ricketts was one of two Soviet wives who married British subjects during wartime who remained under the protection of the embassy. Of approximately forty at one time, all the rest had gradually dropped out of sight so far as the embassy is concerned. . . .

The abduction was regarded as one of the most scandalous occurrences affecting the diplomatic colony in Moscow in some years.

There was no doubt in the minds of any foreigner in Moscow which branch of the Soviet government had engineered Mrs. Ricketts' disappearance. . . .

219

What the Soviet government or its police agency hoped to accomplish by this intentionally outrageous conduct was difficult for the most astute analysts to conceive. One suggestion voiced in the diplomatic colony was that it was designed deliberately to embarrass any Soviet advocates of better relations between East and West.

Dispatch to New York Times
October 18, 1951

The Soviet Union said in an important policy declaration today that all efforts to end the war in Korea would meet its complete and energetic support. Foreign Minister Vishinsky also said that Russia was ready to discuss all outstanding causes of dispute with the United States.

Mr. Vishinsky's statement was in response to a presentation submitted to him by Ambassador Kirk at his farewell interview October 5 before departing for America. . . .

October 19

I have complained most vigorously about delays in transmission of the Vishinsky story. Of course, this merely helps to relieve my indigation, although, since the communications' foul-up affects the Foreign Office, they can be depended upon to give the telegraph office a major rocket.

Censorship is about as tight as it has ever been. I don't believe a story in the last two weeks has gone through without cuts. I have also had three dispatches killed in entirety—after a whole summer in which only two dispatches were killed.

October 21
Letter to Harry Schwartz, New York Times

I should have long since replied to your note of August 22. Time seems to have provided an answer to your inquiry about "what to take along" if you get a visa for Russia. The summer's honey and treacle seem to have vanished with the first Moscow frosts. It doesn't look now as though any visas will be coming through for a long while, until the next whirl of the "friendship" wheel. . . .

October 24
Cable to Turner Catledge, New York Times

Appreciate continuous and fast informative all developments Tass FBI case stop As you probably can imagine theres considerable concern among correspondents here that this action may produce similar or more drastic action by Russian equivalent organization against ourselves regards.

Dispatch Killed by Censor
October 30

Three outstanding Soviet specialists in physics, cosmic, and nuclear research have come under sharp attack by colleagues of equal eminence who have challenged the validity of the discoveries which brought them renown and prizes.

The challenged scientists are academicians Abram I. Alikhanov and Artyom I. Alikhanyan of the Institute of Physics of Armenia, brothers and leaders in Soviet cosmic-ray research, and Professor Georgi Latyshev of Leningrad.

The situation was brought to light in the Party organ *Bolshevik* in an article by Yuri Zhdanov.

Latyshev won a 200,000-ruble Stalin first prize for physics in 1949 for his nuclear studies. Alikhanov and Alikhanyan shared a 200,000-ruble prize in 1948 for their demonstration of the existence of the so-called varitrone, described as a cosmic particle having a variable mass.

Zhdanov reported that Latyshev's work was retested in another institution which disclosed its mistakenness. With regard to Alikhanov and Alikhanyan, it was said that with better equipment and improved methods of work they demonstrated in 1950 that all the previous studies on which they postulated the existence of varitrones were invalid. . . .

November 1
Letter to Director, Administration for Services
*to the Diplomatic Corps**

I wrote you on August 2 requesting that you provide me with a chauffeur since I was compelled to discharge my chauffeur for failure to fulfil his duties.

---

* Henceforth *Burobin,* nickname derived from the Russian name for this agency.

Three months have now passed and despite many promises, assurances, etc., by various of your personnel with whom I have been in telephonic communication, I am still without a new chauffeur. . . .

Dispatch to New York Times
November 2, 1951

A diplomatic exchange between Britain and Russia expressing a desire for understanding on basic conflicts occurred at the Kremlin when the new British ambassador, Sir Alvary Douglas Frederick Gasgoigne, presented his credentials to Nikolai Shvernik, president of the Presidium of the Supreme Soviet. . . .

Dispatch to New York Times
November 6

Lavrenti P. Beriya, one of Stalin's closest associates, tonight declared that the Soviet—as a result of recently solving a series of important problems of "economic and defense interest"—now leads the world in science.

Beriya for the first time delivered the important pre-November 7 speech at the Bolshoi Theater. Ten members of the Politburo were present. Only Stalin and Molotov were absent. . . .

November 7
Letter to Press Censor, Glavlit

I am writing to ask that you take action to pass for publication my dispatch numbered 302100 and 302115, which has now been in your hands for more than a week.

As is readily evident, this dispatch is based upon the article of Yuri Zhdanov in *Bolshevik*, No. 21, and upon collateral material to be found in the *Journal of Experimental and Theoretical Physics*, Vol. 21, No. 9, of this year. . . .

It should be apparent that by this time, or very shortly, copies of these journals will arrive in the hands of subscribers in New York. . . . I fail to understand the lengthy delay. . . .

November 7
Letter to Harry Schwartz, New York Times

Here is a rather delicate matter which I think you should be filled in on.

I notice that the *New Leader* has picked up your open letter to the *Guild Reporter* and republished it with some flourishes, and I understand that the case of the three American correspondents, "prisoners of the Kremlin," has been coupled by some with the Oatis case.

This is rather disturbing to the correspondents for the following reason. Although the prospects certainly appear discouraging, hope has by no means been given up that it may prove possible to do something by diplomatic means to ameliorate the problem— that is, that eventually permission may be obtained for their wives and families to leave the country.

There is a very strong feeling that if such efforts are to be successful, the cases must be handled with utmost discretion and without publicity. . . . We must avoid the spectacular kind of publicity indulged in by the British in the case of their wives which, it is generally agreed, ruined any chance of getting positive Soviet diplomatic action. . . .

November 15
Letter to Turner Catledge, New York Times

I am disturbed at the number of critical letters which have appeared in the *Times* in recent months, taking issue with various points in my dispatches.

In general, these letters make two points: that I am naïve and ill-informed and that I deliberately or inadvertently am a mouthpiece for Soviet propaganda.

I think it is very bad for the *Times* and very bad for me personally that such impressions should be held by any considerable number of readers. . . .

In virtually every instance the "point" which the letter makes is a point not against me but against the Soviet censorship. . . .

Every day my dispatches, pruned by the censors, are published by the *Times*. Mr. L. and many like him come to think that the *Times* correspondent in Moscow is a red or a pink or naïve or stupid.

I don't think that is good for the *Times*, and I know it is bad for me—particularly with the feeling as it is in the U.S.A. right now.

What can be done about it?

One protection to the reader of the *Times,* to the *Times,* and to its Moscow correspondent would be what I have so often and so vainly urged in the past—the publication of an editorial note above every dispatch from Moscow, informing the reader that it has passed through the Soviet censorship. . . .

November 16, 1951

All summer long I rusticated. Really rusticated. Puttering in the garden, sunning for hours, swimming a bit, lazy walks in the birch and pine forests, and hours and hours and days and days and weeks and weeks of talking and talking and talking. Good.

Now I am back in town. But we have kept the dacha for the winter, and it is an escape hatch. I can pop on the train and be there in three-quarters of an hour. Just as far from Moscow as if I were in Siberia. All snow and pine forest and smoke from the wood stoves and sun gleaming on the snow crystals and at night the moon turning the whole country blue and green and mysterious.

It has been very good for me. There has not been too much work—well, probably there would be more if I worked at it. But my energy comes and goes. I have whacked away at my Russian until I can read the papers. Dispensed with my secretary and like it a lot better getting my own news.

Gradually I'm evolving my own ideas about people. Very simple. Let them do what they want. Help them to find out what they want. Let them shear off all the incrustation and filth of environmental mores and be honest and be good and be kind and be thoughtful and love them. I don't like the way that sounds, written out. Too Tolstoyan. But simplicity and ease and quietness are the keynotes.

That is the kind of influence that life in a Russian village has on me. It would be the same, I suppose, in an American village. . . .

Dispatch Killed by Censor
November 18

Generalissimo Stalin plays a direct personal and intimate role in the development of new Soviet weapons. He consults closely with designers and resolves controversies over types of arms himself. He witnesses tests and demonstrations of importance. Accounts of his work in the field of armaments were published in connection with Soviet artillery day. From them there is no doubt of Stalin's leading role in development of the newest weapon in the Soviet armory—atomic arms. It was hardly open to question that demonstrations of these weapons have been carried out in his presence. . . .

XVII

Kennan Is Named Ambassador

November 22, 1951

I am both pleased and disturbed at the talk about Kennan. Pleased because there is no one whose judgment with regard to Russia I respect more highly but disturbed because I believe there is very little possibility of *agrément* for him as ambassador.

If anything were needed to strengthen my belief that the Russians will not accept him, it was provided by last night's note of protest against the $100,000,000 fund in the Mutual Security Act. It hardly seems likely in view of George's connection with the Free Russia Committee or whatever it is called that they will agree to his taking up his post here. Which is a great pity both from our standpoint and theirs.

We miss Kirk here. He and Mrs. Kirk did a hell of a lot to maintain morale in this rather dreary spot. I think his final talk with Vishinsky had considerably more impact than might appear, in part because the Russians tried publicly to minimize it. I think it had a real effect on the negotiations in Korea where it seems quite obvious that in their stumbling way the Commies are trying hard to get off the hook. I will not venture any predictions, but the tone of comment here has changed decidedly since the Kirk-Vishinsky exchange. Beriya employed the word *"vyekhod"* or "exit" or "way out" in discussing the possible end of hostilities in Korea. This was a far cry from Bulganin's laborious analogy of last November comparing the Korean situation to that of the Bolsheviks when they were fighting the interventionists.

Domestically, the stress is on two things—the big Stalin construction projects and peace. One domestic situation intrigues me, but I can't get my fingers on a real indication as to what has happened. This is the big consolidation program for collective farms. The topic has simply dropped out of the press. I can't figure out why.

And here is another funny thing. Not a single speech by Khrushchev has been published since the much delayed one last March which carried the note, the next day, that it was presented for discussion only. Not that he hasn't been making speeches. Hardly a month goes by without Moscow *Pravda* or one of the papers reporting a meeting of kolkhozniks or something which he addresses. They report all the other speeches and wind up with a note that Comrade Khrushchev addressed the meeting. But never print a word of what he says. Once several months ago Moscow *Pravda* reported such a meeting and said his speech would be reported later. But it never appeared.

Frankly, I don't know what to make of it except that obviously there must be some kind of Politburo disagreement, presumably over the consolidation program and presumably over Khrushchev's part in it. Both he and Andreyev have been prominent on the platform at every Politburo occasion this year. But there has been no mention of Andreyev in the press in any other connection.

After writing my story on Beriya's speech, I felt that I and everyone else had missed the boat. The headline obviously should have been: Russia is making 4,000,000 tons more of steel and 3,000,000 more soldiers every year.

Those are the figures that we should keep in mind. I am getting more and more concerned at the tendency of statesmen, particularly State Department spokesmen, and newspapers (including, unfortunately, the *Times*), to play up alleged weak spots in the Soviet and to play down and minimize all factors indicating their growing strength.

To me it is a hell of a lot more important that Beriya's figures show Russia is going to hit Stalin's 1960 goals for steel, oil, and coal ahead of time than that the Muscovites still have to pay eight or nine times our price for a pair of shoes.

I had the same feeling about our published reaction to their new atom-bomb tests this fall. I am sure that we are way out in front in atomic weapons. But I would rather overestimate their gains than underestimate them if I had to pay for my mistakes on the battlefield.

It is my theory that they may well be a lot closer to us in the field of tactical atomic weapons than our experts surmise. I make that deduction entirely from the known facts about Stalin's attitude toward air power and particularly his attitude toward tactical and strategic bombing. If you study what has been published about Stalin's theories of warfare, you find that No. 1 emphasis has always been on maximum firepower applied against concentration of troops at the battlefront and at the breakthrough point.

So, when they come to develop atomic weapons, where are they going to put the emphasis? I think it is almost certain they had two instructions from scratch. First, produce atomic bombs as quickly as possible. Second, concentrate on devising tactical bombs.

By leapfrogging have they almost gotten up to us on tactical weapons? I don't know but I wouldn't take the negative side of that bet. . . .

There is a developing difference between Soviet-American relations and Soviet-British relations. While the Russians habitually couple the British with us, the main weight of their propaganda falls on us. For example, recently they stopped saying Anglo-American imperialists and started to say Americo-Anglo imperialists. Tiny but significant.

Dispatch Killed by Censor
November 23, 1951

The Soviet air force early in November intercepted an American military plane which was charged with flying over Far Eastern territory, it has been learned. . . . Full details of the incident were not available in Moscow. . . .

Dispatch to New York Times
November 23

At the bottom of the left-hand column of *Pravda* today was published an announcement of the award of the Order of the Red Banner to two members of the Soviet naval air force for "exemplary fulfilment of their service duty."

[Such awards are not ordinarily given such prominence. The

last occasion when the newspapers published an announcement like this was on April 14, 1950, when four members of the military air force were given the Order of the Red Banner. . . .]

Dispatch to New York Times
November 26

Soviet physicists have set themselves the task of constructing a completely "materialist" quantum theory, breaking entirely from what they call the "barren flowers of theocracy," represented by such scientists as Albert Einstein, Niels Bohr, and Heisenberg. . . .

Dispatch to New York Times
December 3

Diplomatic observers regard with seriousness Soviet charges concerning an American plane forced down in Hungary. . . . There seemed little doubt that the latest plane incident would be utilized as a dramatic object lesson to underscore [not only] Soviet charges concerning American airmen [but also the fate which perpetrators of such alleged acts may expect to meet].

Not the least important fact is the Soviet charge that the spying and diversionary activities were linked with Yugoslavia. . . .

December 4
Letter to Turner Catledge, New York Times

As you may know, when I came over originally I agreed with Mr. James to stay, first, for two years, and then, later, for three years, or, more specifically, until around the end of this year. . . .

I am quite willing, if it is the desire of the *Times,* to stay here for a considerable period of time, and particularly if it seems that war may be coming at any time in the relatively near future, I should want to stay on until the final moment. . . .

December 7

I want to make an important generalization which apparently hasn't been grasped in the U.S.A. and which must be kept in mind not only with regard to agricultural figures but to economic material of all types.

There is increasing evidence that Moscow, in general, is tending to understate somewhat rather than overstate its production.

This tendency runs through Beriya's November 6 speech. Take his statements about grain having in recent years run over seven billion poods—or 114,500,000 metric tons. Actual figures for 1948, 1949, and 1950 were 115, 124, and 124.5 million tons. In other words, he deliberately used a figure below the best estimates of production for the last three years.

Or, take steel. Beriya claimed a gain of only 4,000,000 tons for the year. This is the identical increase reported for 1950 and somewhat less than the 4,700,000 tons by which 1949 increased over 1948. . . . I suspect this figure is on the lower side.

Beriya's coal figure also seems suspect. The coal industry this year may not equal its plan figure—whatever that may be—but I can't read much meaning into Beriya's statement that for several years output increase has averaged 24,000,000 tons. In 1950 production was 26,000,000 tons above 1949 and 1949 was 28,000,000 over 1948. In 1946 and 1947 there was a boost of 60,000,000 tons.

Beriya's oil figure is also misleading. He says production has increased on the average 4,500,000 tons annually. But 1950 production increased 4,300,000 tons over 1949; 1949, 4,100,000 over 1948; and in the two previous years about 10,000,000 tons were added. . . .

From visual observation of crops in the field and from detailed information in the agricultural and provincial press, several agricultural specialists were convinced that last year's plan figure actually was met. They suspect that the total was deliberately understated to conceal stockpiling by the government.

I have read most of the evidence about padding of Soviet figures, and I certainly agreed that there has been plenty of it in the past, but I think that people like Jasny have carried their calculations past the point of common sense, and I believe the opposite tendency—the tendency to conceal the true extent of production gains—is what we must be on guard against now and increasingly in the future.

December 8, 1951

I have just finished reading Baldwin's *Operation Strangle* about Korea. It has long been my impression that far too little attention has been paid to objective study of the strategy and tactics of the Germans and Russians on the Eastern front and in particular to Russian use of air power.

It has been customary to say that Russia's concentration on tactical bombing was a choice of necessity. I believe there is considerable truth in this. But it is also true that basic Soviet military doctrine is founded upon concentration of saturating fire upon the battlefield breakthrough point.

This is emphasized over and over and over again and is the key to what they call "Stalinist military science." This doctrine holds that air power is essentially artillery power of greater range and flexibility.

I have often thought that a decision to integrate our air force —except for strategic bombers—with our ground force on the marine corps model would cause more concern in the Kremlin than a decision to build another hundred groups of atom-carrying long-range bombers.

On the Eastern front, if the Russians couldn't present a concentration of air power sufficient to outweigh the Germans, they held it back or concentrated on another point. That meant Soviet troops often fought without air support. Somewhat the same pattern seems to have developed in Korea.

I have tried on four different occasions in the last eight weeks to get a dispatch through hinting even in most innocuous terms that Stalin thinks of air power as a tactical weapon and that it would be reasonable to suppose that he thinks of the atom in similar terms.

December 9

The chances for *agrément* on George Kennan's appointment as ambassador are not very bright. I think this is highly unfortunate because I think Kennan's appointment would be a wonderful first step toward extricating our Soviet policy from the state of sterile "you're another" tactics into which it so often falls these days.

By no means the least advantage to be gained from Kennan's appointment would be the weight and influence which his observations and analyses would carry back in Washington. This is probably more important than some imagine since there appears to be a steadily widening gap between actual conditions here and the impression given by many of the statements, reports, etc., issued in Washington.

It is my firm conviction that almost all of the bad errors of Soviet foreign policy in the postwar period stem from a stereotyped impression of the world beyond Russia's frontiers, from faulty diplomatic reporting, and from equally faulty analysis in the Foreign Office here. Only too often we are falling into a similar pattern.

It has been amusing to note the disappearance from the Soviet press of the notorious warmonger Winston Churchill and the emergence of that somewhat cryptic figure "Y. Churchill, leader of the Conservative Party." Churchill hasn't drawn an adjective, an expletive, or a single qualifying phrase since election day.

December 12, 1951

Here it is almost Christmas and I am just getting around to a little Christmas spirit. Not so good when you have packages to send thousands of miles away. They are bound to be late. Not that I am sending anything much.

We have had no real winter so far. The thermometer hovers around the freezing mark, a little above in the daytime, a little below at night, and there has been little snow—not really enough for decent skiing in the country.

Dispatch to New York Times
December 14

In the broad plate-glass windows of Gorki Street—the nearest Soviet equivalent to Fifth Avenue—and in crowded Petrovka, Kuznetsky Most, Stoleshnikov and Negliniya—the heart of the Moscow shopping center—an expansive old gentleman with cherry red cheeks, a flowing white beard, and a long belted coat of fur and wool is the center of interest these days.

He is Dedya Moroz—Grandfather Frost—and his appearance in the shop windows is a signal to every Muscovite that the holiday season is at hand and that it's time to start Christmas shopping.

The holiday season starts a bit later in the Soviet Union than it does in the United States because it is the traditional Russian custom as in many European countries that the principal holiday and time for gifts is New Year's Eve.

There are more and prettier Christmas ornaments in Moscow

than since before the war—many of them lovely products of famous Bohemian glassworks. Russian Christmas trees are decorated about the same as American ones except they are usually topped by a red star instead of a silver or gold one.

Dispatch to New York Times
December 19

Announcement of the execution "by shooting" of two men on charges they were parachuted into Russia by Americans to act as spies and diversionaries was expected to have considerable impact on Soviet public opinion. It was also expected to have further repercussions on badly strained American-Soviet relations. . . .

December 20

In this alleged land of ice and snow we have had a lamblike winter so far. Don't think the temperature has been down to 20° above yet, if that. And only a trickle of snow. But I suppose old man weather will get in his licks come January.

Life is not very exciting right now. We are rather insulated from all the fuss of war scares, and I must say I enjoy the peace and calm. This past year I've spent a lot of time out in the country—really just the Moscow suburbs but surprisingly close to my picture of a Russian village. You don't have to go far into the countryside to be in real country around here. That is one of the curious things—the sharp and very real dividing line that separates the kind of life led in Moscow and that led just across the city limits. You step almost from one age into another.

Every year the world situation seems bad and every year it seems to get worse, and yet it doesn't seem to me that folks on this side of the Atlantic are in any mood to come to blows over anything. On the other hand I don't see much prospect for any early clearing of the atmosphere. Just more of the same.

Before many months roll by I surely hope to get back to the U.S.A. for a little vacation.

Dispatch to New York Times
December 20

Quietly and with no special ceremony [except perhaps a glass or two of robust Georgian wine with a few old, close, and intimate comrades], Generalissimo Stalin will tomorrow mark his seventy-second birthday.

If tradition is followed there will be no public ceremony—not even a small paragraph in the newspapers.

The repercussions of the celebration of two years ago have still not completely died away. The Pushkin art gallery, one of Moscow's principal museums, is still devoting its entire space to a display of only a small part of the great collection of gifts sent to Stalin. The daily press has not yet completed publishing the list of all the greetings sent Stalin—a list so enormously long that some have wondered whether it actually can be complete [before the Generalissimo is ready to celebrate his eightieth birthday]. . . .

Stalin gives every impression of energetic good health.

Dispatch Killed by Censor
December 26, 1951

Hope that the Soviet government would accept George Kennan as next U.S. ambassador to Moscow was dashed today by publication in *Pravda* of a sharply worded attack on him. . . .

Dispatch to New York Times
December 27

Soviet acceptance of George Kennan as U.S. ambassador was greeted as one of the most encouraging developments in recent months. The news frankly surprised many Moscow observers. . . .

It is the first time in history that the American embassy in Moscow has been headed by a man who has specialized in precisely this field. . . .

Some veteran Moscow diplomats took the view that the United States would not have named Kennan to Moscow nor would the Soviet have accepted him if there was not on both sides a realization that no opportunity should be overlooked in exploring possibilities, however slight, for in some measure reducing tensions. . . .

Dispatch to New York Times
January 2, 1952

Maxim Litvinov, whose voice in the epoch between the first and second World Wars has been called "the conscience of the world," was buried today in a quiet corner of Novo Devichiye cemetery beside the icy Moskva River.

Litvinov's death on the last day of the old year at the age of seventy-five was announced by *Pravda* in a brief, black-bordered, unsigned notice. Respects were paid by members of the Foreign Office. The pallbearers were led by Vice-Minister of Foreign Affairs Andrei A. Gromyko and deputy ministers Zorin and Gusev. Among the mourners was Litvinov's English-born wife, Ivy Low, grief-stricken but composed in her trim gray karakul coat and gray karakul hat. . . .

Litvinov was an old Bolshevik in the true sense of the word. His membership in the Party dated from 1903.

[Few of his comrades of that date survive, and few persons old enough to have been his contemporaries attended the funeral. Nor do many statesmen of the era of the great Litvinov days in Geneva survive. Naturally, none were in Moscow for the funeral. Nor could they—in the brief interval between today's *Pravda* announcement and the burial at 2:00 P.M.—have sent messages of condolence. As Litvinov's coffin was carried down the Foreign Office stairs, it seemed to me less like the end of an era than a fleeting intrusion of past and almost forgotten days into an alien present. . . .]

Dispatch to New York Times
January 2

Martin Niemöller, the famous German anti-Hitlerite and World War I submarine commander, arrived in Moscow today. . . .

[One question which Niemöller is most anxious to discuss is that of German war prisoners. There exists a sharp discrepancy between the numbers of Germans missing and the numbers which have now returned. . . .]

Dispatch to New York Times
January 6

A sermon of peace on earth and good will toward men was preached on this snow-spangled Orthodox Christmas Eve in Moscow's Evangelical Baptist church by Martin Niemöller. . . . Boughs of fragrant fir and strings of red, blue, white, and yellow Christmas lights decorated the church. The services began with the silver notes of "Silent Night, Holy Night," sung in Russian by the white-frocked choir.

Outside the church the crowd stood against high-banked snow-drifts and waved white handkerchiefs to Niemöller.

["When they waved farewell to me," said Niemöller, "I could not help thinking of the same natural kindness and friendship which I saw in the United States. It might just as well have been Pittsburgh or Cleveland as a little church in the heart of Russian Moscow."]

Dispatch Killed by Censor
January 7, 1952

Pastor Martin Niemöller concluded a five-day visit to Russia today with some measure of success in his effort to obtain a return to their homeland of Germans now employed in the Soviet Union.

He emphasized to Soviet authorities the benefit to relations between the countries which would flow from return of all Germans to their country after years in which their families have had no word of them.

But he expressed no great optimism that very substantial numbers of former German prisoners of war would be returned to Germany. . . .

Dispatch to New York Times
January 8

The whole Soviet press publishes prominently on page one a large photograph of Georgi M. Malenkov together with fiftieth birthday greetings from the central committee describing him as "a true pupil of Lenin and co-advisor of Comrade Stalin."

There is no doubt that within the inner circle of advisors of Stalin, Malenkov's counsel, particularly in matters of prime domestic importance, carries a weight equalled by few if any others. The use of the words "co-advisor of Comrade Stalin" gave unique emphasis to his position. . . .

[While Malenkov's service on the Politburo is considerably shorter than that of some of his colleagues, he has been intimately associated with Stalin for nearly twenty years. It seemed apparent from the manner in which his birthday was commemorated that he is destined to occupy a leading role in the Soviet government for years to come. . . .]

Dispatch Killed by Censor
January 9

It was reiterated to Pastor Niemöller that no German prisoners of war are now held by the Soviet. Germans working in Russia, it was emphasized, are Germans who agreed to accept employment here voluntarily and of their own free will.

It was agreed that among these Germans it would not be surprising if there were some who were once prisoners of war. But they were said to prefer the Soviet to their homeland and hence to have sought employment here.

Niemöller was given to understand that with regard to technicians recruited in Germany at the end of the war these contracts in most cases are being liquidated as rapidly as possible. He received the impression that few such German workers would remain in the Soviet at the end of this year—or even sooner.

January 13

There has been much discussion stirred up by the Oatis case* and, since Moscow is now the only Iron Curtain point where American correspondents remain, their situation has a special interest.

The U.S. press corps includes five Americans—Eddy Gilmore and Tom Whitney of AP, Henry Shapiro of UP, Andrew Steiger of Reuters, and myself. All of the correspondents except myself have been here many years and have become top specialists in Soviet affairs. The five of us together total about fifty-five years' residence in the Soviet Union. Thus, the correspondents are well equipped to cover Russia intelligently and accurately, and I believe they carry out their assignment quite well given the handicaps imposed by the Soviet government.

A special question is not infrequently raised. This is how the reporting of the four other American correspondents is affected by the fact that each has a Soviet wife and two of them Soviet children. My considered opinion is that the "wife factor" does not color the work of the correspondents. I have seen no evidence

* The arrest and trial in Prague of William Oatis, Associated Press correspondent.

that they curry favor with Soviet officials or pull their punches in hopes of preferred treatment for their wives and children.

On the contrary, I am impressed by their courage and honesty, regardless of possible reprisals.

Nor have I seen any direct or indirect pressure brought on the correspondents or their wives, although the opportunity is present and obvious. Actually, the correspondents and their wives live in the Western diplomatic community in Moscow, associating with Westerners. The Russian wives have little or no more contact with the Russian populace than other members of the diplomatic colony. Psychologically, the situation is difficult. They live on hopes for the future which are hard to maintain in the deepening tensions of the cold war. It upsets them to see suggestions in the U.S. press reflecting on their loyalty and reliability. Even without personal ties one's morale is likely to sink in Moscow—as I myself well know. There is bound to be some loss of initiative, some defeatism, some decline in aggressiveness.

External conditions of correspondence have changed little in my three years. Censorship, while still heavy, is perhaps a bit lighter. Statistical sources have dried up. Travel restrictions are unchanged. Facility visits and interviews are practically non-existent. Travel over a fairly wide area is still possible and profitable. Soviet officials treat correspondents courteously and correctly.

The net effect of censorship and other restrictions is to produce a news report which is rather consistently out of focus because it is only a partial report. This is unfortunate and, sometimes, possibly dangerous.

XVIII

The Freeze Deepens

Dispatch to New York Times
January 16, 1952

The Foreign Office has advised all embassies in a circular note that effective January 15 restrictions have been placed on travel to twenty-two cities. . . .

Soviet cities placed on the restricted list by the new circular include Poltava, Kharkov, Kirovgrad, Pskov, Vitebsk, Gomel, Yaroslavl, Shcherbakov, Bryansk, Chkalov, Novosibersk, Stalinsk, Ufa, Omsk, Tomsk, Igara, Cheremkhovo, Cherapovets, Yakutsk, Saratov, Astrakhan, and Makhachkala. . . .

The new regulations permit travel within forty kilometers of the center of Moscow. The old regulations permitted travel within fifty kilometers. . . .

[It formerly was possible for diplomats to make the very popular Volga River steamboat trip from Saratov to Astrakhan on the Caspian. This is no longer possible. . . .]

January 23

There is a certain fascination about living, as Kirk once phrased it, in "the eye of the hurricane." I could never forgive myself if I moved out of this hot spot just as things are working up to a climax.

So I have suggested to the *Times* that I am prepared to stay on in Moscow—under certain circumstances—for what we might call the "duration of the cold war."

I am looking forward with great anticipation to Kennan's arrival here. I am interested to see what his opinion will be after he has had time to check his studies against fresh, firsthand impressions. I want to correlate his opinions with mine.

The new travel restrictions strike me as a subject of irritation rather than profundity. I am angry that I decided to wait until this winter before going out to Siberia. Now, I suppose I will never get to see beautiful (?) Novosibersk and lovely (?) Omsk again. Let alone Baikal as I had planned. That was about the only trip in permitted areas which was worth taking which I had not made. *C'est la guerre.* There is always Leningard, which is ever a delight.

Not the least annoying restrictions are those on driving around Moscow. We already were constricted enough. The new rules cut out all three of the three decent drives and apparently eliminate the dacha at Saltikovka. I haven't yet pried a ruling out of Burobin, but it looks like the dacha is five hundred yards within a newly forbidden zone.

From what I know about the areas that have been cut off around Moscow, there probably is no real security consideration involved, although maybe they plan to install some additional and heavier antiaircraft defenses. Moscow is virtually ringed with airfields. Every road you drive out has at least one and often two or three. They are of all types—some are training fields, some are fighter fields, some are paratroop fields, and some are heavy bomber fields. The jets and B-29's for the Red Square shows are based on two—or maybe more—fields about twenty-five miles out of town. One of these is perhaps three or four miles from the dacha at Saltikovka. Before the Red Square shows we watch them practice formation flying twice a day. There are also small antiaircraft batteries on most of the highways just beyond the city limits. They are constantly manned and are located close to the highways. They are radar-equipped. Now, possibly they are about to put in some more and heavier batteries. This would seem sensible if the batteries are to be militarily effective and not just for show.

As for the cities added to the forbidden list, someone just went over the country and cut out all the places where diplomats have gone in the last couple of years plus a few others which it hadn't occurred to them to put on the list in 1941. The censorship deleted the fact that the list was first issued in 1941.

My guess is that the restrictions are retaliation for the activity which they claim we are indulging in in parachuting lads into Russia and the satellites. I see nothing particularly ominous in the new restrictions. In the present state of relations it has surprised me to see so much country open to travel.

The Pospelov speech* was very light on America. But there were points of interest. First, the very fact that he laid off the United States. Why? Possibly to avoid giving Truman another talking point in bucking his big arms program through Congress. The Russians in Moscow are restraining themselves from gratuitous name-calling. This was noticeable in Beriya's address November 6. Now, Pospelov does the same. His concentration on Asia may be significant. I think it is. That's where the Russians stand to make progress this year and maybe for years to come. The Party's interest has been firmly fixed in that direction. It suggests that Europe may be becoming a holding operation and that the real business lies in Asia. It is a good switch just as we are getting beefed up in Europe. Pospelov's third point was a reassurance to the home folks that they are moving into communism from socialism. How? Well, the Great Construction Projects of the Stalin Epoch, and the Great Stalinist Plan for the Reconstruction of Nature—that's how. So maybe it is going to turn out that communism is socialism plus PWA-REA-TVA and CCC. Instead of free bread. Interesting.

Dispatch to New York Times
January 30, 1952

The year's most important achievement in agriculture is the restoration of Soviet livestock herds to somewhat more than their strength of 1941. . . . Livestock holdings now are not only larger in bulk than before the second World War but are greater than those of 1916, the last year of czarist statistics. . . .

[Shoe production has increased sufficiently to give every man, woman, and child in the Soviet Union a pair of new shoes last year with several million surplus.]

* The annual speech on the anniversary of Lenin's death, given January 21, 1952.

241

February 1, 1952
Letter to Director, Burobin

I want to make an application for an apartment of four rooms or possibly of three if they are fairly large. I am presently occupying a rather large room at the Metropole Hotel as living quarters and a smaller room for my office. What I desire is an apartment suitable for both living and office purposes.

You will find in your files that I applied to you for an apartment answering the above description nearly two years ago. . . .

Dispatch to New York Times
February 2

Pravda devoted nearly one-quarter of its space today to Herbert Hoover's January 28 address* which it called prime evidence that "alarm has seized a wide strata of Americans" over present U.S. foreign policy. . . .

Dispatch to New York Times
February 3

Why did *Pravda* publish Herbert Hoover's speech? Possibly the most important factor is an obvious Soviet conviction that the United States is not irrevocably committed to the Truman foreign policy, which the Russians have often stated will inevitably lead to a third world war. . . . Another conclusion is that the Soviet is by no means convinced that a third world war is inevitable. . . .

February 7

So far as I can assess the situation here, there is no material increase in Russian concern about the possibility of war—at least not in recent weeks and months. The publication of Hoover's speech certainly is not any such indication. Indeed, *Pravda's* comments lead in the opposite direction.

---

* Herbert Hoover proposed that the United States withdraw its troops from western Europe and rely on hemispheric defense, based on air and sea power.

Dispatch to New York Times
February 9

The navy paper *Red Fleet* noted today that Russia's industrial potential is now more than double the plant capacity which enabled the Soviet to resist successfully Hitler's war machine. It said, "The significance of this fact is hard to overestimate." . . .

[It should not be forgotten that the Soviet is able to mobilize for military needs a considerably greater proportion of her industrial plant than the United States. For instance, in the case of steel the chief customer of the U.S. steel industry is the giant auto industry. The Soviet auto industry is only a fraction the size of that of the United States. Almost all of Russia's steel is available for military use.]

February 15

I understand that the Russians are planning to give visas to foreign correspondents to come in for the International Economic Conference, which opens April 3. I hope Cy will be able to come in at that time.

A serious misunderstanding has developed in New York about my attitude which I haven't been able to clear up in letters. What has been maturing in my mind has been the idea of taking on the Moscow assignment on a permanent basis—or as permanent as such things can be regarded in these troubled times. But, naturally, I want a more precise idea of how the *Times* would view such a project. I was afraid it would be hard to work this out by correspondence, and I find that I was right—the idea has taken root that I am hell-bent to get out of Moscow. I've told Cy to put the whole thing on ice until I can talk to him.

February 18
Letter to U. P. Frantzev, Press Department

I would appreciate information on the following questions:

1. Do the new restrictions on travel of which the Foreign Office advised the embassies on January 15 apply to correspondents as well?

2. Is the dacha rented by Mr. Whitney and myself in the vil-

lage of Saltikovka within the restricted zone? It appears to be very close to the line—possibly two hundred yards or so from a line drawn between Nikolskaya and Saltikovka.

Incidentally, in recent days, I have found it virtually impossible to reach Mr. Khlopikov or any responsible officer of the press department by telephone. . . .

February 19, 1952

There is nothing very exciting to say at the moment about life here. Things are quiet and peaceful—a fact which continues to astound people from the U.S.A. but which is nonetheless true. So long as this state prevails I cannot really believe that the world is about to go up in flames the day after tomorrow. But perhaps I am wrong.

This winter quantities of oranges, lemons, and bananas have appeared in the stores. A small thing, perhaps, but a pleasant one.

I shouldn't want to give the impression that there is no concern here about the world situation. That there is. But nothing like the constant "crisis" atmosphere which seems to permeate the American press.

Niemöller has arrived in the U.S.A. for a tour. What is likely to astonish Americans as much as it surprised Russians is his feeling of great similarities between Americans and Russians— he felt the similarities were much more striking than the differences. He also thought the difference between the spirit of the regime here and that of the Hitler regime was much more important than any superficial resemblance.

Dispatch to New York Times
February 20

The blood-chilling mating call of Tarzan is echoing from the sound screens of twenty Moscow first-run movie houses this week. . . . The Tarzan which is thrilling Moscow filmgoers is an early Johnny Wiessmuller version. . . .

February 27
Letter to Emanuel R. Freedman, New York Times

I want to make the following change in the message set-up in event of Stalin's death.

244

Should this event occur, and should I have reason to suppose that censorship has been imposed, I will file the following messages:

Freedman final expense account mailed today regards Salisbury

Catledge regarding expense account please check with Freedman Salisbury

The messages will be filed "LC." If the death occurred the day before the message is filed, the message will say, "Final expense account mailed yesterday." If two days previously—the message will read appropriately, etc.

Anyone who might be in charge of the cable desk in your absence should be advised of this message set-up as should Catledge and his office.

Frankly, I think it is a thousand to one shot that anything will be known in advance of the official announcement, which almost certainly will be released for publication abroad as soon as it is made here.[*]

The old man's health appears very good, to judge by external appearances, and I think it would be wise to query me before putting into print any rumors about it such as the very silly item from Amsterdam which AP carried, a clipping of which I attach. It was only a few days later that Stalin appeared at the Bolshoi for the Lenin anniversary meeting in obvious good health and spirits.

Dispatch Killed by Censor
March 3

Serious concern has been expressed by the Uzbek government and Party leaders over preparations for the 1952 cotton crop which is hoped to exceed that of last year by 400,000 tons. . . .

March 10

It has turned out that the dacha is not in a restricted zone. So we will have it again this year. For a month we did not use it because we thought it had been put out of bounds.

Now, like all good gardeners, our thoughts have turned to spring, which is almost here—just as in Minnesota (I hope). I have asked Janet to send me some early maturing seeds, the ones

---

[*] In fact when the announcement finally came at 4:00 A.M., March 6, 1953, an outgoing censorship was imposed. Not only did censorship hold up my cable on Stalin's death—they delayed the coded cable as well.

with the shortest growing season—seeds which would be suitable for northern Minnesota. With each package of seeds must be inclosed a certificate from the Department of Agriculture certifying the seeds are free of disease.

I don't expect to be getting back to the States this spring. My guess now is in the autumn. It is now practically decided that I am to remain in Moscow indefinitely, with home leaves, of course.

Dispatch to New York Times
March 11, 1952

The most important feature of the new Soviet proposals on Germany is the declaration that formation of a unified all-German government must precede the final preparation and signature of the German peace treaty. . . .*

Dispatch to New York Times
March 11

One of the great spirits of Russia's Revolution, Alexandra Kollontay, is dead at the age of eighty. Thirty-five lines of type on the back page of *Izvestia* this morning reported the death two days ago of the woman whom her comrades called "the red rose of the Revolution." . . .

[It was evident from *Izvestia*'s brief note today that her passing makes no more ripple on the surface of Soviet life than the death a few weeks ago of two of her great collaborators in the early days of Soviet diplomacy, Maxim Litvinov and Jacob Suritz. All three have quietly departed from the Russian scene this winter without fanfare or ceremonial. . . .]

Dispatch Killed by Censor
March 12

It appears that Georgi M. Popov, who until two years ago was mayor of Moscow, one of the four secretaries of the central committee of the Bolshevik Party, and a rising star in the Soviet

* Generically, this Soviet proposal for a German peace treaty, four-power talks, withdrawal of foreign troops, liquidation of bases, etc., started the intermittent East-West German negotiations which were to continue over the next five or six years.

galaxy, no longer holds any high government post. . . . Popov was replaced in Moscow by Nikita Khrushchev. . . . Popov was given a job as agricultural machinery minister, but now he has sunk below the horizon entirely. . . .

March 14

Things seem to be brightening up a bit from the news standpoint after the long hibernation of the Moscow winter. The last month of winter always seems the longest to me, but this year we have had a fine mid-March thaw which reminds me of Minnesota. Probably next week will bring blizzards again.

March 15
Letter to Glavlit, Soviet Censor

On March 3 I submitted to you a dispatch dealing with the cotton growers of Tashkent. Up to this moment there has been no action on this dispatch. . . .

It has been my experience over a period of nearly three years that for reasons which are obscure you have great difficulty in either passing for publication or deciding what to do with cotton dispatches based on the Central Asiatic press. . . .

Dispatch to New York Times
March 21

For the ninth day in succession mass meetings were held today in cities, towns, and villages all over Russia backing Soviet charges that the United States is employing bacteriological weapons in Korea and Manchuria. . . . The last occasion on which mass meetings were held on anything like this scale was just after the outbreak of the Korean war. . . .

Dispatch to New York Times
March 24

What Russia needs today, *Pravda* observed recently, are new Gogols and Shchedrins, armed with the sharp scalpel of satire and capable of letting the "fresh air of criticism" into the dark, backward, and stuffy corners of this country.

Pravda's remark has become something like the slogan of the day since the announcement of the annual Stalin prizes for out-standing plays, theatrical productions, and the like.

For the first time in many years the committee found no play worthy of receiving a first prize. Second prize went to a Chinese play and third to a playwright from Yakutia. . . .

Actually, the most popular playwrights on the Moscow stage this season have been none other than Nikolai Gogol, Lev Tolstoi, Maxim Gorki, and Victor Hugo. . . .

The search for a new "Soviet" opera is still under way. Last year two major efforts were made—the first was the Bolshoi Theater production of *From the Depths of the Heart*. But it was withdrawn after *Pravda* said it had "an extremely low artistic level." A second effort was made by the Ukrainian playwright, Alexander Korneichuk, with his opera, *Bogdan Khmelnitsky*. But it drew such ire from *Pravda* that it was promptly withdrawn. Because of these difficulties, the Bolshoi's only new opera this year has been *Aida*. . . .

Dispatch to New York Times
March 26, 1952

The Supreme Soviet of the Russian Federated Republic met tonight at the Kremlin. Members of the Politburo present were Molotov, Malenkov, Beriya, Voroshilov, Mikoyan, Kosygin, Bulganin, Shvernik, Andreyev, Khrushchev, and Kaganovich. Sitting between Khrushchev and Kaganovich was Mikhail A. Suslov, secretary of the central committee. [It is not known whether Suslov's presence with the Politburo indicates that he has become a candidate member. . . .]

March 28

For the last three or four weeks all the leading hotels in town —the Metropole, National, Grand, Savoy, and Moskva—have been undergoing refurbishing preparatory to the big economic conference in April. Some streamlined new furniture made in Leningrad has been substituted for the massive old Metropole pieces. The Metropole has three big new oil paintings—including one of Stalin and Lenin. The halls have been recarpeted and a big parking lot set up outside the hotel for the limousines of the delegates.

Dispatch Killed by Censor
March 29

A general reduction of Soviet retail prices, effective April 1, was widely anticipated in Moscow tonight. . . . Business in stores —except for foodstuffs—was extremely slow. . . .

Dispatch to New York Times
March 29

Generalissimo Stalin appeared fit and vigorous tonight at the concluding session of the Russian Federated Republic Supreme Soviet.

Stalin wore a beige-colored generalissimo's uniform with gold-embossed shoulder-boards and a generalissimo's sash of a contrasting shade of beige.

He was given a standing ovation. He walked to and fro with a firm step and his features appeared ruddy and healthy. His appearance gave the lie to recent rumors in the European press concerning his health. . . . .

Dispatch to New York Times
March 31

The government tonight announced price reductions of 10 to 30 per cent on forty-eight principal categories of food products, including meat, butter, sugar, eggs, bread, and flour. . . .

[Foreign observers had anticipated that prices would be cut on textiles, clothing, leather goods, and shoes, but the reductions were limited to foodstuffs.]

Dispatch to New York Times
April 1

Oliver Vickery, apostle of American free enterprise, arrived in Moscow today for Moscow's International Economic Conference. He was ensconced in a three-room luxury suite in the brand-new Sovetskaya Hotel, a dreamlike hostelry of white marble and imitation green malachite. . . . Vickery's bedroom is paneled in cloth of gold tapestry. "It doesn't cost me a cent," Vickery said. The hotel has been created by extensive remodeling of the building which housed the famous old Yar restaurant of czarist days.

[Although the conference opens Thursday, no decision has yet been made whether foreign newspaper correspondents will be admitted.]*

Dispatch to New York Times
April 2, 1952

Stalin today gave powerful impetus to a new Soviet drive which observers believe is designed to effect a reduction in world tensions and achieve settlement of the German question.

In reply to questions from a group of American editors, he affirmed his belief that a third world war is not appreciably nearer, supported the new Soviet proposals on Germany, and said a meeting of the heads of state of great powers might prove useful at the present time. . . .

[There was no doubt in the minds of Western observers in Moscow that the Soviet proposals on Germany are directed against West Germany's adherence to the North Atlantic Pact grouping.]

April 3
Letter to Director, Burobin

On February 1, I wrote you requesting that you provide me with an apartment. I did not even get the courtesy of a reply. On March 15 I wrote again.

I have heard nothing further from your administration. . . . I would like to know at the earliest moment when you expect to fill my request. . . .

April 3
Letter to Mr. Yeregin, Telegraph Office

I should like to bring to your attention the following facts concerning transmission of my cables of yesterday, 020515, 020530, and 020545, dealing with Generalissimo Stalin's statement.

In order that the cables might be handled as fast as possible I marked each of them for transmission at the urgent rate.

Although these were urgent cablegrams, the girl at the *kassa* laid them aside in order to count wordage and forward four ordinary rate telegrams. Meantime, the girls at the *kassa* counted

* After much vacillation a decision was made not to admit foreign correspondents.

and recounted the wordage of my two cables. While I watched, they counted the words no less than *ten* times!

As a result the cables were delayed in transmission forty to forty-five minutes. I must protest that such a delay makes mockery of the term "urgent press." I should like to ask what is the purpose of having an "urgent" rate?

The fact is, of course, that you have assigned to the *kassa* several new, inexperienced girls just at a time when there is a great volume of important urgent news. . . . Frankly, I am shocked at the laissez faire manner in which your personnel handled the Generalissimo talin news yesterday. . . .

Dispatch to New York Times
April 3

The International Economic Conference convened today in the Hall of Columns. The former Nobleman's Club has been transformed for the occasion. New blond birch desks have been installed and a six-way simultaneous translation system with headphones for each delegate. . . .

April 5

Even an American plumber would have to give grudging admiration for the gleaming tile bathrooms in the new Sovetskaya Hotel. The whole place has been outfitted with a lavish magnificence—white marble, malachite columns, crystal chandeliers; tables groaning with caviar, sturgeon in jelly. Siberian game, mounds of butter, heaps of Israeli oranges, tender beefsteaks, and God knows what else.

Dispatch to New York Times
April 6

Stalin believes all outstanding world problems are capable of settlement by discussion and negotiation and regards suggestions for a meeting of the chiefs of state with an open mind.

This conclusion was reached by Moscow diplomats after several developments, the latest of which was a frank and open discussion last night between Stalin and the retiring Indian Ambassador, Dr. Sarvepolli Radhakrishnan. . . .

[Among the matters discussed was the question of the stalemate in the Korean truce negotiations.]

Dispatch to New York Times
April 12, 1952

The International Economic Conference ended tonight after effecting a substantial trade rapprochement between Britain and Russia, China and East Europe. Trade deals in the neighborhood of $200,000,000 were concluded. . . .

Dispatch to New York Times
April 23

Moscow diplomats feel certain that when and if the chiefs of state assemble to discuss global problems Russia will insist on the right of China's Mao Tse-tung to sit at the council table.

This was the conclusion drawn from close reading of an important communiqué issued by the official Tass News Agency, denying certain reports carried by the Indian press. . . .

April 25
Letter to Mr. Yeregin, Telegraph Office

I want to thank you for the new and expeditious system of handling press telegrams which has now been instituted in the Central Telegraph Office. Having repeatedly criticized your organization, I believe it only fair to place on record my appreciation of the present system which has considerably speeded up the transmission of telegrams.

April 25
Letter to S. Kilgast, Burobin

I should like to know what progress is being made on my request that you provide me with an apartment. . . .

April 29
Letter to Director, Burobin

I want to direct your attention to several repairs which are necessary to the dacha which Mr. Whitney and I rent from you at Saltikovka.

First, the dacha is badly in need of painting. Mr. Whitney and I have obtained sufficient good quality oil paint to paint the house. We would appreciate it if you could fix an early date at which your workmen could paint the house.

Second, the second floor of the balcony is quite shaky and should be inspected to see if it is safe.

Third, a number of cracks have appeared in the stove. It looks as though it may be in danger of collapse.

Fourth, the debris from the toilet which was cleaned out during the winter should be removed from the premises immediately as it is unsightly and a menace to health.

Fifth, several boards in the porch floor and steps have rotted and should be replaced.

Sixth, wire screening should be provided along certain parts of the fence to prevent the constant incursion of goats, chickens, and geese from surrounding dachas. . . .

Dispatch to New York Times
May 1

Stalin stood atop Lenin's Tomb in Red Square today, witnessing the May Day demonstration of Russian armed might and a parade of 1,000,000 civilians carrying the slogan "Stalin is Peace!" Stalin looked fit in his beige generalissimo's uniform.

XIX

Kennan in Moscow

Dispatch to New York Times
May 6, 1952

George F. Kennan, the United States outstanding specialist on Russian affairs, arrived at Vnukovo airdrome this afternoon to assume his post as American ambassador. His purpose, as he said before leaving the United States, is to seek the "reduction of existing tensions and the improvement of the international atmosphere."

He told correspondents he comes not as the bearer of any special assignment or intrusted with any extraordinary responsibilities. . . .

His philosophy is that diplomatic negotiations and relations between states should not be influenced by emotional considerations but should be founded on realistic assessment of national interests. . . .

Dispatch to New York Times
Zagorsk, May 10

Jews, Roman Catholics, Moslems, Calvinists, Baptists, and other Russian religious faiths joined today in calling on their co-religionists throughout the world to work for peace and oppose bacteriological weapons.

The appeal was made at a conference in the Troitski-Sergeivsky Lavra, the medieval citadel of Russia's fighting monks. . . .

Among the speakers was the chief rabbi of Moscow, Solomon Shliffer. He said that Jewish religious leaders did not occupy themselves with political questions but could not stand aside from issues of life and death.

The Soviet Union under the leadership of the great Stalin, said Shliffer, "is carrying out a foreign policy based on peace and friendship. Jews everywhere must join the struggle for peace against the atomshiks and hypocritical pharisees who are unacceptable to God because their hands are stained with blood. . . ."

Canon Strode, the deputy of the Roman Catholic bishop of Riga, called upon Roman Catholics everywhere to join the peace movement. He called Stalin "the great wise leader of our state. . . ."

May 18

The seeds got here about April 20—just as Tom and I were about ready to start on the garden. Now we have it almost all planted. The weather has been warm and pleasant since May 1. The seeds came through intact except for the corn which the inspectors took out—apparently afraid of corn borers. Or, perhaps, because it was pelleted seed and they didn't know what it might be.

Things are quiet. We are spending more and more time in the country getting the dacha going for the summer and working in the yard. We put in berry bushes and some shrubs and fruit trees this spring.

It is good to have Kennan here after being without an ambassador for some six months since the departure of Kirk.

Dispatch to New York Times
May 19

The office of the American ambassador in Moscow is a severely functional room, twenty-five by twenty feet, and considerably less impressive than that of a deputy price administrator in Washington.

Its only decorations are two blown-up photographs, one of President Truman and one of Franklin D. Roosevelt. In one corner is a mahogany desk. In another a brown leather couch and two brown leather arm chairs around a glass-topped coffee table.

There is nothing in any way remarkable about the office except the view. The view is magnificent. The ambassador looks out a broad picture window across the acre or so of black asphalt pavement which is Menege Square. He can peer over a thirty-foot wall of faded rose brick right into that storybook melange of four centuries of Russian architectural tastes—the Kremlin.

No foreigner in all Moscow has such a view. And no foreigner in all Russia is closer, physically, to the Kremlin than the American ambassador in the embassy building on Mokhovaya Street.

In a way George Kennan is responsible for the fact that this view exists. As a young State Department specialist in Russian affairs he handled much of the negotiation which resulted in the acquisition of the Mokhovaya Street building. . . .

The man who stands at the window on Menege Square today is a man who can see more than the colorful façade of buildings beyond the pink walls of the Kremlin. Not only does he look with trained eyes, but he has the trained mind to interpret what goes on before his eyes. When he walks down a Moscow street, the signs and posters and placards are not a mere gibberish of strange letters and even stranger words to him. If any straws are being blown about by the Russian wind, Kennan's keen eyes can be counted upon to observe them.

Dispatch to New York Times
May 20, 1952

If you want to telephone the Kremlin, the number to call is Center 6–7571. That's the telephone number of the Presidium of the Supreme Soviet whose offices are in the Kremlin, and it is the first telephone listed in the new Moscow city telephone directory. The directory weighs three and a half pounds and carries listings of about 52,600 individual telephone subscribers and 15,000 other numbers of offices, stores, schools, etc.

[Members of the government like Stalin, Molotov, Malenkov, Beriya, Voroshilov, and Mikoyan are not listed. The Ministry of Internal Affairs is listed but not the Ministry of State Security. There is just one Stalin in the book—P. M. Stalin, living at Bolshaya Devyatinskaya, No. 4. His phone number is Dzherzhinskaya 2–1298. There are seventy-nine Romanovs listed.]

May 29

There has been a lot of concern and anger and nasty words in the papers this week about the signing of the Bonn and Paris agreements. But it has not disturbed the average Muscovite's satisfaction over the glorious spring weather.

It has been a rather backward spring in central Russia, and when spring is late it takes something very sharp and very alarming to distract the Muscovite from his belated enjoyment of the sun's warm rays.

Dispatch to New York Times
May 31

For the second time within a little more than six weeks a great series of mass meetings is being held to express public indignation and anger at the American conduct of the war in Korea. The newest campaign is directed against American treatment of Korean prisoners of war. . . .

[The accusations are calculated to arouse the deepest horror and revulsion in the minds of Soviet listeners. It does not seem likely that the participants in these meetings can retain any very friendly thought toward Americans.]

Dispatch Killed by Censor
June 2

An extensive reorganization of the Communist Party leadership and government in Soviet Georgia has been carried out apparently under the personal supervision of Politburo member Lavrenti P. Beriya.

The changes, reported by Tbilisi newspaper *Zarya Vostoka,* were ordered in mid-April by a plenum of the central committee of the Georgian Party attended by Beriya. Beriya, who for many, many years led the Communist Party of Georgia, personally participated in the work of the plenary.

A series of party resolutions thanked Beriya for his action in coming to Tbilisi to assist the plenum.

Among the causes cited for the Georgian changes are failure of vital industries to meet production quotas, slowness in carrying out agricultural plans, violations of collective farm statutes,

257

criminal squandering of funds, graft, bribery, and other disorders. Ideological and political work was said to have fallen into decay.

The most important change was the release as secretary of the Georgian Party of Kandid N. Charkviani, who had held that post since 1938 when he replaced Beriya. His successor was Akaki Ivanovich Mgeladze. Z. Ketzhkoveli was named president of the Council of Ministers to replace Z. N. Chkhubianishvili. Others who lost their posts were V. B. Gogua and K. E. Razmadze, deputy minister of state security. But General Alexei I. Antonov continues as commander of the Trans-Caucasus military district with General N. Rukhadze as his chief lieutenant.*

Dispatch to New York Times
June 6, 1952

Pravda today put considerable blame upon former secretary of the Communist Party of Georgia, Comrade Shaduri, for the failures and lapses uncovered by the mid-April plenum.

[A large number of other Party secretaries and lesser officials have also been released from their posts. *Pravda* mentioned no other names but that of Shaduri, but it was sweeping in condemning the shiftless and irresponsible attitude which it said was general in the Georgian Party and government.]

Dispatch to New York Times
June 7

Soviet historians have undertaken another major reassessment of history—this time dealing with Crimea. It is said that the importance of the Crimean Khans has been exaggerated in the past out of a feeling of deference to Tatar bourgeois nationalists.

[Soviet historians are in no mood to defer to Tatar nationalist feelings. These elements made common cause with the Germans during World War II. Following the recovery of Crimea by the Red Army, large numbers of Tatar nationalists were removed from the region and sent to Siberia.]

---

* The purge of the Georgian Party was the first public hint of any diminution of influence for Beriya and the first public indication of the maneuvering which went on inside the higher echelons of the Communist Party in the months immediately preceding Stalin's death. In fact, of course, the significance of the Georgian shake-up was not apparent for some months.

Dispatch to New York Times
June 13

Einstein's theory of relativity was attacked today by Soviet scientific spokesmen as a cul-de-sac of contemporary physics. [The backwardness of Soviet physical theory was blamed upon the persistence among Soviet scientists of Einstein's beliefs.]

Dispatch to New York Times
June 15

Pravda informed its readers today that the presidential candidacy of General Eisenhower stems from a plot by the Democratic party to insure the continuance of Truman's policies regardless of whether the Republicans or the Democrats win the 1952 elections. . . .

Dispatch to New York Times
June 19

Ambassador Kennan is concerned over the current campaign in the Soviet Union charging American mistreatment of prisoners of war in Korea.

It is believed that Kennan has conveyed to Soviet officials some indication of his views. The ambassador is leaving Moscow Saturday for a brief trip to western Europe.

He believes that given time and patience it may prove possible for the United States and Russia to work out accommodations on many basic problems. This has not been modified by anything which has developed since he arrived in Moscow in early May. . . .

June 20

From such talks as I have had with Kennan, I believe I am safe in saying that his ideas and mine about conditions in Russia coincide to a very remarkable degree. He is not optimistic, of course, but he is by no means pessimistic or defeatist. I must say it is very, very good having him here. He is off by air early tomorrow morning for a week's trip in western Europe where he will be talking with Acheson and giving him a firsthand report of his impressions. He believes that now is the time for thoughtful and quiet conversation far from the spotlight of world publicity, and he is carrying on his diplomacy here on the basis of this principle.

Dispatch Killed by Censor
June 26, 1952

Diplomats do not see how the Soviet propaganda campaign about alleged American atrocities in Korea can fail to increase the support which the ordinary Soviet citizen gives to his government's foreign policy.

This is especially true since he is told that the Soviet government is fighting against the perpetrators of horrendous crimes.

Diplomats feel this strengthens the hand of the Soviet government for any steps it may consider necessary to combat the "barbarous depredations of the Americans."

Dispatch to New York Times
July 1

Izvestia reported today the plight of a beekeeper named Obratzov, of the Grozny region, who has been investigated by some twelve commissions. So far they have found nothing wrong, but as *Izvestia* notes Obratzov hasn't yet succeeded in proving that he never thought of doing anything wrong. . . .

Dispatch to New York Times
July 9

The witch of Balashikhinsk no longer plies her craft, Moscow *Pravda* reports, but only after repeated complaints prodded local authorities into action. The witch, Feliksa Andreevna Stefanovich, amassed a hoard of money, gold, wool, and silk by telling fortunes, prescribing charms and potions, and curing toothaches. . . .

Dispatch to New York Times
July 10

In their flats down by the stables next to the National Hotel,
    Beneath the blood red Kremlin stars we know so well,
    Sing the Mokhovayans. . . .
                —Lines from an old Moscow song.

No American now resident in Moscow remembers who first put those words to the music of Yale's Whiffenpoof song and set the chorus ringing in one of the high-vaulted apartments in the seven-story tan stone building at No. 13, Mokhovaya Street.

No. 13, Mokhovaya Street has been the address of the American embassy in Moscow since July 5, 1934, but in a few months from now "the Mokhovayans" and Mokhovaya Street will be only a memory.

The American embassy has received notice that by the end of this year it will have to move to new quarters and give up the famous building that fronts on Menege Square. . . .

Dispatch to New York Times
July 27

American Ambassador Kennan deliberately absented himself from the Soviet air show today to underline his formal protest against Russian posters depicting Soviet fighter planes warding off incursions by American planes over the Soviet air frontier. . . .

Stalin reviewed the air show. He alighted before the airport from his great black limousine and mounted the steps with a jaunty air. He carried one of his famous pipes and during the show he puffed in relaxation and occasionally pointed with the pipe to the air acrobatics.

Among the Politburo members present were Molotov, Malenkov, Beriya, Voroshilov, Bulganin, Kaganovich, Mikoyan, Andreyev, and Khrushchev. . . .

July 29
Letter to Director, Burobin

I understand that in the near future the American embassy will be giving up the apartments which it now occupies in the Sadovaya building. This will release a number of apartments and should make it possible for you to fill my long-standing request. . . .

Dispatch to New York Times
July 30

Discussing the nomination of Adlai Stevenson for the Presidency, Soviet commentators said that the November elections will be "for Wall Street a lottery in which it cannot lose."

261

July 31, 1952
Letter to Brooks Atkinson, New York Times

I thought you might be interested to see the use to which the *Literary Gazette* put your summation of the dismal events of the past season on Broadway.

The Metropole is quite spruced up since the days of Mrs. Atkinson's famous *Over at Uncle Joe's*. They put a new carpet on the floor of old 317 the other day without so much as a by-your-leave from me—a rather gaudy purple number which gives the room a certain tone. Or perhaps I should say an uncertain tone.

Curiously enough, were I to write a summary of the past Moscow theatrical season, I'm afraid I should have to use a good many of the same phrases which you tagged onto Broadway— particularly if I wrote about the plays on current themes. And I would only be echoing the criticisms of the Soviet press which takes an equally dim view of the season here. The only really enjoyable productions have been revivals. The Moscow Art Theater has done a beautiful job with Tolstoi's *Fruits of Enlightenment,* a period piece which is precisely suited to their talent for lovingly reproducing mid-nineteenth-century Moscow. Another revival which has been very, very popular and which I enjoyed was Lermontov's *Masquerade*—pure melodrama but with something of the grand style about it.

The more I see of the Moscow theater, the more I feel that my grandfather would have found himself right at home in most of the productions—barring, of course, the so-called modern problem plays and the rash of American spy melodramas which now, thankfully, seems to have run its course.

The state of playwriting and production is a source of great concern to the Party. Every year that I have been here there has been a general beating of breasts and an outbreak of bitter criticism. The theater is on the horns of a real dilemma. As you know, it must be moralistic and it must show the triumph of good over evil. But at the same time evil must not be attractive and good must be lifelike. As the critics correctly note, the good characters tend to be stereotypes and the evil ones steal the spotlight. This earns the playwright a drubbing for failing to make

262

his good people alive and for depicting "untypical" or "un-Soviet" types in his gallery of bad characters. . . .

July 31

The censorship has killed a fairly decent story which I wrote from Leningrad about the progress of their subway system. It is very curious that this big project which has been under way since the end of the war receives almost no publicity. The censorship almost invariably kills any reference to it. I simply can't fathom their reasoning.

Incidentally, censorship is very light these days—has been, in fact, since early spring. One thing they are very touchy about is the great Party shake-up in Georgia. My first and fullest account of that was killed entirely. Subsequent sharply toned-down versions, including the very revealing mention of Beriya's presence at the Party plenum, did go through.

August 1

The garden has been terrific. The squash has flourished as I had never dreamed. We have bushels of peas and beans and soon will have more tomatoes than we will know what to do with. We have corn—some of it Russian and some from seeds left over from last year. We have done great work fixing up the dacha. We have a fireplace—a big undertaking because the Russian stove-builder never heard of one. The place has been painted, and I wish I could stay there all the time. I hope in the next couple of months to get out of the Metropole and into an apartment.

Dispatch Killed by Censor
August 9

The newspaper Kazakhstan *Pravda* reports that plural marriages are common in the October region of northern Kazakhstan. One farmer is said to have taken six wives. . . .

August 10

I must say I am proud of our summer cottage. We have put in a great deal of work, and it has paid off. We have a gas stove—gas from tanks—an electric refrigerator and water from either of two wells, each about two hundred yards distant, and a glassed-in front porch with colored glass—topaz and deep blue in the top and side panes. A pretty and lovely thing. In the front yard we have dahlias, gladioli, larkspur, asters, marigolds, zinnias, phlox, tobacco, the prettiest pansies you ever saw, bachelor's buttons, petunias, and half a dozen other kinds of flowers.

The other day Tom got a lawnmower—one of two or three in all Russia. We have cut the lawn—that is, Tom has, because I seem to have had my fill of lawnmowing in my youth. We have painted the house white and blue outside. I don't believe anyone in Russia has a nicer dacha, and few people have better summer cottages in the States. It is a joy and a pleasure. We have corn a foot higher than my head now, and it is still growing.

This summer I have been able to lead a quiet and pleasant life in the country—only going to town once or twice a week. The chauffeur brings the papers out, and I write my stories at the dacha and he takes them to the telegraph office. In any other place this kind of life would be impossible. But there are seldom press conferences or anything which requires one's personal attendance. Mostly it is just reading the papers and the magazines and sucking your thumb.

The weather has been good. One pleasant hot clear day after another. We have a pond (muddy and not too clean) half a mile away where we can swim if we wish. Last year we went to a beautiful lake five or six miles away with a lovely sand bottom and few people around. But this year it is out of bounds, unfortunately.

This is a life conducive to peace, quiet, and ease of mind. But, of course, no one knows how long it will continue.

August 11, 1952

I have been pondering lately about some petty and trivial incidents of what might be called anti-correspondent feeling over on Mokhovaya Street. Nothing important but more than a little annoying.

However, that water is over the dam now, and thank goodness we have a new and good ambassador who is running things with an iron hand and who is completely frank and open in his relations with correspondents. He is not a great source of news because he has decided ideas of how the embassy's business should be conducted. But he plays fair and square and does what he says, or tells you why he can't do something.

I see a good bit of him as he has taken a great liking to coming out to the dacha. So, I am no longer worried about any little nastinesses which might make life less pleasant.

There is little difference between Kennan's public and private views. He has a real if perhaps rather fatalistic notion that he may be the chosen instrument of achieving some mitigation of relations. He is working at that in his own way, which is not anything spectacular and may, of course, never bear any fruit. He is being careful and correct, and he has knocked a lot of moonshine out of the heads of some of our people here who, I must say, often arrive with wild and woolly ideas picked up from the less reliable daily papers or by too close study of Senator McCarthy. Drew Middleton had a piece a month or so ago which gave a fairly accurate picture of how Kennan sizes up some conditions here, based, I noted, largely on his impressions from strolling around the village where the dacha is located. About the time he went to London to see Acheson in June, the Alsops, *Time* magazine, and probably some others published rather scary versions of his impressions. Those reports were not correct. He does not take an alarmist view. He is annoyed by the propaganda but does not think it betokens any radical shift. He probably is more annoyed because this propaganda makes what he wants to do more difficult.

We are really in the dog days so far as news is concerned. Of course, the quiet will be broken one of these days by a new note on Germany (or possibly on any number of other things). . . .*

* On August 12, 1952, some twenty-four victims of an alleged conspiracy of Jews against the Soviet state were executed. Of these charges, the trial, and the execution nothing was known in such Moscow circles as I had access to.

XX

The Pace Quickens

A change in the atmosphere of Moscow occurred late in the summer of 1952—a sudden quickening of the pace of events. Chou En-lai arrived to negotiate a new Soviet-Chinese agreement. The Nineteenth Party Congress, first since 1939, was announced for October. A new five-year plan was proposed. Signs became visible of maneuvers within the Soviet political hierarchy. To those of us in Moscow, no real pattern was apparent behind these diverse events, but there was a sense of swift and dangerous undercurrents—a sense that deepened after the Nineteenth Party Congress with the ever broadening sequence of charges, countercharges, allegations of ideological sins, the fantastic "doctors' plot," and the whole miasma of terror that was to precede Stalin's death in March, 1953.

Dispatch to New York Times
August 18, 1952

The Soviet Union and China have opened diplomatic negotiations to broaden their military and economic collaboration. The discussions will review questions of threats to peace both in Europe and the Far East. China's foreign minister, Chou En-lai, has arrived for talks with Politburo members Molotov, Mikoyan, and Bulganin. . . .

August 19

Everything seems peaceful and quiet except the newspaper columns. The countryside is lovely in its late summer aspects.

The harvest is pouring in. New buildings are going up. New dams are functioning, and there is a New Deal aspect to things.

Behind that façade, however, I feel there is a little grimmer feeling, a hardening conviction that it is going to be a long time before there is any meeting of minds between East and West.

I don't think there is a feeling that the outcome of our election is going to make any material difference.

The big news, of course, is the arrival of Chou and his Chinese entourage for the Big Talks. We will know no more about those than we are told in the communiqué, but my guess is that their principal purpose is what happens if things get worse. There is room for closer and more practical military arrangements than those of the 1950 treaty. After all, the Far East is not the only danger point. Possibly a full-fledged military alliance will be an outcome as well as military arrangements for the build-up of China's forces and heavy industry. Things will be put on such a footing that both countries will be in shape to meet any "emergency." Then, it would be logical to take another whack at settling Korea.

There is a conviction here that the present situation is frozen for an unpredictable period.

Life from the personal standpoint is pleasant. Particularly in the summertime when it has a Westchester–Lake Minnetonka aspect. The dacha is only twenty kilometers from town but it could be fifty so far as atmosphere is concerned. We have all the peace and quiet one could ask. Sweet corn ripening on the stalks. Lots of tomatoes, cucumbers, squash, beans, peas, potatoes, onions, turnips, beets. There's a wonderful farmers' market in the village and as uncomplicated an existence as you could find. All we lack is a deep freeze. Maybe we'll have that next year. . . .

Dispatch to New York Times
August 20

In his capacity of secretary of the central committee of the Communist Party, Stalin has announced a call for a general Party congress October 5.

The congress will act on proposals to eliminate the Politburo and will hear Georgi M. Malenkov deliver the chief report. It is difficult to overestimate the importance of the congress. It is the first to be held since the war. It is the first time since 1925 that Stalin will not present the principal report.

[But these are not the only significant features of the first Party congress in thirteen years. An outstanding proposal to come before the congress is that for general revision of the Party statutes, eliminating the Politburo and the Orgburo and setting up a new Presidium. The report on the statute changes will be presented by Khrushchev. Thus, the chief announced roles at the congress will be played by Malenkov and Khrushchev. . . .]

Dispatch to New York Times
August 20, 1952

Soviet heavy industry has been pointed to the greatest quantitative expansion in Russian history with publication of the goals of the fifth five-year plan, which will end in 1955.

The program puts terrific emphasis on boosting the output of steel mills, smelters, coal mines, oil fields, power plants, and heavy machine and tool factories. . . .

By 1955 the steel industry should be turning out well over two-thirds of the 60 million metric tons which Stalin has set as the goal to be achieved in 1960. . . .

Even more important is the enormous project for power expansion which will carry electric production up to 162 billion kilowatts compared with 102 billion last year. . . .

August 21

What strikes most people in Moscow about the Nineteenth Party Congress is the fact that Malenkov is going to deliver the chief report for the first time, instead of Stalin, and that Khrushchev, who came up to Moscow from the Ukraine only three years ago, is also playing an important role.

The replacement of the Politburo by a Presidium seems to be more of a semantic than a practical change. Of more importance is the fact that the Orgburo's powers will be vested in the permanent secretariat. Some people expect the Presidium to comprise a wider membership than the Politburo. Expansion of the secretariat, two of whose leading members are Malenkov and Khrushchev—along with Stalin—also seems to be of great significance. The biggest speculation centers around Malenkov's role.

There has been very little published about the Chinese negotiations except for Chou's formal meeting with Stalin at the Kremlin on Wednesday.

Dispatch Killed by Censor
August 21

The Soviet has launched construction of a mighty new industrial complex in the heartlands of Siberia along the Angara River not far from Lake Baikal.

A brief outline of the new base has been given in the new five-year plan. It may be the most significant and in some respects the most important new project in the plan.

The Angara plan calls for eight hydroelectric units with total capacity of 9,000,000 kilowatts—larger than any other development in the world.

This will provide great quantities of cheap electric power necessary for processing such modern chemico-metallurgical elements as aluminum and others of present-day consequence. . . .

Dispatch Killed by Censor
August 22

Future biographers may well note the year 1952 as one of exceptional significance in the career of Georgi M. Malenkov. . . . Year by year he has taken on greater and more serious responsibilities. The events of this year have left little doubt that his career will go forward and that he is properly considered to be a man with a broad and open future, a man who shares Stalin's confidence and tasks of leadership. . . .

Dispatch Killed by Censor
August 22

At least until 1955 the Soviet government will continue to place chief reliance on railroads for transportation, with motor vehicles playing only a secondary role. . . . By 1955 Soviet motor production will approximate 500,000 units annually, more than 80 per cent being trucks. There is no indication of any intention to go in for mass ownership of automobiles. . . .

Dispatch Killed by Censor
August 23

The Soviet proposes to double by 1955 the state material and food reserves in order to put itself in a position of security "against any eventualities."

This is a plain indication that Russia does not plan to be caught short in any eventuality requiring a sudden and unexpected drain on her basic production facilities. There is no indication of the extent of stockpiles which she proposes to assemble. . . .

In some postwar years the Soviet has appropriated as much as 10 billion rubles for increasing state reserves. . . .

August 25, 1952

A week or so ago I had two very interesting conversations about Nenni's* famous interview with Stalin, first with Kennan and then with Di Stefano, the Italian ambassador who had talked with Nenni.

My curiosity had been aroused at the reports which the agencies and the Alsops carried about the Nenni conversation. I was suspicious of the substance of the reports. Even if Stalin believed the division of Germany to be final and further negotiations to be useless, it did not seem likely that he would say this to anyone outside the inner circle since it cuts so sharply across the Soviet propaganda line. Second, Di Stefano had played the Nenni thing very close, only passing on the information about Stalin's interest and what the Alsops call "his surprising grasp" of Italian affairs. So it seemed apparent that the Washington reports must be based on information passed back by our embassy.

I talked with Kennan and found that Di Stefano had filled him in on Nenni's talk. Although Kennan did not note any particular divergencies in the substance of the Alsop report, he was of the opinion they were not basing themselves on what he told the Department. (He was quite definitely wrong on that score, as it developed.)

Kennan felt that Stalin's opinions were not surprising. As to why Stalin would utilize Nenni, he suggested (*a*) that the old man often talks quite frankly with persons whose opinions he has some respect for and thus the remarks may have been made in a naturally developing conversation, or (*b*) that he did not wish Nenni to be under any illusion as to the realities of the European situation.

* Nenni, the Italian left-wing Socialist leader, visited Moscow in July, 1952, and had an interview with Stalin, the nature of which gave rise to rumor and conjecture.

Kennan reasoned that Italy is the one country where the Party still has hopes of returning to legal participation in the government through elections; that the elections are coming up next year and that if anything is to come of the Party's hopes the closest liaison must continue with the Nenni group; therefore, he wanted Nenni to understand that no easing of the German or European situation was in prospect.

I asked Kennan his personal opinion of Germany, and he said he thought our position was very strong, stronger than the Russians now realize, but he felt this would become apparent to them by next winter or early spring. He said he expected continued pressure on Berlin but of a more tactful kind than that which inspired the airlift, and he did not think our position there could be shaken. So long as Berlin is maintained, he believes, it will be impossible for the Russians to construct an East Germany which is completely reliable because Berlin provides a vent in the Iron Curtain.

In general, his feeling is that Russian policy is running up a blind alley and that there must be a man (within the leadership group) who understands this and who will become increasingly aware of it as time goes on. He feels that the November election will play a big part in showing them the light since it insures not only continuance of our foreign policy but more principled and efficient administration of this policy.

He feels the next administration is bound to be more intelligent in applying foreign policy. He thinks the Russians are bound to realize that the conflicts between England and France and the United States are in the nature of family quarrels and that it is impossible actually to split the West. And he points out that there is no reason for them to count on an economic depression in the U.S.A., even if the Korean thing is settled, because the adjustment which would follow would be much less than that which followed the war and we had no depression then. (There may be room for some argument on his economic point.)

Thus, he takes the fairly optimistic view that eventually the Russians will find it necessary and profitable to talk to the West. He is not discouraged by the current anti-American manifestations. He feels his complaints on that score have done some good, as evidenced by the touchiness of Russian reactions (in the *News*, *New Times*, and *Pravda*) to the "hate" charge. But he does feel

271

somewhat frustrated because one of his pet projects is to get both the U.S.A. and the U.S.S.R. to tone down their propaganda. Before coming over he made the Voice of America promise to lay off Stalin and carry no derogatory items about the Generalissimo. He would like to get the Russians to call a halt on their propaganda for a while. Then, he says, he personally would see if he couldn't get some of our more important media to reciprocate. But, as he notes, he is hamstrung on this so long as the Russians, instead of laying off, step up their drive.

And he is hamstrung on another count by inability to talk to really responsible government people. (He doesn't put Vishinsky in that category.) He thinks that the Foreign Office privately sympathizes with him on propaganda and has an idea that they were against it but, naturally, aren't in a position themselves to complain. He deduces that when he complains this enables them to voice their own private convictions. (I think he may be somewhat optimistic on that count.)

He is quite ready to sit here and wait for quite a time until the over-all factors which he thinks will produce a desire on the part of the Kremlin for a change in policy produce the desired effect. I should judge that he thinks another seven or eight months will be required for this.

Now, as to Nenni. Di Stefano was appalled when I showed him the Alsop and agency clips. He had filled in Kennan and no other diplomat in Moscow, and Kennan had promised him complete secrecy. (Kennan confirmed this to me and said he had passed the information to the Department with a request for full secrecy.) Di Stefano is convinced the Department leaked the material, and I fully agree with him. But there is something worse. The report with its quotations of Stalin, etc., represents, in the main, deductions by Di Stefano with some additions by Kennan but not statements by either Nenni or Stalin.

The substance of the Nenni–Di Stefano conversation was as follows: Nenni told about Stalin's interest in Italy, etc. Di Stefano asked whether they discussed Europe. Nenni said yes. Di Stefano said, Does Russia consider the solution of the German problem an essential issue? Nenni said, No, not in the light of recent events. (Di Stefano deduced these "recent events" to be the ratification by the U.S. Senate of the Bonn compact and the nomination of Eisenhower.) Nenni then went on to say that last winter he was in Berlin and talked with Pieck and Grotewohl. He found them very glum. They told him they were going to have to follow the Italian example, meaning relinquish their majority position and go over to the opposition situation of the Italian Communists and left-wing Socialists. He said he saw them again in Berlin in July when he was en route to Moscow, and they told him last winter's plans were now "out"; that they didn't expect anything to come of the note exchange. (Di Stefano deduced from this that Pieck and Grotewohl reflected a change in Russian policy and that Russia has abandoned hope of any negotiations and now relies on a "balance" in Germany, balancing East against West Germany, and that since there will be twelve divisions in West Germany, East Germany will build up to that level.)

That was all the talk between Nenni and Di Stefano on Germany and, obviously, what the Washington reports represented as Stalin's statements were, in fact, deductions by Di Stefano, albeit possibly correct ones. Di Stefano felt, and quite possibly correctly, that Nenni wouldn't have talked this way if the Kremlin held a different position.

Then came an interesting sidelight. Nenni asked Di Stefano whether he knew Kennan. Di Stefano said he did, quite well. (Di Stefano has known Kennan for a long time, having been here as a young attaché in the mid-thirties when Kennan was ditto.) Nenni wanted to know Di Stefano's opinion—was Kennan sincere, was he interested in improving the situation between the U.S. and the U.S.S.R., and did Kennan reflect his government's policies correctly? Di Stefano assured Nenni on these points. (Di Stefano drew the inference that Nenni had been asked to sound him out on Kennan. That may be true. The Kremlin sometimes utilizes very roundabout means of acquiring information, and it might in an indirect way have been letting Kennan know that it was aware of his presence in Moscow.)

Thus, the "Stalin interview," in fact, adds up to a series of plausible deductions. I sent Stalin a series of questions, based on the Alsop report, with the idea if his position had changed he might want to get it on record officially. Unfortunately, I drew a blank.

Poor Di Stefano is in the switches. He got me to carry a denial and even considered asking for his recall. But finally he calmed down a bit.

One other aspect of this is interesting. This is the fourth occasion since Kennan got here that one of his reports has leaked out of the Department—each time in a quite distorted fashion. I don't know who is responsible for this, but it is not doing the ambassador's position much good.

Dispatch to New York Times
August 26, 1952

The Communist Party central committee has ordered all Party units to initiate a broad discussion of the proposed changes in Party rules which will be submitted to the Nineteenth Party Congress by N. S. Khrushchev. . . .

August 27
Letter to Raymond Daniell, New York Times, London

I have a problem which perhaps you can help me with. Not infrequently stories break here, either from Tass or in the morning newspapers, between 4:00 A.M. and 8:00 A.M., Moscow time. "Urgent Press" transmission is too slow to make New York for anything but a very late makeover in case of something really important.

Between the hours 2:00 A.M. to 6:00 or 7:00 A.M., telephone service from Moscow to London is usually quite fast and efficient. Is London staffed to take dictation from me in that period? If so, I will arrange to use the telephone on such breaks with considerable savings in time and tolls.

August 27

Here are some preliminary thoughts about the Nineteenth Party Congress and related events.

First, with regard to the succession. The emphasis on Malenkov is marked. Not only does he present the report which Stalin has delivered at each congress since he consolidated his grip on the Party but neither Molotov nor Beriya is listed for a principal address. The contrast in Molotov's case is particularly striking. In 1939 he was the *rapporteur* on the five-year plan. Thus, suggestions that in the staging of the Nineteenth Party Congress Stalin will make clear the succession are not improbable. Undoubtedly all the Politburo members will make speeches, but the spotlight has been focused on Malenkov in unmistakable fashion. This will be particularly true if, as may turn out, Stalin himself does not appear at the congress. Frankly, this possibility seems remote, but Stalin always is in Sochi in October and may not alter his routine.

However, in studying Malenkov's position it must be remembered that the Politburo listing remains constant in this order: Stalin, Molotov, Malenkov, Beriya, etc. There has been no exception to that order since I have been here. I notice that something has been made in stories about photos for Air Day in July. *Pravda*'s picture showed Budenny on Stalin's right and Beriya on his left, with Malenkov next and Molotov third. The May Day picture showed Govorov on Stalin's right and Malenkov, Beriya, and Molotov in that order on his left.

But the listing continued to be Stalin, Molotov, Malenkov, Beriya—regardless of the position in which the photo was snapped. Thus, it seems quite clear that Molotov still is No. 2 and Malenkov No. 3.

What I think this means is that if Stalin should die in the immediate future, Molotov would succeed to his "parade" positions—president of the Council of Ministers and, presumably, chairman of the soon-to-be-created Presidium of the central committee.

Malenkov, however, would assume the general secretaryship of the Party and the real power.

Some support for that analysis is provided by the proposed organizational changes in the Party apparatus. This follows, if, as I suspect, the new Presidium proves to be a somewhat broader body than the Politburo. The censorship has passed my suggestions to this effect. So long as Stalin lives we can expect that the Politburo or Presidium will show unanimity. However, in event of Stalin's death it will make a considerable difference if the Presidium is a fairly large group of, say, sixteen to twenty individuals as compared with the present compact twelve.

It has been the history of Party apparatus that power is steadily concentrated in smaller and smaller groups. It is no accident that Stalin was able to utilize his control of the compact secretariat to win out over the more diffuse Politburo.

If the Presidium is broadened, the secretariat will be an even more effective fulcrum of power. The present secretariat comprises Stalin, Malenkov, Ponamarenko, Suslov, and Khrushchev.

Here Malenkov's dominance is very clear. He is the only member, with the exception of Stalin, who has held his post there since 1939, and I think there is no doubt he exercises the effective daily control of the office in Stalin's name. Ponamarenko is the next senior member, dating from 1946 or thereabouts. I don't know his precise function and affiliations. Suslov, of course, specializes in propaganda. Khrushchev came in, in 1949, when he was brought up to replace Popov and take over the Moscow organization. I am still in doubt whether he was brought in to balance Malenkov or as a tail to Malenkov's kite.

But what is important about the secretariat is the absence of Molotov and Beriya. This, I believe, gives Malenkov a relatively free hand, which should more than balance any combination Molotov and Beriya could bring against him. I suppose you could postulate an army-police-Molotov combination versus a Party group. But it doesn't fit with anything we know about the inner Party workings.

The disappearance of the Orgburo and merging of its functions with the secretariat is, I think, merely recognition of a change which has already occurred.

As to composition of the new Presidium, I should expect it to include the present Politburo plus Ponamarenko, Suslov, Shkiryatov, and a few others—possibly one more military man (Budenny?) and two or three Party functionaries.

As to the general character of the changes in Party statutes—I am impressed by three things. First, the introduction of national and state concepts; second, the emphasis on "vigilance" and preservation of "state and Party secrets"; and third, the effort to tighten Party discipline and cope with bureaucratic abuses.

Over-all, I suppose the strongest impression one gets is that the Revolution happened a long, long time ago. When "Bolshevik"* follows "commissar," "Red Army," the "Internationale," "military commissar" army rank, commissariat, and the rest into oblivion, you don't have to look at the calendar to see how many years it has been since 1917.

Comparison of the new rules with the earlier ones shows how state and national concepts are almost imperceptibly replacing the earlier Party and international concepts. I don't for a minute

* The new Party statutes proposed to drop the word "Bolshevik" from the official Party name.

mean that the Party is tending to disappear, but I do mean that slowly and gradually it seems to be becoming the instrument of the state rather than vice versa. The day will come when the Party will wither away into an appendage of the state, long before any withering away of the state itself.

The tightening-up process is part of the eternal fight with bureaucracy and natural sloth and human cussedness. One more example of the constant effort in Russia to try to control the backwardness of the extremities by increasing the authority of the center. It is exactly the kind of expedient the czars tried time and again. It will produce temporary results, but since all local initiative is stifled the tendency will continue as at present—the generation of more and more bears' corners in the provinces.

We have a wonderful picture of how this works out down in Georgia where there has been a marvelous housecleaning ever since April when Beriya went down and threw out the old Party leadership and installed a new one. Everything is being cleaned up, and after a while the drowsy Georgian atmosphere will begin to creep back and things will slide and slide until another Beriya comes down from the center and launches another housecleaning.

It has been suggested that the rules changes may be preliminary to a new "purge." I don't believe so. The break with the "purge" technique was, I think, final.* What we will see, however, is intensification of local clean-up drives—the kind of thing which is now going on in Georgia. I believe the Party will remain about constant in its present membership of 6,000,000-odd for some time. I believe for the sake of prestige they will always maintain a larger membership than China—if possible.

Several excellent stories of mine on the five-year plan are still jammed in censorship and probably will be killed. One is on the big Angara River power and industrial center which is to be constructed in the Irkutsk region. There have been indications that at least one of the big dams out there has been built or is nearly finished. This, of course, is one of the leading guesses as a center for production of nuclear products. A second dispatch dealt with the decision to double the state reserves of grain and industrial materials to secure the state against "any contingencies." We

* In reality, purges had been going on almost continuously since I reached the Soviet Union in 1949 and preparations for an even greater one were currently under way.

don't know how large these strategic reserves are, but they already probably are quite large. The decision to double them provides some guess as to how the government rates the war danger in the years just ahead.

Another story deals with the automobile industry, which is being held down sharply. It may not even reach the projected 1950 goals in 1955. Much the same is true of the tractor industry. Obviously, they don't want to allot the steel, rubber, gasoline, and machine tool and instrument production to a mass auto industry in the present state of the world.

September 2, 1952
Letter to Director, Burobin

Just seven months ago, on February 1, I wrote you resubmitting a request for an apartment. . . .

September 2
Letter to Director, Burobin

For the past three years Mr. Whitney and I have rented a dacha at Saltikovka from you.

During that period we have been harassed by failure of the village authorities to put into order a small length of dirt road, about a quarter of a mile long, connecting our dacha with the Stone Highway.

Your officials have come to Saltikovka time and again to "inspect" the situation, to "confer" with village authorities, and to promise that the condition will be remedied.

But the only result is that the road is today in poorer shape than it was three years ago.

For nearly two months a worse situation has existed. Some dacha residents have dug large ditches in front of their dachas at the worst spots in the road. These ditches make it impossible for a car to circle around the holes, which in wet weather are bottomless pits. The *dachniki* dug these ditches to make the road so impassable that, like it or not, the village authorities would be compelled to repair it.

This action has had no effect on the village authorities. . . .

What is to be done? Two men, working for five or six hours, and a load or two of gravel or cinders, could correct the situation.

What must we do to get action? Do you suppose it might have

278

an effect if I wrote a dispatch for the *New York Times,* telling how Soviet authorities handle such a simple problem?

September 3
Letter to Emanuel R. Freedman, New York Times

It is often, as you know, extremely difficult to get through the censorship stories which are cast in a negative tone. For example, in the course of a year I write six or seven stories from the provincial press, reporting cases of polygamy, kidnapping of brides, and even the bartering of girls out in Central Asia.

These are cases published in *Kazakhstan Pravda* and *Pravda Vostoka,* etc. Not more than one in four or five passes the censor. The only method I have found that will get this kind of story through is to put it in a "positive" framework, avoiding so far as possible red-flag words like "polygamy," etc.

I have to follow that same technique on some economic stories, and I think this is responsible for some misunderstanding on the New York desk. I did a story last winter about Soviet livestock production, giving a lot of concrete figures. There was some criticism of the piece for presenting the Soviet cattle position in too glowing terms. But, actually, buried in the story was the key to what I was trying to get across—a sentence saying that production was "even greater than czarist production of 1916." I was trying, of course, to show that after thirty-five years of running full speed, Soviet livestock production had managed to get back to where it started before the Revolution.

Every time a copyreader lifts his eyebrows at a lead of mine of what seems to be something off-key, he should look very carefully for some clue to the point I'm trying to make.

Dispatch Killed by Censor
September 4

Paulina Soldatenko, a Russian housewife, spoke her mind today about some of the things which she felt the government might do in its five-year plan to improve household life in Russia.

Writing in the newspaper *Trud,* she said that Russian housewives want small washing machines, small refrigerators—at cheap prices—better repair services, cookbooks, sewing instructions, and radio advice on how to do their housework.

"I have much cleaning to do," she wrote. "At evening I sit and think and, sometimes, the thought arises—all this could be done quicker and better. . . ."

September 6, 1952

At six o'clock of an August morning Saltikovka is a pretty quiet place. A few commuters are hurrying to catch the early trains for Moscow. Here and there someone is looking to his cow or his goat or his chickens, but that is about all.

So it was the morning of August 20 when the telephone awakened me at the dacha. It was Tass calling to report that the Nineteenth Congress of the Communist Party had been summoned to meet on October 5 to consider the new Soviet five-year plan and changes in the Party statutes.

The telephone call from Tass did more than shatter the early morning calm of Saltikovka. It provided me with one of my biggest news stories in a long, long time.

And it brought the summer dacha season to an abrupt end. There won't be any time for relaxation until after the Party congress—and by that time it will probably be winter.

Dispatch to New York Times
September 13

The Soviet Academy of Sciences has sharply called to account Ivan M. Maisky, onetime Russian ambassador to London, for his responsibility in connection with the publication of an unsatisfactory book on the "bourgeois falsification of history" by Boris E. Stein of the Foreign Office higher school of diplomacy. . . .

Dispatch to New York Times
September 15

The magazine *Smena* today explained to its readers that the American national sport of "beizbol" is a "beastly battle, a bloody fight involving mayhem and murder." Moreover, beizbol is just a Yankee perversion of an ancient Russian village sport called *lapta*. . . .

September 16

Things have been extremely busy since mid-August what with the Chinese in town and preparations for the Party congress. This busy state will continue through the first half of October. It is welcome because we had had a long dry spell without much news. Naturally, I haven't gotten to the dacha for the last month.

Dispatch to New York Times
September 16

China and Russia announced early today an agreement on measures to strengthen peace and security, including continued joint use of the Port Arthur naval base. Both powers warned that conditions dangerous to the cause of peace have been created by Japan's failure to conclude a peace treaty with her two Far Eastern neighbors.

Stalin tendered a Kremlin banquet for Chou En-lai and the Chinese negotiators, attended by nine members of the Politburo and Mongolia's Premier Tsendenbal. . . . Among those present was S. D. Ignatiev. . . .*

September 17
Letter to U. P. Frantzev, Press Department

It has long been obvious to me and other correspondents that the liaison between the censorship and the Foreign Office and, indeed, other responsible departments of the Soviet government leaves much to be desired.

Repeatedly when important news has been announced, the censorship has no knowledge of this fact and transmission of the news is delayed because the censors were not provided with texts of the official documents involved.

I cannot help thinking that it is a commentary on the work of a Soviet office, like the censorship, when it sits with folded hands and does not transact business until it is provided by a foreign correspondent with a copy of an official Soviet announcement. . . .

Dispatch to New York Times
September 18

Ambassador Kennan leaves Moscow tomorrow for consultation with American diplomats in London. . . .

He had no statement to make before his departure, but it is

---

* This was the first indication that Ignatiev had taken over an important government job. In fact, he had succeeded Viktor S. Abakumov as minister of state security and was to hold this position during the last months of Stalin's life and the notorious "doctors' plot."

known that he does not hold any alarmist views regarding the immediate future. He is convinced that for the time being there is comparatively small likelihood of a new outburst of aggression. On the other hand he is deeply concerned about the long-term implications of the present policies of the world powers.

His firsthand observation of Russia has strengthened a deeply held conviction that the so-called containment theory is the soundest and possibly the only effective policy which the United States can follow under present circumstances. . . .

He has been deeply impressed with the tendency in Moscow to view the world as if it were divided into two parts—one good and the other evil, a tendency to view all Western governments in varying shades of darkest tints.

The U.S. ambassador sees little possibility in any diplomatic approach to Soviet-American problems so long as this tendency to view the world in only two colors—black and white—persists. . . .

He will return to Moscow on the eve of the Communist Party congress in order to give that event his personal study. . . .

As regards Russia and China, Kennan has seen in the latest negotiations no grounds for changing his belief that each is a great power with a certain natural community of interests as well as areas in which their views are subject to certain natural national divergencies. . . .

XXI

The Nineteenth Party Congress

Dispatch to New York Times
September 20, 1952

Pravda announces the award of orders and medals to 134 individuals associated in building the Volga-Don Canal and the Tzimlyanskaya power and irrigation project.

The Order of Lenin was bestowed on [Minister of Internal Affairs] Sergei N. Kruglov and [Deputy Minister of Internal Affairs] Ivan A. Serov. Others included Nikolai K. Bogdanov, Sergei Y. Zhuk, director of the "hydroproject," Stepan S. Mamulov, Yakov D. Rapoport, Vasily A. Barbanov, and Georgio A. Russo. . . .*

Dispatch Killed by Censor
September 21

The world's largest construction organization has been created in the Soviet Union for erection of five great projects including the Volga-Don Canal, the Stalingrad and Kuibyshev dams on the Volga, and a number of others.

This organization is known as "Hydroproject." It is headed by the Soviet's famed construction chief, Sergei Y. Zhuk. . . .

The Ministry of Internal Affairs, headed by Sergei N. Kruglov,

* This was the first positive evidence that the "Great Construction Projects of the Stalin Era," as they were called, were being built with the active aid of the secret police and, presumably, in part, with forced labor.

is playing a major role in carrying out these enormous hydroelectric, inland waterway, and irrigation projects. The list of those honored for constructing the Volga-Don Canal includes ten of the twenty-six signers of the obituary of V. V. Chernyshev, deputy minister of internal affairs, who died September 13. . . .

Kruglov has headed the Ministry of Internal Affairs since he succeeded Beriya in January, 1946. The State Security Ministry is headed by Viktor S. Abakumov.*

Dispatch to New York Times
September 22, 1952

The Georgian Communist Party has been put on warning that Georgia's exposed location requires special vigilance because of hostile activities of the United States from Turkey. The warning was given by Georgian Party Secretary A. I. Mgeladze. [He charged that the former leaders of the Georgian Party allowed a situation favorable to activities by foreign spies, agents, and diversionists to develop.

He said that the expelled Party leaders had permitted conditions under which "local chiefs" flourished, and this, "in the final analysis, would have led to the division of Georgia into individual princedoms."]

September 25

With the big Party meeting coming up in October, I have no profound thoughts on the international situation. More and more of the same, I guess, for quite some time. The Russians are busy sawing wood, confident that each month's sawing increases their relative strength vis-à-vis the West, and it is hard to disagree with them. So far as diplomacy is concerned, there is no prospect of its being effective so long as present conditions prevail. People here hardly have much to complain about because every year things get a little better, and they like that—probably because of their mysterious Russian souls.

* In fact, Abakumov probably was relieved of this post as early as February or March, 1952. By September Ignatiev is known to have been occupying this position. The release of Abakumov may have been the first blow at Beriya's power.

284

Dispatch to New York Times
September 26

Pravda today branded Ambassador Kennan "an enemy of the Soviet Union, a slanderer under the mask of a diplomat and a violator of the elementary rules obligatory for a diplomat."

The charges are sufficient under the usual norms of diplomatic procedure to call for a declaration that he is *persona non grata* and to ask for his recall from Moscow. . . .*

Dispatch to New York Times
September 28

Speaking at a Ukrainian Party Congress in Kiev, L. G. Melnikov, the Ukrainian Party secretary, charged that Ukrainian nationalists are "spies, diversionists, and agents of imperialist intelligence services" who have sold out to the Americans and British. . . .

Dispatch to New York Times
September 28

Warning his listeners that the United States is preparing a new world war directed against the Soviet Union, Nikita S. Krushchev has called on the Moscow Party organization to display heightened vigilance against foreign espionage. . . .

He acknowledged mistakes made as first secretary of the Moscow regional Party, particularly in the emphasis put on efforts to resettle collective farmers in large farm settlements instead of putting emphasis on boosting farm production. He revealed the central committee of the Party had intervened to correct the situation. . . .

September 30

It is curious—but the place where there is the least anxiety and concern over Moscow is in Moscow itself. Year by year, no doubt, the international situation deteriorates a bit. But the difference is really quite slight in so far as it can be felt in Moscow. And there is nothing in the atmosphere to suggest an early change either for the better or the worse.

---

* The charge was made after Kennan, in an interview at Tempelhof Airdrome in Berlin, compared conditions in Moscow to those in Hitlerite Berlin.

Stalin believes that war between the capitalist countries is still inevitable under present circumstances. He said experience shows that conflict between the capitalist states over markets is a stronger force than the "contradictions between the camp of capitalism and the camp of socialism." He set forth his ideas in a fifty-page statement in the magazine *Bolshevik.* Comrades who think that conflict between capitalism and socialism is so sharp that wars between capitalist countries no longer are inevitable "are mistaken" he said. "They see phenomena twinkling on the surface but they do not see those deep forces which determine the course of events. . . ."

October 3

George Kennan's career as ambassador to Russia has been tragically cut short. Vishinsky declared him *persona non grata* today. Kennan is one of the few Americans with deep, intimate knowledge of contemporary Soviet society and Russian history. He has said time and again that Soviet-American problems cannot be solved by name-calling and propaganda but by realistic examination of each other's position. In his few months here he was concerned by the deepening and widening of the antagonisms between the Soviet and the United States and made his opinions known to Soviet officials with whom he could get in contact. It will be a long time before the United States sends to Moscow another diplomat so well equipped to talk sense to the Soviets.

October 4

In expelling Kennan the Kremlin is telling the world—and its own people—let Washington storm and rage, let the winds of the cold war howl and blow—we are strong enough so that we need not worry. A great propaganda move on the opening of the Nineteenth Party Congress!

Dispatch to New York Times
October 5

The Nineteenth Party Congress opened with a speech by Georgi Malenkov. A sixteen-member Presidium was elected, including Stalin, Molotov, Malenkov, Beriya, Voroshilov, Bulganin,

Kaganovich, and Khrushchev. The initial Tass announcement listed only eight of the sixteen members of the Presidium of the congress.

[The names included only eight of the twelve members of the Politburo. Mikoyan, Andreyev, Kosygin, and Shvernik apparently are not included. Ordinarily the Presidium of any Soviet meeting includes all twelve Politburo members and Ponamarenko, Suslov, and Shkiryatov as well. . . .]

Dispatch to New York Times
October 6

Georgi Malenkov told the Nineteenth Party Congress Sunday night that the United States has borrowed Hitler's mantle and proposes to use force to gain world domination.

[His attack on the United States was the sharpest—without any exception—ever delivered against America by a high Soviet leader.]

Malenkov said the United States had decided to break the peace and prepare a new world war.

Molotov opened the meeting with a charge that American ruling circles are plotting a world war directed at Russia. . . .

Stalin seemed in good spirits and health but did not speak. . . .

A. N. Poskrebyshev, chief of Stalin's secretariat, heads the Congress secretariat. . . . The eight non-Politburo members of the Presidium are regional Party chiefs. . . .

October 8

Beriya was the third Politburo member to speak to the Nineteenth Party Congress. He continued the general attack on the United States.

October 9

Bad as relations are now between the United States and the Soviet, Western diplomats do not believe they will deteriorate to the point of formal rupture.

Dispatch to New York Times
October 14

A special eleven-man committee has been named to draft a new basic program for the Communist Party, founded on Stalin's economic theses. It is the first revision of the Party program since 1919. Stalin heads the committee. Other members are Beriya, Kaganovich, Kuusinen, Malenkov, Molotov, Pospelov, A. M. Rumyantsev, M. Z. Saburov, D. I. Chesnokov, and P. F. Yudin.*

Dispatch to New York Times
October 16, 1952

A group of thirty-six men was elected by the new Party central committee as members and candidates of the Presidium which replaces the old Party Politburo. At the same time a ten-man secretariat was named in place of the former five-man body.

Stalin heads both the Presidium and the secretariat. The Presidium is made up of twenty-five full members and eleven candidates. It includes ten Politburo members as full members and one, Kosygin, as an alternate. A. A. Andreyev was dropped. . . .

Dispatch Killed by Censor
October 17

There is no question of Stalin's pre-eminence in the Party. Not only has he been chosen chairman of the new Presidium, but he is first among the ten Party secretaries.

Equally apparent is the eminence of Malenkov, chosen both to the Presidium and to the secretariat. The only other member of the old Politburo to be picked for both Presidium and secretariat is Nikita S. Khrushchev. . . .

The new Party leaders have been picked largely on the basis of vigorous leadership either in regional Party organizations or in basic industries. But the core of leadership clearly remains precisely where it was before—in the person of Stalin and nine of his former Politburo associates customarily described here as his "closest comrades at arms."

October 18

I have just been reading a rather snide account in *Time* magazine of the International Press Institute report on "The News from Russia."

* In July, 1961, Khrushchev finally announced a new Party program to be submitted to the Twenty-second Party Congress in October, 1961. For nearly ten years following Stalin's unsuccessful effort, the Party had had no contemporary statement of program.

It seems more than strange that such a report should be compiled without any effort to check with the actual correspondents in Moscow. After all, Moscow is not the moon, and there is no substitute for the old copybook maxim, "If you want to get your information and get it right, go to the source."

Just a few of the inaccuracies presented in *Time:*

1. "Soviet censorship has been steadily tightened until it is now absolute."

Fact: Soviet censorship is materially lighter than it was when I first encountered it during the halcyon days of the war.

2. "Until 1946 reporters could still talk with Soviet citizens."

Fact: Ordinary contacts very, very sharply restricted. But no bar to casual conversations in certain milieu, for example, neighborly talk around the summer dacha, ordinary talks with train passengers, in restaurants, theaters, etc. What is barred is not conversation but friendship.

3. "Until 1946 reporters could still telephone the outside world."

Fact: Reporters telephone "the outside world" every day to dictate their copy to London and Paris. They telephone their friends, relatives, and offices in the United States.

4. "The Russians blandly insist that there are no censors."

Fact: No Russian official I have ever encountered in any responsible position has ever made such an assertion. Glavlit, which handles censorship, is a department of the government, attached to the Council of Ministers.

5. "Correspondents in Russia never see what changes are made in their dispatches before they are sent."

Fact: The correspondent has the privilege of seeing every piece of copy after censorship and before transmission.

6. "Even mailed stories are censored and then retyped to give the home office the impression that the copy was uncensored."

Fact: Mail stories must be retyped if there are substantial deletions. I would assume the reason is to prevent the editor from guessing what has been cut. Every piece of mail copy bears the censor's beautiful rubber stamp and signature.

7. "It is understandable that the men with Russian wives should constantly have personal considerations [in mind] in regulating their behavior."

Fact: If there is any tendency among the Moscow correspondents, it is to lean over backwards in the other direction in the interest of that "objectivity" in covering all aspects of the news which so excites *Time*'s scorn.

October 22, 1952

We have now concluded two months of the fullest news period which I have encountered since coming to Moscow.

Going back to the start of the period, we have the arrival of Chou En-lai in August and the lengthy Russo-Chinese negotiations. There is still a large group of Chinese here, presumably negotiating trade arrangements, technical assistance, military equipment, and credits. There may eventually be some announcement about economic questions. On the other subjects probably nothing will be said.

My guess is that Chou engaged in hard practical bargaining and that both sides got about what they wanted. Certainly, the Russians made some concession to the Chinese in return for the Port Arthur arrangement. Who knows what it could have been? Maybe they washed out some of the bill for jet fighters—or agreed to provide more equipment.

I would guess they came to full understanding on the two questions in which they have the greatest joint interest—Korea and Japan. I suspect that some tempting economic proposals will be made to Japan, provided Japan will sign a peace treaty. The offers will be designed to embarrass the Japanese government with its strongest supporters—the industrialists who have not lost hope of getting back their markets in Manchuria and the China mainland.

I don't profess to understand what they may have decided about Korea. Maybe the UN debate will throw more light on what Russia and China really think and, equally important, whether they actually think alike.

A word or two about Kennan. It is a shock to lose him and particularly in the way it happened. What a difference to have him here. To be able to carry on adult and knowledgeable conversations about Russia and to know that for once in a lifetime Washington was getting from its embassy a perceptive, intelligent, sensitive analysis. Not to mention the rare and special pleasure of having him use the dacha as his private retreat and to listen by the hour as he sprawled in front of the fireplace arguing about

Chekhov or the latest development in the *bez-konflitni* discussion.*

I can't honestly say that if George Kennan had stayed on he would have been able to do anything spectacular about Soviet-American relations. There is just a chance—but not a very big chance and probably not as big a one as he thought when he took the assignment. So long as he stayed, he provided a healthy corrective to the naïveté which permeates so much official thinking about Russia. Had any opening developed for constructive conversations he would have been ideal. My opinion is that from about mid-summer he began to feel more pessimistic—not so much because anything had really happened but because, for all his inborn pessimism and desire to be realistic, he had held too optimistic hopes when he arrived.

Of one thing we can be certain. He did not expect his mission to end in a way that brought more strain on Soviet-American relations—acute strain, to be precise.

And there exists a certain mystery as to how things worked out as they did. The mystery lies in why Kennan came to make those remarks at Tempelhof Airdrome. The afternoon before he left we had an hour's conversation, at his initiative. He expressed concern over the fact that he had been liberally quoted when he made his trip in June to see Acheson. He said that wasn't going to happen this time. This time he was talking to us in Moscow before he left, and he would not do any talking while out of the country. He asked us to suggest the questions he would be asked by reporters in Berlin and London, in order, as I understood him, to be able to parry them effectively.

I left the conversation with the firm impression that he felt it advisable not to say anything more than innocuous platitudes while out of Russia. I do not understand how he came to make the statement he did at Tempelhof. The whole thing puzzles me.

As soon as *Pravda* picked up the quotes it was obvious that the fat was in the fire. Even so, I can't help feeling that the Foreign Office action might not have been taken if it had not been on the eve of the Party congress. It provided a strong gesture of self-confidence and one whose significance could hardly be lost on

---

* An ideological argument was then raging as to whether plays should present conflicts or not. The theory was that since "conflict" had now been eliminated from Soviet society it should not be presented on stage.

either the Party secretary of Krasnodar Krai or the fraternal delegate from Indonesia.

I am sure Kennan is deeply distressed by the turn of events.

October 23, 1952

The outstanding impression which I received from the Party congress—the meeting itself, the Stalin theses, the Republican congresses, the new five-year plan, the changes in the Party statutes and, finally, the Party elections, is one of *power* and *confidence*.

And, I might say, it is a very strong impression.

I do not get the impression that this is power which is being directed at the Western world, per se, or that it is being designed for aggressive military action or as support for revolutions to seize control of any given country.

Rather, I have the impression that the Kremlin believes it is now strong enough to carry on *without limit* its economic and social development, first of all, within Russia and, second, within the bloc which includes China and the Soviet share of eastern Europe.

In many ways the most significant thing which Malenkov said was his nearly concluding remark that Russia "no longer is a lone island encircled by capitalist lands."

Now, for general consumption, and particularly to keep from relaxing in defense and "vigilance," the theory of "capitalist encirclement" is publicly maintained. But, if I read my Malenkov correctly, the Kremlin itself has finally broken with the psychology of encirclement.

I believe that the Kremlin feels it has now safely crossed that most dangerous of postwar periods—the period of genuine weakness in industrial potential and badly strained social fabric and is safely advancing along the clear road of unlimited industrial expansion, based on a capital goods capacity fully adequate to double and redouble itself within very short periods of time.

Of course, as Stalin would be the first to admit, "accidents may happen." But it seems clear that he feels that Russia is already too strong for any power grouping to approach war with her lightly and that the Soviet industrial base is large enough not only to meet arms race competition but to produce the extremely large quantities of the means-of-production necessary to bring

Russia up to something like parity with the United States and, also, to provide actual improvement in the real standard of living.

What does this really mean? I believe it means a *de facto* policy of isolationism, of concentrating on production in Russia, China, and East Europe while carrying on *pro forma* internationalism. They will take advantage of every chance to broaden schisms in the capitalist world—trade bait for England, mutterings about common interests with France on the German question, and encouragement of Arab nationalism and Malay communism. But any one of these things could fail or be abandoned and still the Kremlin would feel perfectly confident that it is growing too strong to be attacked successfully.

Another way of putting it would be that the Russians will not worry too much if we put eight more divisions into western Europe in 1953 so long as they increase in 1953 their output of steel by 4,000,000 metric tons.

Soviet steel production today may be around 40 per cent of U.S. production (it was only 25 per cent of ours as recently as 1949 when I came to Moscow). But what can Russia do with a ton of steel? I think one ton of Russian steel production from the military standpoint is worth three tons of U.S. steel. Maybe more. To see how far the Russians can stretch a ton of steel production, it is only necessary to reread Voznesensky's report on Soviet economy in the Great Patriotic War and note, first, what a tiny steel production the Germans left Russia by 1942;* second, what proportion Russia was able to devote to war purposes; and third, how many guns and tanks they made.

Or take another revealing factor: machine tools. If there is a real index of modern industrial capacity, it lies in the census of machine tools and the capacity to produce machine tools. Malenkov made a significant statement in this connection. He said that since the war the Soviet machine tool park had grown 2.2 times. This means that Russia has close to 1,500,000 machine tools, well above the level of the first postwar plan which was to boost machine tools to 1,300,000 (a larger total than the United States had in 1940).

The Russians are now producing close to 100,000 machine tools each year, and it is planned to double this output in the present, fifth, five-year plan.

* Less than 10,000,000 tons.

When you analyze such facets of Soviet industry, the real basis of Soviet power begins to show itself. Certainly there are soft spots. But the hard spots are what count—steel and coal and oil and electric power and machines and railroads. The soft spots are in secondary or light industrial lines—timber, housing construction (a perennial headache), and consumer lines. But after a long slow lag consumer goods output is beginning to climb.

Their hydroelectric program is extremely important. Quite a few of the new dams have been quietly under construction for a long time. That is true of the Mingechaur Dam, on the Kura in Armenia, which was started at the end of the war. Probably this dam was dropped to low priority in 1950 and only recently restarted. Ust-Kamenogorsk, on the Irtysh, is in much the same category.

Not the least interesting aspect of the hydro program is the big way they are tackling development of the Siberian rivers—the Ob, the Irtysh, and the Angara. The most spectacular is on the Angara, where 9 billion kilowatt capacity of power is available. There have been reports that the Angara Dam near Irkutsk is well under way.

What connection the big hydro program might have with atomic energy is hard to say. These Siberian points are a long, long way from anywhere. On the other hand, if they had enormous significance it would be easy to keep them secret. In one dispatch I suggested that they might use the Angara resources to develop atomic power and, in turn, use nuclear power to aid the great dream of turning Siberian river flows southward to irrigate Central Asia. The censor didn't leave much of that suggestion in the story. Possibly in the next, the sixth, five-year plan they may begin to turn the Siberian waters into Central Asia.

Another aspect of the dam-canal program which is not well understood is the role of the MVD. The fact that a number of high MVD officials were connected with building the Volga-Don Canal has been taken to mean that this project was constructed by forced labor. Now there is evidence that forced labor must have played only a minor role in that canal.

The canal widely advertised for labor and specialists all over the country—free labor, that is, which was offered contracts and specified pay, living conditions, and terms. There was considerable recruitment of Komsomols, much publicity about their activity, etc. Also, this was a highly mechanized construction job. New excavating machines, especially built and developed for this work, were employed, together with large numbers of *buldozeri*. A study of the use of labor and machines on the canal by Rapoport, chief of construction (and apparently an official of the MVD), has been published in *Voprosi Ekonomiki*. Rapoport says that 346 excavators, 900 scrapers, more than 300 buldozeri, 37 "earth-sucking machines," and seven large "automatic" cement plants were used. Comparing it with the Moscow-Volga Canal (built with forced labor), he said Moscow-Volga excavation was more than 50 per cent hand labor whereas Volga-Don was almost fully mechanized.

Thus, Volga-Don doesn't sound like a forced labor job, although some such labor may have been used.

What seems to me important is not that the MVD carried out another forced labor job but that the MVD carried out a great non–forced labor job. More than that. It can be established by cross-checking of published names that the MVD is also building the South Ukraine Canal and has major planning (if not administrative) responsibilities for a whole series of large dams. What seems significant is that the great MVD construction organization and technical apparatus built up and used for such forced labor jobs as White Sea and Moscow-Volga canals have now been intrusted with important almost "pure" civilian responsibilities.

So, without regard to its continuing prison responsibilities, the MVD, which already had wide civil responsibilities such as highways, bridges, fire and police, etc., has imperceptibly expanded into another sphere of activity and become an even more important and powerful factor in the general Soviet economy.

I have filed the essence of this, but the censorship has twice killed my dispatches.

November 3, 1952

I have hardly turned a hand on the news front since the Party congress. After spending something over 16,000 rubles in telegraph tolls in the first fifteen days of October (about what I spend in four months of normal Moscow reporting), I figured the *Times* could stand a little easing up!

Dispatch to New York Times
November 5, 1952

The portraits of ten leading members of the Soviet government, headed by Generalissimo Stalin, today were mounted on walls and buildings throughout Moscow in preparation for the celebration November 7 of the 35th anniversary of the Bolshevik Revolution.

Those whose pictures were displayed were Molotov, Malenkov, Voroshilov, Bulganin, Beriya, Kaganovich, Khrushchev, Mikoyan, Shvernik—Stalin's "closest comrades-at-arms," as they are called.

[The last previous display, on May 1, had incorporated pictures of Molotov, Malenkov, Beriya, Voroshilov, Bulganin, Kaganovich, Khrushchev, Mikoyan, Andreyev, Shvernik, and Kosygin. . . .]

Dispatch to New York Times
November 6

In the presence of Generalissimo Stalin a stern warning to American aggressors not to forget the existence of the "unconquerable" Soviet army was delivered at a meeting honoring the 35th anniversary of the Bolshevik Revolution.

The warning was delivered by Mikhail G. Pervukhin, deputy premier and one of the twenty-five members of the new Party Presidium.

[It was the first occasion since the end of the second World War that Stalin had attended the big October Revolution ceremonial. In former years he has been accustomed to take a brief vacation at the Black Sea resort of Sochi.]

Stalin appeared hale and hearty. He sat in the second row on the platform with Molotov at his right hand and Bulganin on his left. Other principal figures of the government present were Malenkov, Beriya, Kaganovich, Khrushchev, Mikoyan, Shvernik, Ponamarenko, Suslov, and Shkiryatov. . . .

Dispatch to New York Times
November 7

Atop Lenin's Tomb to take the salute of crack troops and hundreds of thousands of civilian demonstrators was Generalissimo Stalin today, clad as he was last night in a dove-colored generalissimo's uniform.

Also on the reviewing platform were a number of his closest comrades-at-arms, including Molotov, Malenkov, Bulganin, Beriya, Kaganovich, Khrushchev, Mikoyan, and Shvernik. Voroshilov was not present. . . .

Numerous portraits of Soviet government leaders were carried by the civilian marchers. First came pictures of Stalin followed by those of Molotov, Malenkov, Voroshilov, Bulganin, Beriya, Kaganovich, Khrushchev, and Shvernik, in that order. [This sequence was repeated hundreds and hundreds of times. . . .]*

* The repeated mention of the new order of listing of the Stalin "comrades-at-arms" was designed to draw attention to the fact (which the censorship would not pass) that Beriya had suddenly been dropped down a couple of notches—a political development of obvious if obscure significance. The new order was first indicated in the portraits put up on November 5.

XXII

The Plot Begins

November 16, 1952

I want to try to analyze some of the political aspects of the Nineteenth Party Congress and the events which have followed.

The initial conclusion—one which was widely noted abroad—is that Stalin, rather than showing any inclination toward retirement, has still got *all* the power firmly in his own grasp.

There was no particular need to stress that aspect *inside* the Soviet Union, since there was no shadow of doubt about this fact.

The procedure whereby Stalin stated his theses a few days before the opening of the congress and then refrained from speaking except to present a brief exhortation to the foreign comrades was designed to emphasize the grandeur of his position—not only standing at the head of Party and State but standing above Party and State, a figure only half-visible to earth-bound mortals.

I don't feel that the question of the succession was greatly illuminated. The selection of Malenkov to make the main report put further emphasis on his No. 1 position (after Stalin) in the Party hierarchy. But that has been apparent since the death of Zhdanov.

Malenkov's status was also emphasized by the composition of the new Party secretariat in which he retained his pre-eminent post as Stalin's chief deputy.

There is independent (and inadvertent) evidence from the Party itself of Malenkov's primacy. Most of the Republican Party congresses and the congresses of Moscow and Leningrad which preceded the All-Union Congress elected members of the Politburo and the three associates, Ponamarenko, Suslov, and Shkiryatov as delegates to the congress. But this was not a uniform process. I compiled a table showing the frequency with which the various men were selected. This shows that in all cases Stalin was picked. Malenkov was runner-up with one less vote and led the next man, Molotov, by two votes. Then came Beriya, Voroshilov, and Kaganovich in that order, separated by a single vote each. At the end of the list was a tie between Andreyev, Ponamarenko, and Suslov, with Shkiryatov trailing.

This action may be taken as corroboration by the local Party groups of Malenkov's position. This does not mean that Malenkov put Molotov in the shade. Molotov, in opening the congress and delivering, in essence, a brief keynote speech, was himself lifted a few degrees above the Party discussion. I think that Molotov has a little of the Stalin aura. And his pre-eminent general position is emphasized by the fact that his name always follows Stalin's and always precedes Malenkov's. And in the November portrait display, the Moscow Hotel layout, which is the No. 1 layout in the city, put Stalin above them all with Molotov directly below him and the others of the present "ten" spread out to Molotov's right and left.

It is fairly clear that should Stalin die in the present period Molotov would succeed him as head of the state, Malenkov as head of the Party, and the actual power would be held in varying degrees by Molotov, Malenkov, Beriya, Bulganin, Voroshilov, and, quite possibly, Khrushchev.

That is a larger group than is generally envisaged and, inevitably, it would polarize first around two individuals and ultimately around one.

A word about Beriya. The November 7 portrait displays dropped him down two notches. The order now runs: Stalin, Molotov, Malenkov, Voroshilov, Bulganin, Beriya. Previously for several years Beriya was listed next to Malenkov. Unless Stalin exercises his "jovial humor" to mystify foreigners by rearranging the portraits—which I seriously doubt—this should mean a tip of fortune away from Beriya. Possibly because of the scandal in the Georgian Party. But that happened and was cleaned up last spring, and there have been plenty of opportunities before November 7 to demote Beriya.

Possibly the change is designed to hint at increasing importance of the military—Voroshilov and Bulganin—at this time. Possibly A-bomb production isn't coming up to Beriya's planned goals. I don't know the reason, but I think it more likely to indicate a downward trend for Beriya than an upward trend for Voroshilov and Bulganin.

Not, I must say, that it seems to have the slightest effect on Beriya's public behavior. At the November 6 meeting and again in the square the next day, he was, as usual, the most jovial of the leaders, constantly engaging the surly featured Malenkov in conversation which, at a distance, had all the appearance of a running fire of Georgian anecdotes. Beriya is the only one of the leaders who indulges in this comrade-like conduct.

The Politburo has not been replaced by the new Presidium of the central committee. That body of twenty-five men and eleven candidates is very clearly an official, rubber-stamp body which will meet periodically, if at all, to approve decisions by a much smaller group.

The nature of the smaller group was made perfectly clear when the pictures went up for November 7. It is the old Politburo shorn of Andreyev and Kosygin. This group of ten men, including Stalin, has no formal name and no formal existence. It is, somehow, rather typical of this country and this regime that it should carefully wipe out all formal and legal basis for the existence of the body which rules the state.

I do not think that the elaborate device of eliminating the Politburo and replacing it with a Presidium was invented *solely* for the purpose of allowing Stalin to reshuffle his inner cabinet a bit. However, with the Politburo no longer in existence it will be much easier to vary the composition of the inner body, utilizing, for example, one combination of men for one purpose and another for another.*

There is no great significance in the dropping of Andreyev and Kosygin. Andreyev has been moving out of the charmed circle ever since immediately after the war and has had to take all the

* Although I had no knowledge of it, this, according to Khrushchev, was exactly what Stalin was doing, employing groups of five, six, or seven Politburo members for varying purposes and playing them off against each other.

lumps for the mistakes (not really very serious) in farm policy. He was named to the central committee, and he was on the stage at the Bolshoi November 6 and below the podium on the tomb on Red Square November 7. So, finally, a formula seems to have been found which enables a man to be removed from a high post without going before a firing squad.

There was even less of a step-down for Kosygin. He made the candidate ranks of the Presidium, and his picture was carried quite frequently by various light-industry groups in the November 7 demonstration.

Stalin's nine associates have no formal name. They are called rather loosely "his closest comrades-at-arms" by the press.

A very important tendency has been revealed in the selections for the Presidium. This tendency is to honor with highest Party rank men, primarily technicians, whose careers have been confined strictly and almost exclusively to government jobs.

If you take the thirty-six candidates and members of the Presidium, you find that fourteen of them are the old Politburo plus the three associates—Ponamarenko, Suslov, and Shkiryatov; five are big shot regional Party chiefs; two are Party philosophers; five are now local Party wigs drafted to the secretariat; and almost all the remainder are government people, including four deputy chairmen of the Council of Ministers and four more men of top cabinet rank.

The most interesting of these groups are the five new Party secretaries and the eight government men.

The government men are no Johnnys-come-lately. All but two were on the central committee as long ago as 1939. But they have stuck closely to their government tasks. These include: V. A. Malyshev, whose specialty is shipbuilding and heavy machinery; M. G. Pervukhin, specialist in machine-tool production; M. Z. Saburov, head of the State Planning Commission, and I. F. Tevosyan, specialist in ferrous metallurgy.

All but Saburov were full members of the central committee thirteen years ago. There are two others whose names should become more important (providing their assignments emerge from obscurity). The first man is S. D. Ignatiev, whose present post hasn't been announced. My files list him a couple of years ago as a central committee representative for Uzbekistan. Before that he was a Party secretary somewhere in Central Asia. He's been in the Su-

preme Soviet since 1937 and most recently turned up in the delegation of ministers which dined at the Kremlin with Chou En-lai. He
is obviously a man of considerable importance with rank close to
that of a deputy chairman of the Council of Ministers. The second
man of some mystery is I. G. Kabanov, who was released last year as
minister of the electrical industry in connection with transfer to
other duties, the nature of which was not stated.

By doubling the size of the secretariat and bringing in five new
men, its importance may have been increased; but it is too early
to draw any deductions. Actually, it may have been weakened by
dilution. The five new men are definitely second or third rank.
Aristov is a No. 1 local Party secretary from Chelyabinsk. Brezhnev has had only a bit more than a year as Moldavian Party
secretary, having previously been at Dnepreges. (He is interesting
because he is obviously a Khrushchev man, and Khrushchev is
also on the secretariat. Counting Brezhnev and Khrushchev, the
Ukraine Party has a minimum of four and, possibly, five votes on
the Presidium.) Ignatov is a former Krasnodar Krai Party secretary. Pegov is the former Maritime Provinces boss who used to
live next to our consulate in Vladivostok. The fifth new secretary
is Mikhailov, who at the age of fifty has finally given up as Communist Youth leader!

I think it is well to keep in mind the existence of this Ukrainian bloc both in the Presidium and the secretariat. It may eventually become more important. People are apt to overlook
Khrushchev. I wouldn't do that. After all, he is the Moscow Party
boss. That is the biggest single boss position in the country, and I
don't know of a Party position where you are more likely to shine
—if you really have ability—than Moscow. And Khrushchev obviously has his finger firmly on the Ukrainian pulse. *I think he
ranks much higher than he seems to*. The number of Ukrainians
on the Presidium is not mere lip service to the Ukraine. No other
nationality is so honored.

The ages of the Inner Ten interest me. The fascinating thing
is that Malenkov, who was fifty last January, is the baby of the
Inner Ten. New people take a long, long time to get to the top.
Look at the postwar situation. Three men, Ponamarenko, Suslov,
and Shkiryatov, have come up to the outer circle. But they never
made the grade as alternate members of the Politburo. And those
men are all over fifty. Ponamarenko and Suslov were fifty this

year. Shkiryatov is sixty-nine. Kosygin at forty-eight was the youngest member of the Politburo—and he was dropped! Andreyev was fifty-seven.

If you average the age of the Ten, you get 60.4 years. If you average the age of the Politburo of ten years ago, you get 49.5. The rate of loss among younger leaders is much higher than among the older ones—i.e., Kosygin, Voznesensky, Zhdanov, and Shcherbakov against Kalinin and Andreyev.

The main point is that Stalin is still running things and looks like continuing to do so for quite some time. And the other point is that the government now provides just as good and perhaps a more effective road to power and position as does the Party organization.*

Dispatch to New York Times
November 25, 1952

Pravda today cited the Slansky trial in Czechoslovakia as evidence of the nefarious activities of American foreign espionage and subversion organizations which, it noted, included the Ford Foundation, "which was once headed by the notorious George Kennan."

Pravda said the real business of the Ford Foundation was the "sending of spies, murderers, saboteurs, and wreckers" into East Europe. . . .

November 27

There is a curious case here of an Englishman named George Bundock, a clerk at the British embassy. In 1948 a Russian girl brought charges that he had infected her with syphilis. The charge was false. Nevertheless, the case was tried in open court.

Bundock was convicted and sentenced to eighteen months in prison. The sentence was imposed, *in absentia*.

Since then Bundock has never left the premises of the British embassy on the Sofiskaya Embankment. There have been repeated efforts to obtain permission for him to leave the country—all unavailing.

In the past there have been quite a few minor diplomats who have been permitted to leave after brushes with the law. The

* This did not prove true. After Stalin's death Khrushchev and his adherents, grasping the key Party positions, prevailed over Malenkov and his adherents, who based themselves to a greater extent on government positions.

difficulty in the Bundock case is that it was treated as a propaganda case by the Russians (it occurred during the agitation over the Russian wives of British employees whom the Soviet would not allow to leave the country. It was obviously Soviet counterpropaganda).

There is still one "British wife" left in the employ of the embassy. She leaves the building only when accompanied by several staff members, only in British staff cars, and only when going to another British building.

The French have a dual-nationality family living on the embassy property. The Greeks have two or three such employees and would have several hundred if it could put the applicants to work. There is also the son of a former Chilean ambassador who married a Russian girl and stayed behind after the sensational Russo-Chilean break in relations. He and his wife live in the National Hotel, and he works for the Argentine embassy. I guess the Argentines have stopped befriending former Spanish Loyalists since the unfortunate trunk-smuggling episode of several years ago.*

Dispatch to New York Times
November 28, 1952

Izvestia revealed in a page-one editorial that losses to the state from production of bad and substandard goods reached a total of 3 billion rubles, or $750 million, this year.

Izvestia in the past ten days has devoted great attention to reports of commercial crime and violation of state economic rules.

The drive follows a demand by the Nineteenth Party Congress for the strictest measures to bring an end to embezzlement, corruption, theft, and substandard production. . . .

November 29

The editorial board responsible for the journal *Kommunist* has undergone considerable change. The latest issue lists two chief directors, D. I. Chesnokov and S. M. Abalin. Chesnokov is new. He is a member of the eleven-man commission named by the Nineteenth Party Congress to draft a new Party program. An-

---

* Soviet authorities discovered a Loyalist Spaniard in the trunk of an Argentine diplomat as the luggage was being put aboard a plane to leave the country.

other new member is L. F. Ilyichev, editor of *Pravda* and a candidate member of the central committee.

Dispatch to New York Times
December 1

A special military court in Kiev has sentenced to death by shooting as "enemies of the people" three men who were convicted of "counterrevolutionary wrecking" in connection with a criminal conspiracy in the field of trade in the Kiev region.

Their crimes were estimated to have cost the state "hundreds of thousands of rubles."

[A vigorous campaign has been launched all over the Soviet since the Nineteenth Party Congress against commercial crime. The government newspaper *Izvestia* has reported stiff sentences in such cases almost every day in the past week or so.]

The Kiev report is the first occasion in which a military tribunal has been summoned to act in the field of commercial crime.

[It is the first time that a newspaper has reported the imposition of death sentences for crimes of this kind since the death penalty was reintroduced in the Soviet Union two years ago for what were then described as "traitors to the Motherland, spies, and subversive diversionists."]

Pravda of the Ukraine explained that the Kiev offenders were judged by the military tribunal under paragraphs 54–7 and 54–11 of the Criminal Code of the Ukraine "for counterrevolutionary wrecking in the field of trade and trade turnover."

Names of the "enemies of the people" were given as K. A. Kahn, Yaroshetsky, and Gerson. The group had its center in the chief office of Kiev light industries. . . .

Dispatch Killed by Censor
December 5

The newspaper *Soviet Tadzhikstan* reports from Stalinabad that a local Red Crescent chairman has been brought to trial under the State Secrets Act for losing a document containing a state secret. The arrest is part of a drive for greater "vigilance" in line with the edicts of the Nineteenth Party Congress.

The newspaper also said that "certain responsible persons" were carrying on telephone conversations in which they talked about state secrets.

A former chief deputy of trade administration, Shonin, has been arrested. . . .

Dispatch Killed by Censor
December 6, 1952

The Kiev newspaper reports that the local Party organization has raised the question of the Kiev trade organization's being "cluttered up with thieves and scoundrels." The question was brought before a plenum of the city Party committee a few days after a special military tribunal imposed death sentences upon three persons connected with the Kiev trade organization. The Party organization said the situation with respect to personnel in Kiev trading organizations was "particularly bad."

In one factory the chief of the cadre section, Mendelsohn, was described as fixing up his relatives with responsible jobs. At the Fourth shoe factory former Director Raigordetsky was said to have participated in large-scale production thefts. He appointed his relative, Rosen, chief of the factory guards.

Dispatch Killed by Censor
December 14

Pravda said today that failures in personnel selection by the trade ministry, the Central Co-operative Union, and other trade branches have permitted "thieves and rogues to penetrate into the Soviet trade apparatus. . . ."

December 15

I wish that I might be getting back to the States for Christmas. But that is not to be. Nor is there any certainty when I can get back. That must depend on the way events develop here—and as to that there is great uncertainty.

December 15

Pravda says that the daughters, sisters, and other close relatives of grafting officials often reap big benefits from these defalcations. It demands that such individuals be brought to punishment. It is the duty, *Pravda* said, of members of families of embezzlers and thieves to maintain vigilance and assist society in exposing such crimes. . . .

December 16

I have asked the press department whether the Soviet Labor Law of June 26, 1940, has been repealed or modified by a decree of July 14, 1951. The 1940 law applied severe penalties, including imprisonment, against workers who left their jobs without permission.

The curious thing is that there is no mention of this July 14, 1951, decree in *Vedomosti,* the official law journal—and yet I am sure there was such a decree. The Criminal Code for 1952 does not mention the 1940 law, although earlier editions carried both the text of the 1940 law and commentaries on it. Nor has there been any mention of the repressive law of 1940 in recent discussions of labor discipline.

December 17

The Chinese delegation which came to Moscow with Chou En-lai to negotiate a new economic agreement last August is still in Moscow. Diplomats believe that major conflicts are involved in the Russo-Chinese talks, but nothing is known of their nature.

Dispatch to New York Times
December 17

The editorship of *Pravda* has been placed in the hands of Dmitri Trofimovich Shepilov who for many years has been a top Party specialist in agitation and propaganda. His immediate predecessor was Leonid F. Ilyichev. . . .

Dispatch to New York Times
December 18

Izvestia charged today that thefts and embezzlements of more than 30,000,000 rubles have occurred in Khabarovsk Krai because the regional prosecutor and his assistants are protecting rather than prosecuting criminals. . . .

December 21

Stalin celebrated his seventy-third birthday today, but no public notice was taken of it. So far as anyone knows, Stalin seems to be in good health and vigor with every prospect of more years of active work. He comes of hardy Georgian mountain stock where longevity is the rule rather than the exception.

Dispatch to New York Times
December 22, 1952

The bi-weekly Party pamphlet, *Agitators' Notebook,* defines Zionism as "a reactionary trend of the Jewish *bourgeoisie"* which acts as a faithful agency of American imperialism.

Zionism carries out espionage and subversion for the benefit of the United States, declares the pamphlet, issued for the use of Party political workers. It provides a text for some 45,000 such agitators in the Moscow region alone and is designed to acquaint them with the Party position on leading questions. It was inspired by the Slansky trial in Prague.

The significance of the statement lay not in its criticism of Zionism—the Communist Party has always been strongly opposed to Zionism—but in its firm identification of Zionism with American imperialism and alleged American subversion.

[Furthermore, the *Agitators' Notebook* revealed an equally antagonistic attitude toward the state of Israel. There no longer is any Jewish press or Jewish theater in the Soviet Union, although both such institutions existed as late as the latter part of 1948. There are several persons of Jewish parentage among the leaders of the Soviet state although by no means so many as in the early days of the Revolution.]

December 23
Letter to Director, Burobin

It is now just a few days short of eleven months since I wrote you last February concerning an apartment. . . .

Dispatch to New York Times
December 24

Secretary Mikhail A. Suslov, of the Communist Party central committee, has sharply criticized P. Fedoseev, former editor-in-chief of the magazine *Bolshevik,* for his failure to mention in two recent articles in *Izvestia* mistakes which he made in 1949.

Suslov pointed out that Fedoseev's errors in economic and political ideology led to his removal from the editorship of the top Communist Party organ.

He said Fedoseev's articles in *Izvestia* which dealt with Stalin's new economic theses were correct in substance. But he suggested that Fedoseev might be "playing sly" by not mentioning the sharp criticism to which he was subjected.

The criticism arose from Fedoseev's mistaken treatment of N. A. Voznesensky's work *The War Economy of the U.S.S.R. in the Period of the Patriotic War*.

Voznesensky, former head of Soviet Planning, was dropped from the Politburo in the winter of 1948–49.

In support of his criticism Suslov made public the full text of a central committee decree of July 13, 1949, concerning *Bolshevik*. This previously unpublished decree revealed that Fedoseev was removed as editor for mistakes connected with publicizing Voznesensky's views and that Georgi F. Alexandrov and M. T. Iovochuk were also dropped from the editorial board.

The decree also sharply criticized Dmitri T. Shepilov, then chief of Communist Party propaganda and agitation. He is now editor of *Pravda*.

Dispatch to New York Times
December 26

Generalissimo Stalin appears to some Moscow diplomats to have offered General Eisenhower an excellent opportunity of making an important and practical test of what so often is referred to by Western diplomats as "Soviet good intentions."

The chance, the diplomats feel, arises from Stalin's responses yesterday to questions from James Reston of the *New York Times*.

The diplomats were not very sanguine over the possible outcome of such a test. But they felt that President Eisenhower should not overlook the fact that the new administration represents to some extent a fresh sheet on the diary of world history. . . .

December 29

The British have been told they must move out of their embassy, just across the Moscow River from the Kremlin, within three months. The British embassy is the third to be ordered out of a prominent location in recent months. In July the United States was informed it must remove from its building on Mokhovaya Square across from the Kremlin. At the same time the Indian embassy was advised it must give up its building near Arbat Square on Kalinin Street.

XXIII

The Doctors Arrested

Dispatch to New York Times
January 2, 1953

President Nesmeyanov, of the Academy of Sciences, said today that Soviet nuclear physicists now occupy the leading place in the world.

His claim of nuclear superiority goes much further than any previous claim. . . . If what he says is true, presumably this would apply to developments connected with utilization of hydrogen just as it would to uranium, plutonium, etc. . . .

Dispatch to New York Times
January 2

The *Teachers' Gazette* charges that Israel has created in Palestine ghettos for Arabs similar to the Jewish ghettos Hitler created in Poland.

The creation of the Arab ghettos was said to be part of the "racist policy of the United States." The *Teachers' Gazette* said that "the bosses of the Jewish state sold their country for dollars to the American imperialists."

Dispatch to New York Times
January 2

Pravda publishes a letter in which P. Fedoseev, former editor of *Bolshevik*, apologizes for the "shortcomings" of the articles for which he was criticized by Mikhail Suslov. . . .

January 3

A ridiculous situation has developed over my efforts to find out what has happened to the labor law of June 26, 1940. I received an inquiry about this from New York on December 14, and I asked the press department next day to advise me whether the decree had been repealed or modified. At the same time I launched my own inquiry, which turned up the fact that there had been no recent mention of the 1940 decree.

Up to this time the press department has not provided me with any information. On December 26 I finally filed a story containing such factual information as I had been able to obtain. The censor has not permitted this story to pass nor did it pass a number of messages to New York about the situation.

On December 30 New York asked me why I had filed no dispatch. I replied December 31 with the following message which was passed by the censor except for the bracketed material:

"31183 Freedman responsive yours anent December twelfth inquiry dispatch has been filed and is presently under consideration stop press department still been unable to obtain requested information but has promised to do what it can [to assist in expediting dispatch which I filed]."

Needless to say, this message brought a sarcastic reply from New York.*

Dispatch to New York Times
January 3

What the war ministry described as the "untimely" death of the fifty-six-year-old army general M. A. Purkaev on New Year's Day was announced by the newspapers *Red Star* and *Red Fleet* today.

Purkaev died on New Year's Day, but his death was announced only today along with plans for his burial.

[The use of the phrase "untimely death" usually denotes death in an accident or by some other unexpected means. . . . Purkaev's obituary was signed by almost a who's who of high Soviet military leaders, but it was by no means complete. For example, among

---

* In the end neither was the dispatch ever released by the censor nor did the press department ever provide any information relative to the repeal of the law. Not until more than two years after Stalin's death was it established conclusively that the law had, in fact, been modified in 1951.

those not listed was such a prominent marshal as Georgi K. Zhukov.]*

Dispatch to New York Times
January 12, 1953

Pravda today demanded that Soviet economists overcome fully "and to the end" the persistence of alien and mistaken subjectivist distortions connected with former Politburo member N. A. Voznesensky.

Pravda named three prominent Soviet economists as "purveyors of the mistaken theories of Voznesensky." They were A. Leontiev, I. A. Gladkov, and G. Kozlov.

Pravda's demand followed by twenty-four hours a three-day meeting of nearly 1,000 Soviet economists who have been discussing their errors in praising Voznesensky's book back in 1948. . . .

[*Pravda's* editorial made plain that this question of economic heresy is a major ideological issue and that the Party leadership is not going to be satisfied until the economic heresies are finally and fully cleared up.] *Pravda* compared the struggle against Voznesensky's views to that which was carried out against "the Trotskyist adventurers and right capitulators."

January 13

There is an echo of the grim days of Yezhov and Yagoda in Moscow today—and of the plots of the mid-1930's. The papers this morning announced the arrest of nine "doctor wreckers" who are said to have been preying on the highest echelon of Soviet government and military leadership—at the direction of Jewish-American-British intelligence.

The "chronicle"—as it was called—was carried by every newspaper in Moscow, and it chilled my blood. The accused doctors have been the most respected and honored in the Soviet medical profession.

This is serious business. Very serious business. No one who read the item—the simple workmen who crowded around the *Pravda*s pasted on the billboards or the diplomats in their comfortable chancelleries—could fail to realize how important it is.

---

* There has been speculation that Purkaev's death might in some way have been connected with the complex train of events which preceded the death of Stalin on March 5, 1953.

The question which flew into many minds was: What of the health and safety of the members of the Soviet government? By a circumstance which is probably not fortuitous the answer to this question was provided on the front pages of the same newspapers which reported the "doctors' plot." It transpires that only last night Stalin, Molotov, Malenkov, Beriya, Voroshilov, and Khrushchev chanced to go to the Bolshoi to listen to a special concert by some Polish artists. The announcement lists the government leaders at the Bolshoi in that specific order.

We correspondents were at the Bolshoi, too, and saw Stalin and his associates in the big government box at the left side of the stage. The view wasn't good, but everyone present seemed to be in good health and spirits.

The health of Stalin and his aids is not the only question which has entered our minds. Will there be an open public trial after the fashion of the 1930's and the recent treason case of Slansky in Prague? And we are wondering whether the plot will involve other persons prominent in Soviet life. Will members of foreign embassies, past or present, be linked to the case? Or correspondents?

It is fair to say that not all diplomats thought that today's "chronicle" was the opening page of another horrible and dangerous period such as swirled around the plotters and wreckers of the mid-1930's. But there is no way of being certain. There is more than one parallel between today's announcement and the 1930's. Then, as now, there were charges of criminal plotting by some of the best known Soviet physicians directed at some of the most famous figures in the Soviet Union.

And the Tass announcement made clear that more is to come. What attracts my attention is the sharp words directed at the failure of Soviet security organizations to "uncover in good time" the plot.

In fact, *Pravda* brought out the parallel with the failure of security agencies to prevent the untimely deaths of Gorki, Kuibyshev, and Menzhinsky.

What caused more confusion and terror in the 1930's than any other fact was the successive involvement of two chiefs of state security, Yagoda and Yezhev. It was not until Beriya took over in 1938 that the situation was brought under control.

All of the physicians who are supposed to be involved in the plot are well known in Moscow. The Mikhoels who was named is assumed to be Solomon Mikhoels, a leading actor of the former Jewish theater in Moscow, famous for his interpretation of King Lear and a leader in the Jewish Anti-Fascist Committee which was dissolved in 1948. The Jewish theater was dissolved at the same time. Mikhoels is supposed to have been killed near Minsk in an automobile accident attributed at the time it occurred—the winter of 1947–48—to anti-Jewish elements. Mikhoels was given a prominent funeral in Moscow, and among those who played a leading role in the obsequies was Ilya Ehrenburg, who is intensively anti-Zionist.

Among the arrested doctors is Professor Vladimir Vinogradov, one of the most respected figures in Russian medicine. Less than a year ago, on his seventieth birthday last February 26, he was awarded the Order of Lenin. He signed the death certificate for President Kalinin in 1946 and for Georgi Dimitrov in 1949. Another signer of the Dimitrov certificate is Professor P. Egorov, first doctor listed in the chronicle and chief of the treatment administration of the Kremlin. He also signed the death certificate of Mongolia's Choibalsan last January.

Dispatch Killed by Censor
January 14, 1953

There was no relaxation today of the concern which has been spread by the announcement of the "doctors' plot."

For the second time within twenty-four hours the papers give front-page mention to Stalin's activities. Yesterday he received at the Kremlin the chairman of the Chinese-Soviet Friendship Society, Sun Tsin-lin, and the president of the Chinese Academy of Sciences, Go Mo-jo. . . .

There was no diminution of the general feeling of apprehension among citizens. Soviet citizens are fully aware from past experience of the dangers which lurk in such plotting even after it has been exposed. . . .

It is apparent that the entire story of the plot has not yet been made public. The participation of others is by no means excluded. The most important question is the failure of Soviet security agencies. Where the ramifications of this may lead is not certain. It might lead to involvement of Soviet citizens who have secreted themselves in high positions and possibly to connections with foreign agents who might have acted under cover of diplomatic immunity. It might involve persons who even today continue to occupy positions of rank and responsibility.

The Party organ, *Kommunist,* in an article written by Frol R. Kozlov, a secretary of the Leningrad organization, invokes the famous central committee warning issued after the assassination of Sergei Kirov, one of Stalin's closest associates, December 1, 1934.

Kozlov reveals that "a number of alien and foreign elements" have already been exposed and purged from the Leningrad organization, including persons connected with what he calls middle bourgeois, nationalist counterrevolutionary parties such as the Jewish Bund, as well as Trotskyites and kulaks.

Kozlov said that by exposing and eliminating Trotskyites and Bukharinites in the mid-1930's Russia rid itself of a fifth column. The same thing, he said, is now going on in the drive against the "Rajks, the Kostovs, the Slanskys," all of whom were identified as agents of American imperialism.

One of those whom Kozlov singled out for special criticism was Professor A. N. Bernstam, who was said to be guilty of gross political errors. . . .

The conclusion drawn by Moscow diplomats was that the revelations thus far are only the beginning of a complicated horror story. . . .

Dispatch to New York Times
January 15

Once again the well-known Soviet economist Eugen Varga has publicly admitted his errors and acknowledged his indebtedness to the "genius work of Comrade Stalin."

Varga's latest apology was made at a special session of the Scientific Council of the Institute of Economics held in November to consider economic problems in the light of Stalin's new theses. . . .

January 15

Today *Izvestia* strengthened the criticism of Soviet security agencies which was voiced by *Pravda* two days ago. *Izvestia* says the leaders of Soviet security organs lost their vigilance and became infected with what is called *rotozeistvo*—loafing.

This makes it perfectly plain that the responsible members of the security agency will be appropriately punished. There are few crimes more serious than that of a sentry sleeping on guard duty —that is what the "responsible" security leaders are accused of.

What Moscow diplomats are now talking about is that the heads of the security agencies will be brought into the plot. All the Moscow papers are talking about "vigilance" and American "fifth columns."

Pravda went out of its way today to denounce the "zoölogical racism of the Hitlerites." This is probably a backhanded reply to charges published abroad that the "plot" is anti-Semitic in character.

Muscovites are reading their newspapers with more than usual avidity. If such a "plot" can be exposed in the shadow of the Kremlin, what other crimes may be in progress? What everyone is worrying and wondering about is—where will it lead?

Dispatch to New York Times
January 16, 1953

Pravda demanded that Party organizations take increased vigilance against enemy intrigues directed against Soviet scientists and Soviet intelligentsia.

It published sharp criticism of a number of scientists for "subjective and idealistic" distortions. This included a number of physiologists, astronomers, and physicists who were said to be under Western influence.

[The attack appeared to be a natural result of the exposure of treason on the part of nine Soviet medical men who had occupied positions of high Kremlin trust.]

A meeting of the Party's top agitators and propagandists was convened in Moscow. A four-day meeting of the All-Union Society for Dissemination of Political and Scientific Knowledge was opened, and a meeting at the Marx-Engels-Lenin Institute has just been concluded.

A number of participants in these meetings acknowledged their errors in connection with the 1947 book of N. A. Voznesensky, the former member of the Politburo. . . .

Ivan Maisky, former ambassador to London, and a number of other Soviet historians, including Boris Shtein, I. I. Mintz, D. A. Baebsky, and L. I. Zubok, have been criticized in the discussions about Voznesensky. . . .

Dispatch to New York Times
January 18

Nominations for local Soviets—the equivalent of city councils—are going on now throughout the Soviet Union. *Pravda* published the nominations of Stalin and Malenkov on page one. On page two were Beriya, Bulganin, Voroshilov, Molotov, and Khrushchev. [Among the prominent government leaders who have not been nominated yet are Mikoyan, Suslov, Ponamarenko, Shkiryatov, Kosygin, and Andreyev.] Those nominated in Leningrad were Stalin, Malenkov, Beriya, and Bulganin. At Tbilisi: Stalin, Beriya, Malenkov, and A. I. Mgledze. . . .

[There is a widening movement against all types of security and vigilance violations, including the arrest of an official of the Ministry of Nonferrous Metallurgy and discharge of several Ukrainian officials.]

Pravda revealed that A. I. Korshun, of the metallurgical ministry, has been implicated in the mysterious disappearance of a secret document.

Red Fleet exposed a criminal named Greenberg and his partners Mefodovsky and Lebedev. The Kiev newspaper reported dismissal of two Kiev Party secretaries and widening hatred among the people for "all these Kahns and Yaroshetskys, Greensteins, Kaplans, and Polyakovs" responsible for crimes.

[The Kiev newspaper spelled all these names with small letters and put them in a category described by Stalin as "spies and traitors if not worse."]

Dispatch Killed by Censor
January 19

The Vilnaus newspaper reports that bourgeois nationalists and members of Jewish Zionist organizations have penetrated local institutions and establishments. . . . The *Turkmenian Star* reported similar crimes in Ashkabad. . . .

January 19

The famous Marx-Engels-Lenin Institute has a new director. Professor G. D. Obichkin has replaced Peter N. Pospelov, who has headed it for several years.

Dispatch to New York Times
January 21, 1953

The journal *New Times* said today that the entire Jewish Zionist movement has "sold out to American intelligence" and is assisting in creating a fifth column in the Soviet Union and the people's democracies. . . .

The attack coincided with the announcement of the award to Dr. Lydia Fedoseevna Timashuk of the Order of Lenin for her services in uncovering the "doctors' plot."

Speaking in the presence of Stalin and high Soviet leaders, Nikolai Mikhailov told the Lenin Memorial meeting that the Party will "mercilessly drive out all degenerates or double-dealers."

Newspapers reported that the Bolshoi Theater meeting was attended by "leaders of the Communist Party and the Soviet government." [Newspaper accounts did not specify which leaders of the Party and government were present. In past years it has been usual to publish photographs of the Bolshoi Theater stage, showing the government and Party leaders on the platform. Today's papers published no photographs of the meeting.]*

Dispatch to New York Times
January 22

The newspaper *Byelo-Russia* in Minsk has published an exposé of seven doctors whom it charged with malingering and engaging in a false-illness racket. They were named as Drs. Asya Epstein, Tsilya Nisnevich, Regina Blok, Kantorovich, Slobodskaya, Kokash, and Dora Moiseevna Paperno. . . .

Dispatch to New York Times
January 23

Izvestia publishes almost a full-page article attacking leading members of the Institute of Law of the Academy of Sciences and the All-Union Institute of Juridical Science. Among those named were A. Trainin, B. Mankovsky, E. Korovin, M. Strogovich, N.

* The press published pictures of the leadership group attending the November 6, 1952, meeting at the Bolshoi and also of those atop Lenin's Tomb, reviewing the parade November 7, 1952. However, on both occasions the customary listing of Party leaders present in presumed order of rank was omitted. The January 21, 1953, meeting carried this one step further by dropping even the picture.

Alexandrov, N. Farberov, A. Lepeshkin, N. Polyansky, A. Piont-kovsky, A. Gertzenson, S. Gringaus, N. Durmanov, I. Isaev, B. Utevsky, D. Genkin, I. Novitzky, R. Eisenstat, N. Rabinovich, and A. Karp. . . .

January 24

Mikoyan has finally been nominated for a place on the Moscow city council along with Suslov and Kosygin. However, he is described merely as a "member of the Presidium." Suslov is identified as "a true and firm son of the Communist Party." Kosygin is identified as "a member of the Presidium." . . . Other government leaders were described as Stalin's "closest comrades-at-arms."

The newspaper Komsomolskaya *Pravda* reports the case of a blind Fagin named Cohen who has succeeded in obtaining a series of orphan boys from Moscow children's institutions to lead him around and carry out his commands.

The modern Fagin's name is Alexander Lazarevich Cohen. He claimed to have been blinded as a soldier in World War II and obtained some 21,000 rubles in state grants on this account.

Cohen applied to Moscow children's institutions for youngsters to work "jointly" with him. He promised to see that youngsters received normal schooling.

But the newspaper revealed that Yuri Pankov, the latest child to be supplied to Cohen, was kept out of school and used by him to guide him around town and carry out his every whim.

January 25

The *Ukraine Pravda* has exposed another Kiev scandal—this one involving a "family business" which Jacob Davidovich Mailman established at Kiev's glass thermos factory.

Mailman's relatives and friends are without number, the newspaper said. "They all work in the family business." There's Nephew S. Mailman, Uncle Vintman, Haplerman, Kagansky, Faibisovich, Kleiman, Obukhovsky, Singer, Shor, Shvartzer, Shenker, "and so forth." . . .

Dispatch to New York Times
January 27

The newspaper *Medical Worker* reports new medical scandals including the case of Myra Israilevna Chernyakova (Bloch) who in a year's time tossed more than 500 tumor samples into the ash-can instead of carrying out biopsies. The other scandals involved M. Z. Izrailit and one Zaitsev. . . .

The newspaper *Pravda* of the Ukraine reports that Kiev Party secretaries Zinitz, Ilin, and Petychenko and bureau member Davidov have been sharply criticized in connection with the Kiev criminal ring, some members of which were shot. . . .

The newspaper reported another racket in the Kiev publishing house involving Radyansky, Pismennik, U. Dolda Mikailik, E. Adelheim, and U. Mokreeb.

Dispatch to New York Times
January 28, 1953

The journal *Kommunist* [attacking a number of philosophers, economists, and historians for their support of former Politburo member N. A. Voznesensky] warned that "carriers of bourgeois views and bourgeois morals" are enemies of the people. . . .

Among those attacked were Georgi F. Alexandrov, P. Fedoseev, M. Iovchuk, A. Leontiev, L. Gatovsky, S. L. Ronin, A. Gertzenson, S. Greengaus, N. Durmanov, M. Islev, B. Utevsky, and E. A. Kosminsky. . . .

The newspaper *Erevan Kommunist* exposed a million-ruble fraud perpetrated by Garush (Mnatzakan) Samuelyan. . . . The newspaper *Trud* reported crime in small Moscow shops, citing the case of A. Levitas and L. Lumer. . . .

Dispatch to New York Times
January 30

The *Medical Worker* exposes another medical scandal, a case of nepotism, bourgeois theories, Freudian beliefs, and alien ideas in the Institute of Forensic Psychiatry, formerly headed by Professor T. M. Feinberg. . . .

Among Feinberg's "many friends and relatives from Odessa" brought into the institute it listed the Khaletzky, Kalashnik, Korsunsky, Turubin, Freier, and Borevsky couples, Luntz, Shtiller, Zaturolovsky, Usevich, and others. . . .*

---

* The purpose of these frequent lists of names was to show the high percentage of Jewish victims of the drive—a fact which the censor would not permit to be stated directly.

Dispatch to New York Times
January 31

Pravda reports the exposure in Soviet Lithuania of a band of Jewish and Lithuanian bourgeois nationalists engaged in espionage and diversion at the behest of the Americans.

It also said that the former minister for nonferrous metallurgy, S. M. Petrov, is guilty of blatant laxness and carelessness in connection with important secret documents.

A. I. Orlov, *Pravda* said, has been exposed by the Ministry of State Security on charges of treason in connection with stealing a document. Another violator of state security was named as I. G. Khanovich, head of the Krylov Academy of Leningrad. . . .

G. L. Zaslavsky, official of the geology ministry, is said to have taken valuable secret materials from the vaults and told outside persons about them. A similar case was cited involving M. G. Kazhdaev, former oil ministry official. . . .

A. N. Nesmeyanov, president of the Academy of Sciences, read a lesson in political vigilance to his colleagues. He called particular attention to the seriousness of ideological mistakes of "an idealistic subjective character."

February 2
Letter to Director, Burobin

Precisely one year ago I wrote you requesting a three- or four-room apartment. I have not yet received that apartment. . . .

Dispatch to New York Times
February 2

The Kiev newspaper says that the United States has organized attempts on the lives of Jacques Duclos, Maurice Thorez, Palmiro Togliatti, the Japanese Communist Tokuda, and the Chinese Communist leaders.

[No details of the plot directed at the Chinese were provided.]

The newspaper said the Slansky trial and the "doctors' plot" showed that Zionism and Jewish bourgeois nationalism have sold out to American intelligence agencies. . . .

A. A. Snechkus, Communist Party secretary in Lithuania, called for a drive against all secret enemies in Lithuania, including [Christian Democrats, Social Democrats, Zionists, SR's, Tautinists, and Lyaudininists].

February 3, 1953

The censorship is getting touchy about the articles on vigilance, graft, etc. A whole series of cables which I filed January 31, based on *Pravda*'s leading editorial and a lengthy *Pravda* article, citing instances of arrests and security violations were subject to lengthy delays—although ultimately passed without change. It is difficult to understand why it takes a censor so long to decide whether a straight report lifted verbatim out of *Pravda* should be passed or not.

Dispatch to New York Times
February 3

Foreign Minister Andrei Ya. Vishinsky, speaking as a law academician, has excoriated the Soviet legal profession for its "serious mistakes" in failing to cope with "bourgeois pseudoscience."

The Soviet legal profession has been under critical examination since an address delivered at the Nineteenth Party Congress last October by Lieutenant General Alexander Poskrebyshev, chief of the Kremlin secretariat.

The same meeting of the Academy of Sciences heard P. F. Yudin, Presidium member, again attack P. N. Fedoseev for "dodging and slurring over" his error in supporting the economic views of former Politburo member N. A. Voznesensky. Economists L. A. Leontiev, L. M. Gatovsky, and K. V. Ostrovitianov and philosopher G. F. Alexandrov apologized for their errors in the same connection. . . .

XXIV

The End Nears

February 5, 1953

I have been out to the dacha, and all I can say is that I wish the world were as quiet and peaceful as it appears around Moscow now. Everything is covered in a deep blanket of white, white snow. There is a very strong frost—close to 30° below, centigrade, and the sky is pale winter blue. The air is crisp and horses' and humans' mouths are quickly covered with hoarfrost. The country is sleeping quietly under its white blanket, the peasants are busy with winter chores, the youngsters' skates ring on the village ponds, and the forests stand dark green and silent and a little frightening.

It looks and is a simple kind of world.

But, unfortunately, I do not think we can consider this a symbol of the state of this country in these parlous days. Nevertheless, I do have a feeling that once this time is past the countryside and the forest and the people will still be there, still quiet, still filled with deep winter calm. . . .

February 6

Here is the news of the day. *Pravda* announces the arrest of three persons whom the United States is supposed to have sent into the Soviet for espionage and subversion. One of them is S. D. Gurevich, described as a veteran Trotskyite who was educated in the family of a Bundist Menshevik. He was in the United States from 1914 to 1917, returned to Russia, became a Trotskyite, and established connections with foreign intelligence services in 1939. He sounds vaguely familiar to me. He is supposed to have implicated a woman employed in the Academy of Sciences named E. A. Tartuta who stole secret documents for him. Two other agents were named—K. F. Romanov and T. A. Saks. . . .

I will not put down any golden thoughts about these latest developments on the international scene. As the *Literary Gazette* says in its captions over the pictures of starving children and lynched Negroes in a certain unspeakable and unmentionable land: "Comment Unnecessary."

Dispatch to New York Times
February 6, 1953

The Jews do not constitute a nation, Zionists are agents of American-English imperialists, and Israel is being turned into an American war base.

These are some of the conclusions advanced today by the official Soviet encyclopedia. The same volume describes life in the Jewish autonomous *oblast* of Birobijan as busy, productive, and growing.

The article says there is no such thing as a Jewish nation because the Jews do not represent a historic, concentrated, stable community of people with common language, territory, life, and culture. . . .

As for Birobijan, it is described as a happy, prosperous region, busy cutting marble for the new Moscow subway stations and rapidly expanding its woodworking industry. There is said to be a library named for Sholem Aleichem with 80,000 volumes and two newspapers, one in Russian and one in Yiddish.*

Dispatch to New York Times
February 8

Argentina's new ambassador, Louis Bravo, reports that Stalin appears to be in excellent physical and mental condition. His general state of health belies his seventy-three years. Bravo spent forty-five minutes with Stalin at the Kremlin last night. The last Western diplomat received by Stalin was French ambassador Joxe last summer. . . .

* When I visited this library in 1954, it was no longer named for Aleichem, and it had no Yiddish books on its shelves.

Izvestia reported that security agencies have liquidated a nest of American spies established at Vladivostok by former U.S. naval attaché George Roullard in 1947. The Vladivostok consulate was closed in 1949. . . .

Izvestia said the United States smuggled weeds harmful to man and beast into Russia in innocent-looking lettuce seed packets during the war. The packets were filled with quack grass and jimpson weed, designed to "deal a dagger blow at the Soviet rear."

Izvestia said that all American diplomats now work for the U.S. intelligence agencies, and that there have been a number of cases of intelligence agents "operating under the mask of journalism."

It cited as examples the cases of Anna Louise Strong and Robert Magidoff. . . .

Dispatch to New York Times
February 10

Fifteen hundred candidates for the Moscow city council have been nominated—a roster which is a veritable who's who of the Soviet Union. . . .

Among those nominated is Semyon D. Ignatiev, whose name has been advanced by members of the Ministry of State Security. Another candidate is Ivan G. Kabanov, former Minister of the Electrical Industry, now listed as chairman of the State Committee on Material-Technical Supply.

[Among those not nominated is Viktor A. Abukumov, listed since 1946 as Minister of State Security. Lieutenant General Vasily Stalin, who was elected in the last election in 1950, is not a candidate for re-election. . . .]

February 12

It seems to me that severance of diplomatic relations between Israel and Moscow—announced by Vishinsky to Minister Eliashev in a note about 1:00 A.M. this morning—forecloses any remaining possibilities for emigration of Jews from Russia or eastern Europe to Israel.

Nor would it be surprising if the satellite governments followed Moscow's example and broke off, too. Relations have been getting worse and worse since the Slansky trial in Prague with its allegations of Zionist plotting.

As soon as we heard that a bomb had gone off in the Soviet legation in Tel Aviv, we assumed that the break in relations would follow. The next thing will be some effort to tie in the bomb explosion with the "doctors' plot."

Israel and Russia have maintained relations since the founding of the Israeli state May 16, 1948. The first Israeli minister, Mrs. Golda Myerson, arrived here in September, 1948, and established headquarters in the Metropole Hotel. Hundreds of Moscow Jews swarmed to the hotel to pay their respects—not that all Moscow Jews had such a friendly attitude. Ilya Ehrenburg has always been an outspoken enemy of Zionism, and when he met Mrs. Myerson at a reception soon after she came here, he spoke to her with withering sarcasm.

Dispatch to New York Times
February 13, 1953

The Kiev newspaper reports the discovery of a "vile nest" of Zionist, bourgeois Jewish nationalists at the Odessa State University. . . . The *Medical Worker* attacks Drs. Rabinovich, Meller, and Raikh as "scoundrels and rascals. . . ."

Pravda bitterly criticized a new novel by the famous Soviet war correspondent Vassily Grossman. It said his book was permeated by a new ideological sin called "pythagorism." It particularly found fault with his characters Professor Shtrum, Dr. Sofia Levynton, and a certain Shaposhnikov.

[Grossman is one of the leading Soviet writers of Jewish origin.]

February 14

Early this morning the radio reported the death of Lev Z. Mekhlis, former minister of state control, one of the few Jews who had remained in a high government office. He will be buried today with a state funeral in Red Square.

Dispatch to New York Times
February 15

Some of the important Chinese economic officials who came to Moscow last August—six months ago—with Chou En-lai are still here negotiating with their Soviet counterparts. However, the high Chinese air officers who were here at the time of the November holiday have gone back home. . . .

February 16

Vassily Grossman, the famous Jewish writer whose popularity as a war correspondent was so great that the Red Army picked him to write about its battle experiences, has now been attacked by *Kommunist* magazine as "a prisoner of the ideology of bourgeois nationalism and racism. . . ."

Dispatch to New York Times
February 18

Moscow diplomats believe there is a possibility of new efforts to bring the Korean war to an end. This speculation has arisen after conversations at the Kremlin last night by Stalin with India's Ambassador K. P. Menon and Dr. Saiffudin Kitchlu. Stalin talked with the men separately.

Dr. Kitchlu said he had "a frank free full talk on all the leading questions of the day," including Korea. . . .

Both Kitchlu and Menon described Stalin as being in excellent health, mind, and spirits. . . .

February 20

Red Star tries to draw a line between anti-Semitism and anti-Zionism. Anti-Semitism seems to be something which exists in America, whereas anti-Zionism is "defense against American spies, diversionists, and undermining agents."

"Thus," says *Red Star*, "they are two different things, as different one from the other as heaven and earth."

Other Moscow papers carried items about Israeli Moiseevich Joffe who got a job in the Ministry of Light Metallurgy through a certain Shapironsky. Others who got jobs through friends and relatives were named as Leonid Moiseevich Roitblat, David Shabelevich Abramovich, M. P. Feinberg, and Y. I. Furman. One Abram Yankelevich was accused of immoral conduct with a series of women. . . .

February 21

I heard today that the Soviets have agreed to accept Charles Bohlen as U.S. ambassador, succeeding George Kennan.

We learned this afternoon that Marshal Sokolovsky has replaced General Shtemenko as chief of staff. The change showed up when military attachés got their invitations to the Red Army Day reception on Monday. The cards were signed by Sokolovsky instead of Shtemenko. Sokolovsky was a World War II commander who had been closely associated with Marshal Zhukov. Shtemenko was one of the men named as an intended victim of the "doctors' plot." There is no indication of what has happened to him.

There also seems to be a new commandant of the Moscow military district air force. Stalin's son Vasily held the post until recent months. The last time he appeared publicly as district commander was at the air show last July. Judging from the candidates in the municipal election districts, the new air force commander is General Ivan Galitzky.

February 22, 1953

This has been a frosty winter Sunday, and I have spent a good many hours just strolling about the streets of Moscow. I left the Metropole about noon and wandered over toward the Red Square. Lots of traffic in the streets—most of the cars mass-production Pobedas but some new pastel-tinted Zims and a few of the old high-bodied Zis cars, which look like the Packards of the 1930's.

The white-smocked ice cream girls were doing a brisk business in Eskimo pies and ice cream sandwiches. I never get over being surprised to see a Muscovite strolling along in 20° below weather eating a Russian Good Humor.

Around the Revolution Place subway station the kiosks were busy—one selling soft drinks, another paper and wax flowers, another cigarettes, and another chocolate bars. I bought a ten-ruble bar that carried a wrapper designed to persuade youngsters to clean their hands. On the wrapper was this verse:

> You must, you must wash
> In the morning and the evening.
> Don't be an unclean chimney sweep—
> Shame, shame on you.

The line of people waiting to get into Lenin's Tomb already stretched back toward Alexandrinsky Park. Seeing Lenin is a favorite Sunday family occupation,

Even though the sun was shining and it was really pleasant, as Moscow winter days go, a battalion of heavy snowplows and trucks stood in the lee of St. Basil's, ready for action at the first hint of a snow cloud. And a crew of snow sweepers was shoveling off the roof of St. Basil's.

On the big fence along the Zaryadnaya excavation below St. Basil's where it is proposed to put up Moscow's tallest building, there were a lot of advertising posters—two for champagne, two for caviar, two for cheese, three for ice cream, and others for kvass, real coffee, toilet soap, margarine, face powder, and corn-flakes. Mikoyan has been trying for years to get the Muscovites to buy cornflakes, but he can't seem to succeed.

I walked down Razin Street, one of the oldest in Moscow. Once it was known as Barbarian Street and even earlier, a hundred years before Christopher Columbus, it was known as All Saints Street.

In this street is the old Romanov house—the sixteenth-century house where that ambitious merchant family lived before Michael was called to the throne. I was interested to see whether the new construction project would disturb it. I found the house shuttered and gloomy as ever. Some youngsters had made an icy slide in the courtyard, and across the street was an Agitpunkt for the municipal election. As far as I could see, the new building will not disturb the old landmark.

Then I walked along the Moskva River—firmly frozen from shore to shore—glancing down-river to the fairy towers of the new twenty-four-story apartment on the Kotelnikovskaya embankment and upstream to those of the new Smolenskaya building which houses the Foreign Office and foreign trade ministry. I skirted the Kremlin walls, past the Borovitskaya Gate, and entered Kalinin Street, which used to be called Komintern Street and before that Vozdvizhensky or Holy Rood Street. This is a terribly ancient street which used to be the main route to Novgorod in the days when Novgorod was a great city and Moscow just a wilderness trading post.

This street connected the Kremlin with the "Orbat" or medieval trading settlement which is now the Arbat quarter. Here before the Revolution rich merchants and industrialists lived. Embassies and legations now occupy many of the houses.

I window-shopped along Kalinin Street. In a bookstore I noticed a 1915 edition of Ivan Bunin's works. Bunin has not been republished lately, and his books are hard to come by. Next to Bunin was a tattered paperback edition of a book by "Dzhek" London, the all-time American favorite in Russia.

A government car came swirling down the street, bound for the Kremlin. It stirred up hurricanes of snow in its wake.

In the Central Military Department Store there was a display of silk yard goods at prices of 105 to 140 rubles a meter. A silk dress was priced at 595 rubles.

Watching passers-by, I was impressed by the extent to which the *valenki* or traditional Russian felt boot had been supplanted by rubber boots and rubber overshoes. Valenki are clumsy and ugly but probably the warmest footgear invented. In the years immediately after the war 90 per cent of the men wore valenki in winter.

At the big Art Movie Theater in Arbat Square a picture called *Friends and Enemies of America*, a 1939 Hollywood production originally called *Let Freedom Ring*, was showing.

I plunged into narrow Arbat Street, one of the busiest in Moscow. Every few steps posters had been put up for the election. Several people stopped with me to peer into the frosted windows of the pet store. The birds, puppies, and goldfish had been removed to warmer spots. The Vakhtangov Theater, one of the few Moscow buildings destroyed in wartime and now newly rebuilt, was advertising *The Gray-haired Maiden*, a Chinese play. It is also showing *Dve Verontzov*, which I suddenly realized is *Two Gentlemen from Verona*.

By now the towers and battlements of the great Smolenskaya building loomed overhead. There are eight of these tall buildings in Moscow. I crossed Smolensk Place where after the Revolution "the former people" used to sell their possessions. Now the site is occupied by a vegetable store, a shoe repair shop, and a hair-dyeing establishment.

In an icy courtyard I saw a red-cheeked youngster busy chopping a small log into kindling. Just beside him was a poster advertising a memorial concert for Feodor Chaliapin.

I walked across the windy Crimean Bridge to the winter fairyland of Gorki Park, filled with music and rinks and iced paths and hundreds of youngsters.

On the walls of the park were dozens of posters, freshly put up for the Red Army holiday. They depicted a Red Army man with a tommy gun and a series of insets showing the enemies he had defeated—Wrangel and the White generals of the Civil War, interventionist foreign troops, the Poles in 1920, the Japs in 1937, the Finns in 1939–40, the Nazis and Japanese in World War II, and finally a portrait oval which was blank. It simply said: "Reserved for those with bad memories."

As I rode back to the Metropole Hotel on the subway, the impression which came back to me most strongly from my Sunday walk was that of the blank oval in the Red Army Day poster—the one for "those with bad memories."

Dispatch Killed by Censor
February 23, 1953

Semyon Denisovich Ignatiev, member of the Presidium, has become minister of state security. . . .

February 24

Before he left early today for a trip to Central Asia and his return to India, Dr. Kitchlu gave me a rundown of his talk with Stalin just a week ago.

Stalin talked at length about the United States, Kitchlu said. He said that the Americans had made some great contributions to the world in the past. For instance, the American Revolution was an inspiration to other peoples in their struggle for freedom. The American policy of isolation and non-involvement in the affairs of other countries was a good thing, but two wars have given the American capitalists a taste of profits and now they want more. That's what's behind U.S. foreign policy—profits for the capitalists.

Dr. Kitchlu said that he wished he could tell the American people everything that he learned from Stalin. "It would surprise and please them," he said. He added that Russia does not want war with the United States.

Stalin described Eisenhower as a good military man who was much better able than Truman to judge the world situation. He had a good record in World War II. But the people around Eisenhower, the capitalists, are not good. One trouble with Truman was that he was too much influenced by Churchill. Churchill got him under his thumb. Churchill's Fulton (Missouri) speech got Truman on the wrong track.

Stalin said he was surprised at the English. He thought the English had a spirit of sportsmanship. Russia saved England's hide in the war. It would only be fair for England to support Russia now. If the English don't want to play fair, then you can't blame the Russians for going it alone.

If war comes, Stalin told Kitchlu, England will be smashed. War will be bad for Russia and the United States—very bad, indeed. But it will be fatal for England. If it really comes down to cases, the English can't support the United States in war. They know it means their finish. The same goes for France. England and France can't go on indefinitely supporting the United States. They are going to break. This is bound to happen.

Stalin doesn't entirely understand Nehru's position. Kitchlu tried to explain it, but Stalin still didn't feel that he understood India. He said he could see that India had more to learn from China than from Russia and that it was natural for India and China to have more intimate relations. Stalin does not feel that there is only one path of political and economic development open to a country. Each country has its individual peculiarities, and these are marked in the case of India. America's efforts to "buy" India will not succeed. However, Chester Bowles (then U.S. ambassador) is a very clever man. Kitchlu told Stalin that Nehru would like to have a meeting with him. This is very much on the q.t. Kitchlu said he had not even told Ambassador Menon about this. He also said he might not tell Nehru everything that Stalin told him.

So far as Korea is concerned, Stalin said that his words of reply to Reston were not idle. That, in fact, Russia was ready to co-operate in a new diplomatic effort to end the Korean war. This is not just talk, Stalin said. It has a concrete meaning which will be disclosed in due time. Russia doesn't want war with the United States and can't afford to have a war. It would jeopardize everything that's been built up in the last thirty-five years.

Kitchlu was much impressed with Stalin. He said the General-issimo was extremely well informed, seemed to have all the facts at his finger tips, and spoke most freely and frankly.*

* Kitchlu's interview, February 17, 1953, was the last Stalin had with a foreigner before his death. It is notable that the general structure of his thinking, as reported by Kitchlu, closely resembles many of the major foreign policy premises of Khrushchev eight years later.

February 24, 1953

The *Medical Worker* discloses that there was a first class row over Lydia Timashuk's suspicions which touched off the "doctors' plot."

She is a grandmother whose son was badly injured as a World War II aviator. She works as an electrocardiograph specialist in a hospital, and her suspicions were first aroused when she discovered a distinguished professor apparently misreading and misdiagnosing the condition of a patient on the basis of her electrocardiograph. She called the doctor's attention to what she thought was a simple mistake and was sharply reprimanded. She then carried her battle to higher levels. The accused doctor was supported by many other doctors, equally distinguished, who challenged what the paper calls Timashuk's "political maturity and honesty." The battle went on for a long time "in very difficult and complex conditions," but finally Timashuk won out.

February 25

General Shtemenko has turned up in Berlin. He attended a reception, but his post was not stated. Still no indication what has happened to Vasily Stalin.

February 26
Letter to Generalissimo Stalin, the Kremlin

General Eisenhower is quoted as having said in Washington yesterday that he is ready to meet with you and that he is prepared to travel halfway around the world for that purpose provided such a meeting will contribute to the cause of peace and freedom.

May I take the liberty of inquiring:

Whether you are prepared to meet in the near future with General Eisenhower? What place would you suggest as suitable for such a meeting?

Do you believe a meeting of heads of state of the Soviet Union and the United States might have positive results with respect to such questions as Korea and Germany?

XXV

The Death of Stalin

Dispatch to New York Times
March 1, 1953

The central committee of the Communist Party, in a resolution front-paged by the newspapers today, demands from all the highest political vigilance. It charges the United States with sending into Russia a stream of spies, wreckers, and murderers. . . .

Telegram to New York Times
March 3—3:00 a.m.

Anything doing on dictation backstops London or Paris yet?

Telegram from New York Times
Received March 4—00:52 a.m.

Dubious about setting up London Paris dictation posts simply for late breaks Moscow but still awaiting results of cost inquiry.*

Dispatch to New York Times
March 4—8:30 a.m.

The government announced shortly before eight o'clock this morning that Generalissimo Stalin on Sunday night, March 1-2,

---

* The matter of establishing a dictation system to expedite transmission of late, hot news breaks had been under consideration since late August, 1952. I was becoming increasingly nervous, because it was obvious that something big and probably unexpected was about to occur in Moscow. I did not, of course, realize that the break was only a few hours away.

suffered a [massive] brain hemorrhage with paralysis of the right hand and leg, loss of speech and of consciousness.

The illness was called "heavy" in a joint announcement in the name of the Council of Ministers and the central committee.

Stalin is said to have been stricken in his quarters in the Kremlin on Sunday night. The illness affected the most important brain centers, disturbing the functions of the heart and lungs.

The announcement was issued thirty-six hours after the onset of the illness.

The medical bulletin was signed by ten physicians, headed by the new health minister, A. F. Tretyakov. Daily bulletins will be issued. It is said that Stalin will not be able to participate in the government for a considerable period.

[So far as the bulletin indicates, the illness has not yielded to the remedies employed thus far. The news spread through the city like wildfire, passing by word of mouth from one passer-by to another among the Muscovites going to work. Even before the radio announcement word was sweeping the city that Stalin was ill.]

Those who have seen Stalin lately—Ambassador Bravo of the Argentine and Ambassador Menon and Dr. Kitchlu of India—had the impression he was in robust physical and mental condition. But it is undeniable that Stalin has been under unusual strain in the past six months.

[Not the least important strain was the announcement last month of a plot of leading Soviet doctors directed against leading figures in the government, allegedly carried out at the behest of American and British intelligence agencies. With all this going on, Stalin did not take his customary Black Sea holiday at Sochi last autumn.]

Telegram to New York Times
March 4—9:00 a.m.

Believe in view this mornings news better establish that standby for dictation in London or Paris which I have been asking for stop at least can't we put dictation man on temporary basis while things are hot here? I hope this can be done tonight and will proceed on that assumption barring word from you to contrary.

335

March 4—4:30 p.m.

There is no indication of the slightest connection between the "doctors' plot" and Stalin's illness. But rumors of some connection have circulated nonetheless.

Those doctors whom I have talked with tell me that a hemorrhage of the extent indicated in the communiqué would have been sufficient to kill outright most men of Stalin's age.

In the interregnum the direction of Soviet affairs has been taken over by that group called Stalin's "closest comrades-at-arms." They have called on the people to display "unity, solidarity, a firm spirit, and vigilance."

This group is headed by Georgi Malenkov, Stalin's deputy and right-hand man, Lavrenti Beriya, Nikolai Bulganin, Molotov, and several others. When Lenin fell ill in 1923 and 1924, a similar role was played by Stalin and his closest associates.

No one knows when the next medical bulletin will come out. Radios are turned on constantly. There were long lines at the kiosks—sometimes a hundred and more—to buy papers. Many believers have gone to the churches to pray for Stalin. The patriarch issued a general proclamation asking for prayers for Stalin and is to conduct a solemn service himself in the Yelokhovsky cathedral. At seven o'clock this evening the chief rabbi will hold special services at the Central synagogue.

March 4—9:00 p.m.

The chief rabbi called for a day of fasting and prayer in the Jewish community tomorrow that Stalin's life might be spared.

At the big cathedral the patriarch called on God to spare Stalin's life. The congregation chanted "Amen." Acolytes held aloft the Bible in its golden case, and the patriarch with his golden rod and gown of gold and purple slowly passed through the multitude of praying believers. Around the altars hundreds of tiny candles burned like golden stars of hope. All over Russia this scene was repeated in one form or another.

Telegram to New York Times
March 4—9:00 p.m.

Please instruct London place phone call for me at midnight London time and hourly intervals thereafter until I instruct discontinue stop London can instruct phoners that I will be waiting at Moscow International call office to receive call when it is put through stop please confirm.

Telegram from New York Times
Received March 4—10:00 p.m.

Effective date living allowance increase awaits your request.

Telegram from New York Times
Received March 5—12:30 a.m.

Supplementing earlier message living allowance we suspending action thereon pending your advice on mailing of final expense account.

Telegram to New York Times
March 5—Midnight

Excellent going on living allowance increase stop will advise you on effective date soons make necessary local calculations.*

March 5—1:00 a.m.

The atmosphere of the city is quiet and concerned. After dark a light snow began to fall. The day had been brilliant with March sunshine.

Snow-sweeping crews went into action in Red Square where the usual block-long queue of citizens earlier in the afternoon had visited Lenin's Tomb. Spotlights tonight played as always on the red flag flying over the offices of the Supreme Soviet in the Kremlin, and lights burned in the Kremlin offices. The big Council of Ministers' building on Hunter's Row, across from the Moskva Hotel, was a blaze of lights. But this is not unusual. Lights burn in these offices every night of the year.

After I finished filing the initial flashes of the story to New York this morning, I left the telegraph office in the heart of Moscow and walked down to the Red Square. The sun was shining brilliantly on the Moskva River. It was the height of the morning rush hour. Thousands upon thousands of citizens were going to work. There was nothing unusual in the square. Small groups of tourists were being taken around to see the

---

* This exchange of telegrams alerted my New York desk and myself to the code which I had advised New York a year earlier would be employed by me in event censorship was imposed upon Stalin's death.

sights. It was hard to realize that just behind the beautiful crenelated Kremlin walls, rosy and golden in the bright March sun, the leader of the Soviet state lay fighting for existence.

Here and there as I went around the city during the day, I saw a woman sobbing as she read the news of Stalin, or a man hastily wiping away a tear. It is hard to describe just what Stalin has meant to the ordinary Russian. But certainly he has never seemed a mere man.

Dispatch to New York Times
March 5—7:00 a.m.

The government announced just before 7:00 A.M. that Stalin's condition has undergone little change in the past twenty-four hours. As of 2:00 A.M. this morning his condition has undergone no material change either for better or worse. . . .

Pravda called on all citizens to stand firm and close ranks behind the Party and government in this difficult hour.

This morning's bulletin reports that there have been serious interruptions in Stalin's breathing. In addition to oxygen he has received camphor preparations, saffine, strofantin, glucose, and penicillin. There has been a sharp increase in white blood corpuscle count. . . .

March 5—4:00 p.m.

By a curious fate one of the last communications to reach Stalin obviously was my letter of the 26th which arrived on his desk twenty-four hours or so before he was stricken. It probably is still lying there in the last batch of unanswered mail.

I suppose this is the fiftieth or sixtieth letter I have written Stalin. I don't know how many letters Stalin got per year from correspondents. He always managed to answer one or two, but never one of mine.

March 5—6:30 p.m.

Stalin still lies unconscious while a team of ten medical specialists fight for his life. There is no sign of any turn for the better. Leeches are being used to reduce blood pressure. The press continues to call for all citizens to rally behind the government and maintain "revolutionary vigilance." Queues surrounded the newspaper kiosks, and prayers go on in the churches.

338

March 5—9:00 p.m.

A new medical bulletin on Stalin's condition as of 4:00 P.M. says it has grown worse and continues "extremely heavy."

At 8:00 A.M. this morning there was a sharp circulatory collapse. A second heavy collapse occurred at 11:30. There have been central changes in the back wall of the heart. At 4:00 P.M. his blood pressure was 160 over 120, pulse 120 per minute, and respiration 36 times a minute.

March 5—10:00 p.m.

The lights are blazing in the windows of the yellow-painted empire buildings of the Kremlin. Heavy traffic flows past, and an icy March wind sweeps across the Moskva River.

I made a circuit of the Kremlin just before 9:00 P.M. The night was bitter, and the wind hurled snow flurries across Red Square and into Menezhnaya Square. The ruby stars as always glowed red above the Kremlin towers.

*Telegram to New York Times***
March 6, 1953

During this crisis period you would be well advised to give my copy same kind of careful treatment which agencies give theirs stop eye am not overlooking any salient aspects of medical communiques or any other development here stop eye am not filing in brief flat takes because eye think that is very acceptable way of doing it but because eye want you to have story without delays which might make it quite useless to you paragraph with regard to that living allowance matter which you raised eye have sent off final accounts closing books as of last night march fifth regards.†

March 6—7:30 a.m.

The official announcement of Stalin's death was made just after 4:00 A.M. this morning, but only now has the censor begun

---

* Filed at approximately 4:00 A.M. Transmitted at 6:20 A.M. Received in New York at 9:24 A.M., Moscow time.

† This message contains the coded information of Stalin's death. It was delayed in censorship and in transmission so that it was not received in New York until more than five hours after the bulletin on the death had been transmitted by Soviet official radio shortly after 4:00 A.M., Moscow time.

to pass our dispatches. Death is said to have occurred at 9:50 P.M. last night.

We have spent the night at the Central Telegraph Office. At 8:00 P.M. Tass advised us that a bulletin would be ready soon. We got it just before 9:00. It said that Stalin's condition was extremely grave. Obviously the end was near.

At about 9:30 P.M.—just twenty minutes before Stalin is said to have died—I made a circuit of the Kremlin. There were many cars in Red Square and lots of lights in the buildings.

From 10:00 to 11:00 P.M. I was busy preparing advance copy in anticipation of Stalin's death. I listened to the news broadcast from 11:30 P.M. to midnight. Nothing new. At 12:05 A.M. I circled the Kremlin again. Some cars—government cars—were just returning.

At 3:30 I drove around the Kremlin again. Saw some government cars in front of the Moscow Soviet building. The woman at *Izvestia* said the paper would be "very late." Just after 4:00 A.M. the chauffeur who was listening to the car radio outside the telegraph office brought in the word of the death.

I have toured the central part of the city several more times in the last two hours. Until daylight all was serene. Guards stood duty at Lenin's Tomb, militiamen stomped their feet against the cold, and the sharp March wind blew the light snow in whirls and eddies.

March 6—9:00 a.m.

Pravda has just appeared with broad black borders around the front page, which is devoted entirely to Stalin. There is a large photograph, the official bulletin, the medical reports, and announcement of a funeral commission headed by Khrushchev.

The body will lie in state in the Hall of Columns at a time which will be announced.

Shortly after dawn the building porters and superintendents—*dvorniki* as they are called—began to put up black-bordered red flags, symbol of mourning.

Before the Spassky Gate of the Kremlin in Red Square a crowd of citizens rapidly grew. There were several hundred by 7:30 A.M. On the Hall of Columns a huge portrait was being put up. The red flag which always flies on the Supreme Soviet building behind Lenin's Tomb was lowered to half-staff.

March 6—4:30 p.m.

By the time I ventured into Red Square on foot at midmorning the crowds had grown to several thousand. They stood on the sidewalks opposite Lenin's Tomb and in a long half-moon some distance from the Spassky Tower, right in Red Square itself. There were men and women, both young and old, and some children. I had never seen anything like this in Russia before—a *spontaneous* crowd. The throng stood quietly, hardly speaking.

In the stands at either side of the tomb, crews of women were busily removing snow. Guards stood at attention as always before the mausoleum. I noticed a small sign saying that it was "closed for the day because of necessary preparations."

Throughout the morning the crowds in the center of the city grew. They were quiet and serious. As early as 7:00 A.M. there was the beginning of a queue at the Hall of Columns in anticipation of Stalin's lying in state. By midmorning that line was several blocks long, and militia were forming the citizens into orderly ranks stretching up Pushkin street. By midafternoon hundreds of thousands of citizens had assembled, and the lines extended back as far as the first garden boulevard.

There were throngs, too, in Sverdlovsk Square. I spent a couple of hours at the hotel window watching them decorate the Hall of Columns with bunting and fresh-cut evergreens. Several troops of beautifully mounted MVD cavalry, sabers gleaming and harness sparkling, clattered up. Other MVD detachments began to route traffic and pedestrians away from the center of the city. During all this time there was hardly a word spoken by the waiting crowds.

In the Metropole I surprised several elderly maids and housekeepers sobbing.

By 2:00 P.M. the Hall of Columns had been garbed in mourning and powerful floodlights had been installed. MVD regiments had completely cleared out the surrounded central squares.

The Moscow radio was playing solemn and melancholy music —Tchakovsky, Scriabin, Rachmaninoff, Dvořák, Mussourgsky, and Chopin. The aching tones of Dvořák's *New World Symphony* and Rachmaninoff's *Second Symphony in E Minor* haunted the Metropole Hotel corridors.

A little before 3:00 P.M. all was in readiness. A single vehicle moved swiftly out of the Kremlin by the Spassky Gate and, circling the center of the city, drew up before the Hall of Columns. Stalin's coffin was borne by a blue vanlike vehicle of the Moscow City Sanitary Department.

Between 3:00 and 4:00 P.M. the leaders of the Communist Party and government entered the Hall of Columns to pay their final respects. At 4:00 the doors were thrown open, and the long, long procession of mourners started past the bier.

It seems to me that the shock has been so great as to paralyze and subdue normal reactions. The throngs in the squares just stand voiceless or wander aimlessly. They are like people who have suffered a heavy blow the nature of which they have not been able to analyze and the effects of which they are not yet aware of. Even children in the parks seemed to catch the mood and play with extraordinary quietness.

The weather was typical for March—alternating between brief spells of bright sunshine and gray overcast.

March 6—7:30 p.m.

Thousands upon thousands of people are filing past Stalin's open funeral bier. He lies amid a bank of flowers in the handsome gilt and marble building.

The throngs waiting to view the body stretch back for several miles in a number of serpentine lines. How many people there are no one knows. But it must be millions.

The government is moving briskly and resolutely to demonstrate to the people that the transition from Stalin to new leadership involves no loss in momentum. The watchword is vigilance, vigilance, vigilance—both in internal and external affairs.

March 7—Midnight

A communiqué has just announced that Georgi Malenkov now heads the Soviet government. He was also listed first in the new Presidium of the central committee, which comprises ten members and four candidates.

The communiqué said the government changes had been effected to make certain "uninterrupted and correct leadership" and to avert "any kind of disorder or panic."

Standing beside Malenkov in the new government are four

342

veterans who were named first deputy chairmen of the Council of Ministers—Beriya, Molotov, Bulganin, and Kaganovich.

Beriya takes over the security ministries. Molotov again is foreign minister. Bulganin goes back as defense minister with Marshals Vasilevsky and the famous World War II commander, Georgi K. Zhukov, as his deputies.

The announcement said that in order to permit Khrushchev to concentrate on "the work of the central committee" he has been released as first secretary of the Moscow Party.

It was announced that Stalin will be buried Monday and that his body will lie beside that of Lenin in the mausoleum. It will be embalmed, just as was Lenin's.

March 7—1:00 p.m.

Pravda did not reach the Metropole Hotel today until just before 1:00 P.M. It is a six-page issue instead of the customary four pages.

The most interesting feature is a deep, six-column photograph showing Stalin lying in the funeral bier with "the leaders of Party and government" standing at his side.

The photograph shows, from left to right in the first row, Molotov, Kaganovich, Bulganin, Voroshilov, Beriya, and Malenkov. Behind them are Khrushchev, Mikoyan, and Marshals Vasilevsky, Zhukov, Sokolovsky, and Konev.

I presume this is designed to demonstrate that there are no rifts between the Soviet leaders—civil or military.

March 7—4:00 p.m.

Hour after endless hour it goes on—the march of Moscow's mourning millions past Stalin's bier. It started at 4:00 P.M. yesterday and will go on until 2:00 A.M. Monday morning. There has been nothing quite like this before—except when Lenin died in the cold January days of 1924.

I went through the line today. Some of our young embassy people have been through two or three times. The columns converge on the hall from all points of the compass.

The people are fed into the hall eight abreast. Each of the beautiful crystal chandeliers is darkened by gossamer wisps of mourning crepe. In the corridors are countless wreaths. As we ascend the broad staircase, a solid file of guards stands at attention.

The deeper one penetrates, the deeper becomes the ceremonial atmosphere of mourning. Enormous floodlights illuminate the columns. There are cameramen, both movie and still. In the great hall Stalin lies against a bank of thousands of flowers—real, paper, and wax. A symphony orchestra plays funeral music. The line moves swiftly, and it is difficult to see in the dazzling lights who is standing honor guard. Stalin lies, his face placid and quiet, wearing his generalissimo's uniform and the ribbons of his orders and medals. On small pillows of deep maroon velvet at his feet are the decorations themselves. There is an air of repose about his figure. Almost before I realize it I am out in the open air.

March 7—5:30 p.m.

By a series of extraordinary measures the government has transformed the heart of Moscow into a kind of citadel in which almost nothing is going on but mourning for Stalin at the Hall of Columns.

I have never seen anything like the rapidity and efficiency with which authorities commandeered the heart of this great city.

By establishing cordons against movement into the central areas such as Red Square, Menezhnaya Square, Revolution Place, Sverdlovsk Square, Theater Square, etc., they have created a city within a city.

The whole operation was carried out in a few hours on Friday morning. It cleared the center of the city and severed its connections with the remainder of the metropolis. It provided an impressive first demonstration of the efficiency of the new government.

The maneuver was accomplished not by simply throwing lines of MVD troops across the main thoroughfares. It utilized a technically complex but very effective method of checkerboard parking of motor trucks in such a fashion that they created an actual physical barrier across the main avenues. Later this was reinforced by tank units.

Once this checkerboard pattern was in place it was possible to seal off the center almost hermetically. All normal service and retail institutions were closed—stores, theaters, movies, offices, etc.

The center suddenly became extraordinarily quiet and solemn.

Nothing was moving in the big squares except for swift Zis government cars and trucks bringing in troops.

Thus, there was not the slightest possibility of any "disorder or panic" among the millions of citizens being swiftly moved in and out of the Hall of Columns.

March 8—12:30 p.m.

Sometimes a man's name tells more about him than many words of formal biography. That's the case with Georgi Maximilianovich Malenkov.

Malenkov's middle name, or his patronymic, shows that his father was called Maximilien. This means his grandparents were nonconformists, possibly revolutionary sympathizers who showed their scorn for religious custom by giving their son a name not found on the calendar of saints. The name they picked is that of France's most famous revolutionary, Maximilien Robespierre. Malenkov is descended from a family which has been inspired by revolutionary sympathies for at least two generations. He almost certainly is descended from the middle class or petty nobility.

March 8—3:30 p.m.

Today is Sunday, and I went over to Red Square just about noon and stood before Lenin's Tomb, watching a band of workmen prepare the mausoleum for Stalin's sarcophagus.

It was an unforgettable experience. The great expanse of the square was empty as I walked up the little hill between the Lenin Museum and the State Historical Museum. Behind me I could hear the distant echo of the crowds thronging to the Hall of Columns.

But inside the great square it was so quiet that each blow of the workmen's hammers rang out like the crash of brass cymbals. Entry to the square was almost blocked by an enormous collection of funeral flowers and wreaths—thousands of them, deposited around the historical museum.

I have often before stood near Lenin's Tomb. But only when the square has been jammed with humanity. Walking across the great space had the quality of a nightmare. But this was no dream. Drawn up before the red and marble mausoleum were three generators. Long cable lines had been run across the square. Inside the tomb workmen were busy. Outside they were replacing the letters on the front which now will spell out Lenin-Stalin instead of just Lenin.

There was a special atmosphere about the city today. I rose just after dawn, intending to take the suburban train to Saltikovka to see how the villagers were reacting. The subway was not yet running, and because of security arrangements the only way to the railroad station was on foot. I walked up Dzerzhinskaya hill, past the Lubiyanka Prison. There was hardly any traffic. Only a few knots of people at the barricades. The sun came up rosy in the eastern sky, and I could feel a hint of spring in the air.

Here and there bands of MVD troops were swinging their arms and stamping their feet after a night in the frosty air. Most stores were closed.

When I reached the B-Circle at Krasnaya Vorota, I found for the first time something like normal traffic movement. I finally got to the Kursk station after an hour's walk. But I could have saved myself the trouble. At the suburban ticket office there was a knot of people. A broad-shouldered woman spoke to me: "*Grazhdanin* [Citizen], you can only buy tickets to the country but not for return. Look at the notice which is posted up."

On the bulletin board a hand-lettered notice said that the trains from the Zheleznodorozhnaya and Gorki directions "will not run today."

Apparently the authorities don't want people from the outlying regions crowding into Moscow on the eve of Stalin's funeral. Of course, many have already gotten into Moscow. They have poured in by the thousands. Trains from Leningrad are said to have arrived with people clinging to the roofs, covered with frost and half-frozen.

March 8—8:00 p.m.

All day long the radio has reiterated a single theme—the steel unity and monolithic solidarity of the people behind the Party and government leadership.

Special orders of the day have been broadcast to the armed forces calling on them to close ranks behind the central committee and the government.

I noticed that Bulganin's appeal was Prikaz No. 35 and that

of Admiral Kuznetzov was No. 21. The last published prikazes of the army and navy were Nos. 30 and 15, respectively, issued for Red Army Day, February 23. I wonder what the intervening ones may have dealt with? Special security measures in connection with Stalin's death?

There are rumors that Molotov is not well.

Stalin will be laid to rest precisely at noon tomorrow.

I have seen nothing in the atmosphere of Moscow to cause the government to be so concerned—as it obviously is—lest there be "disorders or panic." This is the constant theme of propaganda. Does this hark back in some way to the "doctors' plot"?

March 9—6:00 p.m.

A few hours ago Stalin was laid to rest in Red Square.

The hour was high noon, and the funeral speeches were over. In the square where the multitude had gathered, there was a moment of utter silence. Then the great golden hands of the clock in Spassky Tower pointed straight up.

The iron bells of Spassky and the steel salute guns of the Kremlin began to speak. Crash! went the bells. Boom! went the cannon. Crash . . . boom . . . crash . . . boom. . . .

Lifting the crimson and black-draped coffin to their shoulders, Stalin's comrades-at-arms bore it inside the mausoleum.

In this last moment they were all there—Malenkov with a deep sadness on his almost youthful face; Beriya, a solid man and solemn; Chou En-lai, flown all the way from China to walk the last steps with Stalin's coffin; Voroshilov, every inch an old comrade; the handsome military figure of Bulganin and the others, Khrushchev, Kaganovich, and Mikoyan.

There were thirty roars of the salute guns—ten per minute—and during those three minutes everything was silent throughout Russia. Every moving vehicle stopped. Every train, every tram, every truck. A single sparrow left its nest high in the Kremlin wall and swooped gracefully over the tomb, its small and gentle chirp sounding strangely loud.

Then roared the voice of General Sinilov, commander of the Moscow garrison, ordering the march-past to begin. There was a shuffle of feet. The crack troops began to move. The military band struck up the triumphant fanfare of Glinka's *Hail to the*

347

Czar! The red flag on the Kremlin was suddenly raised to full staff once more.

Stalin had been laid to rest.

The square had been filled since 8:00 A.M. At 10:20 A.M. the sound of the funeral procession from the Hall of Columns was audible. The strains of Chopin's funeral march came louder and louder.

First came Sinilov, striding with the agonizing slow pace of the funeral march. Then the flower bearers, a sea of green and pink and purple wreaths that brought a sudden touch of spring into the square. Then fourteen marshals of the Soviet Union, led by Budenny, each carrying one of Stalin's high orders on a crimson velvet cushion. Then a single black lead horse and six more black horses drawing the funeral cortege—an olive-drab gun caisson bearing the black-and-red closed coffin.

When the cortege reached the center of the square the coffin was placed on a simple dais. It remained there while the funeral orations were spoken—first Malenkov, then Beriya, then Molotov in a voice that time and again choked and broke until I wondered whether he would be able to complete his speech.

After the march-past, Malenkov led the procession down from the mausoleum for a final look inside the tomb at Stalin's bier. With Malenkov walked Chou En-lai, Beriya, and Molotov. Behind came the others.

In his speech Malenkov pledged that the new government would maintain peace and bring to the people a higher standard of living. Beriya pledged that the Soviet government would maintain the rights guaranteed by the Stalin constitution. Civil liberties, he said, would be preserved. Molotov added that Soviet armed strength was the best defense against any foreign intrigues and called for vigilance.

Malenkov's words of peace and better living had an extraordinary impact on the Soviet civilians.

March 10—10:00 a.m.

One final vignette. The hour was 3:30 this morning. Once again I had finished my work at the Central Telegraph Office and had walked out into Gorki Street. The tumult and the shouting had died away. The streets were quiet again and empty.

The thought entered my mind that precisely at this hour a week ago I had been sitting in the same telegraph office reading a dull Russian book on Mongolia, impatiently glancing at my watch and wondering why *Pravda* was so late.

I strolled slowly down Gorki Street this morning. A few cars swished past. The traffic lights by the Hotel National and the Moskva Hotel winked red, then amber, then green, then red again.

Moscow was sleeping. I walked up the little hill between Lenin Museum and the historical building and into Red Square again. All was quiet. There were a few lights still burning in the Kremlin buildings. The sentries stood duty as always. At the mausoleum there was a small group of people, a dozen or so, just standing there with heads lowered.

I wandered out of the square. A few women *dvorniki* were sweeping the sidewalks with their long-handled brooms as I walked past the Moskva Hotel and into Hunter's Row. The street was hushed, but I was not entirely alone. Half a dozen workmen were busy at the Hall of Columns, some on the little balcony at the second floor, some on the sidewalk below. They were taking down Stalin's great portrait. One workman said: "*Ostorozhny* [Careful there]." Another replied, "Never mind. We'll not be needing this one again."

XXVI

First Maneuvers

March 10, 1953—6:00 p.m.

Diplomats feel that Malenkov's speech at Stalin's bier is an effort to open a way to a new effort at resolving differences between East and West. He said that it was "the holy duty" of his government to prevent a new war.

What struck diplomats particularly was the stress he laid on settlement of world problems. None of the trio—Malenkov, Beriya, and Molotov—mentioned the United States by name.

One Westerner said he thought it would be most natural in the light of Malenkov's declaration if he and Eisenhower should sit down together in the not-distant future and try as practical men to work out a way for America and Russia to live together.

Malenkov appears to be moving to improve relations with China. V. V. Kuznetzov, named deputy foreign minister only last Friday, will be sent to Peking as ambassador. And Mao Tse-tung in Peking has pledged his full confidence in the new regime. Together with this statement *Pravda* published a photograph showing Stalin, Mao Tse-tung, and Malenkov together at the time of the signing of the Sino-Russian alliance, February 14, 1950. It had never appeared before. It shows only the three men.*

---

* The photograph was a crude fake. Originally it had been a group photo showing many individuals. As it appeared in *Pravda,* it had been cropped and repasted to show only Stalin, Mao, and Malenkov apparently alone together.

March 10
Letter to Chairman Malenkov, Council of Ministers

For the first time in the hundred years of its existence the *New York Times* held its presses until 6:00 A.M. yesterday in order to bring to the American people your words a few minutes after they were spoken in Moscow.

May I suggest that the moment is unusually appropriate should you desire to send any special message to the people of America. I would deem it a great privilege to have an interview with you, however brief, to that end, etc.*

March 11

Again today *Pravda* returned to the theme of vigilance. Meetings are being held all over the country at which this is the theme. On Saturday the Supreme Soviet will meet.

Sir Alvary Gasgoigne, the British ambassador, called on Molotov today. He found him strained and tired but thought his health was holding up.

Today I have had a chance to look back a bit and think over the last few months. There has been a gradual increase in the tempo of events here ever since last August. It started August 16 with the arrival of Chou En-lai and the Chinese delegation, quickly followed by the call for the Nineteenth Party Congress, the new five-year plan, and Stalin's economic theses.

All through September there was a rise in the volume if not the quality of developments—the convening of Republican Party congresses and preparations for the Nineteenth Party Congress.

October was even busier—the Party congress and Kennan's ouster.

Two things now stand out with regard to the Party meeting.

The first is the great impression of strength and confidence. True, there was an obverse side—much talk about slackness, particularly by Poskrebyshev. But it was not a major point.

The second was the curious set of elections—the Presidium and the new secretariat. So large were these bodies that it was apparent they served to conceal any emerging line with regard to the succession. The Presidium was impossible as an executive body. The

---

* Similar letters were sent Chou En-lai, Molotov, Beriya, Mikoyan, Kanganovich, and Bulganin. No replies were received.

secretariat was another kettle of fish. It could have had much meaning.

There were signs of a breaking up of the Politburo group—the dropping of Andreyev, Kosygin's demotion, and other minor ups and downs. There was the sudden emergence of Ignatiev, whom I had first noticed in the guest list for the Kremlin banquet for Chou En-lai.

Next came the November holidays. The dropping of Beriya below Bulganin and Voroshilov, the use of Molotov's picture in a single line directly below Stalin's, and Pervukhin's selection as the November 6th speaker—evidence of rising importance of the Younger Guard (fiftyish fellows).

The next month, two important events—the plot in the Kiev trade network and use of a military tribunal to try the criminals, mostly Jews, and their death sentence. The other was appearance of the attacks on Jews and Zionism in the *Agitators' Notebook* and the *Teachers' Gazette*.

And on December 24 Stalin replied to Reston's questions.

On January 13 there was significant news—the "doctors' plot." Up to this date little more has been adduced as to what is the target of this plot. The local offshoots took the form in most cases of drives against commercial crime, expropriation, hypothecating of funds, etc.

There has been a deliberate effort to emphasize the Jewishness of the criminals. Case after case of Jews has been singled out.

The political ramifications of all this were (and still are) uncertain.

But there was a development in December to which all this may have been related. This was the sudden interest in Voznesensky and his almost forgotten 1947 work on the war economy of the U.S.S.R. This developed into a mass phenomenon in which the economists and historians, etc., apologized for having had anything to do with him and then struck out at other cosmopolitan sins. It looked like a re-run of the bourgeois cosmopolitanism thing of the late 1948–49 period.

At this point (January–February) came the local elections. They confused the picture. There appeared to be a deterioration of Molotov's position. He almost didn't show in the Moscow nominations. He wasn't nominated in Leningrad or several Union republics. Everywhere it was Malenkov, Malenkov, Malenkov. It looked as though Mikoyan was being eased out. There was a further build-up of the Younger Guard—Pervukhin, etc. The ministers of health and state security had been dismissed. Ignatiev had the state security job. Vasily Stalin didn't show up, and there was a big gap in the agricultural ministries, which looked as though they were in the hands of Budenny—of all people.

This was the general news picture on the eve of the Stalin story. I had a very strong feeling that big news would be forthcoming, presumably in reference to the plot. There was so much nervousness on every hand. By mid-February Whitney, Steiger, and I had an arrangement under which each of us, working alternate weeks, listened to the Tass dictation-speed broadcast at night and worked the telegraph office and the newspapers. With the help of the Foreign Office we finally started to receive *Pravda* at the telegraph office. I was trying to set up a system for dictating late breaks direct to London. We talked a bit about what might happen if one of us should get involved in the "plot." There didn't seem to be anything to do but wait for developments.

March 12, 1953

There was a fresh fall of snow around Moscow last night, and this morning I went out to the country to see how the villages are faring.

I found everything covered with a blanket of white and sparkling like diamonds in the morning sunshine. I had not been out of metropolitan Moscow since the announcement of Stalin's illness.

Passing through the villages, I saw few signs of the great events. Each railroad station flew a red-and-black mourning flag, and in the waiting rooms there were small rosettes of black and red decorating Stalin's portrait.

But I saw no other sign connected with the death of Stalin. Passengers on the train were mostly peasant women who had brought produce in to sell at the big Moscow markets and were going back home, their string bags full of bread and other items from the Moscow stores. Across the aisle sat three peasant women and one man. One fat, red-faced woman had seen Stalin's body as it lay in state, and she was telling her neighbors about it. The man went on reading his book and paying no attention. Other passengers were eating ice cream, talking of the weather, the coming spring.

Walking about Saltikovka, it was difficult to believe anything out of the ordinary had happened. There was the same busy village market, gay and animated. Half a dozen low-lying Russian sledges, drawn by horses with the familiar big yokes, had brought in supplies of sweet-smelling hay. On the long wooden outdoor counters were heaps of potatoes, onions, carrots, cucumber pickles, sour cabbage, and garlic. Typical products of a typical winter market. An old man had a long string of dried mushrooms slung around his shoulders. Peasants were selling freshly painted pink and blue and black plaster-of-Paris cats and oilcloth decorated with red, yellow, and purple flowers. There were fresh oranges and lemons from God knows where. Wormy green apples. And, of course, many peasants with bulging gunnysacks of *semichki*, sunflower seeds.

In the butcher stalls lay heaps of freshly slaughtered meat and mounds of fresh and salted fish brought out from the city. In the hardware stalls the farmers talked about plans for spring planting and speculated on the weather. Some railroad girls were knocking icicles off the station roof.

Life in the Russian village was going on just as it always has—and, no doubt, always will, regardless of who lives or dies in Moscow.

March 12, 1953
Chief, International Section, Ministry of Communications

On the morning of March 6th, I observed a serious violation of the elementary rule of giving "urgent" handling to "urgent" cables.

Clerk Vasileyvna was in charge of the window. I noticed around 6:00 A.M. that she had allowed an enormous number of urgent telegrams to pile up on the desk—telegrams which already had been given three word-counts, and, even after this delay, she merely tossed them in careless fashion in a heap about six inches high. When I pointed out that she was delaying transmission of these telegrams, she told me in rude fashion that this was "not my business." I told her it was my business; that the *New York Times* spent thousands of dollars each year with the post office for the purpose of obtaining "urgent" transmissions.

To this she retorted by slamming her window shut.

May I ask what is the purpose of maintaining an "urgent" rate if your clerks are permitted to delay transmission of such telegrams forty minutes or an hour?

354

March 13

The first issue of *Kommunist* to appear since Stalin's death devotes considerable attention to the central committee, which it says is "the incarnation of the wisdom of our Party." It notes that Stalin often emphasized the importance of the central committee and quotes him as saying "in collective work, in collective leadership, in monolithic unity which is characteristic for our Party and its central committee lies the greatest strength of the leadership of the Communist Party."

March 14

The Supreme Soviet meets tomorrow. There is extreme interest among diplomats as to whether Malenkov will give any indications about negotiations with the West and particularly with regard to a meeting of the chiefs of state.

Today I repeated the walk which I took through Moscow shortly before Stalin's death. I wanted to see what changes there might be.

I saw the first in Red Square. No line of citizens waiting to inspect the tomb. It has been closed since Stalin was interred. But there was another change too—one of atmosphere. I found possibly two thousand persons in the big square, quietly sauntering across the expanse of paving blocks, standing in front of the mausoleum and wandering about. Someone had laid a small bunch of yellow mimosa on the balustrade in front of the tomb—probably a child. An old man in blue cotton-padded jacket was polishing the railing.

It is hard to describe the atmosphere of the square. But it was relaxed and easy. A hundred years ago the Russians used to have *gulyanie* or promenade in the square at this season. That was the atmosphere I found today. Two weeks ago, of course, the citizens would not have been permitted to walk about like that.

In the bookstore on Kalinin Street the 1915 edition of Ivan Bunin's works which had caught my eye on my earlier walk was gone—I had bought it myself the next day. In its place was an almost equally rare complete edition of Dostoevski.

Just beyond the Central Military Department Store I saw a rare sight for Moscow—a fire. Apparently in the basement of a bookstore. Four of Moscow's big red engines were drawn up, and as I watched there appeared a fire buff's dream—a Moscow fire chief car, almost a block long, all shining crimson, gleaming chrome and nickel. A beautiful thing.

The menacing Red Army posters were gone from Gorki Park. In their place was a new poster—the huge figure of a Russian workingman. He thrusts away from him a hand trying to grasp his on which is stamped a dollar sign. It bears the legend "Vigilance—Our Weapon."

Dispatch to New York Times
March 15, 1953

Premier Malenkov, in his inaugural address to the Supreme Soviet bid for peace between Russia and America, said any and all troublesome and unsolved questions may be resolved by peaceful negotiations. A number of diplomats characterized Malenkov's statement as an open invitation to the United States to solve conflicts between East and West by diplomatic means. Beriya formally moved Malenkov's nomination as premier. . . .

March 16

A few more notes about the Stalin story. . . .

We had managed to make arrangements for the delivery of *Pravda* and *Izvestia* to the Central Telegraph Office fairly quickly after they left the presses—which might be at any hour after 3:00 A.M. Ordinary days the papers are out at 3:00 to 3:15 A.M. But big news may delay them to 5:00, 6:00, or even 8:00 A.M.

I think one reason they made the arrangement was that someone became concerned when they found Whitney and myself prowling around *Pravda*'s rear entrance at 3:00 A.M. looking for a copy of the paper.

Thus, on the night of March 3–4 I was drowsing away at the International Call Office waiting for the papers to come out. But they did not come at 3:00 or 4:00 or at 5:00. I telephoned Whitney and Steiger they had better come down since it looked as though something was up. At 6:00 A.M. the papers still had not come out, and the girl at *Izvestia* said they would be "very late." But Tass had no information. A few minutes before 7:00 A.M., Tass still was insisting nothing was up. But five minutes later they called and said to come for a bulletin, that Stalin was extremely ill.

It was about 8:00 before we actually got the Tass bulletin. I had to file by urgent press as I had no telephone arrangements, but an emergency setup was made later in the day.

The Russians, of course, made no special press arrangements on the story. We could not, for instance, even find out when or if medical bulletins would be issued. The story became a twenty-four-hour deathwatch from the moment of the first break. Fortunately, not a long watch.

It was a most extraordinary sight to watch the security forces take over the heart of Moscow. At 10:00 A.M. on March 6 it was still possible to move up and down Gorki Street and into Red Square, but cordons had cut off Hunter's Row and Theater Square where the Metropole is located. I had a hard time getting inside the Metropole cordon, but from that vantage point I watched as larger and larger numbers of troops, truckloads of security forces, ordinary militia, and mounted battalions concentrated in the squares and then began to move people out. By 2:00 P.M. there were heavy barricades made up of thousands upon thousands of trucks. The barricades controlled the movement of every person within the inner ring.

This was all done in the name of the lying-in-state ceremonies. But it was also a demonstration of the ease and power with which the security forces, garrisoned all around Moscow and working from time-tested disposition plans, could take over the heart of Moscow any time it was deemed desirable.

I cannot describe the next three days in detail. They have a nightmarish quality, dominated by the fantastic spectacle of hundreds of thousands of people moving through the Hall of Columns —the funeral dirges, the klieg lights, the perfumes of the flowers. the stench of sweat—it was a phantasmagoria out of Dante by Dali.

Every step I made through the city—and I had to be on the run and on foot constantly—was made through military and police lines. There were no passes. Every block was an adventure. The militia were good-natured for the most part. It was almost always possible to get through their lines with a mixture of bravado and haughtiness. But to go through meant scrambling under huge military trucks with roaring motors, climbing over engine cabs, squeezing through crevices and around building corners. There were fifteen security barriers between the Metropole and the telegraph office. Even *Pravda* delivery trucks couldn't get through, and no papers reached the center of town until midafternoon.

Amid this, strange things were possible. For instance, on Sunday before the funeral I walked right into Red Square, which was protected by the most formidable barriers of all. I simply walked through the lines of troops and up to Lenin's Tomb, and no one asked me a question.

Of course, not a word about military control of the city, the cutting off of train service, etc., was permitted to pass the censorship.

The almost immediate announcement of the new government and Party changes on Saturday caught the people by surprise, as was intended. Together with the efficient, iron control of the Moscow center it fixed the tone of the new government—new, efficient, practical, and *different.*

This impression was reinforced by Malenkov's speech in Red Square Monday, which struck people as refreshing in content and style. It seemed so to me also. It was quite a contrast to hear good Russian and good delivery.

I was able to dictate to London an eyewitness account of the Stalin funeral by about 4:45 A.M., New York time. This was possible because as soon as Stalin's body was placed to rest and the final military parade started, I simply ran out of the square, down the hill past the historical museum, into Menezhnaya Square, across the open spaces, up Gorki Street for two blocks and into the telegraph office. I don't quite know how I accomplished this, fighting my way against the stream of a military parade, battling through spectators fifty deep, and scrambling under a barricade of trucks.

Dispatch to New York Times
March 18, 1953

Pravda published another important article on vigilance today by D. Chesnokov, editor of *Kommunist.* So long as "capitalist encirclement" continues, he writes, all measures must be taken to strengthen Soviet power. . . .

March 19

Contrary to his photographs, Malenkov makes, surprisingly, a rather appealing appearance. His manner has just a touch of shyness and boyishness about it. He is a good speaker—a melodious speaker. His voice is light with qualities of warmth and vigor. He speaks crystal-pure Russian.

He is not an orator, but he contrasts sharply with the dry, statistical delivery favored during the Long Reign. His dark lock of forehead hair is a favorite affectation of Russian intellectuals. His pathetic hands and fat-boy figure add up to something more human than we have seen on the Soviet podium in many a year.

I stress this because it is in direct contrast to the boorish, greasy, unappetizing Malenkov of the photographs.

Last summer the Italian ambassador lectured me on how impossible it was for Malenkov to succeed Stalin because of his unaesthetic appearance. Of course aesthetics have nothing to do with Soviet politics. But the premise was wrong anyway. Malenkov is not unattractive. His writing style goes with his speaking style—fresh, unpretentious, good Russian.

From all indications I think the assumption that Malenkov is of bourgeois origin is probably correct.

So far Malenkov has not been given much personal build-up. There have been just three pictures—each showing him with Stalin. This includes the phony Mao Tse-tung picture. Incidentally, the Mao declaration supporting the new regime has been published in every Moscow paper and all the provincials in big type, ten or twelve point, for emphasis. This shows how important it is felt that everyone know that China continues to stand with Russia.

The importance of Russian-Chinese relations is equally clear from the prominence given to Chou En-lai and the naming of the new ambassador, Kuznetzov.

My deduction is that Chinese-Soviet negotiations have been bogged down for a long time and that relations have now been taken out of the Foreign Office where they were subject to typical Molotov pettifogging and directly attached to the Kremlin. Ambassador Panyushkin (who has been recalled) was an able man and a specialist in the Far East, but he held the same post with the Chiang government, and I think there was a not-too-subtle snub involved in naming him to Mao.

All of this fits the pattern of second-rate treatment given by the Foreign Office to the Chinese last November 7 and the curious handling the press gave to an item on Red Army Day about Chou's visit to Port Arthur. I happened to be monitoring the Tass dictation broadcast that night, and I heard them dictate twice a lengthy item about Chou visiting Port Arthur. The next morning not a single Moscow paper published this report, although it got a big ride in China and the East. Three days later all the papers published a two-paragraph squib about Chou. Someone put the freeze on this news.

The papers are not quoting Malenkov's speeches as doctrine in the fashion they quoted Stalin's. I think the reason for the lack of build-up for Malenkov is that he is only one man in a triumvirate.

In the triumvirate Molotov has very little power. There are three sources of power in this country—the Party, the police, and the army. Molotov has none of these. All he has is years of service and prestige.

Beriya is playing it very cute. He is the great kindly uncle. He is the man who put Malenkov into nomination at the Supreme Soviet, calling him a "talented pupil" and a "true comrade-at-arms" of Lenin and Stalin, respectively. That was a delicate way of showing his own superior age and authority, I thought. Beriya it was who gave the pledge at the funeral bier for respecting civil rights. This was Beriya pledging that there would not be a new purge. It was his frank recognition of what the people fear from him, and you could almost hear the sighs of relief when he uttered the words. He may not keep his promise, of course. But the Russians are very serious about promises made in public over the dead body of the leader.

Both on the day of the funeral and at the Kremlin Sunday Beriya in a rather hard-to-put-into-words manner seemed to be speaking for the army as well as the secret police. That is a very important impression for him to give. I may have caught the nuances wrong, but I think not. And I am not at all certain that he *does* speak for the army or that the army likes him to speak for them. Because if Beriya is playing a game and holding back his cards, the army is being even more coy. The army seems more interested in the substance of power than the trappings of office.

I think that the army's real weight is shown by the Zhukov appointment with all that it implies. In the end it may turn out that the military is a bigger power than the Party. I know that is a radical thing to say, but in recent years the power which the Party for so long exercised in the name, for instance, of the army, or the police, or the church, has been flowing back to the original and basic depositories.

Today the army is giving Malenkov its support. The army is an independent force, and what is given can be taken away.

One more note about Beriya. He contrived to give both Malenkov and the army a striking demonstration of how important it is to be on his right side at the time of the funeral. This was by means of the action under which he took over control of the central city. It was Beriya's troops which held the city inexorably in their grasp for the period of the funeral. It was a grasp so tight it could have been broken only by an air force willing to employ dive bombers.

I don't know how this impressed those in the Kremlin. Perhaps they were too busy to notice. But it impressed me. And I will bet it impressed Malenkov and the army and made them realize that, after all, they have no troops in Moscow except for the cadet corps and the specialized personnel of the military academies, which are no match for Beriya's thousands of MVD troops deployed in huge camps dotted all around Moscow's periphery.

My estimate of Beriya is that he holds most of the high cards at the moment but is content to let Malenkov play front man. He himself has emerged from the shadows, but there is no sign that he, as yet, wants to be king. King-maker, yes.

But it is obvious that these forces are not and cannot by their nature be stable. There seems to me nothing explosive in the situation. It can go on for a long time. But eventually like all du-ates or triumvirates it will begin to crumble. I think Molotov can drop out without affecting the power basis. But there exist the makings of a police-army conflict.

The dominating motive of the present government is to secure its power. I think they were afraid the people might think that the death of Stalin meant the death of government. The people were so stunned and dopey for several days that it was easy to imagine them suddenly awakening and saying: "Well, Stalin is dead. There isn't any government." That is why the government talked about "disorder and panic." I think Isaac Deutscher, in the *London Times,* was right in suggesting that the government wanted the people to feel it had not only a government but a new government.

And it is brisk and business-like. The session of the Supreme Soviet lasted one hour and seven and one-half minutes by my watch. There will be more departures in ways of doing things, designed to emphasize that it is a new regime.

I believe the muted notes of peace are related to the desire of the government to establish its authority most solidly. It wants no international adventures, no wars, no big conflicts. I think it is an "isolationist" government. Both Malenkov and Beriya have "isolationist" tendencies. They want to keep what they have. But they don't want to risk anything for the sake of more.

I think Malenkov is willing to go quite a way to stay at peace with the U.S.A. I don't think he is fooling. The new Russian team is conservative by character and circumstance. It will fight like hell to hang on to what it has, and I think it can do that successfully.

There is an almost complete hiatus in the hate-America campaign. It is absent from the speeches, and it has disappeared from the press. Vigilance is still stressed, but this drive was under way when Stalin fell ill.

I have the impression they don't know what to do now with the big "doctors' plot." I expect the thing will be put on ice for a time. It certainly had its role in the inside maneuvering around Stalin. Now we have this unexpected and potentially explosive situation of the Old Man dying just the kind of death the Kremlin doctors were said to dish out.

What ammunition is created in this for one Kremlin faction to use against another faction if it wishes! But the factions have not developed that far as yet.

Domestically, I think that Malenkov and Beriya implied some diminution of the heavy industry drive to satisfy consumers' needs. So perhaps they can do more for the home folks.

I gather that people in the field of the arts are breathing a sigh of relief and expecting at long last to be freed from the strait jacket of provincial Tiflis taste of 1890 at long last. I hope the sighs are not premature.

March 21, 1953

Malenkov has been released from his duties as secretary of the central committee at his own request and a five-man secretariat headed by Nikita Khrushchev has been set up. The action was taken at a plenary held on March 14, just the day before the meeting of the Supreme Soviet.

Khrushchev was listed first among the new secretaries. Malenkov's action in divesting himself of the secretaryship marks a differentiation between the posts he will hold and those which Stalin occupied.

In Party affairs the role of Khrushchev appears to be of the greatest significance. The man who is listed first among the Party secretaries has traditionally held a very, very important post. The other secretaries are Suslov, Peter Pospelov, N. N. Shatalin, and Ignatiev.

The question now is whether Malenkov in the role of chairman of the Council of Ministers will prove to hold a more important role than Khrushchev in the Party secretaryship.

XXVII

The Thaw

March 22, 1953

Small but tangible signs of a better diplomatic atmosphere have appeared. There is a general absence in *Pravda* and *Izvestia* of "cold war" materials. Other small signs: an expression of sorrow by General Chuikov, Soviet commander in Germany, over the death of some British fliers; notification that the Soviet is willing to utilize its good offices in the repatriation of British personnel from Korea—a matter which has been hanging fire two and a half years; a "conciliatory" attitude by the Foreign Office in the American Bering Sea plane incident.

March 26

Russia and China have finally signed a new trade agreement. It was worked out by Mikoyan and the Chinese and witnessed by Chou En-lai before his return to China. Diplomats believe the Russians and Chinese made considerable progress in settlement of the many differences which were unresolved at the time of Stalin's death.

Dispatch to New York Times
March 28

The first prisoners to be freed under the new government's sweeping amnesty marched out of Soviet prisons today. All persons serving sentences of five years or less—with a few exceptions—are being freed. Some seventy women with children were released today from Moscow's big city prison, Butyrskaya. Men are expected to be let out tomorrow.

Thousands of persons recovered their civil rights under today's decree. [But persons living in exile or in forced residence are not affected by the edict. Hundreds of persons gathered around Butyrskaya today waiting for the release of their relatives. Similar scenes occurred all over Russia.]

The amnesty is the broadest since the time of the Revolution.

Dispatch to New York Times
March 31

Sir Alvary Gasgoigne is leaving for London Tuesday morning. He has been called back for pressing consultations on the situation here and on Chou En-lai's new proposals for a Korean settlement. . . .

Dispatch to New York Times
March 31

Price cuts on 125 categories of retail products including 10 per cent cuts in the prices of food and 5 to 15 per cent cuts in clothing prices were announced by the government tonight. . . .

Dispatch to New York Times
April 1

Foreign Minister Molotov in his first official statement gave full Soviet support to the new Chinese proposals on Korea. Diplomats take this as one more sign of the new and active Soviet policy to move for solution of East-West issues. They believe some fundamental changes are in the making. . . .

April 3

This evening a group of American and Soviet newspaper editors have been exchanging toasts to Premier Malenkov and President Eisenhower at the Arogvy restaurant. I cannot recall an evening of more friendliness on the part of Russians and Americans.

April 4

It was announced early today that the "doctors' plot" was based on false evidence. The doctors as well as six other persons accused in the affair have been released, and those responsible for the charges have been arrested. The announcement blamed former workers of the Ministry of State Security for the plot. Two of the doctors originally arrested were not listed as having been released. It is reported they died in prison.

There is fluidity and an air of rapid change in the Moscow atmosphere such as I have never seen. Many experienced and tough-minded observers are beginning to think seriously of the possibility of *rapprochement* between East and West.

The announcement in the "doctors' plot" case probably clears the way for resumption of normal relations between Russia and Israel.

One of the latest moves of the Foreign Office is to advise the British and the Americans they may keep their present embassies if they so desire. Unfortunately, the U.S. has decided to go ahead and give up the wonderful Mokhovaya location on Red Square. The British, of course, are sticking to their fine embassy across the Moskva River from the Kremlin.

British and French citizens are being repatriated from North Korea through Soviet good offices. George Bundock is expected to be permitted to go back home shortly.

Soviet officials are beginning to emerge in friendly contacts which remind me of the kind we used to have during World War II.

Dispatch Killed by Censor
April 4, 1953

There were dramatic scenes at the Central synagogue tonight when the congregation heard that the "doctors' plot" had been declared a frame-up. Chief Rabbi Solomon Shlieffer offered prayers for the leaders of the Soviet government. Tears sprang to his eyes as he spoke.

Many persons are speculating whether there will be a public trial of the persons responsible for the false plot. Another question which arose is: Who were the responsible officials who permitted the case of the Kremlin doctors to be developed?

Presumably, Beriya is not responsible since he has just taken over the portfolio of state security. But it is not known who was in charge of state security when the plot was developed. Viktor S. Abukumov is known to have been released from the post some time ago. Presumably, he was succeeded by Ignatiev who is now a secretary of the central committee, which would indicate that he is not the responsible one.

April 5

George F. Kennan is a major prophet who is experiencing the unusual sensation of living to see his prophecies come true. His judgment on what lay ahead in Soviet-American relations is being confirmed with remarkable accuracy almost every day.

In private conversations he repeatedly insisted that the first necessity in American-Soviet relations was to create a change in the atmosphere which would make it possible for statesmen to sit down at the same table for intelligent talk.

He told the Russians the requisite for this was a cessation in name-calling. He proposed a cease-fire on the propaganda front. That precondition has actually begun to be put into effect by the Soviet press and radio. There has been a remarkable diminution in anti-American material.

Thus far, the second step—reciprocal action by the American press—has not occurred, but perhaps an initial step is evidenced by the visit of a group of American editors to Moscow. They are seeking to avoid controversial and inflammatory materials.

Kennan believed that once the propaganda standstill had been achieved it would be possible to move naturally to the next step—examination of particular issues from a realistic viewpoint.

He was deeply disappointed last summer when, instead of getting a cessation of propaganda, there was an intensification of Soviet attacks on the U.S. But he was profoundly convinced that a change in Soviet policy toward the United States and the West would be forthcoming. He was not such a prophet as to predict the death of Stalin. But he was convinced that policy would change.

Only two weeks before he left Russia last September, Kennan told me that he thought the cold war was nearly at an end. He said he expected Soviet policy would continue unchanged through the winter but when spring came there would be a change. He was absolutely confident of this. He did not make the prediction on the basis of mysticism but simply on the hard facts of Soviet-American relations. He took the view that Soviet leaders are first and foremost realists.

"When spring comes," he said, "there will be a change because it is in the logic of the situation. When it comes it may come with startling rapidity. I am willing and ready to sit here for events to mature because when the time comes the United States must be prepared to act and to act decisively. It is in the interests of both sides to avoid war. War means suicide for both countries. The day will come when the Soviet will frankly recognize this. We must be ready to act intelligently and realistically when that time comes."

Dispatch to New York Times
April 6, 1953

Pravda reports that former Deputy Chief Rumin in the state security ministry has been arrested on a charge of responsibility for preparing the false "doctors' plot." It blamed former Minister of State Security Ignatiev for "political blindness and gullibility" in connection with the case. It seems obvious that Ignatiev will be dismissed from his post in the Party secretariat. . . .

April 6

Pravda's custom of buttressing its editorials with frequent quotations from the works of Stalin and other prominent Party leaders has undergone modification.

For example, this morning's editorial about the "doctors' plot" is presented in *Pravda*'s own words with no quotations from any source. This is typical of *Pravda* in recent days. Examination of *Pravda*'s leading editorials since April 1 shows no use of quotations. References to personalities are equally rare. There has been only one mention this month of Stalin's name. Quotation of Malenkov is scant.

Another innovation is a suggestion by *Pravda* that the Bolshoi include Wagner in its repertoire. Nothing of Wagner's has been presented in Moscow for many, many years.

Things are popping so fast that I literally don't have the time to write about all of them.

Dispatch to New York Times
April 7

It was announced today that Ignatiev has been released as Party secretary. There was no announcement that he had been arrested. *Pravda* editorially appealed today for racial tolerance and against any race feeling in the Soviet. . . .

April 8

I went out to Gorki Park today. Everyone is hard at work getting it ready for the grand spring opening May 1. It is going to be opened with a spring *gulyanie,* a long-abandoned Russian custom. I noticed that the billboards which displayed Red Army men in February and Vigilant Workers in March now advertise Karandash, the perky little Soviet Charlie Chaplin.

April 8

I want to put down a hasty and somewhat disorganized report of the way things are developing. The first point is the *extreme fluidity* of the situation.

It resembles the upper Mississippi River as I used to know it as a boy when spring came. The upper river was used for timbering operations. All winter long the logs would accumulate in the woods and along the tributaries. Then, spring suddenly came. Fast, as it does in the north. The ice would begin to move out with explosive rumbling that could be heard for miles around. The ice would break and then the logs would start moving downstream in a twisting, tangled mass, end over end, into constantly clearer water. A dangerous, exciting, spectacular performance.

Something like that *seems* to be happening here. I say "seems" because no one can tell for sure just what is happening and how far it will go. But we can say that there is every outward sign that after twenty-nine years of bowing to the iron will of a Victorian-minded and (it is evident) psychopathic and morbidly suspicious Georgian, the country is suddenly shaking loose from many of its bonds.

When a giant has been tied, hand and foot, for as many years as has this country, and suddenly awakens—the results are bound to be sensational.

I do not want to suggest that there is any sign that anything is yet out of control. There is not. Life is going on smoothly and more pleasantly. But you can't go around curves as fast as these people are doing in such a heavy vehicle as Russia without a good deal of strain.

I suppose the first sign that something spectacular in policy change would accompany the new administration was given to Gasgoigne when he saw Molotov the day after the funeral. However, there was every reason to play things carefully since it was obvious that it would be to Soviet interest to split the United States and England, per the Stalin formula.

However, the British with their usual acuity had already sensed that something was up and immediately put their influence behind a "give these people a chance" thesis. They said they were frightened that the United States would in a blustering manner start to drive the turtle back into its shell just as it stuck its head out.

Actually, we have played it very carefully and sensitively and Eisenhower's statements have been phrased in the right counterpoint to encourage the Russians to proceed on their new foreign policy line.

The first sign the Americans had of a change was, I believe, March 19 when Malik advised us out of the blue that if we would rather stay on at Mokhovaya than move into the new Chaikovsky building, why please do. They offered to take back the Chaikovsky building and pay us for the money we had spent on it.

But this small swallow was followed by a whole flock of major diplomatic moves—Germany, Korea, the UN—and small gestures, release of the French and British internees in North Korea, release of a British seaman under the amnesty, indications that Bundock would be allowed to go home, permission to American newspapermen to come in, etc.

What is sensational is the development in the last ten days of a domestic policy which fits the new foreign policy.

The first symptom was the sudden diminution in attacks on the U.S.A. (I reported this in a long and very interesting dispatch to the *Times,* complete with a detailed survey of *Pravda,* comparing the periods February 19–23 and March 19–23, but for some reason the New York desk thought it wasn't news.)

The change in press treatment has been erratic. Some papers haven't been able to get their signals straight. For instance, *Krokodil* in its first issue after Stalin's death, dated March 10 but only appearing March 29, had as its lead cartoon a Kykriniksy drawing of a Soviet bureaucrat with a fatuous smile looking through an enormous pair of rose-colored glasses at an American diplomat who looked like Dulles but who had swastikas for eyes. Viewed through the rose spectacles, the American appeared benign and pleasant.

Published on that date it constituted a savage commentary upon Malenkov, Molotov, and Co., who were viewing American diplomats in just that fashion. (I reported this, but the *Times* used only a short bite in an early edition.)

The next issue of *Krokodil* on April 4 had its lines straight. The initials U.S.A. were not to be found in the magazine.

There have been other blunders of this kind, including that of the *Young Kommunist* which appeared on the day of *Pravda's* revelation of the falsity of the "doctors' case" with an editorial eulogy of Lydia Timashuk who the same day had to turn back her Order of Lenin.

An equally startling press development which I have not managed yet to get through censorship is the *disappearance* of Stalin's name.

I have found Stalin mentioned editorially only twice in *Pravda* since April 1. And only mere mention of the name on each occasion. He is mentioned a little more often by some lesser papers—probably because the editors haven't got the line down pat yet.

Fitting this pattern is *Pravda's* sudden suggestion that the Bolshoi Theater repertoire include the best Western classics, in particular Wagner, who was anathema to the Old Man.

I think I must revise my previous concept of the "doctors' case." My present guess is that the case had its origin in an attempt to get Beriya. It would seem to have started at least a year ago and possibly even longer. This is based on reports that one of the doctors named Kogan has been dead for at least that long (presumably, this is B. G. Kogan, who was not listed as having been released). Whether Abakumov was still minister of state security at that time I don't know. There were reports whose origin I never knew that Abakumov had been dismissed or shot last spring.*

In any event it is evident from *Pravda* that the "doctors' case" was under way before Ignatiev took over the ministry. He probably came in sometime last summer. Presumably, he held the post at the time of the Kremlin dinner he attended for Chou En-lai last September. He went into the Presidium in October. In January he was tacitly announced as minister of state security when

* Abakumov's execution on a charge of complicity in the "Leningrad affair" was announced in December, 1955.

the papers published his nomination to the Moscow City Soviet. I reported this about four times before it finally impressed New York enough so that Schwartz wrote a piece about it. What with the delicacy of reporting such items in fashion to clear censorship, the chances are fifty-fifty that they will miss the attention of the New York desk.

Obviously it wasn't Ignatiev to whom *Pravda* had reference last January 13 when in announcing the "doctors' plot" it took a swipe at persons responsible for state security who had "over a long period of time" permitted this plot to develop.

Pravda was talking, probably, in particular, about Abakumov and Beriya.

If you fit that with the sudden purge in Georgia last spring just a year ago, and Beriya's going down there, personally, to handle it and fire a lot of Georgians who were his own appointees and probably his best friends, you can well imagine someone was moving ruthlessly to get him.

This fits Beriya's demotion in the posters of last November 7.

How better to get Beriya than to find that he permitted a doctor's plot directed at an old man who was probably more worried about his health (at his age) and about plots (since he had plotted so much himself)?

And what better angle to introduce than the anti-Semitic one because of Beriya's known *partiality and friendliness to Jews?* There has long been a rumor that Beriya himself is a Jew. Regardless of the rumors it is undeniable that when he was secretary of the Party in Georgia he conducted a policy of aid and assistance to the poor Georgian Jews who probably had few equals in depression and persecution.

Beriya's Georgian record is not well known, but it is no secret. I was put onto it by the Israelis who had been astonished to find in Tbilisi a special Museum of Jewish Culture, complete with photos of Chaim Weizmann, Einstein, and Sholem Aleichem. Beriya conducted a liberal and helpful Jewish policy in Georgia, very different from that to be found in other parts of the Soviet Union.

So, it seems, the parts of the scheme fit together like nicely jointed cabinetwork. Anyone as astute as Beriya must have seen the portents. So Stalin's death may well have come at a most fortuitous time for Beriya and—literally—have saved him.

372

What has since happened, I think, bears out my feeling that of the parties to the ruling triad Beriya has made the greatest contribution of personal force. I would not say that everything of liberalizing nature springs from Beriya. Molotov may well have been equally fed up with the Old Man's phobias. And Malenkov, too.

But this leaves unanswered the $64 question. Who was trying to get Beriya? Possibly Malenkov. But my instinct suggests that it wasn't he. It may be someone we can't put our finger on because he has never emerged far enough from the shadows. Who knows, for instance, what kind of a man was Poskrebyshev, for so many years Stalin's head of secretariat, and a man who was little mentioned in Stalin's lifetime and not at all since Stalin's death?

There is another possibility too—fantastic, yet perhaps there is more reason to believe in the fantastic than in the prosaic.

It seems to me that when Stalin removed the Politburo members from direct control of their respective ministries in March, 1949, he may have kept them at arm's length and with Georgian cunning deliberately encouraged the subordinates to report directly to him. Thus, he could have encouraged an atmosphere of rivalry and dissension which would allow ambitious men in the security ministry, for instance, to move against Beriya, particularly if, as many believed, Beriya's personal influence was exerted on the side of an easier, more Georgian kind of policy. We probably will never know the whole story, but it is plain that Beriya has been moving as rapidly as possible to consolidate his position.

It is apparent that the situation was by no means stabilized in the government announcement of March 7. Changes of power and position are proceeding rapidly. For instance, Ignatiev was named to a Party secretaryship only in the decree of March 6, published March 7. He was confirmed at the central committee plenary of March 14, published March 21. But by April 4 the tide had turned. On March 6 Malenkov was named premier and continued in his listing as first, among Party secretaries. On the same date Khrushchev was dropped from his Moscow post into an uncertain limbo of "work in the central committee." But by March 14 Malenkov resigned his secretaryship, and Khrushchev was listed first among those remaining.

If Malenkov, as many people suspect, was behind the machinations against Beriya, it looks as though Beriya has already checkmated Malenkov.

But, as I said before, I am not convinced that this comparatively simple theory is correct.

I think it is possible that all the present members of the government were the victims and targets of these undermining and sinister palace intrigues and plots whose real center could only have been the Old Man himself, since they could not have gone on without his tacit acquiescence. He was not senile, you can be sure of that.

I have made another change in my earlier evaluations. I suspect that Molotov may be the nominee of the army in the triumvirate.

I say that because the foreign policy he is conducting seems to me to have army earmarks. I have long thought that the army was the least politically minded and most Western-oriented group in the power structure and probably the most staunch opponent of aggressive policy. If this is correct, Molotov has a stronger position in the government, and it is more of a Beriya-Molotov than a Beriya-Malenkov government than I thought.

In any event I stick to my thesis that the real power now lies in the hands of Beriya and the army rather than the Party.

Why the hell-bent rush to settle things up in the West?

I can suggest two things. One is revulsion from the years of Stalin's iron control. The other is deep knowledge of division in the upper hierarchy which may have dangerous repercussions. Thus, an effort to reduce external tension before internal tension weakens dangerously Russia's international position. If the men at the top fear that they may be quarreling seriously among themselves, it would be prudent to settle some quarrels abroad while there is time.

Whatever the reason, the result is obvious to us all—the Russians want and want desperately to get back on good terms with the West.

They are full of talk about things having changed, about forgetting "surface" irritations, and are eager, they say, for ideas of how to improve relations. We have given them plenty of suggestions.

374

They have even asked us what they ought to do about the censorship.*

April 9, 1953

A series of mass meetings is being held to discuss friendship of nationalities within the Soviet Union and equal rights among all peoples. This coincides with an *Izvestia* essay about the rights of Soviet citizens. There is a big drive on to liquidate race antagonisms and anti-Semitism.

Dispatch to New York Times
April 10

A number of changes in state-security and interior-ministry posts are being made in the provinces. There have been changes in Azerbaijan, Tadzhikstan, Latvia, Byelorussia, and Uzbekistan. . . .

April 10

The amount of anti-U.S. material in the press seems to have been cut 75 to 80 per cent. So far this month, outside of a handful of joint references to Lenin and Stalin, there have been no references in *Pravda* to Stalin or any other personality.

Instead of individual references, *Pravda* talks of collective decisions of the central committee. There is still no build-up of Malenkov, Beriya, or Molotov. No more photographs of Malenkov. Decrees are not signed by individuals.

But Stalin's picture is still to be found almost everywhere. No one seems to be taking them down.

Dispatch to New York Times
April 11

Charles E. Bohlen arrived today to take up his duties as U.S. ambassador. He denied he brought any special message from Eisenhower to Malenkov. . . .

April 15

Once again it is planting time at Saltikovka and once again the question is whether the seeds I've ordered from the States will

* Censorship finally was abolished in the spring of 1961.

get here. I finally have had a chance to get out in the country again and do a little spading. If the weather holds, we should be planting about May 1.

Dispatch to New York Times
April 17, 1953

In an important declaration of principle *Pravda* excoriates individual leaders who act as if they know everything and take criticism as a personal offense. Communist Party leadership, it says, is based on collectivity and collegiality. The Party has no place for one-man leadership or leaders who don't know how to listen to the opinions of their colleagues.

Pravda published a 1931 quotation from Stalin supporting the principle of collectivity. The paper warned of the danger of the individual leader who "conducts himself as though he knows everything and brooks no criticism of his decisions. . . ."

Dispatch Killed by Censor
April 17

Justice Minister Gorshenin today pledged equality under the law to all Soviet citizens regardless of race or national origin and warned that racial hatred or scorn will be punished by law. . . .

He said that under the amnesty decree of March 27 the criminal code must be revised along humanitarian lines. A. Tarasov, deputy chairman of the Supreme Court, said defendants must be guaranteed their right to defense by lawyers, open trial, the right of subpoena, and the right to present witnesses. . . .

XXVIII

The Downfall of Beriya

Dispatch Killed by Censor
April 19, 1953

A new case involving falsification and fabrication of evidence
has been exposed in Georgia with the arrest of the former Georgian state security minister, General N. Rukhadze, and others, the
dismissal of Party secretary A. I. Mgeladze, and a general re-
shuffling of the Georgian Party. They are accused of fabricating
cases against three leading Georgian Party members. The trio was
released from prison and given important posts in the government. The action was accompanied by a panegyric in honor of
the man who was called Georgia's "best son"—Lavrenti Pavlovich
Beriya.

Apparently the Georgian plot was concocted along much the
same lines as the infamous "doctors' plot."

Among the many changes announced in the Georgian set-up
the most notable was the appointment of Vladimir Georgievich
Dekanozov as minister of internal affairs. He is one of Beriya's
oldest and closest associates. For many years he was active in the
Ministry of Foreign Affairs.

April 21, 1953

D. I. Chesnokov seems to have been released as chief editor of
Kommunist.

Dispatch to New York Times
April 21, 1953

The central committee in its list of forty-seven slogans for May Day places chief emphasis on a declaration that "there is not a single difficult or disputed question which cannot be solved by peaceful means of mutual agreement of the interested countries.
. . ."

Dispatch to New York Times
April 24

Important changes in the Leningrad Party organization are announced. N. G. Ignatov who had been one of the Party secretariat has been named first secretary of the city Party committee.
. . . More changes in republic state-security organizations are reported. . . .

Dispatch to New York Times
April 25

Pravda said today that the Soviet leadership is ready for business-like discussion of international questions directly or through the United Nations but finds no evidence in President Eisenhower's latest speech of an American desire for talks. . . .

For the first time *Pravda* published the full text of an Eisenhower speech. *Pravda's* editorial occupied the whole of page one.

Diplomats regard the statement as the most significant made since the new Soviet leadership came to power. One diplomat was particularly interested in what he called the "collective nature" of the statement, by which he meant the fact that it was not signed and appeared to have been prepared by several hands.

The document contained a strong hint that some positive action might be taken toward signing an Austrian peace treaty. . . .

Dispatch to New York Times
April 25

M. D. Bagirov, for many years secretary of the Azerbaijan Communist Party, has relinquished this post and become premier of Azerbaijan. The Party post has been taken over by T. A. Yakubov, for many years Azerbaijan minister of internal affairs. Other important changes in security personnel have been made in the Ukraine and in Georgia. . . .

Dispatch to New York Times
April 28

The traditional May Day display of portraits of government leaders was put up today. The portraits were displayed in the following order: Malenkov, Beriya, Molotov, Voroshilov, Krushchev, Bulganin, Kaganovich, Mikoyan, Pervukhin, and Saburov.
. . .

April 30

Ambassador Sir Alvary Gasgoigne was advised by the Foreign Office today that George Bundock may return to England.

May 1

Americans paid a sentimental kind of farewell to Red Square today. This is the last holiday on which the embassy will occupy its front-row seat on Mokhovaya Street. There was so much fraternization with Russian paraders that some Americans could hardly keep from joining in the Red Square procession—as invited by their Soviet friends. There had been no such scenes during the many long years of the cold war. In past years militiamen have sternly herded back any Americans who ventured outside even to take pictures.

May 6

The dwindling band of survivors of the Bolshevik era got a pleasant surprise today. Announcement was made of the award of the Red Banner of Labor to Grigor I. Petrovsky in connection with his seventy-fifth birthday. The birthday actually occurred last year. He had been one of Lenin's associates and an important Party leader in the Ukraine. But since the time of the purges of the 1930's he had not been heard of.

May 7

Catledge sends me congratulations on the Stalin coverage. It came at a good time—simultaneous with a nasty fit of hysterics by *Time* magazine, directed against me. I suppose at a time when the Bohlens are called "security risks" and the Kennans are eased out of government, one can hardly avoid this kind of dirty business.

Of course, it is an eternal problem writing from here. I have

379

just been through it again with the Sunday department in connection with a piece I wrote for them, based on my walks through Moscow. They decided not to run the piece. This bothers me since by the haphazard chance of events my walks offered a small footnote to history.

Now they are asking me whether there may be a possibility of doing "more critical" pieces in the future. Actually, of course, the censorship on the Moscow-walk article was light, but so long as it exists it is difficult to write articles which emphasize the critical side. I can get things through if I call a spade a digging implement, but it will be a long time before I can call it a "dirty Communist shovel."

New York felt that the American reader would regard the Moscow-walk article as "Russian propaganda." The feeling arises, obviously, not from the content of the article (a flat and photographic report of Moscow and its streets) but in the absence of moral pointing. The reader is forced to draw his own conclusions as to why, for instance, people now stroll more freely in Red Square, why a small boy should be chopping wood on a main boulevard of Moscow, why it should be news that Wagner concerts are again being given, what the prices of the materials in the Red Army store work out in dollars, etc.

Before Stalin's death the militia hounded people out of Red Square. The small boy should, of course, be in school and not chopping wood, and the room should have steam heat instead of a wood stove. Stalin hated Wagner and wouldn't permit his music to be performed. The censor never passes prices, and those from the department store just slipped by. Small change. Yes. But important small change. And this in a piece which some idiot in New York thought should be called "A Walk through Paradise"!

I can only report the facts—not the commentary. And I must confess this does pose an unusual burden on the reader since he is compelled to think and draw conclusions for himself.

Dispatch to New York Times
May 11, 1953

The Tbilisi newspaper, *Zarya Vostoka*, connects Deputy Minister of State Security Riumin with the fabrications of Georgian

Security Minister Rukhadze. More arrests are expected in Georgia. . . .

Usman U. Usupov, for so many years Party chief in Uzbekistan, has been named chairman of the Uzbek Council of Ministers. There are many more changes in the provincial security ministries—Uzbekistan, Kazakhstan, Lithuania, Estonia, and Byelorussia among others. . . .

Dispatch to New York Times
May 12

Churchill's proposals for great-power conversations looking toward something like a present-day Locarno pact are expected to get a favorable response here. . . .

May 17

The belated honors shown Petrovsky have hit the Russians much like the reversal of the "doctors' case." He is a well-known person to the older generation of Communists. Now they are wondering what other survivors of the 1930's will be honored and how much of the history of the 1930's is going to be rewritten. The Petrovsky case, perhaps, is a symbol. A damn good one.

Dispatch to New York Times
May 17

Diplomatic amenities between the Soviet and Yugoslavia—nonexistent for the past four years—have taken a trend toward normalcy. The Yugoslav chargé has had conversations with Molotov and his deputy Zorin in the last month. Both sides are understood to have indicated a desire to normalize diplomatic relations. . . .

May 18

One of the New York Russian-language papers has criticized my report of *Pravda*'s attack on one-man leadership. Of course the criticism is egregious nonsense. The *Pravda* article made two points—both important. It elaborated on "collectivity and collegiality," which I had previously noted March 11 in my dispatch on the *Kommunist* article. And it coupled this with a very strong attack on "one-man leadership." All the best diplomatic specialists here agree with my interpretation.

Dispatch Killed by Censor
May 22, 1953

Wheat flour has been placed on constant daily sale in government stores in Moscow and other centers.

For years flour has been sold freely only four times a year—just before the November holiday, New Year's, Shrovetide, and May Day. At all other seasons flour was sold only in the peasant markets at high prices.

It has been so long since flour was sold freely in government stores that I could not find a Moscow housewife who could remember when it had occurred. They think it might have been in the early 1930's. I suspect it has not been since the Revolution. . . .

Dispatch to New York Times
May 24

Making plain that it considers the German question the crux of any *détente* with the West, the Soviet has rejected Churchill's Locarno suggestions. . . .

Dispatch to New York Times
May 27

The Ministry of Internal Affairs announced today the violation of the Soviet Ukrainian frontier on the night of April 26 by an American plane which dropped a group of diversionists, terrorists, and spies by parachute. The group has been apprehended and shot, the announcement said. . . .

Dispatch to New York Times
May 29

Pravda rebukes propagandists who are devoting their attention to the problem of "product exchange." It said the Party and government have decided to continue development of Soviet trade on a monetary basis. The product exchange system was first proposed last September by Stalin in his valedictory work, *Economic Problems of Socialism in the U.S.S.R. Pravda* called those advocating the product exchange system "theoretically incorrect" and said they were doing practical harm to the Soviet economic system. . . .

May 30

Thank goodness the Russians have seeds! The ones I ordered from the U.S.A. have gotten bound up in U.S. bureaucratic red tape. This kind of thing sets my bile flowing. I see so much bureaucracy close at hand that it stimulates the flow extensively when I see our own Little Men duly treading their weary footsteps along the same route.

Dispatch to New York Times
June 8

Kommunist attacks what it calls the "cult of personalities or heroes" in a leading article. It says that Marx, Engels, and Lenin strongly opposed development of any personal cult of leadership. It quotes Stalin as having once said that "it is not heroes who create history but the people who push forward history and create heroes."

The article again emphasizes the importance of the principle of collectivity. But the sharpest words of the article were directed against cults which attribute to a particular individual "all the great achievements of a given historical period. . . ."

The article said survivals of this cult persist in Soviet propaganda, books, stories, and lectures. . . .

Dispatch to New York Times
June 8

The changes in security posts continue. Shifts are reported in Latvia, Estonia, and Byelorussia. . . .

June 9

Bohlen has been advised that exit permits will be given to the Soviet wives of Eddy Gilmore, AP correspondent, and Bob Tucker, an embassy employee, and two children of Mrs. Ethel Balashova, an embassy employee. The cases of other Russian wives of American citizens are under consideration. The last such visas were granted in 1946.

Dispatch Killed by Censor
June 13

The ouster of Leonid G. Melnikov as chief of the Communist Party of the Ukraine was evaluated tonight as the most important Party development in the past two months.

He is the first member of the post-Stalin Presidium to be affected by any change in status. It is expected there will be further developments. Alexei I. Kirichenko was advanced to fill Melnikov's post. There are other shake-ups, too. One has affected the central Komsomol secretariat. The other is in Turkmenia.

It is expected that Melnikov will be dropped from the Presidium just as Ignatiev was dropped from the secretariat when he was involved in the "doctors' plot." Melnikov has headed the Ukraine Party since Khrushchev came to Moscow in December, 1949. He has always been closely associated with Khrushchev.

The principal charge invoked against Melnikov was that he encouraged a policy of Russianization in the western Ukraine. The charges in the Georgian scandal also involved false accusations of nationalism and anti-Semitism.

Dispatch to New York Times
June 18, 1953

Reports from Vilnaus say that the Lithuanian central committee is meeting to discuss "major mistakes" in political and industrial work, particularly with respect to "national policy. . . ."

June 19

Four more Russian wives of American citizens, including those of Tom Whitney, Henry Shapiro, Andrew Steiger—all correspondents—and George Adkins, an embassy employee, have been given permission to leave the Soviet Union.

Dispatch to New York Times
June 21

The Foreign Office has advised foreign embassies that travel restrictions have been lifted for vast areas in European Russia, Byelorussia, the Ukraine, the Caucasus, and Central Asia.

The forty-kilometer limit on travel around Moscow is continued.

The new rules provide greater freedom of movement in most areas of the Soviet than has existed in many years.

It is now possible to visit Kiev and Minsk, to travel the length of the River Volga, to ride the Trans-Siberian from Moscow to Vladivostok, and to visit the fabulous cities of Central Asia—Tashkent, Samarkand, Bokhara, and Alma Ata.

But Karaganda, border areas, the Urals, and many big Siberian cities are still closed. . . .

Dispatch to New York Times
June 24

Kommunist said today that the Soviet people should not "fence themselves off from the culture of foreign lands." The leading article was by P. Fedoseev, who was so sharply criticized last December for his support of N. A. Voznesensky back in 1948.

Fedoseev says that Russians should not bow down before Western achievements but neither should they fence themselves off in a chauvinistic fashion and "juggle under the flag of patriotism and national tradition. . . ."

Dispatch to New York Times
June 28

Finance Minister A. Zervev has issued a formal denial that the government contemplates new currency reforms. He denounced rumors of devaluation which have been circulating among the populace.

[It is understood the rumors started some months ago in other Soviet cities and only reached Moscow within the last week or so. Persons anticipating monetary reform have been purchasing consumers goods, particularly valuable articles such as jewelry and objects of art. Many had been withdrawing money in savings accounts in anticipation of devaluation.]

Dispatch to New York Times
June 28—5:00 a.m.

The leaders of the Soviet government and the Communist Party made a public appearance last night at a performance of a new opera called *The Decembrists* at the Bolshoi Theater. They were headed by Georgi Malenkov and Vyacheslav Molotov.

In addition those present included Voroshilov, Khrushchev, Bulganin, Kaganovich, Mikoyan, Saburov, Pervukhin, Shvernik, Ponamarenko, and Malyshev.

[Among the top leaders of the government the only one who was not present was Beriya. Those present included all the members of the Presidium with the exception of Beriya, Leonid Melnikov, and M. G. Bagirov.]

The only non-member of the Presidium listed was Malyshev. The presentation of the new opera was described as a "great success."*

Dispatch to New York Times
June 28, 1953

A new minister of internal affairs has been named in Byelorussia and a number of Latvian nationals have been advanced to important posts in the Latvian Party. . . .

Pravda has published another article attacking the cult of "outstanding personalities."

In recent weeks a whole series of articles emphasizing the role of collectivity and collegiality in leadership have been published.

[A practical demonstration of the collectivity of the present Party and government was given last night when the whole government—with the exception of Beriya—attended a performance of the new opera *The Decembrists* at the Bolshoi. Newspapers listed the twelve members of the government as follows: Malenkov, Molotov, Voroshilov, Khrushchev, Bulganin, Kaganovich, Mikoyan, Saburov, Pervukhin, Shvernik, Ponamarenko, and Malyshev.

It was the first appearance of the government leaders collectively since the days immediately after Stalin's funeral.]

July 1

The other day I went picture-taking at the Kremlin. It was the first time any permanent resident of Moscow has been permitted to take pictures inside the walls.

The pleasant-mannered Kremlin colonel said he would tell me where I could photograph and to take as many as I liked so long as I didn't delay our sightseeing party.

It was a wonderfully brilliant day—perfect for pictures.

"I hope you got some good shots," the Kremlin colonel said as I left.

"I hope so too," I replied. "But I'll be surprised."

There are many rumors in Moscow that after a bit the Kremlin gates will be opened for ordinary visits. There is also speculation

---

* This item was the first indication that Beriya was in difficulty. It broke early on a Sunday morning and was not published by the *Times*. When I repeated the item the following day, it was killed by the censor.

as to whether the government will continue to use the Kremlin for personal offices and residences as in Stalin's and Lenin's times.

The atmosphere of change is in the air, and it would not be too surprising if the Kremlin's great gates were to swing open one of these days to one and all.*

July 6

At long last I have moved bag and baggage out of the Metropole where I was rapidly becoming almost as much of an antiquarian curiosity as the statue of the nude maiden which they had to remove from the lobby because of the scandalous conduct she aroused on the part of the befuddled Red Army major.

I have an excellent four-room apartment at 12/24 Sadovo Samotechnaya, which is a big modern apartment house occupied entirely by diplomats.

I have a fine office here, much cleaner, lighter, and less odiferous than the Metropole.

I hope to leave in a day or two on the first trip of the New Era. This is to the Volga-Don Canal. I have put in for an extensive Central Asia trip as soon as possible and am looking forward to going on leave in America at the end of summer. By that time I will have been in the Soviet Union three solid years without vacation.

A few words about the situation here, in general. The analogy to Alexander II's succession to Nicholas I is so close that I turned to Pares' *History of Russia* the other day and found this passage:

"Nicholas declared: 'My successor must do as he pleases—for myself I cannot change.' Nicholas expired on March 2, 1855, and with him fell in ruins the system of which his personality was everywhere regarded as the incarnation.

"The new sovereign Alexander II had had his political training under the oppressive and reactionary regime of his father to whom he was greatly attached and entirely loyal. . . . His accession was therefore regarded with anything but hope by the Liberals. . . . Alexander gave permission for travel abroad and abolished the obscurantist restrictions introduced in the universities since 1848. These acts of the Tsar were enough to start a new epoch. Without any change in the laws, the censorship ceased, in the

* They did, but not until 1956.

main, to obstruct the Press. . . . The leaders of the public, though, were at first not very definite in their demands. Alexander's first liberal measures were greeted with the greatest enthusiasm, but the public which had not recovered from the pressures of the police regime of Nicholas waited more or less passively for benefits to be thrown to it. . . ."

There is beginning to be a definite parallel between the present "regime of the nameless ones," as they might be called since they prefer the anonymous mantle of collegiality, and that of Alexander.

When you realize that it has been only four months since Stalin's death, you realize that they have gone a long, long way. In the Russian fashion of fluctuation from one extreme to another I expect them to go farther—always providing, of course, that Kirov doesn't get shot again or that some SR does not bump off the German ambassador.*

There seems to be a persistent tendency on the part of some of the single-track American commentators to relate all the easing of restrictions inside Russia to a "peace offensive." I think this is short-sighted. These are dramatic changes put into effect for domestic reasons by people who give every appearance of believing in what they are doing.

If one asks how men who loyally served Dictator Stalin can put into effect a series of liberal policies, I can only point to the parallel of Alexander.

Dispatch to New York Times
July 8, 1953

The newspaper *Soviet Lithuania* has apologized for articles it published last February reflecting on a group of Lithuanian doctors and scientists whom it accused of "alien opinions. . . ." *Pravda* of the Ukraine has made a similar apology. . . .

July 10

Beriya has been dismissed. He has been turned over to the Supreme Court for prosecution on charges of seeking to seize power and trying to turn the Soviet back to capitalist paths.

---

* Sergei Kirov, Communist Party leader of Leningrad, was assassinated on December 1, 1934. Ambassador Count von Mirbach was assassinated in 1918. Both events touched off waves of severe repression.

The announcement reveals that Malenkov made the report on which the action was based to the central committee. Beriya is called an "adventurist" who was only interested in grabbing power for himself.

Thus is removed from high leadership one of the three men who stood on Lenin's Tomb the day of Stalin's funeral.

It was just six days ago—last Saturday night—that the government leaders attended the Bolshoi Theater together—without Beriya. It is obvious that this was a demonstration of unity following the decision to remove the police chief. Sergei N. Kruglov has been named minister of internal affairs.

This comes by no means as a surprise to ordinary Moscow citizens nor to Moscow diplomats. Reports have been flying fast and thick since Beriya was left out of the Bolshoi Theater party. Rumors were all over Moscow: "Beriya is out." Day after day more details were added.

Beriya will be tried and presumably shot. In fact he may already have been dealt with.

There is no doubt that the elimination of Beriya has strikingly enhanced the power and prestige of the government and Party. Beriya disposed vast authority and prestige. He had put the Ministry of Internal Affairs in a position of superiority not only in the center, in Moscow, but in the provinces. It was a kind of supergovernment. Thus, only a government with great courage and confidence could have tackled this problem so forthrightly.

One thing which interests diplomats is whether there is any connection between Beriya and the events in Berlin.*

There is also the question of what bearing the Beriya arrest may have on the "doctors' plot" and the similar fabricated cases down in Georgia.

July 11

The government has handled the Beriya case in a manner calculated to increase its moral authority and to enhance its prestige with the general public. There have been no visible military or defense precautions. Nothing more than the normal police forces are on the Moscow streets. So far as a foreigner can tell, the country is entirely quiet. The propaganda line being taken repeatedly

---

* The uprising in East Berlin occurred on June 16, 1953, immediately before the Presidium's action against Beriya.

reiterates a famous quotation of Karl Marx against "the cult of the individual." *Pravda* says that the Party must take under its systematic and unweakening control the activity of organs of the Ministry of Internal Affairs. A general purge is not expected. However, any individuals too closely associated with Beriya are expected to be duly punished.

There are a number of others who are known to have been his obedient tools in his long-maturing and closely guarded plot.

July 12, 1953

It is plain from the language used by *Pravda* that Beriya is being blamed for a series of basic difficulties in relations between the Great Russians and other Soviet nationalities, particularly relations with the Ukrainians.

Alexander Korneichuk, the Ukrainian writer who is now first deputy chairman of the Ukrainian Council of Ministers, charges Beriya directly with stirring up differences between the Russians and Ukrainians. In this connection it is recalled that Leonid Melnikov was dismissed as Ukrainian Party secretary on charges of attempting to russify the western provinces of the Ukraine. Now the question arises as to whether the charges against Melnikov were genuine or whether they resulted from Beriya's machinations.

In any event it is clear from what *Pravda* says that the Ukraine was one of the prime fields of Beriya's manipulations. Beriya is also said to have delayed solution of the farm problem, but no details are offered.

I have seen absolutely no public manifestations in connection with the Beriya affair. Nor have I heard anyone discussing the matter in restaurants or in the streets.

Beriya is supposed to have lived in a certain house behind a big gray fence just beyond Revolution Place, not more than two or three hundred yards from the American embassy. Not that anyone ever saw him going in or out. I went over to the house after the news was announced to see what I could see. But there was nothing to see—just the same fence and no activity whatever.

But for all the absence of tangible evidence people have certainly been thinking. One thought which is widespread is that there is no place in present-day Soviet life for anyone to set himself up as some kind of superman.

Dispatch to New York Times
July 14

General Antonov, commander of the Trans-Caucasus military district, told a meeting of Trans-Caucasus officers that there is full unity of the army and the central committee in the Beriya affair. . . . The Tbilisi newspaper reported that Beriya Square has been renamed Lenin Square. It used to be called Erevan Square before the Revolution and in the 1920's was called Freedom Square. . . .

Dispatch Killed by Censor
July 16

Two of Beriya's oldest and closest associates have been ousted from the Georgian government and Party on charges of treason in association with Beriya. They are Vladimir Dekanozov, who became minister of internal affairs of Georgia only last April, and Stepan S. Mamulov, Lieutenant General of MVD and a senior police official, who was named to the Georgian Party bureau in April. Another man named as a traitor is Akadi Mgeladze, Georgian Party secretary, who was ousted in April. . . .

Dispatch to New York Times
July 17

Vyacheslav A. Malyshev has been given an important new assignment—direction of the newly created ministry which is given the title of "medium machine construction."

The Council of Ministers has ordered turned over to this ministry a whole series of institutions and establishments. No listing of these establishments is made public in connection with the formation of the new ministry.

[Nor is there any public explanation of exactly what types of "medium machine building" will fall within scope of the new ministry.]*

Dispatch to New York Times
July 19

Mir Djafar Bagirov, chairman of the Council of Ministers of Azerbaijan and a member of the fourteen-man Presidium of the

---

* In fact, as this dispatch sought to hint, this was the Soviet atomic energy ministry, which formerly had been directed by Beriya.

central committee, has been dismissed from his post on charges of grave errors.

[He is the third member of the Presidium to lose his job. The others were Leonid Melnikov and Lavrenti P. Beriya. Bagirov for years has been closely associated with Beriya. He was an old-time Cheka officer.]

Dispatch Killed by Censor
July 21, 1953

A detailed account of last week's plenary of the Georgian Party reveals that seven of Beriya's close associates have been purged on charges of assisting him in a plot to seize power through the Ministry of Internal Affairs.

Among them are Avksenty Rapava, Nikolai M. Rukhadze, S. S. Mamulov, Vladimir Dekanozov, a man named Shariya, Bogdan Z. Kobulov, and Soloman R. Milshtein. Four of these men are top-ranking MVD officers. . . .

XXIX

Khrushchev Moves Up

July 23, 1953
Letter to Chief, International Section, Central Telegraph

I wish to enter the strongest complaint against the fantastically inadequate communications facilities for correspondents. . . .

You have several times assured correspondents that three telephone lines are at their disposal for calls to London—although there are four correspondents and frequently five who desire to talk to London simultaneously.

The actual fact is that it is a very rare occasion when three lines are available to London. Night after night after night the clerk says there is only one or only two lines available.

Why have you promised that three lines will always be available for correspondents when you know very well that your employees never make three lines available unless the correspondents shout their heads off and raise a scandal?

Dispatch Killed by Censor
July 23

Marshal Georgi K. Zhukov is now serving as first deputy minister of defense. He was one of two named last March. At that time Marshal Vasilevsky's name was listed first. Now Marshal Zhukov's name is listed ahead of Vasilevsky's.*

---

* This was the first indication of Zhukov's ascendancy as a result of his support to the Presidium in the arrest of Beriya.

July 24, 1953

A letter from Minneapolis. They haven't heard from me in five months! It seems incredible. But that just about covers the period since Stalin's death. And, of course, I have been going night and day since before that time. Quite literally. My sleeping hours these days are from 10:00 or 11:00 in the evening until 2:30 A.M. and then again from 5:30 or 6:00 A.M. until about 10:00 A.M. It has been that way since February, and it will go on ad infinitum as far as I can see.

I hope to get back to the States in September. I had been planning originally on getting away at the end of March or in early April. But of course the death of Stalin made that impossible.

I am still far from installed in my new apartment. I got a good bit of furniture from the embassy—available because of their move from Mokhovaya. My office is surrounded by bookshelves, reaching almost to the ceiling, laden with *Pravda*s and *Izvestia*s. I do my own translating, clipping, filing, and am forever behind.

The dacha is on its last legs. All the correspondents, except for me, are leaving. Eddy Gilmore, Tamara, and the kids have already left. Inside of a week Tom and Julie Whitney will leave. I have hardly seen the dacha since May. I went out yesterday and pulled enough weeds to pick some peas. The beautiful strawberries went to the birds. The raspberries are going the same way.

Janet is in the hospital. I can think of nothing more absolutely and completely unfair.

July 26

A great relief to talk to Jim yesterday and get his reassurance that all is well with Jan.

Today has been another busy day. A good story this morning. A difficult one, too. A little after 3:00 A.M. when we got the Tass sheets we found a huge batch—about thirty or forty pages—devoted to a history of the Communist Party from 1903 to 1953, actually a full statement of principles of the new government.

It took three hours to digest and report and phone all this to London for the Sunday paper. By the time we got through, it was a cool sunshiny Sunday morning. What hits me most about this document is the absence of references to Stalin. In 7,500 words his name is mentioned only four times. We are used to seeing it scores of times in a simple newspaper editorial.

I never did get to make the trip to the Volga-Don Canal. The Beriya story intervened. But I have a whole series of trips I want to make before I get away in September. With travel opened up in all directions I must take advantage of it.

July 27

The big news story today is the signing of the Korean armistice. Sure hope it sticks. It broke too late to be published here this morning, but I expect it will get a big ride in the Tuesday paper. This is the first fruit of the new foreign policy adopted after Stalin's death.

Dispatch to New York Times
July 28

The machinations of Lavrenti P. Beriya lay behind the dismissal of Leonid Melnikov as Ukrainian Party secretary, and Beriya's hand has been involved in other recent cases of "nationalist errors."

This was seen by diplomats in the government decision to appoint Melnikov ambassador to Rumania. Apparently no very serious fault could be attributed to Melnikov. He was not removed from the central committee or from the Presidium. He participated in the plenary which voted to dismiss Beriya.

[Melnikov has always been regarded as an extremely able administrator and for many years worked closely with Nikita Khrushchev. Just before Melnikov was ousted from his Ukrainian job, Colonel General Andrei A. Grechko, for several years military commander in the Ukraine and member of the Ukraine Party bureau, was transferred out of Kiev to replace General V. I. Chuikov in Germany. . . .]*

July 28—2:45 a.m.

Well, as usual, I am at the telegraph office waiting for *Pravda*. This is where I have been living my life since Stalin's death. The Whitneys are about to leave Moscow—a complicated business. They have been gradually disposing of their furniture and pos-

---

* Actually Melnikov eventually disappeared from the scene, and the closeness of his successor, A. I. Kirichenko, to Khrushchev suggests that Melnikov, although originally a Khrushchev supporter, was drawn in by Beriya in his complex maneuverings for power. Kirichenko also finally fell from grace in January, 1960.

sessions. Now all they have left in their apartment is a bed and a couple of card tables.

There is a bull market in Moscow for any kind of consumer goods. The best demand is probably for women's clothing and next best for furniture. It is startling how much standard American items bring. Of course part of it is the ridiculous rate of the ruble. Nonetheless, nylons command a price of 125 to 150 rubles. Even at ten to one that would be $12.50 to $15 a pair. I don't know why this should be. Except that Kaprons, the local nylon, are rather sturdy and not sheer.

Furniture is in demand because there are lots of apartments opening up and not enough is produced to meet the demand. It is expensive, and my impression is that it is not mass-produced. It is not in good taste—bulky, heavy, and poorly colored. Men's clothing is equally high priced. A man's suit runs 1,200 to 2,000 rubles. Most of the fabric is dark and unattractive. But it wears like iron. One thing doesn't sell well—white dresses, coats, or suits. The reason is simple—punk cleaning facilities. It costs 44 rubles to get a suit cleaned by "fast" dry cleaning—two to four days.

Dispatch to New York Times
July 31, 1953

The Soviet government in a note to the American embassy charged that a U.S. B-50 bomber violated Soviet frontiers in the vicinity of Cape Gamov and flew over Askold Island, not far from Vladivostok, engaging in an exchange of fire with a Soviet plane and then "disappearing in the direction of the sea. . . ."

July 31

I will jot down a few notes and then collapse. This morning at a little before 7:00 A.M. I finally got the Whitneys off for Helsinki, and a little while ago they phoned to say they have arrived in good order with their Siberian cat, Charley, who traveled with them in a specially built small house equipped with a mahogany door. After nine years! They met and fell in love just nine years ago—August 11, 1944.

These last few weeks and days have been incredible. Last night no sleep at all. A thousand and one things to do on top of the usual telegraph stint and two good stories—the Austrian treaty and the Vladivostok plane incident.

Last night a telegram from Mother. Jan doing well. I am so glad.

With Tom and Julie gone I will be able to make my plans about coming back. September is target date. I have a trip to Central Asia up my sleeve which should be a honey. I want to revisit some of the places I went to with Eric Johnston—Alma Ata, Tashkent, Samarkand, plus some others, Bokhara, Stalinabad, Frunze, and maybe Fergana.

August 2

Tonight I saw *The Sea Gull* for the first time in Moscow. It has always seemed a shame that the Moscow Art Theater where it was really born no longer had *The Sea Gull* on its repertoire. All of *The Sea Gull* that remains in the Moscow Art Theater is the emblem emblazoned on the curtain. But this summer the Novosibersk Red Torch Theater is presenting it. The performance was uneven. Several wonderful actors and several hams. The fourth act was excellent. Of course, it is an incredibly difficult play. The only Chekhov play consistently on the Moscow Art Theater repertoire in recent years has been *The Three Sisters*. This year they resumed playing *Uncle Vanya*. *The Cherry Orchard* has been shown nowhere in the last five years.

Dispatch to New York Times
August 4

Beriya's booklet on the history of Bolshevik Party organizations in the Trans-Caucasus has been sharply attacked as "anti-Marxist" and profoundly harmful. It is called a jumble of mistakes and contradictions. There are said to have been particularly serious violations of "nationalist policy" in the Abkhazia and South Osetia districts of Georgia. Abkhazia is the region Beriya hails from. . . .

August 4

Janet is home from the hospital. I've told her I'll be in Minneapolis by October. Yesterday I went to the dacha with the Ekelunds, the Norwegian chargé and his wife and their children. He used to be consul in Minneapolis. We did a little weeding. The poor garden is a jungle. But it is full of peas, beans, cauliflower, tomatoes, and lettuce. I have the Whitneys' dog, Candy. She chased the neighbors' chickens out of the garden.

August 6, 1953

Talked to Janet on the telephone. Good to hear her voice sounding so natural.

As usual I am at the telegraph office in the wee hours of the morning. The Supreme Soviet is meeting and that makes the papers later than ever. It was 8:00 A.M. before I was through today, and it will be close to that again this morning.

We are now surrounded with elegance. They promised us better facilities by the opening of the Supreme Soviet. In "stormavik" fashion they have worked day and night to lay new floors, cover them with fine maroon carpets, panel the walls in birch, set up six new telephone booths for dictation and six booths for writing, each booth complete with folding-leaf desk and electric fan. They have tried in a naïve and rather touching way to give us good facilities, and I must thank them. But, if the truth were known, a little less beauty and a little bigger working desks would have been preferred.

Dispatch to New York Times
August 6

The government has launched a program to encourage peasants to own their own cows and increase the productivity and profits of the peasant's individual farm plot. This is the stated objective of a radical reorganization of the agricultural tax which has been submitted to the Supreme Soviet.

There is nothing to suggest a loosening of the collective farm system, but it does put a halt to rather widely circulated rumors that the government was going to curtail individual farm activity by the peasants. . . .

The fact that the program comes just a month after Beriya was accused of blocking solution of farm problems suggested that he might have opposed such measures in the past. . . .

Dispatch to New York Times
August 8

Premier Malenkov told the Supreme Soviet today that the United States no longer has a monopoly of the hydrogen bomb. He offered no elaboration of his statement. . . .

398

He emphasized that Soviet unity and solidarity have been strengthened by the Beriya affair and that peace by negotiation is permanent Soviet policy rather than a temporary tactic. He said no reasons exist for war between Russia and the United States. . . .

Dispatch to New York Times
August 8

Premier Malenkov told the Supreme Soviet today that Russia plans to boost retail trade 70 per cent over the 1950 average. . . .

A decree dated June 26, relieving Beriya of his posts, was approved by the Supreme Soviet. The date reveals that the action was taken the day before the government leaders went in a body to the Bolshoi Theater to see the première of *The Decembrists.* . . .

Dispatch to New York Times
August 9

For the first time since the start of the five-year plans in 1928 some of the enormous emphasis in the Soviet economy is going to be shifted from heavy industry into consumer goods. . . .

And there are other changes. There will be incentives for peasants to develop livestock, and there is going to be a radical change in methods of evaluating harvests and collection of grain. An end is going to be made of what is called the "biological yield" method of estimating harvests. Under this system the size of the harvest was calculated in the field and the peasant had to deliver a percentage of that total regardless of whether the actual harvest as collected bore any resemblance to the paper estimate. . . .

Dispatch Killed by Censor
August 10

It is apparent from the just-concluded Supreme Soviet session that the great hydroelectric program outlined last autumn as well as some portions of the huge program initiated by Stalin is being held back or delayed to permit more emphasis on consumer goods. . . .

The Kuibyshev Dam was supposed to be finished in 1955 and the Stalingrad Dam in 1956, but these dates now seem unlikely. . . .* It appears that work on the Turkmenian Canal has been abandoned. . . . News of all these projects has practically vanished

* Kuibyshev was finished in 1958, Stalingrad in 1960.

from the press. The Turkmenian Canal has not been mentioned since last March 13.

August 11, 1953

I've gotten another colleague off—Andy Steiger, the Reuters' correspondent, and his wife. That leaves only one more to go— Henry Shapiro of UP.

August 13

Good reports continue to come on Janet, thank goodness.

Stories have appeared abroad saying that Lysenko is finished. I wish I felt this was true. The articles are based on attacks which seem to have been written before Stalin's death. Since then Lysenko has had a big article in *Pravda,* and lately he has been very busy propagandizing a fertilizer campaign in Byelorussia. I do think, however, that the general climate of opinion seems favorable to his ultimate downfall.

Today it turned cold and rainy. First hint of fall. It looks like summer is on its last legs. I hate to see it go. It is so short here in Russia. In the States mid-August is just past the center of summer, and you have two more months of pleasant weather to come, then a glorious October and maybe a wonderful November.

But here when the weather starts to go off in August you have had it. You know that you are going to have gray days in August for the rest of the month and then rain and a coldish September with only a day or two of golden sunshine to make your heart ache for the real autumn, sliding imperceptibly into October's cold and dreary sunlessness. By then it is winter whatever the calendar says, and it stays winter on and on and on until you can't stand it any longer. It is April before the sun bursts through and the streets run gutter full. In a week all the snow is gone and it is spring—a hot short spring—and the course of the seasons all over again.

August 15

Patience is not one of my strong qualities, although God knows I have been called upon to exercise it the last four years. Sometimes, I think I have used up so much patience here that I will have none whatever left for the remainder of my life.

There are so many incidents here that require patience. For

instance, take the matter of the *chorny khod* or the "black way." That is to say the garbage chute in my apartment. In two months I have had to complain four times that the chute is clogged up—choked with refuse which smells so bad you can hardly go into the kitchen.

We have had another rainy weekend. It brought cancellation of the air show for the second successive Sunday. This last weekend was rain, rain, rain. A sodden autumn rain that looks as though it will never stop. I spent part of the weekend reading Proust.

Dispatch to New York Times
August 16

Stepan Emelyanov, Azerbaijan minister of internal affairs, has been released. [He was very close to M. D. Bagirov, an associate of Beriya, who was recently let out as Azerbaijan Party secretary.]

Dispatch to New York Times
August 17

New Soviet proposals looking toward a German peace conference within six months and proposing urgent East and West steps to establish a temporary all-German government and carry out all-German elections have been submitted to the West. . . .

August 18

I am touched by Janet's concern over the long hours I work. I have been accustomed for many, many years to work hard and long and I enjoy it. It doesn't hurt me the least. I manage to get my quota of sleep, even if at odd hours.

I paid a visit to the dacha yesterday. Dozens of tomatoes ripe for picking—so many the neighbors' chickens hadn't been able to deal with all of them. And many cucumbers, ripe and juicy and sweet. Much lettuce. A lot of *kabotchki* or squashes. So I picked and weeded and read Gorki and sat in the sun and played with Candy and ate a lunch and found nothing necessary to call me back to Moscow until six o'clock. And nothing had happened, and I had, indeed, picked a good day to go to the country.

I am hopeful that by the end of the week permission for the Asian trip will come and I will vanish for three weeks or a month.

The government's announcement that a test explosion of a

hydrogen bomb had been carried out recently aroused great public interest. Foreign diplomats speculated whether the announcement might not be followed soon by a new Soviet drive for banning nuclear weapons.

I expect that there will be plenty of skeptics to say the Russians haven't got a hydrogen bomb even though they have set one off. I wouldn't want to play around with that kind of speculation. I think it safest and most sensible to believe they do have one.

But the subject of Bombs with a capital letter is so pumped full of Madison Avenue chicanery that no one in the U.S.A. probably has a clear picture of what it is all about.

There seems to be a continuing notion that God gave only the United States science and industry and the know-how to deal with atoms. But I fear it is a delusion and that just as our efforts were made possible through the contribution of men of all nationalities so these various nationals working in their own countries can, if they have access to a large industry, duplicate our efforts and even outdistance us.

This, of course, is an idea beyond the comprehension of many grass-roots-type statesmen because it is not a pleasant and self-inflating kind of idea like: Only Americans Can Make Atoms. Just as I believe it has been said that Only American Boys Have Mothers.

It is a big world these days, but it is full of little, little men.

So, I venture, it always has been. I can fancy when the first Chinamen set off the first gunpowder how proud they were and how sure that Only Chinese Brains could conceive Gunpowder and only Chinese Know-How could produce it. For a thousand years China must have felt, then, the Celestial Empire will be safe from assault from the outside. Yet it was the very Gunpowder made by Barbarians rather than Celestial Images which provided China with her complete and terrible downfall.

How pleasantly ironical is history.

August 21

As I suspected—Lysenko drew a half-page spread in *Izvestia* a couple of days ago.*

* By January, 1961, Lysenko was back in full favor as Khrushchev's agricultural adviser. On August 8, 1961, he was named head of the All Union Academy of Agricultural Sciences.

Kommunist today attacks Soviet film productions of recent years which sought to idealize reactionary figures like czars and khans who oppressed their own and foreign peoples. It strongly attacked the tendency to glorify "Supermen, Caesars, and Napoleons. . . ."

Dispatch to New York Times
August 28

Today was moving day in Red Square. At every entrance to the vast block of gray stone buildings facing the Kremlin were drawn up big trucks. Workmen were piling them with office furniture. After twenty-five years the "Upper Row" of arcades which was the pride of Moscow's merchantry in the late nineteenth century is going back into use as Moscow's greatest shopping center. . . .

August 29

I am on tenterhooks about my Asian trip. The press department has said it is approved in principle. But they are waiting final word on a few details. It is supposed to come through any day. I am nervous as a cat. I want to make the trip and be off for America by October 1.

The other night I went to the Hermitage, the outdoor gardens, and saw Leonid Utesov. He is the leader of the All-Russian State Vaudeville Orchestra. It used to be State Jazz Orchestra until times forced a change of name. He has often been criticized for Western tendencies and for playing jazz. The other night he borrowed a pair of opera glasses and swept the audience from the stage. "Just wanted to see if that fellow was here," he said, "the one who sits in the first row and applauds and cheers and then writes letters to the papers saying that we are playing jazz."

He then went into a little speech about how Karl Marx never said anything against love. So why don't Soviet writers put some love and kisses in their songs?

It was a little pathetic, but it had a revolutionary tingle, too, because the concepts he was shooting at were some of the most fundamental in what is rapidly getting to be known here as the *ancien régime*. I felt Utesov was getting a lot off his chest. The suppressed bitterness of years was coming out. That is the way things are going here.

Another interesting development. One of the biggest art galleries in town has been devoted ever since January, 1950, to an exhibit of birthday junk sent Stalin on his seventieth birthday. This at last has closed and the museum has a big sign on it: "Closed for Repairs."

Now there is a rumor around town that the famous Russian collection of French Impressionist art, one of the best in Europe, which has not been shown since the start of the war and which was denounced as degenerate, may be placed on the walls where so recently hung the handworked embroidery portraits given to Stalin by the Kirghiz peasants.

September 1, 1953

Yesterday I attended the dedication of the new Moscow University. It is on the same order as the University of Pittsburgh but located on a prairie at the edge of town. There is no good reason for building a skyscraper in that location. It provides plenty of problems in moving the kids back and forth at the end of class periods just as they discovered at Pittsburgh. They have 112 elevators. They will need them. The building houses the scientific faculties. It will be the first thing which visitors see on approaching Moscow from the airport.

The university has a huge red star atop it. It is 32 or 38 stories tall, depending on how you calculate it. But it is no bigger than the University of Minnesota. It has 13,000 day students—about 8,000 of them in the new skyscraper.

Dispatch to New York Times
September 2

The famous collections of French Impressionist paintings assembled before World War I by the Moscow collectors S. I. Shchukin and I. A. Morozov will soon be on exhibit in Moscow again. . . .

September 8

I have suffered a bit from accumulated fatigue this last week but have been able to take things easier. There is a big new deal. In hours—working hours. In Moscow everything is now on a 9:00

404

to 6:00 basis. We get *Izvestia* at 1:00 A.M. and *Pravda* by 2:00 A.M., which is wonderful.

It was all changed when the government changed its working hours. Radio stations have set new hours for broadcasting. Stores open earlier. The Foreign Office doesn't send notes in the evening any more.

This has always been a late town because the Kremlin worked late at night and all the Little Shots had to do the same. They couldn't afford not to be there if Stalin called at 2:00 A.M. As of September 1 all this changed.

September 10

A gentleman whose judgment in things Russian is equaled only by his wizardry on the links has made what I think is the most apt remark I have heard about the local situation. He says: "Malenkov is acting as though he is running for an office he already holds."

And that is exactly the way Malenkov is behaving.

A couple of weeks ago there was a tornado at Rostov Veliki, an old Kremlin town near Yaroslavl. It sheared off golden onions from the cathedrals and unroofed some houses. A few people were killed and some injured, but it was not a large-scale catastrophe. It would not be worth mentioning if Malenkov had not paid the scene a visit, comforted the victims, inspected the damage, and ordered measures for repair just as the governor of Minnesota would if a twister hit Mankato, Minnesota.

The story is being told all over Moscow as an example of how Georgi does things. It hasn't appeared in print, and the censors have stopped it dead.

It really is naïve the way all the ducks and pigeons have swung into line on this new working hours deal. Not only have all local republics ordered similar hours but even the hours of the radio setting-up exercises have been set back forty-five minutes earlier.

Obviously, it was only Stalin's penchant for night hours which had put the whole country on such a silly time basis. And the same goes for the reopening of the "Upper Row" on Red Square. The Old Man didn't think it was "cultured" to have trade on the square.

In this reversal of the Old Man's personal idiosyncrasies, we have a mixture of motives in which the most prominent is a desire to shake off the petty tyranny of a man whose 1890-ish provincial taste had been erected into a kind of national fief.

I am thinking of Utesov's defense of the right of every Soviet citizen to hear the kind of music he wants to. "There is nothing in the Soviet constitution which limits the kind of music which Soviet citizens may listen to," he said. "We play *all kinds* of music." Last winter during the "doctors' case" there were rumors that Utesov had been arrested. The venom with which he speaks makes me think there was truth to the rumors.

The same kind of feeling motivates the present top brass in their drive to extirpate Stalinism. They, too, have felt the cold hand of arrest coming too close to their soft warm necks.

I sent New York an item the other day about the death of Borodin. I got that from Parker, who asked me at the Moscow University ceremonies whether we had ever carried the news of Borodin's death. I said, no—had he died? Yes, he said. He understood it had been reported in the Chinese press. The Chinese are said to have intervened for Borodin, sending a personal letter to Stalin, stressing his contribution to the Chinese Revolution and asking for clemency. Borodin was sent East where he died in the course of the past year. A pity, since people like that are now being let out.

I think this pretty well confirms my observation about Borodin and Anna Louise and all the stink that was going on when I came here in 1949. The censorship passed the Borodin item after forty-eight hours. I said the news of the death was announced belatedly. They deleted "belatedly."

No clue to what impends in the Beriya case. It has vanished like a stone at the bottom of the sea. Even in Georgia things have quieted down. The only ripple is the continuing series of changes in the Republican ministers of interior. Censorship has killed six times a story which I have tried to file about a clutch of top MVD brass who got it in the neck down in Georgia. The gentlemen apparently comprised Beriya's hand-picked inner circle.

It is my impression that the situation has stabilized materially since Beriya's downfall. Ostensibly, at least, the government group is pulling well together. Perhaps there are still facets of relationship to be worked out between the government and the army. If so, we don't know much about them.

Dispatch to New York Times
September 13, 1953

The central committee at a plenary session has elected Nikita Khrushchev first secretary. The election places him in the No. 1 Party position in the country.

He had been listed first among secretaries since Malenkov retired from this position last March. But this was the first time he had been designated first secretary.

The announcement, together with a sweeping agricultural plan of his drafting, was spread across the whole top of *Pravda* and *Izvestia* in the Sunday morning papers.

His plan is designed to remedy grave defects in Soviet livestock production, which in some respects is still below prewar levels and in others is less than it was in 1928. . . .

Dispatch Killed by Censor
September 13

Nikita Khrushchev called on the country to face the fact that livestock production has never regained the losses of wartime and the 1930's.

Cattle production is nearly 9,000,000 head below the 1928 figure, just before the collectivization of agriculture. Russia now has about 16,000,000 head of horses, about 60 per cent of the pre-Revolutionary figure and 27 per cent of the prewar figure. . . .

September 14

I have the trip to Central Asia cleared on a curtailed but respectable basis. I am taking off day after tomorrow for Alma Ata. I expect to leave for America about October 7 or 8.

One day last week I went to the dacha. Lordy, lordy—the mud. Iowa in 1919 had nothing on Saltikovka in 1953. It was bad. It has been raining almost continuously for the last two weeks. Summer is over, and it looks like there will be no fall. There have already been a few snow flurries.

I harvested some more tomatoes and cucumbers and half a dozen enormous squashes. The last harvest, I fear.

Dispatch to New York Times
September 15, 1953

The most revealing, the most frank, the most basic critique of Soviet agriculture ever made public by a Soviet spokesman was published today under the signature of First Secretary Khrushchev.

It was a 25,000-word report to the central committee, and there are few sins of Soviet farm practice of the last thirty-five years which escape his scathing attention.

His conclusion is that livestock production after thirty-seven years [and application of countless new laws and regulations] factually stands at about the level of 1916. . . . The most striking fact about Khrushchev's report is that it pulls no punches and makes no attempt to gloss over the huge deficiencies of Soviet agriculture. . . .

XXX

To Central Asia

September 17, 1953

It is nearly midnight. My apartment on the Sadovo Samotechnaya is in order. My office desk is clear of papers, and just before leaving I pause in the darkened living room to observe an old Russian custom. I sink into an easy chair to sit in quiet contemplation for a moment before starting on a long journey.

A long journey—it is that in truth. Since I returned to Russia in the cold spring of 1949, cold in climate and cold in spirit, I have been dreaming of going back again, once more setting foot on the Golden Road to Samarkand.

Nothing seemed more unlikely then—or even now—than that I should ever again see Samarkand. And yet, here I am, bags and typewriter packed. In a moment the journey will begin.

But the thrill has gone for me. It has been lost in days of arguing about arrangements, in years of waiting, and, perhaps most importantly, in the pounding, grueling task of covering Moscow. The Golden Road to Samarkand! What dreams the words bring back. Nowhere is there a youngster in whose heart the spark of adventure flickers whose eyes do not sparkle at the words—Samarkand . . . the Golden Horde . . . Tamerlane . . . Kublai Khan . . . Genghis Khan. . . . Slant-eyed horsemen, cruel as steel, bending the whole world to their will for a century or two—sitting fat and rich upon Asia's patient back for another half a thousand years. Or nearly so.

When we are young, we think that the Samarkands of the world are golden nuts which we can crack with strong white teeth and within will be The Secret—the kernel of the mystery. But now I wonder. Is there really a Secret? Or is it just something which lives in our imagination?

Nor is this all. Today the world is full of worry. I have my own private worries about those at home. When I first started on the Golden Road, it was a world to conquer. Today nor I nor anyone thinks it a world to conquer. But we hope it is a world to survive.

It is time to leave. To go to the Metropole to pick up Eric. I wait for him on the third floor where I lived so long. This grim and dismal pile, this monstrous abomination of a Russian merchant's taste of 1907, was what I was pleased to call my home. What I know of Russia was largely pounded into my brain within its creepy corridors—corridors I know so well that blindfolded I could walk anywhere in the hotel. I know every smell of these halls and the smell of most of the rooms—musty, greasy, cabbage-laden. I know the onion smell, the garlic smell, the stench of oil and kerosene, the crisp scent of birch logs chopped in the court, the brass polish, the toilets. There is my epitaph: a man knew the Metropole so well he could find his way around by his nose.

Now we are speeding out to the airport. It is cold, and I am tired. Eric is talking, but I do not listen. As the car rushes through the raw night, I think of all the times I have left on trips—the first big trip from home, from Minneapolis to Chicago by sit-up night coach to join the Chicago UP bureau, the first step that led by inevitable progression to this car speeding now to the edge of Moscow and turning onto the highway where the great bulk of the new Moscow University skyscraper rises high and black and finally red against the sky.

The first step. To what? What has it all meant? Twenty years of reporting, twenty years of correspondence. I am not really of a philosophic turn of mind. I ask these questions, but I do not work over the answers until I have them right. Why have I set out on this trip to Central Asia, for instance?

Partly it is romanticism. So few people have been there. So few can go. But I can and will—that feeling. Do I expect to win fame and fortune by it? No. I shall be pleased if the *Times* uses my dispatches. All men are born with a certain desire to be the first to stand on a high mountain peak. To be the first to see the blue Pacific. The first to look on Tamerlane's bones. The North Pole, the South, Everest, the floor of the sea—whatever nature guards and protects; there surely you will find man, wrestling and tugging at nature's hands to grab what she holds.

And so I am driven by these doglike instincts halfway across the globe and into the remote fastness of Asia to find, perhaps, a few bones of history and to try to snatch from nature's careless fingers a jewel or two.

September 18—2:58 a.m.

Air-borne for Alma Ata. . . . Passengers clucked like chickens as we boarded the plane. Now they are quiet and we are still flying over Moscow. . . . Saltikovka just to the north. Moscow is big from the air. Big and diffused and golden in the night. You don't see the red and green of traffic lights or neon signs—it is all softly glowing gold. Now I will sleep, too.

Later . . . . I went right to sleep. The plane was cold but gradually it warmed up. I was restless. Woke at 4:30. The sky just beginning to show a pale light. A bright eastern star. We are headed due east. And now we are flying over a big city which shines very brightly below us—Gorki? I have been thinking how different it is from the last time I headed toward Central Asia. Then it was all excitement and adventure and thrills. I remember the girl *dvornik* outside the Metropole that June morning in 1944—watering down the sidewalk, sprinkling us, and laughing with high spirits. No high spirits tonight. I feel old and worn.

It is 6:15 A.M. We have just touched down on a red earth airport. I wonder where? There is a concrete landing strip laid out in lozenges.

This turns out to be Uralsk, a grim and dreary town on the southern tip of the Urals, just inside Kazakhstan. It is a cold, gray morning. Most of the buildings are of whitewashed adobe—low-lying like cattle barns. The factories of a large city are only faintly visible on the horizon. A gray, gray morning. A few women moving about with gray shawls over their heads, bundled against the chill. In the sky a cloud of migrating birds. The air is full of their caw-caw-caw. But they are not crows—some smaller bird, the size of a thrush.

Airport restaurant: a billboard outside where a three-day-old *Pravda* is posted. (Where is their vaunted air distribution, and this at the airport itself?) A signboard "Tonight on the screen" but in the space to chalk up the attraction—a blank.

Inside it is cosy. Chromo oil paintings on blue walls. A pretty, tight-lipped, tight-sweatered girl with sullen eyes takes a quick order for eggs and tea. The service is fast, and the brown bread, tea, and eggs are good.

Our plane has a stewardess with a bag of magazines and paperback novels and short stories. There is a hot plate and a small refrigerator so that she can take care of a bottle for a mother with a nursing baby.

9:40 A.M. Down through the clouds again to an endless world of rusty steppe. Very like western Nebraska. Great two- and three-mile squares of black fall-plowed earth. Most of the land under grain. It looks like a low yield area. Obviously open steppe until fairly recently.

We come down at Kustanai—a little airport-and-grain-elevator town at the River Tobol. We eat a pale-pink, green watermelon, drink a glass of tea, and take off for Karaganda, home of coal and prison labor. All this is MVD-land. But we see no signs of it so far. In the restaurant an air force officer downs 150 grams of vodka in a single gulp. He will go far.

Looking out over the barren, wind-swept plain, I think of our talks in Moscow—talks of finding a far, far off place and turning our backs on civilization. But not in Russia! Not in Russia! Russia is not arranged for Thoreaus or hermits. The steppe is gray and endless. The land flows on and on like a solid sea. To find a hermitage in this steppe would be like finding a snug harbor in mid-Atlantic.

On the fence at the airport restaurant were the last purple morning-glories of the year. Now we are riding on cotton wool clouds, and I will sleep a little.

1:00 P.M. Still flying over the flat, coppery steppe. The expanse is broken by giant checkerboards of black and chocolate-brown— fall plowing. I am surprised to see so much steppe under the plow. We are flying straight across northern Kazakhstan along the route of the South Siberian Railroad. I have been reading a 1930 Intourist Guide. In it is an advertisement, "The Golden Road to Samarkand." It tells about an American I.W.W., Bill

Shatov, who was responsible for driving the Turk-Sib railroad through. I wonder if there are any of the old I.W.W. crowd left in Russia? That was long ago—another age. Big Bill Haywood jumping bail and landing within the Kremlin wall. If there are any old Wobblies left in Russia, they may be living out in this country. Or in some obscure Moscow back street. But I don't think any survived the purges of the thirties.

2:00 P.M. We land at Karaganda. The very name is sinister. First, we flew over a good-sized city adjacent to a large kidney-shaped lake to the north and east of Karaganda. About five minutes flying time to the east we came to Karaganda, a sprawling industrial town. Great patches of black from mine heads and coal-loading areas. There are factories coated in the gray dust of limestone or gypsum and plants surrounded with patches of red copper—copper refineries, no doubt. It would seem to be a city of 300,000, laid out in perfectly rectangular squares—as regular as cell blocks. There were many large compounds and fenced-in areas. I saw one enormous fence that ran around a plant and many other buildings—several miles in area. Theodore Shabad's Geography shows that the first town I saw was Temir-Tau (Iron Mountain) on a reservoir of the Nura River. It has a steel mill with an annual output of 120,000 tons, blast furnaces, a hydroelectric plant and dam. Twelve miles south of Karaganda is Saran, another coal mining center.

There is warm sunshine in Karaganda, like an October day in west Texas. The air is invigorating. Only a mile east of the airport there is a big copper refinery. Went to a restaurant and ate borscht and veal with rice. The stewardess announced the plane had developed a bad motor and we would stay the night. Later she said a plane was coming up from Alma Ata about 9:00 or 10:00 P.M. to take us on.

A passenger made a wisecrack: "Better notify the militia we are here—quickly. We have no visas for Karaganda, and we do not want to be *rasstrelyat* [executed]!" Another passenger: "Does the hotel here have towels and soap?" Many jokes about the delay and the facilities, which are clean and comfortable. We get hot water and shave. There is hot water for coffee, comfortable beds, and I take a nap.

The woman who runs the airport hotel is a Kiev Jewess. She has been here "since the war." How her brown eyes light up when she starts to talk about Kiev. And how her sunburned face seemed to gray when she began to talk about the building boom, of the "stroitza" here in Karaganda. She alleges that there is a nice Palace of Culture, a theater, and apartment houses. But these we do not see. We see a pleasant, clean, but tiny, room. Two blue-painted iron beds with orange wool blankets. Blue linen portieres with white lace window curtains.

First fruit of the trip—Karaganda. No one ever had this date line before. A good augury. I sleep the sleep of exhaustion for three hours. Now it is 8:30 P.M., local time, three hours ahead of Moscow. The airport beacon swings past the window every minute by my wrist watch.

There is an atmosphere of police and faint apprehension in the air. Yet a few minutes after we landed a high-school teacher led a bunch of Pioneers out to look at the plane. They looked fresh and easy in their red kerchiefs. But I can't help wondering how many former residents of the Metropole now live within the forbidden limits of Karaganda.

9:30 P.M., local time. The plane for Alma Ata will now take off.

It is a clear, sharp night with a white three-quarter moon. Karaganda's lights are a golden chain along the horizon. A dog is howling in the distance. At 1:20 A.M. we come down in Alma Ata—cool, pleasant, fresh—just as I remembered it. Like Denver or Ogden. Limes and poplars at the field. We get pleasant clean rooms at the Dom Delegatov.

September 19—8:30 a.m.

Eric's alarm awakens us to a warm autumn day—blue sky, a faint haze of leaves burning, the soft rustle of poplars outside the window, and a frieze of snow-capped mountains in the distance. The hotel is full of Uzbeks with blue and purple undershirts. There is no bath—until Saturday. Showers being repaired. It was a nervous, troubled sleep. My head aches and my mouth burns.

We found a pleasant young taxi driver who spent seven years in the army, including fighting the Japanese in 1939. He makes 700 rubles a month. Has two suits which cost him 1,300 rubles each. Pays 15–25 rubles a kilo for meat and eats it once a week. He and his brother have a five-room house which took them five years to build. He thinks the peoples of the U.S.A. and the U.S.S.R. must see that their governments don't make war.

414

Alma Ata is filled with pleasant parks, fresh mountain streams, purple asters, white buildings, and much construction. It seems to be a third larger than when I was here in 1944. All day a blimp hovered over the city, edging close to the Ala Tau Mountains. A weather blimp, the taxi boys say.

This evening, coming back from buying our bus tickets for Frunze, we saw a nut-brown old Uzbek bowing down in a garden on Komsomol Street and praying to Allah—to the west!

I gave a handful of change to a rather distinguished-looking beggar who was playing a violin outside Federatzi Park. I had not seen a street violinist since my first evening in Russia in January, 1944, at Astrakhan. Now beggars in Russia seem as natural to me as they do to the Russians. No phenomenon causes more surprise to foreigners than the beggars, especially the filthy, grabbing kind you find around the churches. I don't quite understand the Russian attitude toward begging, but I am trying to. There is much real pity, naïve as we would call it. It makes no difference if a Russian knows the beggar is a fake. Sometimes I think it is because the Russian knows how often life goes up and down and how easily he might be standing there with outstretched hand. The beggar is not looked down on or reviled.

Tonight the moon is almost full. In two or three days it will be full. The air is stirred by a soft breeze. In the distance is music. We went to a restaurant in Federatzi Park. Very cultured. Picture by Shishkin of The Three Bears. Much drinking.

All we had to do to get to Frunze was go to the bus depot and buy tickets. We could have bought them to any place in Russia just as easily.

Russia is foolish not to move her film industry out here. The climate is like that of Hollywood. Big savings. But you never could get the artists to move from the Center.

September 20—7:00 a.m.

Rather chilly, overcast day. We get up, shave, pack, and are off for Frunze by bus. I expect it will be a long, dusty, tiring ride. The bus is a wooden box set on a truck body with holes gouged out for windows. There are wooden benches covered with brown oilcloth. It already is full. We hoist our bags up and sit by the door. We are the fourteenth and fifteenth passengers. No. 16 is "Dedya," a mahogany Russian with leather-smooth cheeks, gray

415

mustache, and beard. The other passengers say he is seventy. He looks not more than forty-five to me. He has just come back from China, he says, where he was working for 350 rubles a month and found.

We start at a brisk clip past a long row of mud-and-wattles houses out onto the broad plateau to the west with the high ridge of the snow-capped Ala Tau Mountains on our left. It is overcast and disagreeable.

We had not got out of Alma Ata before we started seeing old Orientals in their conical hats riding donkeys. A few miles from town there was a big peasant village and a steady stream of donkey carts on the road. Also many horsemen and an occasional horsewoman with her baby strapped to the back, Indian-papoose style. About an hour and a half out we came to a big village market. Four of the Russians and I went to the bazaar. It was a scene out of Genghis Kahn. Scores of horses with their horned saddles and blanket cloths and embroidery. Men in conical fur and felt hats. Loose brown tunics. Women squatting around their cocks and chickens and geese and ducks. Melons and tomatoes, apples and grapes, cucumbers and onions, garlic and red pepper, dried and powdered. Everywhere horsemen of the Golden Horde. Men with beautiful silver belts and daggers and a curious medicine man in gold-rimmed spectacles who looked like Ed Wynn. I started to take pictures and had snapped six by the time the militia interfered. Two uniformed men with broad North-China faces and two men in plain clothes, one a pleasant Russian, one a nasty Kazakh with a white face like the root of a mushroom. They demanded *dokumenti*. The Russian didn't want to make anything of it. The Kazakh did. But two youngsters came to my aid. They talked to the plain-clothes men and in a few minutes all was well. There were smiles and apologies all around. One of the kids' father was *raikom parti*. He threw his weight around a bit and that was it. I couldn't blame the militia. Eric and I were like a couple of men from Mars.

I noticed a uniformed militiaman in each village today. At the outskirts of Alma Ata a half-dozen militia stopped the bus and started joking about "free riders" but quickly waved the bus on. Our youngsters said they had trouble with documents on occasion. I noticed a little chill when the militia stopped the bus. Perhaps only imagination. I saw a rifle-armed MVD soldier guarding two

416

closed vans (not very different from our bus) on the main street of Alma Ata. And today we passed one truck of prisoners under guard. But the rebuilding of the Alma Ata–Frunze road (only surfaced about one-third of the way to Frunze) was being done by free labor.

All the way from Alma Ata to Frunze the people live in hogans. Most are natives, and I can't see that they have progressed much in recent centuries. Now in the autumn the roofs are heavy with drying corn and sorghum and melons and squashes. There are great stocks of mud bricks, dried all summer and now being used in building new hogans. After the village where I was arrested, the country became empty. It was a desert steppe for miles.

Finally we came down a fertile green valley into Frunze, another city of trees, white buildings, and gardens.

Impressions: A pretty Kirghiz girl in pigtails and red dress tamping down a surveyor's pole at a point where the road was being built. . . . At a well a fine-featured Kirghiz woman sitting on a white horse in a white wool dress with a white-dressed baby strapped to her back. . . . The yellow melons and the fabulous colors of the chickens and cocks. . . . A golden eagle high over the pass and mountain goats in the foothills.

At the Restaurant Kirghistan—a twelve-year-old beggar boy. A sign around his neck: "Help Me, Comrades, I am deaf and dumb." Everyone giving him a handful of change. He had to wait quite a while at a table where an MVD officer, his girl, and a friend were drinking goblets of Soviet champagne. Girls dancing together. . . . Boys at tables paying them no attention. . . .

How far, how far, this country has to go! I thought of a comparison today. Kazakhstan is like the United States West would have been if there had been a lot more Indians and half of them were in charge of Western things today. Kazakh ways are those of reservation Indians.

Eric was upset at the camera incident. He is cautious and worrisome.

September 21, 1953

We arranged with a young taxi driver named Ostrovsky to pick us up this morning to show us the town. He came out to work on the Trans-Sib Railroad—the second such we have met. Came from Kiev. There he had a French governess. His mother knew many

417

foreigners—French, Italian, and German. He has a brother in Kiev. During the war he served in the North and saw Americans there. He drove an American truck during the building of the Trans-Sib and had a good friend, Mr. Quinn, a dentist. A very good man. Mr. Quinn went to live in Prezhvalsky, and Ostrovsky never saw him again. He learned a little English from Quinn. "No Parking," for instance.

The best building in Frunze is the church. Everyone goes—high army officers, government officials, young and old. There is also a small white mosque.

Ostrovsky wants to cut down some of the trees, cut back the shrubbery, and widen the streets.

"What makes a city?" he asked. "Greenery, asphalt, and lights. We have enough greenery—too much. We need more asphalt and lights."

I want very much to go to Fergana via Osh. Eric is afraid we will get into trouble. If we don't go, I feel I will never forgive myself. Silly. Before yesterday I never heard the name of Osh. But now it is a symbol of what I want to do—break new ground. Look for that illusive Secret.

I wonder about Mr. Quinn. What ever brought an American dentist to this part of the world? Who was Mr. Quinn? Frunze was not even a provincial city them. It was still Pishpek, a dreary frontier garrison. Ostrovsky said Mr. Quinn spoke perfect Russian. His eyes lighted up as he talked about him. Quinn would look in your mouth and say: "Extraction!" He was here for a while and then went on to Prezhvalsky—the real jumping-off place of the world, perched on the edge of the Tan Shan Mountains. Is he still there—a little wizened man in turned sheepskin coat and round fur hat like the Kirghiz? Was he, too, like Bill Shatov, an I.W.W.? A rebel? I can see him putting a sign on his door. "Out to Lunch. Back in an Hour." And that was all. Mr. Quinn vanished. What did he do next?

Tonight the waitresses at the outdoor café clustered around us like butterflies. They made fun of Misha—a member of the "local intelligentsia," star of the local ballet, and his two friends who make fairy gestures. A character from *The Lower Depths* wolfs his plate of borscht—drinks it down. In the park a poster of a clean Red Army lad liberating oppressed peoples. Under the poster a

418

bench and a dead drunk Kirghiz. The chief waitress came here from Leningrad in 1942. She wishes she could go back.

September 22, 1953

The alarm rings on a day which is still dark and cold and sunless. I stumble out and ask the sleeping girl to bring me some boiling water. A long wait. When the girl returns, she has combed her hair, washed her face, put on lipstick, and looks pert and lively.

We take off at 7:45 A.M. A familiar old DC-3 with side benches. We cross the Kirghiz range near Talass and follow the Talass Valley. A clear, sunny day. Rough, jagged mountains stand out sharp in the sunshine.

I have been thinking about the "Catastrophe at Otrar" in 1218 and the consequences which flowed from it. I suppose Genghis Khan was destined to turn West even if the Khorezm satrap had not seized his camel train. But perhaps not. He might have turned to India and expended his forces there. Suppose that had happened. Would the frontier of Asia have stayed east of the Urals? Possibly not. It seems likely that the economic and military structure of the states like Khorezem and the Byzantine Empire and Persia were not sufficiently virile to have long survived. The Mongols conquered the West because they were a hard, tough, brave, mobile people. They had a more powerful offensive weapon than any other people of that day—the horse. They were the thirteenth-century panzer army.

10:00 A.M. We circle Tashkent. I was surprised at the breadth of Tashkent and vastness of the "old city"—that is, the part made up of mud huts. Fully two-thirds of the city is so housed. I was astounded at the wireless mast. It seemed a good five hundred feet high as we circled it.

As we came to town, I recognized nothing but the streetcars until we passed the railroad station. This afternoon we went out past the textile plant named for Stalin which seemed about twice as large as in 1944. Then to the market—stacks of ruby tomatoes, purple eggplant, green lettuce, green peppers, red peppers, paprika, saffron, celery, walnuts, almonds, and peanuts at a ruble a glass. I bought two glasses. Melons, pears, apples, peaches, dried apricots, plums, and yesterday's *Pravda*. All clean and smelling fresh.

419

Back to the hotel and ran into Blum, the Luxembourg minister, and Scheyven, from UNESCO. They are going to Samarkand and Bokhara, too.

This afternoon I tried to find the old man we visited in 1944. I located the approximate block of adobe huts, but the passageway seemed different, and I couldn't spot the wall of his garden in the maze. I did take a picture of a little kid, really as a kind of memento of Dick Lauterbach, because it was when Dick was taking pictures of a kid that the old man invited us into his garden. He gave us tea (or his bashful wife did) and showed us the picture of his son on the wall in a Red Army uniform and talked a bit about his life. "Before the Revolution," he said with a simple dignity I have never forgotten, "I was nothing. Now I am a man." It was the first and only time I ever met one who had experienced the pride and joy of becoming a man.

A funny thing, progress. To me the old city is picturesque and beautiful. But I can understand the old man and his wife thinking of it as old, uncultured, uncivilized, and yearning to exchange their lovely pool and garden for a two-room apartment on the fifth floor of a concrete building.

Tonight the moon is full in Tashkent just as it was when first I came here. Again it has given the alders, the aspens, the willows, and the poplars a silvery sheen. We stood a while beside the great fountain in front of the new opera house and watched the water play with the lights changing in rainbow hues.

You could imagine that this was some modern Registan and this the emir's pleasure fountain and the boys and girls strolling here members of his Golden Court.

And, perhaps, so it is. But who is the emir? The dead Stalin? The not-yet-clear image of the new Malenkov? Or the faceless mass of the Russian people?

I can't get out of my mind the face of the MVD man in the market place. He had no eyebrows, and his was the baldest face I have ever seen. The planes were flat as an egg. His nose ran straight down the center of his face like a child's drawing—no perspective. . . . A dangerous man.

I was thinking tonight. . . . Here is a small village completely out of the way. There are two uniformed militia. And out of nowhere spring two plain-clothes men and a third, their chief. Five MVD men for such a tiny market place. Multiply the villages by the thousand and ten thousand—how many police? This is the real Stalin teaching on the "National Question." It is the MVD whom he fell back on as the simplest and safest way to handle all problems. And here they are still running the Kazakh villages.

Saw some rugs in the Tashkent commission store. Not very good. The best was a big 20 × 10, maybe larger, 5,500 rubles. Smaller rugs for 1,000–1,500. Poor store. But their electric store was better than Moscow's. Big refrigerators for 2,600 rubles. Electric heaters, electric coffeepots and teapots, irons, lamps—a good selection. But no factual books on Uzbekistan in the bookstore.

September 23, 1953

A good breakfast of fried eggs, bread, butter, and tea at the airport and off by DC-3 for Samarkand. Just as simple as that. I am afraid the Golden Road feeling is gone.

Yesterday the taxi driver kept saying that "soon things would be better." It is true up to a point. But it takes longer than the taxi drivers think. By the time one old city is cleared away, you must start rebuilding the new one. Suddenly the cabbie said: "Excuse me for asking, sir, but why does the Communist Party in America work so badly?" Afraid he was hurting my feelings, he hastily added: "You are a Communist, no?"

"No," I said, "I am not a Communist."

It was a good question. One I wish I could have answered for the driver. Of course the reason why the Communists "work badly" in America is that they have no economic basis for their agitation—or very little. You cannot make Communists out of people who have work, are well fed, well housed, comfortable, secure in their lives, and confident of their future. So long as that is true, no people is going to be agitated into changing its way of life. That is as true of Russia as it is of America. Since life in Russia is becoming more comfortable and secure, there is no realism in the silly talk of émigrés and propagandists about an overthrow of the regime. Russia is a tyranny, but successful tyrants do not fall— they flourish.

XXXI

Samarkand–and Beyond

September 23, 1953

Samarkand. . . . At the Pobeda movie theater, across the street from the Registan: *Tarzan in the West.* In the stores Kreml perfume. . . . The newspaper: *Lenin's Path.* . . . The Hotel Registan —modernistic architecture. . . . In the stores posters: "Parents and School Children Buy Your School Books." In the Park of Rest and Culture: "Ballroom Dancing lessons start Sept. 8. Enroll now."

I have been rereading the notes of my 1944 visit to Samarkand. All I can say is that Samarkand is a place you should visit only once. Then it will stay in your memory like a burning jewel. But don't go back. By coming back to Samarkand, I have quenched a flame that burned inside me, almost a *mystique.* In its place is a tourist's day of sights and places and a visit to the local market.

The only moment of feeling was in the Registan—when I found a circular staircase and clambered to the room where the muzzein once chanted to the faithful. Here I could look over the roofs of Samarkand. *Sur les toits de Samarkande!* A quiet, peaceful spot looking down on an interior courtyard where workmen were making brick just as they did in the time of Uleg Bek.

I did enjoy the market. Bargained with a woman for a *tybeteika.** I got three for forty-five rubles, which was too much. Later I bought a little girl's hat from a Russian girl who asked ten and, when I refused, took five rubles. I was embarrassed.

* A kind of skullcap commonly worn in Central Asia.

422

September 24

Worked late on a story and went to bed ill at ease and disappointed. Up at dawn, about 5:30, and went into the city. It seemed to me that there should be camel trains arriving at the bazaar. I walked a bit. No camels. No caravans. Women were dripping water from the ditches and spattering it over the sidewalk and street. I hopped a bus for the Registan. Fare forty kopecks. Many veiled women, although our Uzbek driver said his wife had thrown hers away.

Bokhara. . . . A short flight. I am lying in the hotel thinking about the ancient city. Outside, the murmur of people softly talking and in the distance the beating of a drum. The radio plays oriental music.

It feels like the Orient. It is the Orient. It is the Soviet Union, too. There is a Palace of Culture in the center of the city with posters about the five-year plan. And they have broken-up trading at the Pavilion of Precious Stones, the Pavilion of Jewelry, the one for velvet and silks, and all the rest. The market is a collective one. Behind the mud walls I don't think much has changed.

For instance, the "boss of the hotel" is a Uzbek and the local MVD bigwig. He told about his marriage. He never saw his bride before the wedding. Because he was poor, they tried to marry him to an old hag. His wife was a virgin. It is Uzbek custom for women to shave all over—and for men, too, I think. They sleep together twice a week. The man stays inside after intercourse. But things are different now, he said. He can sleep with his wife whenever he wants to. Before, his wife was practically in *purdah*. Now she has given up the *paranja*. But he worries about his daughter, because if she isn't a virgin when she marries, it will be a terrible scandal. You can touch a girl to the waist—not below. That is strictly forbidden. If a girl marries and she isn't a virgin, she is cast out of house and home. It is a terrible disgrace for the parents.

But now young people see each other before marriage. They go to movies. They go walking. They go to dances. Everything is changing.

So he said. But change is slow in Bokhara. I saw Lenin's picture along with Stalin's. Not part of the new image—just the old. Lenin was the great leader, and it looked as though they never quite got around to substituting Stalin as a symbol. No pictures of Malenkov or the new men.

This afternoon we went walking with the Boss. He said he would show us an old Jewish synagogue. We got to the Street of Jews and found a bright-eyed Russian boy who showed me the gate of a caravansary which he said had been very beautiful but it was too narrow and was knocked down by a truck. He said there was a very interesting *madrasah* at the end of the street.

The synagogue presents a black wall to the outside. Within, there is an almost barren room, to the right a room with a center altar covered with a reddish altar cloth, and little more. I was so preoccupied taking pictures, I noticed little more. My camera turned out to be the wrong size for the Russian film I bought in Samarkand. I was in despair until I realized I might buy a Russian camera. I went to the Univermag and bought a Lubitel for sixty-three rubles. I hope I have luck with it.

Our host took us to a shoeshine stand across the street from the hotel. This collected a great crowd, including a thin, studious man with a bundle of blue books under his arm. Finally, he approached me and asked: "Do you speak English?" I said yes. He was pathetically glad and said, "I am so happy to meet someone who talks English. I teach English at the school." There is no one else in Bokhara to talk English with. He learned English at the institute in Tashkent. He said he understood me perfectly. He often listens to the radio.

At this point our host came up and said, "What school are you from? The Red October?" Yes, the man said. "What is your name?" By this time the teacher was edging out of the crowd. "Shepnik," he said. "I will say goodbye. I must go now," he said, with alarm in his face. As I watched, two men in blue suits came up to him. They looked more like friends of our host than of his.

September 25, 1953

My impressions of Bokhara are almost as much of a jumble as the city itself. In the first place, I am never comfortable in a place where the chief of police is assigned as my host. In the market Friday morning I saw a dozen women get up from the pavement and run like gazelles when a militiaman wandered in after us, attracted by curiosity.

Just after lunch we went to the pitiful little Univermag to buy film for Scheyven. When we were coming out, a little, thin-faced militiaman stopped Scheyven and wanted to see his permission to photograph. He was a tough, determined little bastard and was quickly joined by a companion. They insisted that we go to their commandant. I refused after much argument. They kept saying, "You're not a child. You know you must come." I said, "How can you, a Soviet militiaman, behave so rudely?"

A great crowd assembled. Twice the militiamen barred our way, but finally we strode majestically back to the hotel, with the crowd trailing us and the militiamen at our heels sputtering and protesting.

At the hotel our host quickly told off the militia. They apologized profusely, and there was much shaking of hands. This incident stirred curiosity in the bazaar. People clustered around us whenever we appeared.

Bokhara did not impress me as a very happy town. The Russians despise being there. You can see hatred in the eyes of the natives. It looks to me as though plenty of harshness and cruelty has been employed to break the necks (perhaps, literally) of the fanatic and fierce Moslems. I think there was good reason to keep Bokhara closed to foreigners, because I think it was fairly explosive for years. It is interesting that they should have dumped so many Poles into the city in 1940. And there were many of them, as our host explained. All now gone, of course. Contrary to what I had heard when we were in Samarkand in 1944, no Germans were sent there. But Germans were used in Tashkent for construction after the war—particularly on the Navoi Opera House.

Nowhere did I see forced labor, and it is hard to imagine present-day conditions as hard as those of the emirate. A great and fairly successful effort has been made to break the power of the mullahs. Yet, the famous madrasah adjacent to the great minaret of Bokhara is being used for its original purpose—the training of Moslem priests. Essentially, the Russians are trying to utilize the Moslems as they do the Orthodox—another string to their bow.

There is still pride in Bokhara for their role as the spiritual center of the Moslem world. Our host was quick to state that Bokhara is still a center of Moslem learning and faith.

About the Bokhara Jews my impressions are less specific and less valuable. The old Street of Jews is in the center of town. It is called "Central Avenue." It is about bullock-cart width and lined with blind mud walls and ancient carved wooden doors of *kara-gach** with tiny passageways leading God knows where.

How firm a hold has ancient Bokhara faith on the younger generation? And how has the Jewish colony survived under Soviet rule? For a thousand years the Jews have lived here unobtrusively. They still live unobtrusively. You see only a few individuals in the Street of Jews—sometimes an almond-eyed, olive-skinned, black-haired little boy or a graceful Jewish maiden in her beautiful gown of rose and jade silk, her dark eyes flashing like a couplet from the Song of Solomon.

But the trade and commerce by which the Bokhara Jews supported themselves are gone. Where there was once trade in pearls from the Persian Gulf, rubies from India, and emeralds from Siberia, and where once furs of Russia and silks of China were sold—now there are only dealers in melons and venders of cheap cigarettes.

Another force is working against old Bokhara. This is government development of other cities. Not much money is spent on Bokhara; the city is dying on the vine.

Still, not many hearts can quietly beat at the sight of the Minaret of Death, rearing against the pale turquoise night, sprinkled with stars sparkling with the same brilliance as when Uleg Bek's astronomers plotted their course. In the pale moonlight the minaret is pure Arabic poetry come to life. At night Bokhara is a quiet city but for the barking of fierce dogs and the resonance of the gongs that sound the hours to midnight. After midnight all is quiet. The radio from Moscow is turned off. The raucous sound of the summer movie is stilled. In the distance is an occasional wail of an Arabic song. But close at hand the city is so quiet you can hear the soft shuffle of slippered feet in the dust and the gentle coughing of hidden sleepers behind pillars and latticed windows.

The aroma of night-blooming vines wafts through the narrow streets to mingle with the stench of horse and donkey droppings and those of humans as well. Bokhara sleeps a gentle sleep, but a bit fitful. In the Pavilion of Jewels under the naked glare of an electric bulb stands a blue-and-red-capped Soviet militiaman who raises his hand in salute as we walk through the small pool of light.

* A variety of elm often used as timber in Central Asia.

426

Back in the hotel the toilet in the back courtyard can be smelled half a block away, even though it is swished out a couple of times a day by a dirty old Arab. A squatting toilet, of course.

Somehow you feel that Bokhara died forty years ago. But no one has yet pronounced the obsequies.

September 26, 1953

We are flying to Stalinabad after a great send-off at the hotel this morning. There must have been a hundred people, mostly kids but some adults as well, including a camera fan with a Leica.

We have been flying over some of the grimmest saw-toothed mountains I ever saw—mountains, desert, and irrigated areas.

I worked until 1:30 A.M. getting my dispatches ready to go back to Moscow with Blum and Scheyven. I am tired and irritated by my company. My energy and enthusiasm are low. I am worried about my people. I would go back to Moscow now if I could. But the schedule has to be carried out, and I will spend a few more days seeing Stalinabad and Fergana.

September 27

All the way to Stalinabad I kept dreaming—suppose at Stalinabad we found a wonderful, clean, comfortable hotel with good service, hot water, no flies, no dirt, no smells. When we landed at a fine clean airport and climbed into a bus that ran through neat, tree-lined streets, my hopes rose. We arrived at a fine new hotel, were shown a suite of two large, clean rooms, a big bathroom and our own toilet, hot running water, neat nickel beds covered with white natural silk covers, white natural silk curtains, red and blue rugs—all spotlessly clean.

"I'll bet," I said to myself, "this is where they have settled the Germans and the Balts."

It was a good hunch.

Last night Comrade Tupilov, chief of the culture department of the local Soviet, showed us the city sights. He is a big hack-faced man, heavy-boned and heavy-minded, who delighted in quoting great hunks of the Short Course of the Party and Comrade Gafurov's History of the Tadzhik People. I was deathly tired, but he walked my legs off. Finally we reached his destination—the Central Park of Rest and Culture named for Lenin. He said the central square was named for the 25th anniversary of the founding of Tadzhikstan, but the hotel manager called it Moscow Square.

When I told him Stalinabad had just as fine buildings as Moscow, he said: "Naturally. Moscow is big, but we are a little Moscow." The park had big picture layouts of the government (Stalin is still very prominent). But our friend quoted Malenkov about the necessity of improving things for the consumer. The talk turned to the press, and I explained to him who we were exactly, which I don't think he had fully comprehended up to that point. This brought no noticeable chill in the air, but this morning he called to say he was ill and canceled a date to show us the rest of the city.

I awakened much refreshed after a hot bath and good night's sleep in a clean soft bed. We had breakfast in a nice dining room, surprising our waitress jumping up and down in front of the hall mirror. She ran like a fawn all the way to the kitchen. The restaurant manager insisted on showing us the local market. It was big and clean and filled with fresh-washed, lovely smelling tomatoes, grapes in wonderful straw panniers, coal-purple eggplant, greens of every kind, pomegranates still a little green, etc.

Back at the hotel I got a taxi driven by a nice-looking blond youngster who asked what nationality I was—Polish? American, I said. He nearly fell out of his cab. "Not really." Yes, I told him. "I'm German," he said. "From the Volga?" I asked. "No, Zhitomir."

"You've lived here long?" I asked. "Just since the war." He whipped out his passport. It showed he was born in 1931 at Zhitomir. It bore the designation "German" as his nationality. His parents were descendants of the colonists whom Catherine brought to Russia. His father was a *tokar,* a lathe operator. When the war came on, it was first decided to send them to Siberia. But they managed to get that changed and came to Central Asia, to Stalinabad. "We are *spetz,*" he explained, as though everyone knew that spetz meant a person whose passport was stamped for special residence and who is only permitted to live in a specific locality.

"When we Germans first came here," he said, "there was nothing here. There was the hotel and the opera house. Nothing else. Everything else we Germans built." He said there were not only many Germans in Stalinabad but Tatars, Estonians, Letts, and Bulgars. "Nearly everyone here is spetz," he said. "But most are

428

German. We built the government building and the other big buildings for the ministries and the housing. We widened the main street and put asphalt on it. We are turning it into a modern town."

"Life is good in Stalinabad?" I asked.

"Life is good in Stalinabad . . . sure," he said, spitting out the words. "There is a whole quarter of the city where nothing but Germans live. Just beyond the botanical gardens."

He showed us the gardens—a lovely wood with no signs, no placards, no loud-speakers. "In the summer the park is full of people," he said. "We Germans all go there." He said he never went to the central park.

"Isn't this a healthy town?" I asked.

"What do you mean?" he asked. He said he had been in the hospital three times with malaria. He took us to see how "we Germans" live. He showed us the house where he, his father and mother, his older brother and brother's wife and child, and two other members of the family live. It was a collection of three small mud-and-wattle huts.

"Here we live just like the Tadzhiks," he said bitterly. "We built good buildings for them, but this is all they will give us to live in."

But the Germans in Stalinabad, he said, are much better off than others on the collectives. He said the Germans had been settled as far east as Tadzhikabad. "That is where it is really bad," he said. "Old people can't stand it. They just die." His family, like all the German families, speak nothing but German at home. They have no German books, and nothing to read in German can be obtained.*

The Germans here are clearly an undigestible mass. For 150–170 years they have kept their German ways, their German nationality.

A thousand questions come to mind after talking with that youngster. How many other cities in Asia and Siberia are populated by spetz? And how many collective farms are manned by uprooted people? The frequency with which one meets such people convinces me that the numbers are great. It is an appalling thought and, as in the case of the young composer and his wife whom we met in 1944 when they were exiled from Leningrad to

* In 1957 publication of German-language newspapers was resumed.

Tashkent, it is so much more impressive when you meet the individual than when you hear statistics about twenty-five million slave laborers.

Slave labor exists in this country, true. But that is not the point. The point is the amount of force used against all individuals and the results it produces. Is there no other way? Surely, there are other ways. Capitalism has tried a good many of them.

Another thing: The farther from the Center the more crude and simplified methods become. I saw yesterday a public example of brutality by a Soviet militiaman. This was on the main street. A Tadzhik was riding a bike at a rapid clip, and the traffic cop whistled to him to stop. He didn't stop. Another militiaman reached out a hand, grabbed the handlebars, deliberately spilling the Tadzhik and his bike to the pavement. When the bruised and stunned Tadzhik got up, the militiaman put his hands on his hips and said: *"Khorosho, khorosho*—very good, very good—and how do you like that?"

People on the street walked along. Russians love street incidents, but this was probably too common to attract attention. In the central park I noticed a decided segregation—voluntary. The Tadzhiks kept to themselves in one part of the park and the Russians in another. At the opera there was only one Tadzhik in the orchestra and possibly one or two dancers. The audience was 95 per cent Russian and German, 5 per cent Tadzhik. A couple of floozies sat behind Eric and me. They did their best to pick us up, but we did not encourage them and they wandered off.

September 28, 1953

We are flying from Stalinabad to Tashkent, and I have been reading Chekhov. Once again I am struck by Vershinin's insistence upon what the world will be like two or three hundred years from now. That is the refrain of this country. Come back five years from now—twenty years from now—you won't recognize it. In a way that is true. The country is building up. But not as fast as they think. Granted that Stalinabad is postwar development. But Tashkent, Samarkand, and Alma Ata are not, and I have no difficulty in recognizing them from my memories of 1944. The Russians are always filled with excuses. Why don't they stop excusing themselves? I think all peoples of the Soviet now have enough to eat. Most places have fair health and sanitation. But living conditions are fearsome even by European peasant standards. It does not have to be like this. You set the Volga Germans down in the filth and disease, and they create a modern clean city. You give the Russians Samarkand or Bokhara, and in fifty years they only scratch the surface.

In the luncheon room at Samarkand airport just now, we saw three senior pilots who had been with us when we did Tamerlane's tomb. *"Barin,"* said a waitress, "how did you like Samarkand?" I had never heard *barin* (lord) used in this Russia except by old people to foreigners. "Just like the kolkhoz," said the pilot in bored fashion. His fellow pilots agreed.

There is a special quality about reporting in Russia which comes very close to what is expressed in Eric's favorite line, "the lust of knowing what should not be known." This is what makes it exciting for a correspondent. So much which you can know in any country just for the asking is to be learned here only by observation, deduction, induction, projection—utilization of all the senses of sight and sound and even of smell.

This is the eleventh day we have been traveling. I am tired and worried. Three more days before we can get back to Moscow. The trouble is traveling with someone else. Eric and I are opposites. I want to be up and about early, and he dawdles until I am driven mad.

6:00 P.M. Tashkent. I decided to bring the trip to a quick end. We bought tickets to go to Fergana at 8:00 A.M., back at 4:00 P.M., and leave for Moscow tomorrow evening.

Scheyven was delighted with his trip. Said he would now be able to answer Arutinyan and the other Russians who attacked Belgian policy in the Congo. He thinks the natives there are treated better than the natives at Bokhara. Perhaps he exaggerates a bit, but I must admit that my assessment of Soviet policy in Asia has dropped from 1944 to 1953.

September 29

At the airport in the "government and generals waiting room" there is a freshly painted (hardly dry) red picture frame with a painting of Khrushchev. I touched it to see if the paint was still wet. In the Bokhara bookshop there weren't even any pictures of Malenkov for sale. But in Stalinabad they had pictures of all the

431

new leaders. Of course, that is a "little Moscow," as our Cultural friend said.

"Now we no longer work at night," he said. "This is the new Soviet law."

"Yes," I said, looking at the blazing lights in the government office building. The time was 9:00 P.M.

The Cultural man had lived in Stalinabad for sixteen years, but he did not know the Tadzhik language!

Thinking of the stupidity of this Communist, I was reminded of the people who sometimes have called me a Communist or pro-Russian. Such people may be ignorant or stupid, but often they are vicious. They are the great opponents of "objective" reporting, which they say is impossible in Russia's case. In other words, do not tell the truth. Distort and lie. The same psychology lies behind the whole current approach to Russia. Answer Russian propaganda with American propaganda, Russian lies with American lies.

The fact is that today as always the way to meet propaganda is with truth.

When Mr. Sulzberger sent me to Moscow, he said: "We don't give our correspondents any instructions. If we didn't trust you, we would not send you to Moscow. Just tell the truth—that is the only instruction I have for you."

And that is what I have done. I have not been able to tell the whole truth. Often I have not known the whole truth. Sometimes I have known it, but the censorship prevented my telling it. Sometimes, because of that, my dispatches have been inadvertently misleading.

And I have made mistakes in interpretation—but who has not?

This is written as I am flying to Fergana, southeast over semi-mountainous country. To return to what I have been writing about—what is the purpose of this trip through Central Asia? Certainly not just to gratify curiosity or to test reporting ability. It is justified only on the broad ground that the more we know and understand about Russia, the better off we are.

It is easy for Americans to see how dangerously Russia deludes herself with pictures of our jobless, our bread lines, and such nonsense. It is not always so easy for Americans to see that frequently we are guilty of the same kind of mistake.

Well . . . now we have seen Fergana, the fertile, the wondrous,

432

and are on our way back and glad of it. Fergana is supposed to be another Vale of Kashmir, lush and beautiful, a land of milk and honey, one of the most beautiful places in the world. Perhaps that is true for other parts of the valley, but not for the Fergana we saw. We flew over barren desert most of the way. The city is a desolate provincial town not much changed since the Revolution or since 1890, as far as that goes. There is no question that Skobelev* would still recognize his town. There are a few fly-bitten droshkies, three taxis, and a couple of autobuses. The market was a shock—the poorest we have seen.

At twelve o'clock we went to the only restaurant in town. The doorman stopped us and said nothing was ready to eat. "The restaurant opens at eleven," he said, "but nothing is ready yet."

We went to a small open-air café beside the muddy river and ordered goulash and a bottle of lemonade. In a minute a character in canvas clothes, very dirty, entered and begged a few kopecks from a neighboring table. We gave him fifty kopecks. A minute later a woman dressed in rags and using a shepherd's crook came in. I gave her a ruble. Two small emaciated girls, one in a ragged pink dress, one in a sackcloth smock, came in. They were about ten years old. We gave them twenty kopecks each.

We walked about town a bit. There was a blind woman begging at the market gate and another on the steps of an open-air sweatshop—a sewing artel set up under a low wooden roof with perhaps twenty women at sewing machines. If there is any resemblance between Fergana and paradise, I did not notice it.

Later. . . . I have been shopping again in Tashkent for a rug. I found a Bokhara about the size and design of one I have for 1,300 rubles, or $160. About twice what I paid for mine at the Fur Auction in Leningrad.

On the second floor of the Main Department Store, I ran into one of the most howling, scratching riots I have ever seen. Several hundred women buying silk yard goods. There was one slow-moving man to wait on the women, and twenty-five cops to keep order.

I noticed in the market at Fergana today wheat flour on sale by the peasants—the first I have seen on this trip. But I have seen in Alma Ata, Frunze, Samarkand, and Bokhara notices saying

---

* General Mikhail D. Skobelev, first Russian governor of Fergana.

that first and second grades of wheat flour are being sold at regular hours.

Yesterday, coming into Tashkent, I had a curious experience. There was a big, flabby-faced man in the waiting room. He looked familiar and got up quickly and said, "Pardon me, but haven't we met in the Metropole Hotel?" Well, we had. About four years ago this man had a room next to Barry Reed of the embassy and picked an acquaintance with Barry. We had breakfast together once. I regarded the man with great suspicion, and when he spoke to me again yesterday I pretended I did not know him. I believe, thinking about it, that the whole thing was quite innocent. Just a coincidence.

I am certain there was no surveillance of us in Alma Ata, Frunze, or Tashkent. I saw no sign of it in Samarkand. But, of course, in Bokhara we were under surveillance all the time. There is no doubt that there are many curious characters to be met out in this part of the country. So many people who have been forced out of Moscow. I noticed today there seemed to be a lot of Jewish-looking people in Tashkent. I noticed the same thing in Samarkand. We were mistaken for "Greeks" in Stalinabad—possibly some of those exiled from the Black Sea. When we were in Tashkent in 1944, we met Nona, the beautiful "house mother" for the American fliers who were interned there. She was an English teacher at the institute and had fallen in love with two of the Americans. At least one of them had asked her to marry him, or so she thought. When we saw her, she was hoping and hoping she would be allowed to go back to Moscow. I thought of Chekhov's Three Sisters. Like them, I fear she never got to Moscow.

September 30—6:00 a.m.

For the last hour we have been flying up through a very heavy overcast after a breakfast stop at Aktybinsk. Next stop: Moscow at 11:00 A.M.

There was a light drizzle when we stopped at Aktybinsk airport, although it was still warm and much the same flowers were blooming as at Uralsk and Karaganda. We have left Kazakhstan now and are back in Russia.

This morning, as we waited to take off, a choleric little air force general came to the ticket window and demanded a ticket. The girl said the plane was full. He demanded that a passenger be removed to make room for him. The girl called in the latest passenger and asked if he would give up his seat. The passenger refused. The general stalked off to look for the administrator. Pretty soon he came back after we were all aboard the plane and disappeared into the forward compartment. A little while later, he emerged and sat down. Apparently the pilot gave him permission to fly even though the plane had its permitted weight load.

While generals are regarded with greater awe in Russia than even in Mexico, I have never seen one pull his rank in this way before.

We have not seen many military on this trip except MVD and green-capped border guards, particularly at Stalinabad.

XXXII

A Last Look at Russia

October 4, 1953

A wild rush to get everything in order to leave. I am sailing from France on the "Queen Mary" on the 15th and will be in New York on the 20th and in Minneapolis a few days hence. I am leaving here on the 8th.

October 6

A final souvenir of Russia. We were called to the Foreign Office for the first time by the new press chief, Leonid Ilyichev. He informed us that henceforth American correspondents will be subject to the Soviet income tax and will pay 10 to 13 per cent on their earnings above 600 rubles ($150). It is in retaliation for our applying income tax to Tass correspondents in the United States. A Foreign Office clerk passed out the new tax forms to us. They are the ones peasants use to fill in their profits from the sale of garden produce.

October 18—Aboard the "Queen Mary"

Some notes on the current situation in Russia:

I

Russian policy since the death of Stalin has been dominated by a single fact, the struggle for the succession to his power. Thus, at present, domestic, internal, and personal Russian political necessities are more and more often providing the clue to foreign policy.

436

It is by no means certain who will succeed Stalin; nor is the nature of the succession state yet crystallized.

The struggle for the succession is still in progress and may continue for an indefinite period. Malenkov has yet to prove that he can last the limit. Khrushchev is moving up.

Nominally, the struggle for power is going forward within the framework of the Communist Party but, in actuality, the participants represent well-defined power groupings, i.e., the army, the police, the Party apparatus, etc.

One fact should always be kept in sight: for many centuries Russian leadership has been episodic; aggressive, powerful personalities like Ivan, Peter, Catherine, and Alexander I have been followed by mediocrity and sloth.

It is too early to say that post-Stalin history will follow the traditional pattern, but some signs of this tendency may be seen.

II

With the death of Stalin the power which he had concentrated in his own person quickly reverted to the basic elements of which it was comprised: Party apparatus, police, army.

The government of last March was a coalition of the three power factors: Party (Malenkov), police (Beriya), and army (Zhukov, *et al.*) Like most Russian coalitions, it was most unstable and was held together, even temporarily, only by the crisis of Stalin's death (and, possibly, by the still unknown events immediately preceding Stalin's demise).

Because of its instability and inherent contradictions, the coalition was markedly weaker than Stalin's "monolithic state" and was well aware of this fact.

Maneuvering within the coalition began the day of Stalin's funeral—if not before. When Beriya spoke at the time of Stalin's death, he sought to establish his primacy among The Three by commending Malenkov to the public as a "talented pupil" of Lenin and, subtly, sought to suggest that he spoke for the army as well as for the police.

III

Beriya did, in fact, have the real power during the days of Stalin's death and funeral, since it was Beriya's special police troops who actually held Moscow in a state of siege.

Beriya was too big for the coalition. The demonstration of

power which he gave at the time of Stalin's death made a secret alliance of Party and army against him inevitable.

Even yet, the extent of Beriya's "empire within an empire" is hardly understood. His power nexus comprised:

All ordinary police, fire, public service, and public security forces in Russia.

The railroad police and all other specialized industrial police forces.

The special corps of frontier troops and special frontier air defense network.

The regular MVD and MGB (police) army.

The secret police with agents in every Russian institution from the Kremlin secretariat down to co-operative shoe-repair shops. Every Party unit and every army unit included Beriya's agents, reporting to his apparatus.

Russia's largest labor force—uncounted millions of political prisoners, ordinary criminals, forced residents, resettled peoples, and unreleased prisoners of war.

Control over every phase of atomic development, nuclear research, and manufacture.

Control of many other higher phases of scientific research in "sensitive fields."

General direction and control of Siberia, the Far North, the Maritime Provinces and Birobijan, Central Asia, all border areas, and all "special regions," such as the Baltic states and the western Ukraine.

Control of the Caucasus through party bosses personally loyal to him in Georgia, Armenia, and Azerbaijan.

General security and policy responsibility relative to satellite states, East Germany, and bordering states such as Turkey, Afganistan, Iran, etc.

Administration and operation of Russia's largest construction apparatus, building scores of large-scale projects such as Volga-Don Canal, Pechora railroad, mines, highways, dams, etc., all over the country.

Direction and control of all Soviet espionage and counter-espionage both inside and outside Russia.

The right of veto over all Soviet domestic and foreign policy proposals on security grounds.

438

Just as no single individual has inherited Stalin's powers, so no one man has succeeded to Beriya's treasure house of functions.

IV

There has been a general curtailment of police authority and functions with a view to reducing police prestige and its effectiveness as an independent source of power. Probably this was the price the army demanded for support of Malenkov in dealing with Beriya.

Elimination of the police as a first-class military organization and transfer of most of its military and paramilitary functions to the army have increased the authority and prestige of the army, *which has now become the sole military basis of the state.*

There has been a parallel strengthening of the Party apparatus, which has regained direct control over large territorial areas (Siberia, Central Asia, etc.) and other spheres of normal civil responsibility which Beriya had seized.

V

Army authority appears to be concentrated in the hands of a small group of leading commanders of World War II—Zhukov, Vasilevsky, Konev, and Sokolevsky. This might be called the "Berlin group," since it was this group of commanders which was responsible for the final assault on Germany.

The army grouping appears to be relatively stable; the first photographs published at the time of Stalin's death showed Party leaders grouped on one side of Stalin's bier and Zhukov, Vasilevsky, and Konev on the other side.

The men of the "Berlin group" are more accurately described as professional army officers, men of the officers corps, than as political or Party figures. Several of them, such as Zhukov and Sokolovsky, have had fairly extensive contacts with the West, particularly with Western military figures.

There is evidence that these Western contacts have left a certain mark on these military men.

Parallel to the rise of the "Berlin group," there are indications that the influence of Marshal Bulganin, former Moscow-Party bank executive and Party leader for the army, is waning in the military sphere.

VI

While it is outwardly stable, the present two-power coalition of army and Party is not likely to prove much more resistant to internal stress than the three-power coalition which preceded it.

The first important crisis may arise over the question of what is to be done with Beriya, with Malenkov favoring a lighter policy in dealing with the police (looking to the rebuilding of the police apparatus as a counterweight to the army) and the army demanding stronger measures.*

The two-power coalition contains the same explosive ingredients which destroyed the three-power coalition. The army has the paramount military force which is capable, in the final accounting, of settling any dispute by force. The Party, however, is in actual day-to-day control of the government. The Party cannot permit this situation to continue indefinitely unless it wishes to become the mere creature of the army.

Inevitably, *the Party will seek by means of intrigue to split and divide the army.* It may be presumed that this process is already under way. However, the Party is subject to the same kind of splitting process.

It cannot yet be determined conclusively whether the rise of Khrushchev as a Party boss is occurring because he is Malenkov's chief lieutenant or because he is Malenkov's most powerful challenger for Party leadership. Possibly, neither Khrushchev nor Malenkov yet knows precisely which way the cards will be played.†

Molotov held (and holds) a special role in the coalition. He represents no power group himself but appears to have been trusted by all to carry out the delicate nonpartisan task of holding the front, internationally, while the struggle for succession goes on at home.

Molotov's technique, so far, has been in the nature of a carefully calculated withdrawal from overexposed positions (Korea)

---

* At the November 7, 1953, reception Marshal Zhukov publicly taunted the Party leaders in a toast to "justice," which was interpreted as a demand for action against Beriya. A few weeks later Beriya was executed.

† Khrushchev first split the Party to win out over Malenkov with army support. Malenkov was compelled to step down as premier in February, 1955. Khrushchev utilized the support of Marshal Zhukov to win out over a combination of Malenkov, Molotov, Kaganovich, and others in June, 1957. In October, 1957, he was able to oust Marshal Zhukov, having split the army with the aid of Marshal Konev and others.

in order to bring Russian foreign commitments more closely into line with the relative weakness of Russian power, which may now be calculated by the formula "X minus Stalin" instead of "X plus Stalin."

This means, in fact, that Russian foreign policy is now dominated by *a realization of weakness* instead of (as in Stalin's time) a presumption of strength.

Translated into specific terms, this means: abandonment of any real hope or effort (although the propaganda may go on) of winning over or "neutralizing" Germany and reliance on a purely military position in East Germany and the satellites—a defense in depth; efforts to reduce military commitments at the periphery, i.e., Korea, and possibly, Indochina (which is closely linked to the next factor); a determined effort to re-establish the historical European balance of power—a Franco-Russian alliance vis-à-vis a rearmed Germany (which offers the dual advantage of recognizing the actual bankruptcy of Russian policy in Germany and splitting the European coalition of anti-Communist forces).

Regardless of propaganda gestures, the above bases will undoubtedly lie at the core of the Russian position in any negotiation with the West. It should be remembered that any victory for Molotov in such negotiations will play a double role, since it is likely to affect positively the relative balance of Party and army forces in Moscow. Molotov may well be more interested at this time in affecting that balance than in achieving anything else.

Should Malenkov be displaced by the army, Molotov is a very likely candidate to succeed to the premiership.

Regardless of who wins the struggle for the succession, Russia is weaker internationally during the progress of this struggle than she will be when one power group or the other achieves supreme control.

Index

Bogdanov, Nikolai K., 283
Bohlen, Charles E., 327, 375, 379, 383
Bohr, Niels, 229
Bokhara, 423, 424–25, 426–27
Bolshevik, 221, 222, 286, 308, 309, 310
Boris Godunov (Moussorgsky), 111
Borodin, Mikhail, 4, 15, 24, 406
Bowles, Chester B., 332
Brassard, Rev. Louis, 33 n.
Braun, Father Leopold, 33 n.
Bravo, Louis, 324, 335
Brest, 144, 145
Britansky Soyusnik, 32 n.
Bronze Horseman, The (Pushkin), 41, 43, 80
Bucar, Annabelle, 18
Budenny, Semyon M., 275, 276, 353
Bulganin, Nikolai, 20, 21, 43, 91, 117, 226, 248, 261, 266, 286, 296, 297, 299, 300, 317, 336, 343, 347, 352, 379, 385, 386, 439
Bundock, George, 303–4, 366, 379
Bunin, Ivan, 329–30, 355
Burlachenko, Y., 13
Burma, 66
Byelorussia, 381, 383, 386

Carinthia, 40
Carpathian Ukraine, 38
Catledge, Turner, 379
Caucasus, 5, 38
Central Asia, 5, 56
Central China News Agency, 62
Champanois, Jean, 34
Charkviani, Kandid N., 258
Chekhov, Anton, 291
Chernyshev, V. V., 284
Cherry Orchard, The (Chekhov), 397
Chesnokov, D. I., 288, 304, 358, 377
Chiang Kai-shek, 3, 30–31
China: Communist, 6, 24, 27, 28, 31 n., 66, 69, 70–71, 81, 90, 95, 100, 109, 132, 139; Nationalist, 51, 62, 66
Chinese Communists, 3, 30, 34, 37, 62
Chinese Nationalists, 30–31
Chinese-Soviet relations; *see* Soviet-Chinese relations
Chkhubianishvili, Z. N., 258
Chou En-lai, 70, 105, 106, 109, 153, 266, 267, 281, 290, 347, 348, 351, 352, 359, 364, 365
Chuikov, V. I., 395
Chukovsky, Korei, 72

Church of St. Louis, 33 n., 44
Churchill, Wiston S., 232, 331, 381, 382
Coexistence, 5, 113
"Collegiality," 381, 383, 386, 388
Cominform, 21
Coronet, 40
"Cosmopolitanism," 12, 15, 22–23, 29, 45
Council of Economic Mutual Aid, 58
Council of Ministers, 10, 27–28, 34, 151, 275, 391
"Cult of Personality," 383, 386, 389–90, 403
Cummings, E. E., 14
Czechoslovakia, 3

Daily Worker (London), 35 n.
Davis, Richard, 25
Dead Souls (Gogol), 25
Decembrists, The (opera), 385, 399
Dekanozov, Vladimir G., 377, 391, 392
Deutscher, Isaac, 361
Diaries (Dostoevski), 2
Dimitrov, Georgi, 42, 43, 60
Di Stefano, 270, 272, 273
"Doctor's plot," 266, 281 n., 312, 313, 314, 326, 328, 335, 336, 347, 352, 362, 365–66, 371–74, 377, 381, 384, 406
Dolmatovsky, Evgeni, 47
Dostoevski, Fëdor M., 2, 355
Dve Verontzov (Two Gentlemen of Verona), 330

Early Days (Fedin), 25
Easter celebration; *see* Russian Easter
Economic Problems of Socialism in the U.S.S.R., 382
Eddington, Arthur S., 45
Ehrenburg, Ilya, 33 n., 314, 326
Einstein, Albert, 229, 259
Eisenhower, Dwight D., 272, 309, 331, 333, 350, 370, 375, 378
Eliot, T. S., 14
Emelyanov, Stepan, 401
Estonia, 381, 383
Evening Moscow, 13, 24

Fall of Berlin, The (film), 111
Fedin, Konstantin, 25
Fedoseev, P., 308–9, 310, 322, 385
Fergana, 432–33
Forced labor, 425, 430
Ford Foundation, 303

Formalism, 45
Formosa, 98
Fountain of Bakchisari, The (ballet), 87
Frantzev, U. P., 71, 85, 150
Freedman, Emanuel R., 16
Friends and Enemies of America (film, *Let Freedom Ring*), 330
From the Depths of My Heart (opera), 248
Fruits of Enlightenment (Tolstoi), 2, 262
Frunze, 415, 417, 418

Galitzky, Ivan, 328
Gao Gan; *see* Kao Kang
Gasgoigne, Alvary D. F., 222, 351, 365, 379
Geis, Bernard, 40
Genetics, 47
Georgia (Soviet), 257, 377, 378, 380–81, 384, 390, 392, 406
German question, 36, 37, 40, 246, 250, 265, 270, 271, 272–73, 382, 401, 441
Germans in U.S.S.R., 427, 428–29
Germany, 28
Gide, André, 14
Gilmore, Eddy, 33, 34, 38, 40, 84, 93, 237, 383, 394
Giselle (ballet), 129
Gladkov, I. A., 312
Glavlit; *see* Soviet censorship
Glinka, Mikhail, 15
Gogol, Nikolai, 247–48
Gogua, V. B., 258
Gorki, Maxim, 248
Gorki Literary Institute, 12
Govorov, Leonid A., 275
Gray-haired Maiden, The (play), 330
Grechko, Andrei A., 395
Greece, 37
Green Street (Surov), 28
Griffith, D. W., 15
Gromyko, Andrei, 85, 213, 235
Grossman, Vassily, 326, 327
Grotewohl, Otto, 273
Guild Reporter, 223
Gusev, F. T., 235

Heisenberg, Werner, 229
Hellman, Lillian, 72
Hermitage collections, 77–78
Hill, George, 74

History of Russia (Pares), 387
Hoover, Herbert, 242
House on the Lane, The (play), 31
Hugo, Victor, 249
Hungary, 3
Hydrogen bomb, 398, 402; *see also* Soviet nuclear physics

Idiot, The (Dostoevski), 25
Ignatiev, S. D., 281, 284 n., 301–2, 325, 331, 352, 353, 363, 367, 368, 372, 374, 384
Ignatov, N. G., 378
Il Tempo (Milan), 63
Ilyichev, L. F., 305, 307, 436
India, 106
Indonesia, 66
Inner Mongolia, 105
Inspector-General, The (Gogol), 111
International Economic Conference, 243, 249, 251, 252
International Women's Democratic Federation, 85
Intourist, 9
Inverchapel, Lord; *see* Kerr, Archibald Clark
Iovochuk, M. T., 359
Isbakh, Aleksandr, 13
Italy, 269, 270
Ivan Grozny (play), 111
Ivanov-Smolensky, A. G., 150
Izvestia, 90, 246, 260, 304, 307, 308, 315, 324, 340, 364, 375, 402, 407

James, Edwin L., 3, 27, 38, 41
Japan, 290
Japanese peace treaty, 34, 91, 102, 123
Jasny, Naum, 230
Jeans, James H., 45
Jessup, Philip, 23 n.
Jews in U.S.S.R., 13, 22–23, 56–57, 255, 424, 425–26
Johnston, Archibald, 32
Johnston, Eric, 150
Johnston affair, 57
Journal of Experimental and Theoretical Physics, 222
Joxe, Louis, 324

Kabanov, I. G., 302, 325
Kaganovich, Lazar, 43, 117, 248, 261, 287, 288, 296, 297, 299, 343, 347, 379, 385, 386, 440 n.

445

449